ASCENT

CENTER FOR TECHNICAL KNOWLEDGE

Autodesk® Revit® 2017 (R1) for Project Managers

Student Guide

Imperial - 1st Edition

AUTODESK.

Authorized Publisher

CONTINUING EDUCATION

AIA

ASCENT - Center for Technical Knowledge®
Autodesk® Revit® 2017 (R1)
for Project Managers

Imperial - 1st Edition

Prepared and produced by:

ASCENT Center for Technical Knowledge
630 Peter Jefferson Parkway, Suite 175
Charlottesville, VA 22911

866-527-2368
www.ASCENTed.com

Lead Contributor: Martha Hollowell

ASCENT - Center for Technical Knowledge is a division of Rand Worldwide, Inc., providing custom developed knowledge products and services for leading engineering software applications. ASCENT is focused on specializing in the creation of education programs that incorporate the best of classroom learning and technology-based training offerings.

We welcome any comments you may have regarding this student guide, or any of our products. To contact us please email: feedback@ASCENTed.com.

AS-REV1701-PMR1IM-SG // IS-REV1701-PMR1IM-SG

Contents

Preface

The Autodesk® Revit® software is a powerful Building Information Modeling (BIM) program that works the way Architects and Engineers think. The software streamlines the design process with a central 3D model. Changes made in one view update across all views and on the printable sheets. This student guide is designed to give you an overview of the Autodesk Revit (Architecture, Structure, and MEP) functionality especially as it pertains to Project Managers.

Topics Covered

- Understanding the purpose of Building Information Management (BIM) and how it is applied in the Autodesk Revit software.
- Navigating the Autodesk Revit workspace and interface.
- Working with the basic modifying and modeling tools.
- Troubleshooting elements in projects.
- Viewing models using plans, elevations, sections, and 3D views.
- Putting together construction documents by adding views to sheets that can then be printed.
- Exporting files to CAD Formats and DXF (the Autodesk® Design Review software).
- Working with schedules.
- Linking and importing CAD files and Autodesk Revit models into projects.
- Using Worksets in a collaborative environment.
- (Optional) Creating details.

Note on Software Setup

This student guide assumes a standard installation of the software using the default preferences during installation. Lectures and practices use the standard software templates and default options for the Content Libraries.

Students and Educators can Access Free Autodesk Software and Resources

Autodesk challenges you to get started with free educational licenses for professional software and creativity apps used by millions of architects, engineers, designers, and hobbyists today. Bring Autodesk software into your classroom, studio, or workshop to learn, teach, and explore real-world design challenges the way professionals do.

Get started today - register at the Autodesk Education Community and download one of the many Autodesk software applications available.

Visit www.autodesk.com/joinedu/

Note: Free products are subject to the terms and conditions of the end-user license and services agreement that accompanies the software. The software is for personal use for education purposes and is not intended for classroom or lab use.

Lead Contributor: Martha Hollowell

Martha incorporates her passion for architecture and education into all her projects, including the student guides she creates on Autodesk Revit for Architecture, MEP, and Structure. She started working with AutoCAD in the early 1990's, adding AutoCAD Architecture and Autodesk Revit as they came along.

After receiving a B.Sc. in Architecture from the University of Virginia, she worked in the architectural department of the Colonial Williamsburg Foundation and later in private practice, consulting with firms setting up AutoCAD in their offices.

Martha has over 20 years' experience as a trainer and instructional designer. She is skilled in leading individuals and small groups to understand and build on their potential. Martha is trained in Instructional Design and has achieved the Autodesk Certified Instructor (ACI) and Autodesk Certified Professional designations for Revit Architecture.

Martha Hollowell has been the Lead Contributor for *Autodesk Revit for Project Managers* since its initial release in 2013.

In this Guide

The following images highlight some of the features that can be found in this Student Guide.

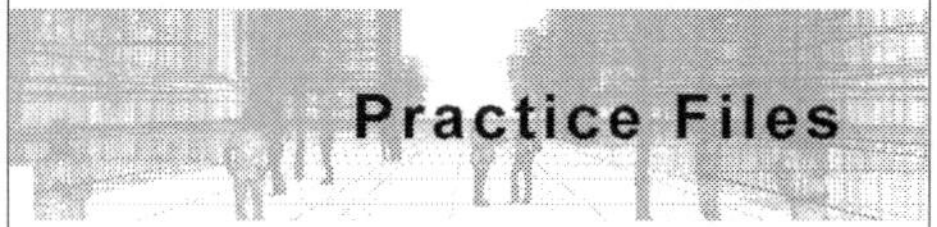

Practice Files

To download the practice files for this student guide, use the following steps:

1. Type the URL shown below into the address bar of your Internet browser. The URL must be typed **exactly as shown**. If you are using an ASCENT ebook, you can click on the link to download the file.

2. Press <Enter> to download the .ZIP file that contains the Practice Files.
3. Once the download is complete, unzip the file to a local folder. The unzipped file contains an .EXE file.
4. Double-click on the .EXE file and follow the instructions to automatically install the Practice Files on the C:\ drive of your computer.

   Do not change the location in which the Practice Files folder is installed. Doing so can cause errors when completing the practices in this student guide.

http://www.ASCENTed.com/getfile?id=xxxxxxxx

Stay Informed!
Interested in receiving information about upcoming promotional offers, educational events, invitations to complimentary webcasts, and discounts? If so, please visit: *www.ASCENTed.com/updates/*

Help us improve our product by completing the following survey:
www.ASCENTed.com/feedback
You can also contact us at: *feedback@ASCENTed.com*

FTP link for practice files

Practice Files

The Practice Files page tells you how to download and install the practice files that are provided with this student guide.

Chapter 1

Getting Started

In this chapter you learn how to start the AutoCAD® software, become familiar with the basic layout of the AutoCAD screen, how to access commands, use your pointing device, and understand the AutoCAD Cartesian workspace. You also learn how to open an existing drawing, view a drawing by zooming and panning, and save your work in the AutoCAD software.

Learning Objectives in this Chapter

- Launch the AutoCAD software and complete a basic initial setup of the drawing environment.
- Identify the basic layout and features of AutoCAD interface including the Ribbon, Drawing Window, and Application Menu.
- Locate commands and launch them using the Ribbon, shortcut menus, Application Menu, and Quick Access Toolbar.
- Locate points in the AutoCAD Cartesian workspace.
- Open and close existing drawings and navigate to file locations.
- Move around a drawing using the mouse, the **Zoom** and **Pan** commands, and the Navigation Bar.
- Save drawings in various formats and set the automatic save options using the **Save** commands.

Learning Objectives for the chapter

Chapters

Each chapter begins with a brief introduction and a list of the chapter's Learning Objectives.

Side notes

Side notes are hints or additional information for the current topic.

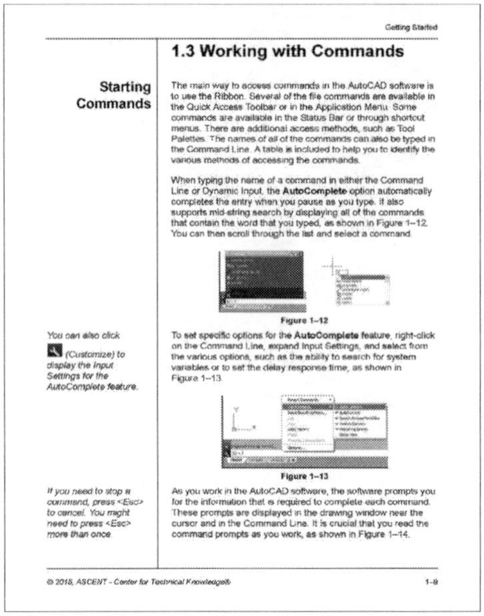
Getting Started

1.3 Working with Commands

Starting Commands

The main way to access commands in the AutoCAD software is to use the Ribbon. Several of the file commands are available in the Quick Access Toolbar or in the Application Menu. Some commands are available in the Status Bar or through shortcut menus. There are additional access methods, such as Tool Palettes. The names of all of the commands can also be typed in the Command Line. A table is included to help you to identify the various methods of accessing the commands.

When typing the name of a command in either the Command Line or Dynamic Input, the **AutoComplete** option automatically completes the entry when you pause as you type. It also supports mid-string search by displaying all of the commands that contain the word that you typed, as shown in Figure 1–12. You can then scroll through the list and select a command.

Figure 1–12

You can also click (Customize) to display the Input Settings for the AutoComplete feature.

To set specific options for the **AutoComplete feature**, right-click on the Command Line, expand Input Settings, and select from the various options, such as the ability to search for system variables or to set the delay response time, as shown in Figure 1–13.

Figure 1–13

If you need to stop a command, press <Esc> to cancel. You might need to press <Esc> more than once.

As you work in the AutoCAD software, the software prompts you for the information that is required to complete each command. These prompts are displayed in the drawing window near the cursor and in the Command Line. It is crucial that you read the command prompts as you work, as shown in Figure 1–14.

© 2016, ASCENT - Center for Technical Knowledge®   1-8

Instructional Content

Each chapter is split into a series of sections of instructional content on specific topics. These lectures include the descriptions, step-by-step procedures, figures, hints, and information you need to achieve the chapter's Learning Objectives.

Practice Objectives

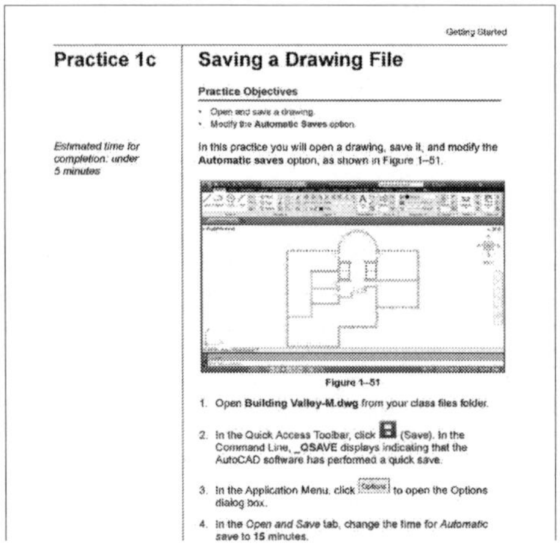
Getting Started

Practice 1c Saving a Drawing File

Practice Objectives

- Open and save a drawing.
- Modify the **Automatic Saves** option.

Estimated time for completion: under 5 minutes

In this practice you will open a drawing, save it, and modify the **Automatic saves** option, as shown in Figure 1–51.

Figure 1–51

1. Open **Building Valley-M.dwg** from your class files folder.
2. In the Quick Access Toolbar, click (Save). In the Command Line, _QSAVE displays indicating that the AutoCAD software has performed a quick save.
3. In the Application Menu, click Options to open the Options dialog box.
4. In the *Open and Save* tab, change the time for *Automatic save* to **15** minutes.

Practices

Practices enable you to use the software to perform a hands-on review of a topic.

Some practices require you to use prepared practice files, which can be downloaded from the link found on the Practice Files page.

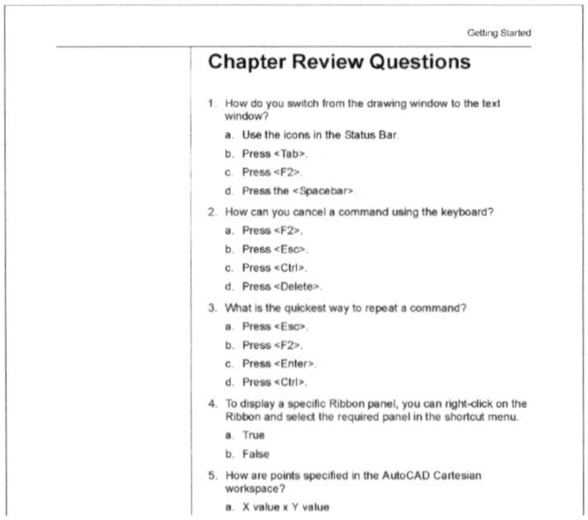
Getting Started

Chapter Review Questions

1. How do you switch from the drawing window to the text window?
   a. Use the icons in the Status Bar.
   b. Press <Tab>.
   c. Press <F2>.
   d. Press the <Spacebar>.
2. How can you cancel a command using the keyboard?
   a. Press <F2>.
   b. Press <Esc>.
   c. Press <Ctrl>.
   d. Press <Delete>.
3. What is the quickest way to repeat a command?
   a. Press <Esc>.
   b. Press <F2>.
   c. Press <Enter>.
   d. Press <Ctrl>.
4. To display a specific Ribbon panel, you can right-click on the Ribbon and select the required panel in the shortcut menu.
   a. True
   b. False
5. How are points specified in the AutoCAD Cartesian workspace?
   a. X value x Y value

Chapter Review Questions

Chapter review questions, located at the end of each chapter, enable you to review the key concepts and learning objectives of the chapter.

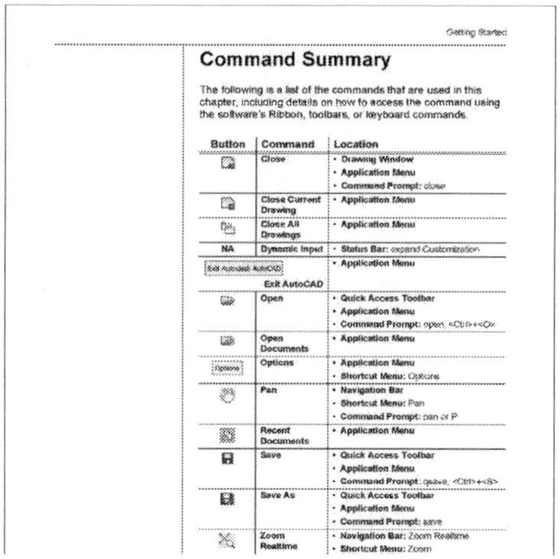

Getting Started

Command Summary

The following is a list of the commands that are used in this chapter, including details on how to access the command using the software's Ribbon, toolbars, or keyboard commands.

Button	Command	Location
	Close	• Drawing Window • Application Menu • Command Prompt: close
	Close Current Drawing	• Application Menu
	Close All Drawings	• Application Menu
NA	Dynamic Input	• Status Bar: expand Customization
Exit Autodesk AutoCAD	Exit AutoCAD	• Application Menu
	Open	• Quick Access Toolbar • Application Menu • Command Prompt: open, <Ctrl>+<O>
	Open Documents	• Application Menu
Options	Options	• Application Menu • Shortcut Menu: Options
	Pan	• Navigation Bar • Shortcut Menu: Pan • Command Prompt: pan or P
	Recent Documents	• Application Menu
	Save	• Quick Access Toolbar • Application Menu • Command Prompt: qsave, <Ctrl>+<S>
	Save As	• Quick Access Toolbar • Application Menu • Command Prompt: save
	Zoom Realtime	• Navigation Bar: Zoom Realtime • Shortcut Menu: Zoom

Command Summary

The Command Summary is located at the end of each chapter. It contains a list of the software commands that are used throughout the chapter, and provides information on where the command is found in the software.

Icons in this Student Guide

The following icons are used to help you quickly and easily find helpful information.

New in **2017** 	Indicates items that are new in the Autodesk Revit 2017 (R1) software.
Enhanced in **2017** 	Indicates items that have been enhanced in the Autodesk Revit 2017 (R1) software.

Practice Files

To download the practice files for this student guide, use the following steps:

1. Type the URL shown below into the address bar of your Internet browser. The URL must be typed **exactly as shown**. If you are using an ASCENT ebook, you can click on the link to download the file.

2. Press <Enter> to download the .ZIP file that contains the Practice Files.

3. Once the download is complete, unzip the file to a local folder. The unzipped file contains an .EXE file.

4. Double-click on the .EXE file and follow the instructions to automatically install the Practice Files on the C:\ drive of your computer.

   Do not change the location in which the Practice Files folder is installed. Doing so can cause errors when completing the practices in this student guide.

http://www.ascented.com/getfile?id=rangifer

Stay Informed!

Interested in receiving information about upcoming promotional offers, educational events, invitations to complimentary webcasts, and discounts? If so, please visit:

www.ASCENTed.com/updates/

Help us improve our product by completing the following survey:

www.ASCENTed.com/feedback

You can also contact us at: *feedback@ASCENTed.com*

Introduction to BIM and Autodesk Revit

Building Information Modeling (BIM) and the Autodesk® Revit® software work hand in hand to help you create smart, 3D models that are useful at all stages in the building process. Understanding the software interface and terminology enhances your ability to create powerful models and move around in the various views of the model.

Learning Objectives in this Chapter

- Describe the concept and workflow of Building Information Modeling in relation to the Autodesk Revit software.
- Navigate the graphic user interface, including the ribbon (where most of the tools are found), the Properties palette (where you make modifications to element information), and the Project Browser (where you can open various views of the model).
- Open existing projects and start new projects using templates.
- Use viewing commands to move around the model in 2D and 3D views.

1.1 BIM and Autodesk Revit

Building Information Modeling (BIM) is an approach to the entire building life cycle, including design, construction, and facilities management. The BIM process supports the ability to coordinate, update, and share design data with team members across disciplines.

The Autodesk Revit software is a true BIM product as it enables you to create complete models and the associated views of those models. It is considered a *Parametric Building Modeler:*

- *Parametric:* A relationship is established between building elements; when one element changes other related elements change as well.
- *Building:* The software is designed for working with buildings, as opposed to gears or roads.
- *Modeler:* A project is built in a single file around the 3D building model, as shown on the left in Figure 1–1. All views, such as plans (as shown on the right in Figure 1–1), elevations, sections, details, and reports such as schedules, as well as construction documents, are generated based on the model.

When a change is made anywhere in the model, all of the views update automatically. For example, if you add an element in a plan view, it displays in all of the other views as well.

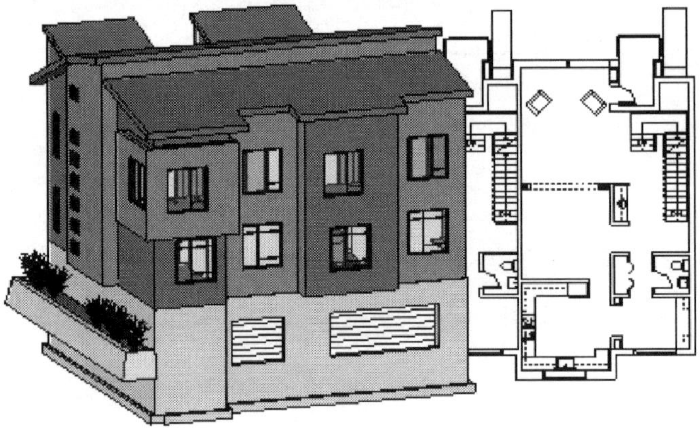

Figure 1–1

- The Autodesk® Revit® software includes tools for architectural, mechanical, electrical, plumbing, and structural design.
- It is important that everyone works in the same version and build of the software.

Workflow and BIM

BIM has changed the process of how a building is planned, budgeted, designed, constructed, and (in some cases) operated and maintained.

In the traditional design process, plans create the basis for the model, from which you then create sections and elevations, as shown in Figure 1–2. Construction Documents (CDs) can then be created. In this workflow, changes are made at the plan level and then coordinated with other documents in the set.

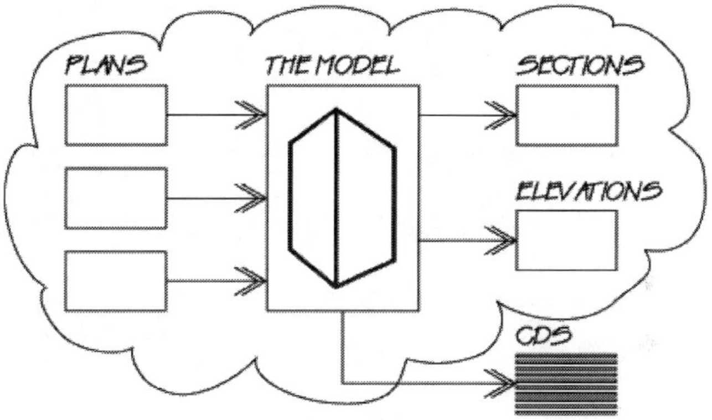

Figure 1–2

In BIM, the design process revolves around the model, as shown in Figure 1–3. Plans, elevations, and sections are simply 2D versions of the 3D model. Changes made in one view automatically update in all views. Even Construction Documents update automatically with callout tags in sync with the sheet numbers. This is called bidirectional associativity.

By creating complete models and associated views of those models, the Autodesk Revit software takes much of the tediousness out of producing a building design.

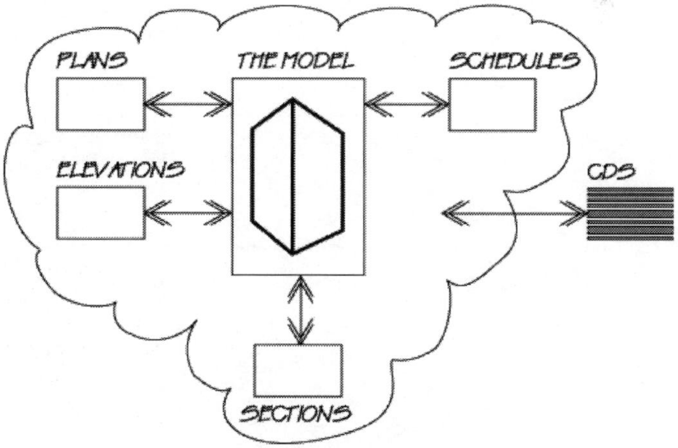

Figure 1–3

Revit Terms

As you start working with the Autodesk Revit software, you should know the typical terms used to describe items. There are several types of elements (as shown in Figure 1–4) as described in the following table.

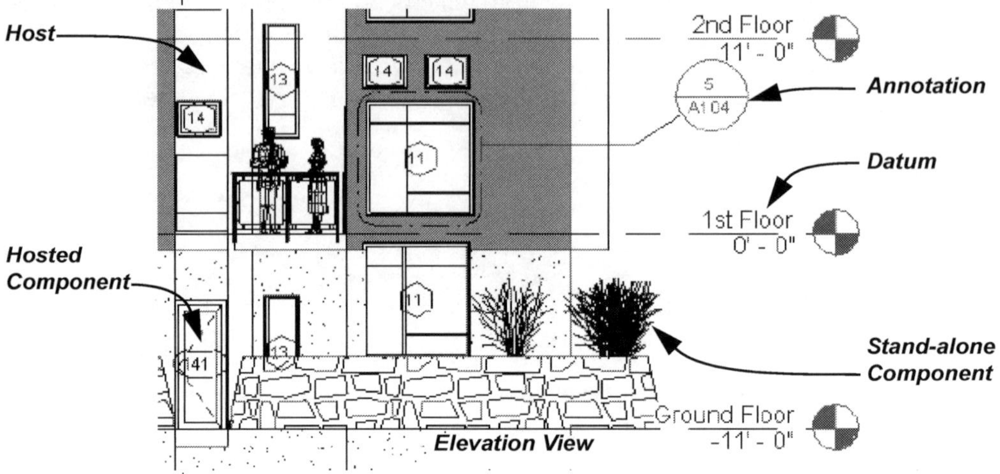

Figure 1–4

Host	Model elements (such as floors, walls, roofs, ceilings, stairs, and ramps) that can support other elements. They can stand alone in the project.
Components	Elements that need to be attached to host elements (such as doors, windows, and railings), as well as stand-alone items (such as furniture and equipment).
Views	Enables you to display and manipulate the project. For example, you can view and work in floor plans, ceiling plans, elevations, sections, schedules, and 3D views. You can change a design from any view. All views are stored in the project.
Datum	Elements that define the project context. These include levels for the floors, column grids, and reference planes that help you model.
Annotation	2D elements that are placed in views to define the information modeled in the project. These include dimensions, text, tags, and symbols. The view scale controls their size and they only display in the view in which they are placed.

- The elements that you create in the software are "smart" elements: the software recognizes them as walls, columns, ducts or lighting fixtures. This means that the information stored in their properties automatically updates in schedules, which ensures that views and reports are coordinated across an entire project, generated from a single model.

Revit and Construction Documents

In the traditional workflow, the most time-consuming part of the project is the construction documents. With BIM, the base views of those documents (i.e., plans, elevations, sections, and schedules) are produced automatically and update as the model is updated, saving hours of work. The views are then placed on sheets that form the construction document set.

For example, a floor plan is duplicated to create a Life Safety Plan. In the new view, certain categories of elements are toggled off (such as grids and section marks) while furniture elements are set to halftone. Annotation is added as required. The plan is then placed on a sheet, as shown in Figure 1–5.

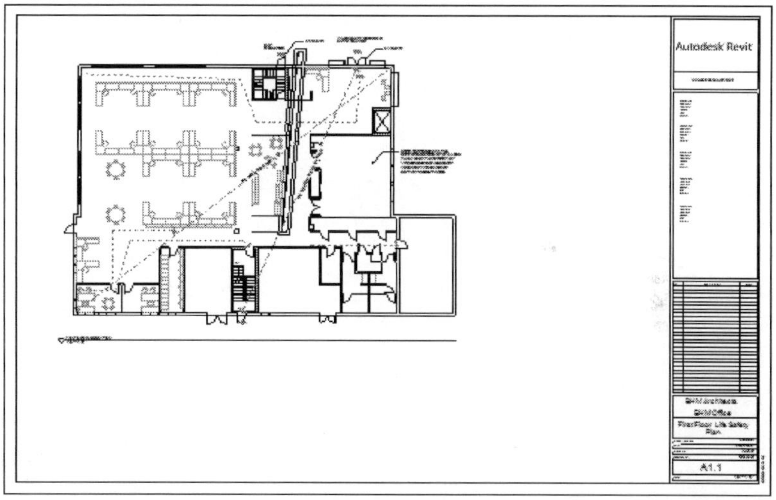

Figure 1–5

- Work can continue on a view and is automatically updated on the sheet.
- Annotating views in the preliminary design phase is often not required. You might be able to wait until you are further along in the project.

1.2 Overview of the Interface

The Autodesk Revit interface is designed for intuitive and efficient access to commands and views. It includes the ribbon, Quick Access Toolbar, Application Menu, Navigation Bar, and Status Bar, which are common to most of the Autodesk® software. It also includes tools that are specific to the Autodesk Revit software, including the Properties Palette, Project Browser, and View Control Bar. The interface is shown in Figure 1–6.

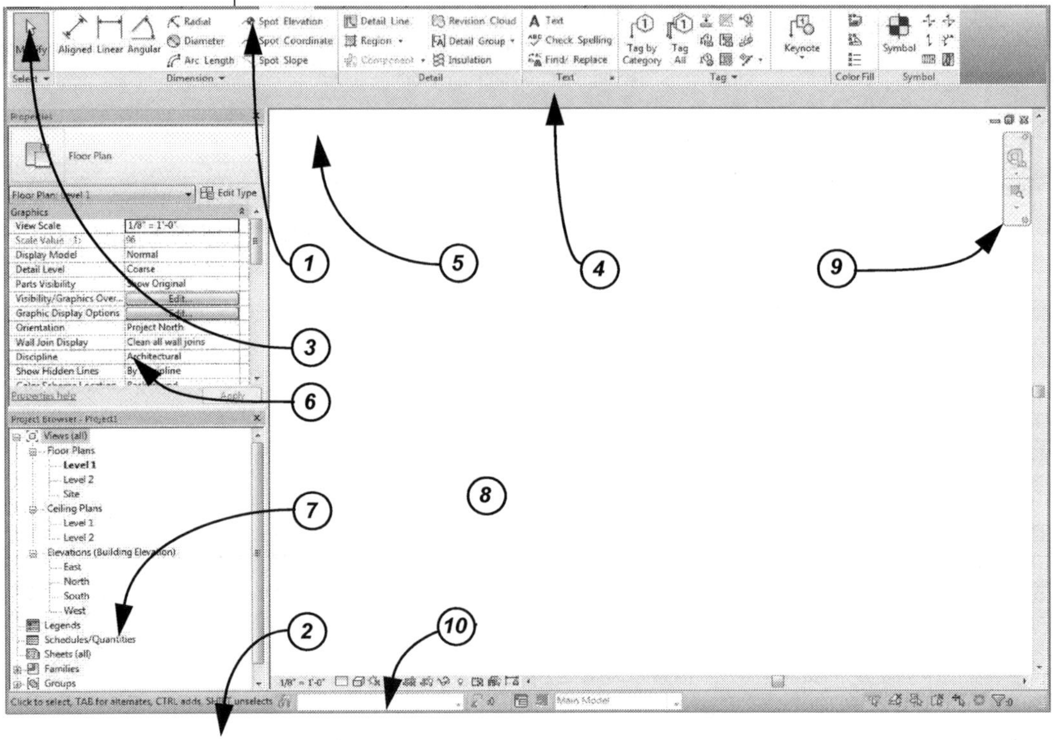

Figure 1–6

1. Quick Access Toolbar	6. Properties Palette
2. Status Bar	7. Project Browser
3. Application Menu	8. View Window
4. Ribbon	9. Navigation Bar
5. Options Bar	10. View Control Bar

1. Quick Access Toolbar

The Quick Access Toolbar includes commonly used commands, such as **Open**, **Save**, **Undo** and **Redo**, **Dimension**, and **3D View**, as shown in Figure 1–7.

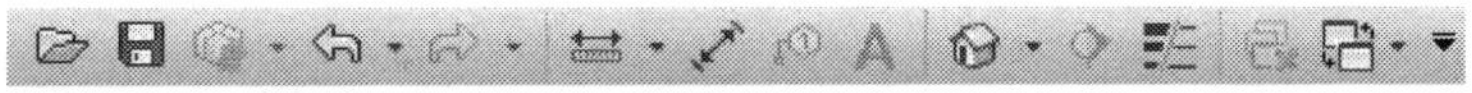

Figure 1–7

> **Hint: Customizing the Quick Access Toolbar**
>
> Right-click on the Quick Access Toolbar to change the docked location of the toolbar to be above or below the ribbon, or to add, relocate, or remove tools on the toolbar. You can also right-click on a tool in the ribbon and select **Add to Quick Access Toolbar**, as shown in Figure 1–8.
>
> 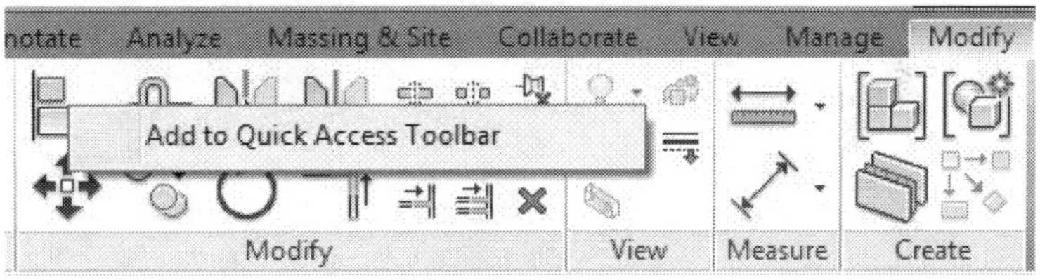
>
>
> **Figure 1–8**

The Quick Access Toolbar also hosts the InfoCenter (as shown in Figure 1–9) which includes a search field to find help on the web as well as access to the Subscription Center, Communication Center, Autodesk A360 sign-in, and other help options.

Click here to collapse the search field to save screen space.

Figure 1–9

2. Status Bar

The Status Bar provides information about the current process, such as the next step for a command, as shown in Figure 1–10.

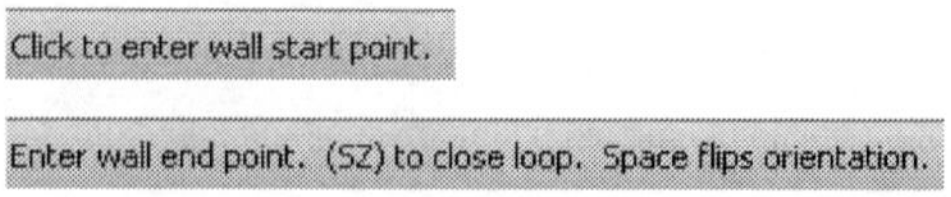

Figure 1–10

- Other options in the Status Bar are related to Worksets and Design Options (advanced tools) as well as selection methods and filters.

Hint: Shortcut Menus

Shortcut menus help you to work smoothly and efficiently by enabling you to quickly access required commands. These menus provide access to basic viewing commands, recently used commands, and the available Browsers, as shown in Figure 1–11. Additional options vary depending on the element or command that you are using.

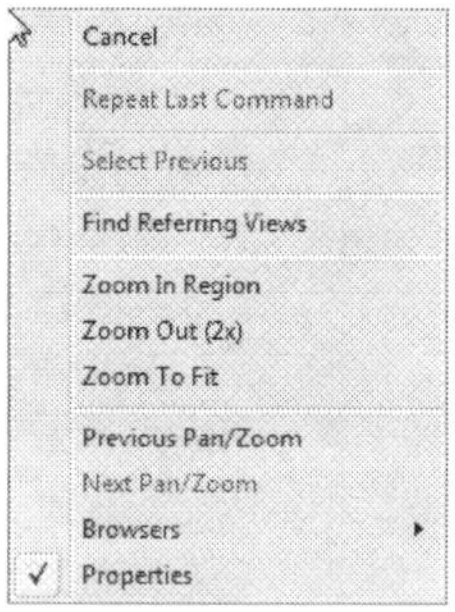

Figure 1–11

3. Application Menu

The Application Menu provides access to file commands, settings, and documents, as shown in Figure 1–12. Hover the cursor over a command to display a list of additional tools.

If you click the primary icon, rather than the arrow, it starts the default command.

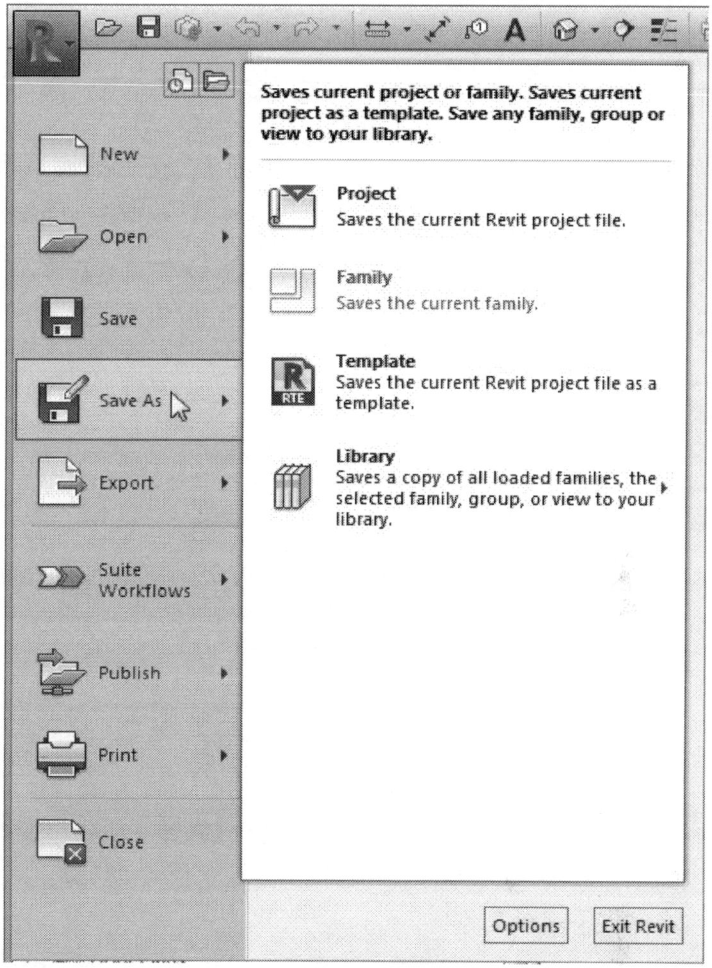

Figure 1–12

- To display a list of recently used documents, click (Recent Documents). The documents can be reordered as shown in Figure 1–13.

Click (Pin) next to a document name to keep it available.

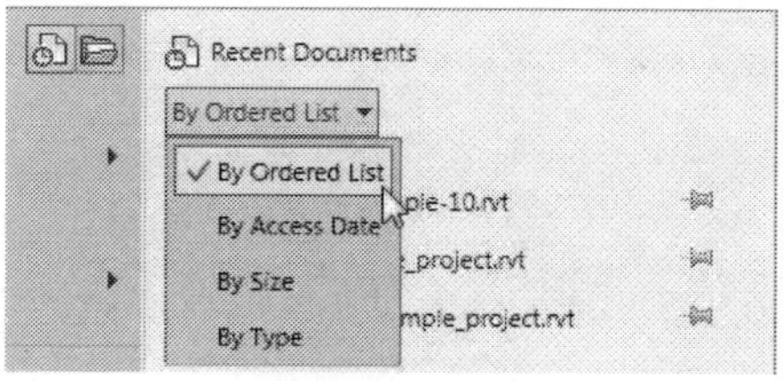

Figure 1–13

You can use the Open Documents list to change between views.

- To display a list of open documents and views, click  (Open Documents). The list displays the open documents and each view that is open, as shown in Figure 1–14.

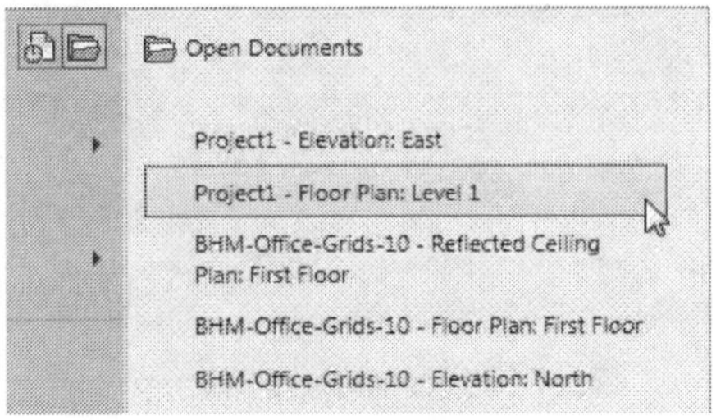

Figure 1–14

- Click  (Close) to close the current project.
- At the bottom of the menu, click **Options** to open the Options dialog box or click **Exit Revit** to exit the software.

4. Ribbon

The ribbon contains tools in a series of tabs and panels as shown in Figure 1–15. Selecting a tab displays a group of related panels. The panels contain a variety of tools, grouped by task.

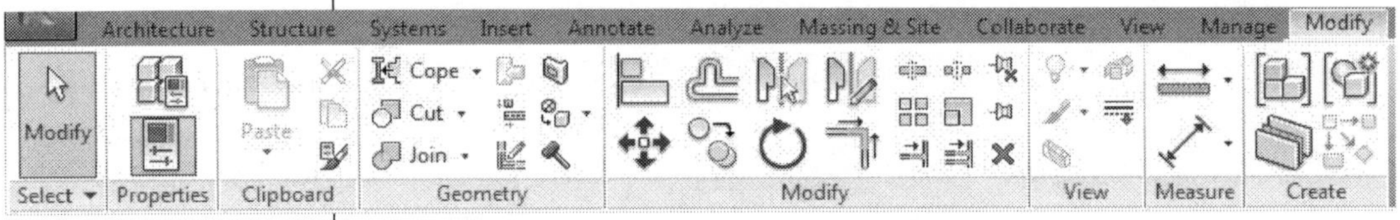

Figure 1–15

When you start a command that creates new elements or you select an element, the ribbon displays the *Modify | contextual* tab. This contains general editing commands and command specific tools, as shown in Figure 1–16.

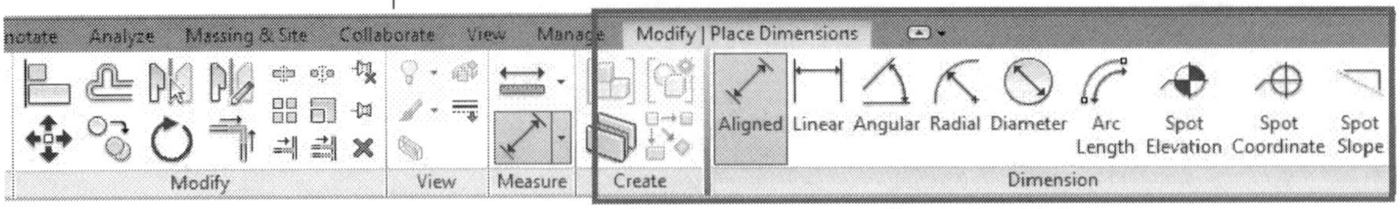

Contextual tab

Figure 1–16

- When you hover over a tool on the ribbon, tooltips display the tool's name and a short description. If you continue hovering over the tool, a graphic displays (and sometimes a video), as shown in Figure 1–17.

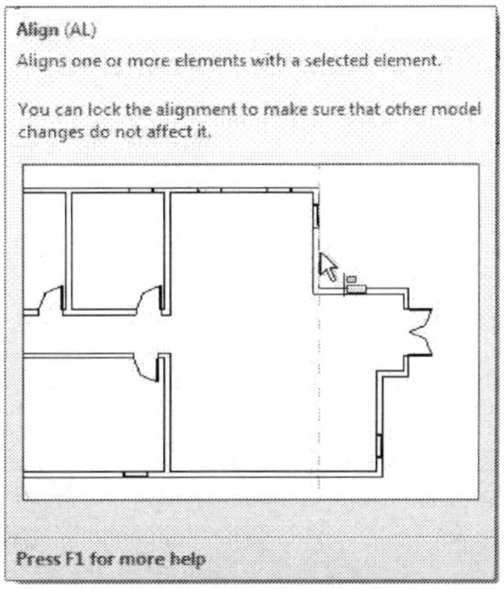

Figure 1–17

- Many commands have shortcut keys. For example, type **AL** for **Align** or **MV** for **Move**. They are listed next to the name of the command in the tooltips. Do not press <Enter> when typing shortcuts.

- To arrange the order in which the tabs on the ribbon are displayed, select the tab, hold <Ctrl>, and drag it to a new location. The location is remembered when you restart the software.

- Any panel can be dragged by its title into the view window to become a floating panel. Click the **Return Panels to Ribbon** button (as shown in Figure 1–18) to reposition the panel in the ribbon.

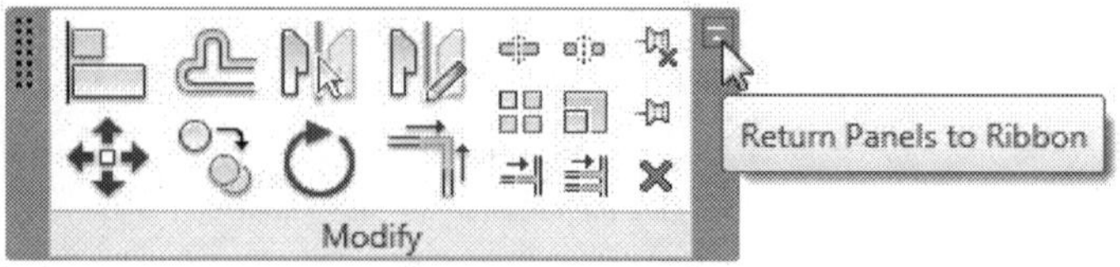

Figure 1–18

> **Hint: You are always in a command when using the Autodesk Revit software.**
>
> When you are finished working with a tool, you typically default back to the **Modify** command. To end a command, use one of the following methods:
>
> - In any tab on the ribbon, click (Modify).
> - Press <Esc> once or twice to revert to **Modify**.
> - Right-click and select **Cancel...** once or twice.
> - Start another command.

5. Options Bar

The Options Bar displays options that are related to the selected command or element. For example, when the **Rotate** command is active it displays options for rotating the selected elements, as shown at the top in Figure 1–19. When the **Place Dimensions** command is active it displays dimension related options, as shown at the bottom in Figure 1–19.

Options Bar for Rotate Command

Options Bar for Dimension Command

Figure 1–19

6. Properties Palette

The Properties palette includes the Type Selector, which enables you to choose the size or style of the element you are adding or modifying. This palette is also where you make changes to information (parameters) about elements or views, as shown in Figure 1–20. There are two types of properties:

- **Instance Properties** are set for the individual element(s) you are creating or modifying.
- **Type Properties** control options for all elements of the same type. If you modify these parameter values, all elements of the selected type change.

The Properties palette is usually kept open while working on a project to easily permit changes at any time. If it does not display, in the Modify tab>Properties panel click  *(Properties) or type* ***PP.***

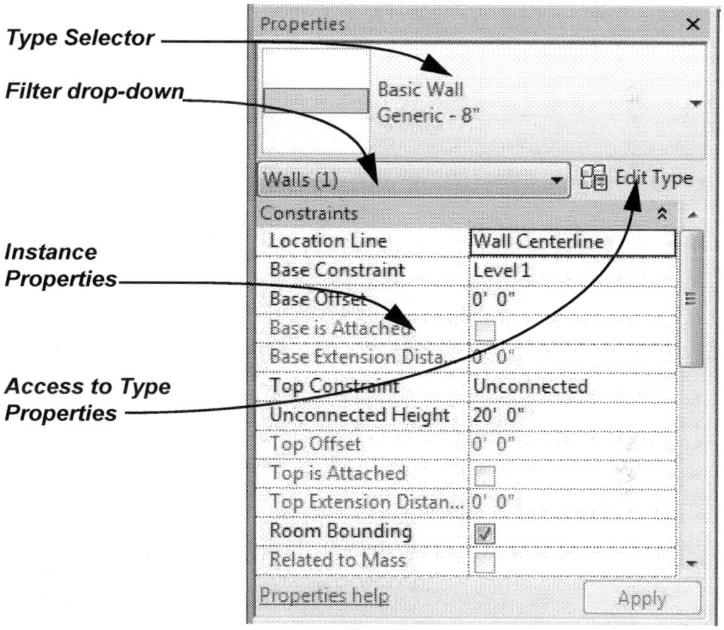

Figure 1–20

Some parameters are only available when you are editing an element. They are grayed out when unavailable.

- Options for the current view display if the **Modify** command is active, but you have not selected an element.
- If a command or element is selected, the options for the associated element display.
- You can save the changes by either moving the cursor off of the palette, or by pressing <Enter>, or by clicking **Apply**.

- When you start a command or select an element, you can set the element type in the Type Selector, as shown in Figure 1–21.

You can limit what shows in the drop-down list by typing in the search box.

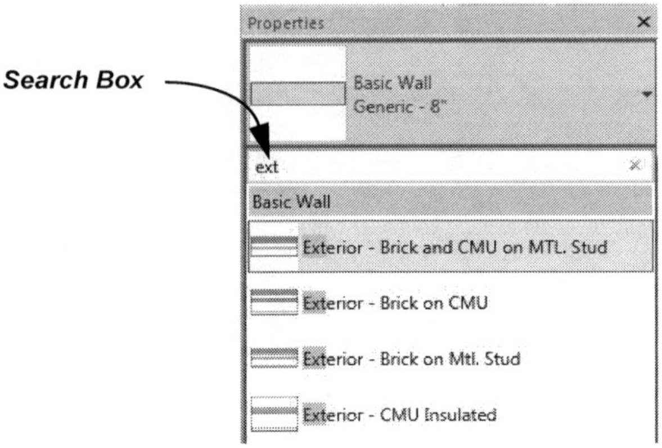

Figure 1–21

- When multiple elements are selected, you can filter the type of elements that display using the drop-down list, as shown in Figure 1–22.

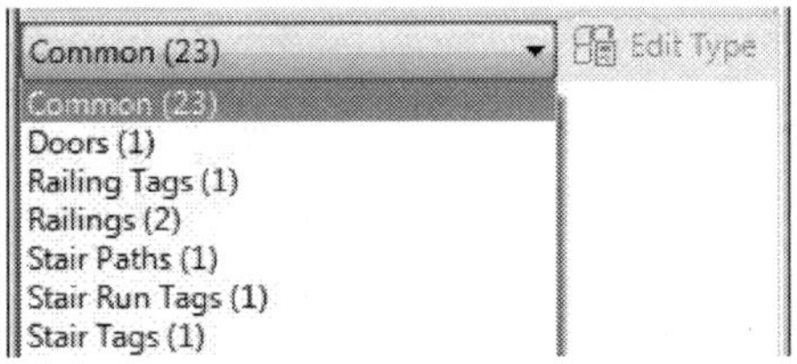

Figure 1–22

- The Properties palette can be placed on a second monitor, or floated, resized, and docked on top of the Project Browser or other dockable palettes, as shown in Figure 1–23. Click the tab to display its associated panel.

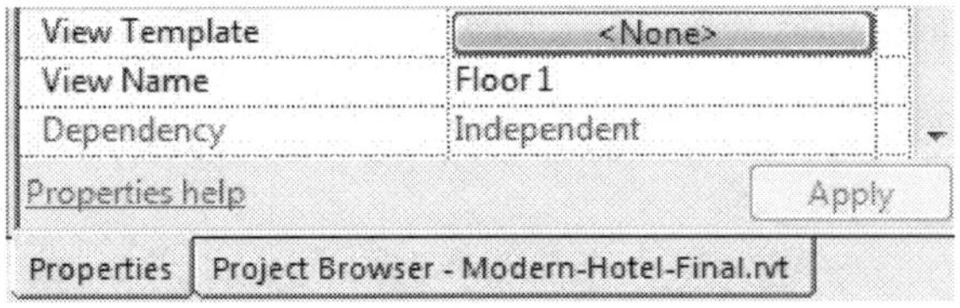

Figure 1–23

7. Project Browser

The Project Browser lists the views that can be opened in the project, as shown in Figure 1–24. This includes all views of the model in which you are working and any additional views that you create, such as floor plans, ceiling plans, 3D views, elevations, sections, etc. It also includes views of schedules, legends, sheets (for plotting), groups, and Autodesk Revit Links.

The Project Browser displays the name of the active project.

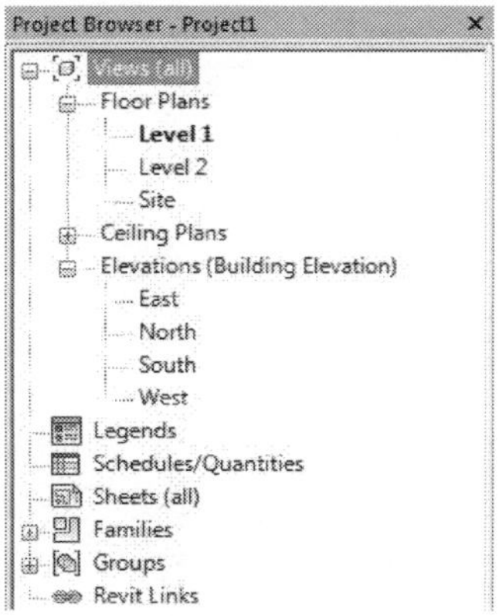

Figure 1–24

- Double-click on an item in the list to open the associated view.
- To display the views associated with a view type, click (Expand) next to the section name. To hide the views in the section, click (Contract).
- Right-click on a view and select **Rename** or press <F2> to rename a view in the Project Browser.
- If you no longer need a view, you can remove it. Right-click on its name in the Project Browser and select **Delete**.
- The Project Browser can be floated, resized, docked on top of the Properties palette, and customized. If the Properties palette and the Project Browser are docked on top of each other, use the appropriate tab to display the required panel.

How To: Search the Project Browser

1. In the Project Browser, right-click on the top level Views node as shown in Figure 1–25.

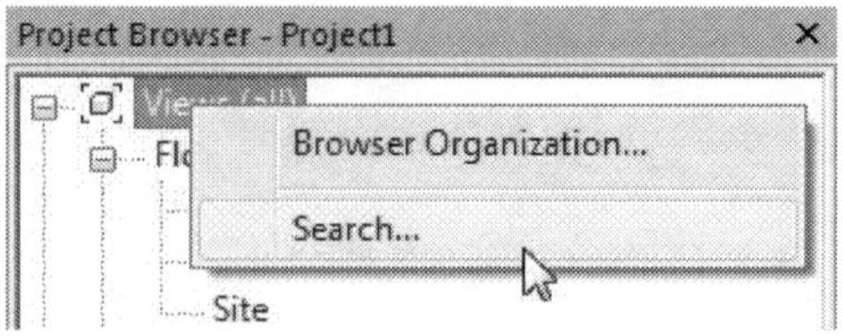

Figure 1–25

2. In the Search in Project Browser dialog box, type the words that you want to find (as shown on the left in Figure 1–26), and click **Next**.
3. In the Project Browser, the first instance of that search displays as shown on the right in Figure 1–26.

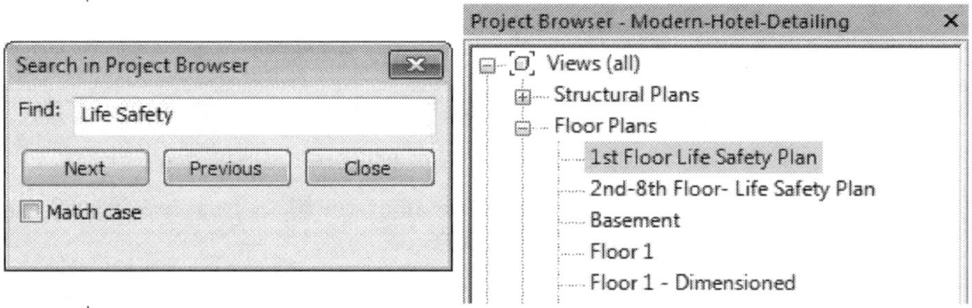

Figure 1–26

4. Continue using **Next** and **Previous** to move through the list.
5. Click **Close** when you are done.

8. View Window

In 3D views you can also use the ViewCube to rotate the view.

Each view of a project opens in its own window. Each view displays a Navigation Bar (for quick access to viewing tools) and the View Control Bar, as shown in Figure 1–27.

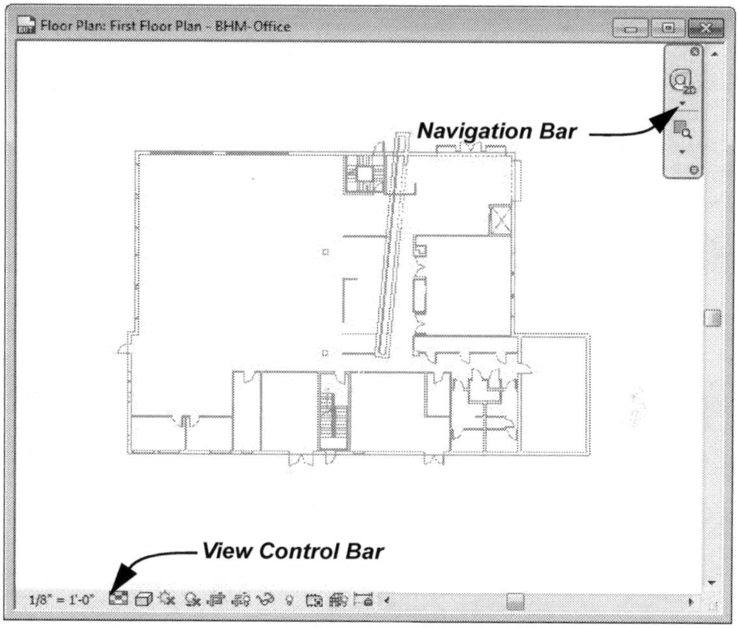

Figure 1–27

- To cycle through multiple views you can use several different methods:
  - Press <Ctrl>+<Tab>.
  - Select the view in the Project Browser.
  - In the Quick Access Toolbar or *View* tab>Windows panel, expand (Switch Windows) and select the view from the list.
- You can Tile or Cascade views. In the *View* tab>Windows panel, click (Cascade Windows) or (Tile Windows). You can also type the shortcuts **WC** to cascade the windows or **WT** to tile the windows.

9. Navigation Bar

The Navigation Bar enables you to access various viewing commands, as shown in Figure 1–28.

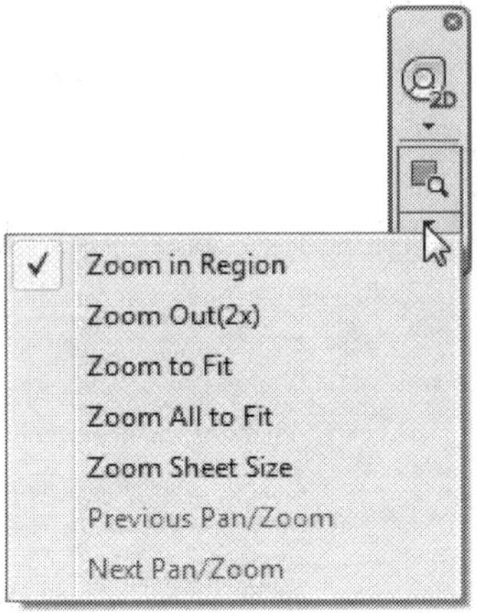

Figure 1–28

10. View Control Bar

The number of options in the View Control Bar change when you are in a 3D view.

The View Control Bar (shown in Figure 1–29), displays at the bottom of each view window. It controls aspects of that view, such as the scale and detail level. It also includes tools that display parts of the view and hide or isolate elements in the view.

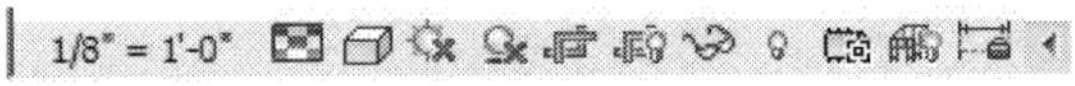

Figure 1–29

1.3 Starting Projects

File operations to open existing files, create new files from a template, and save files in the Autodesk Revit software are found in the Application Menu, as shown in Figure 1–30.

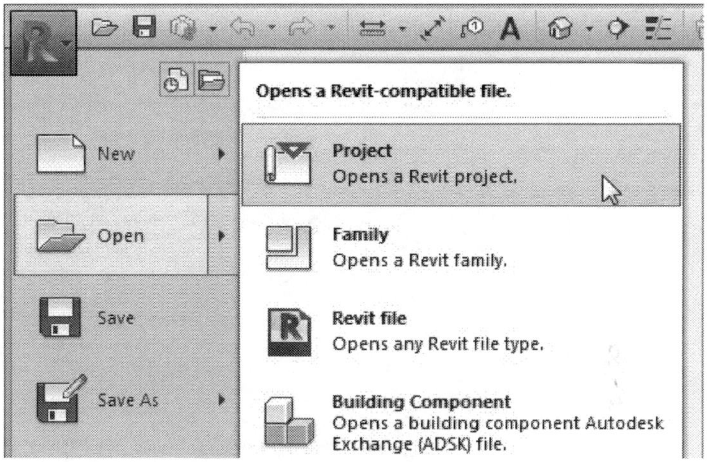

Figure 1–30

There are three main file formats:

- **Project files (.rvt):** These are where you do the majority of your work in the building model by adding elements, creating views, annotating views, and setting up printable sheets. They are initially based on template files.
- **Family files (.rfa):** These are separate components that can be inserted in a project. They include elements that can stand alone (e.g., a table or piece of mechanical equipment) or are items that are hosted in other elements (e.g., a door in a wall or a lighting fixture in a ceiling). Title block and Annotation Symbol files are special types of family files.
- **Template files (.rte):** These are the base files for any new project or family. They are designed to hold standard information and settings for creating new project files. The software includes several templates for various types of projects. You can also create custom templates.

Opening Projects

To open an existing project, in the Quick Access Toolbar or Application Menu click (Open), or press <Ctrl>+<O>. The Open dialog box opens (as shown in Figure 1–31), in which you can navigate to the required folder and select a project file.

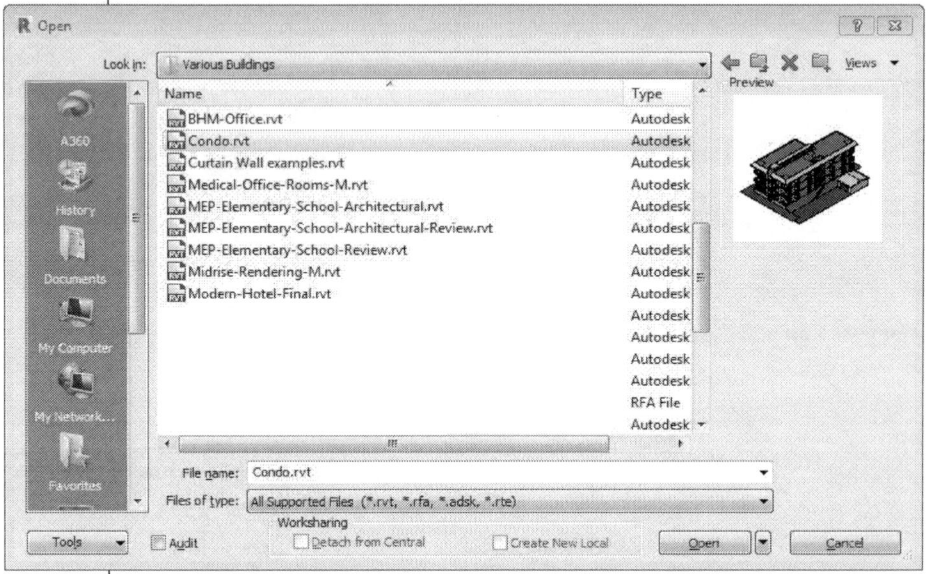

Figure 1–31

- When you first open the Autodesk Revit software, the Startup Screen displays, showing lists of recently used projects and family files as shown in Figure 1–32. This screen also displays if you close all projects.

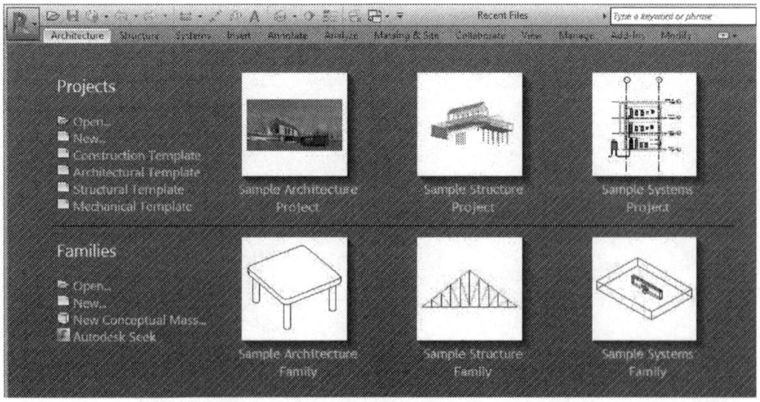

Figure 1–32

- You can select the picture of a recently opened project or use one of the options on the left to open or start a new project using the default templates.

Hint: Opening Workset-Related Files

Worksets are used when the project becomes large enough for multiple people to work on it at the same time. At this point, the project manager creates a central file with multiple worksets (such as element interiors, building shell, and site) that are used by the project team members.

When you open a workset related file it creates a new local file on your computer as shown in Figure 1–33. Do not work in the main central file.

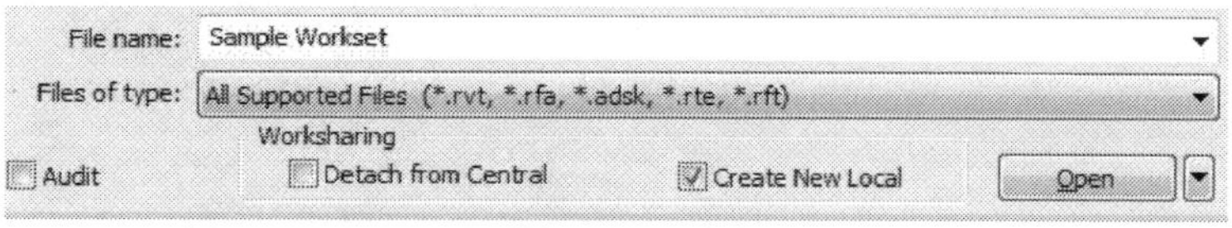

Figure 1–33

- It is very important that everyone working on a project uses the same software release. You can open files created in earlier versions of the software in comparison to your own, but you cannot open files created in newer versions of the software.
- When you open a file created in an earlier version, the Model Upgrade dialog box (shown in Figure 1–34) indicates the release of a file and the release to which it will be upgraded. If required, you can cancel the upgrade before it completes.

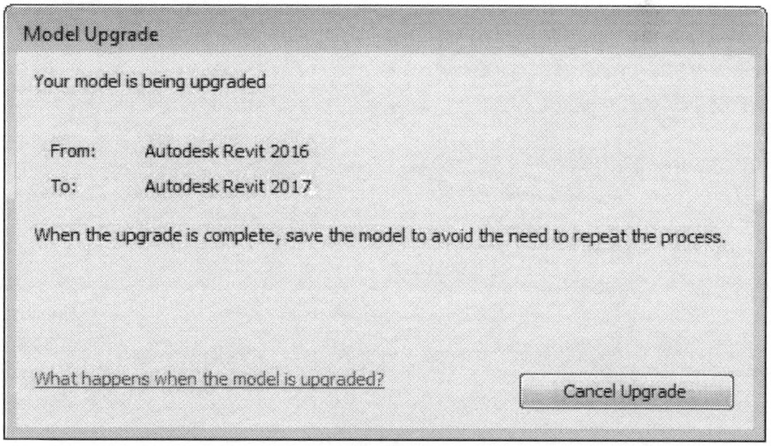

Figure 1–34

Starting New Projects

New projects are based on a template file. The template file includes preset levels, views, and some families, such as wall styles and text styles. Check with your BIM Manager about which template you need to use for your projects. Your company might have more than one based on the types of building that you are designing.

How To: Start a New Project

1. In the Application Menu, expand (New) and click (Project) (as shown in Figure 1–35), or press <Ctrl>+<N>.

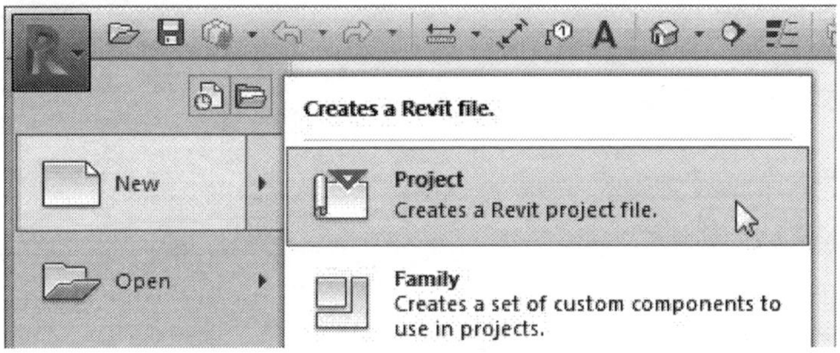

Figure 1–35

2. In the New Project dialog box (shown in Figure 1–36), select the template that you want to use and click **OK**.

The list of Template files is set in the Options dialog box in the File Locations pane. It might vary depending on the installed product and company standards.

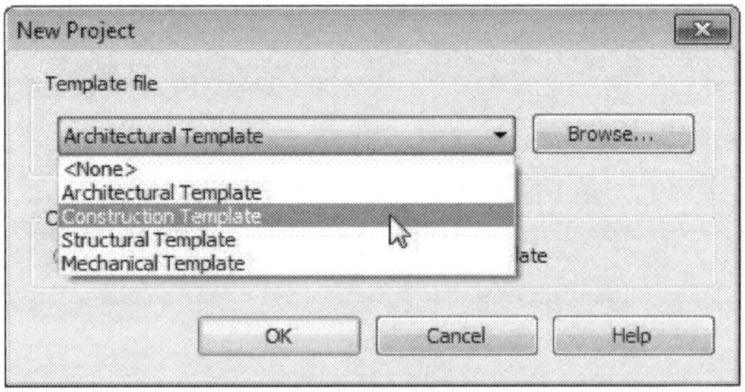

Figure 1–36

- You can select from a list of templates if they have been set up by your BIM Manager.

- You can add (New) to the Quick Access Toolbar. At the end of the Quick Access Toolbar, click (Customize Quick Access Toolbar) and select **New**, as shown in Figure 1–37.

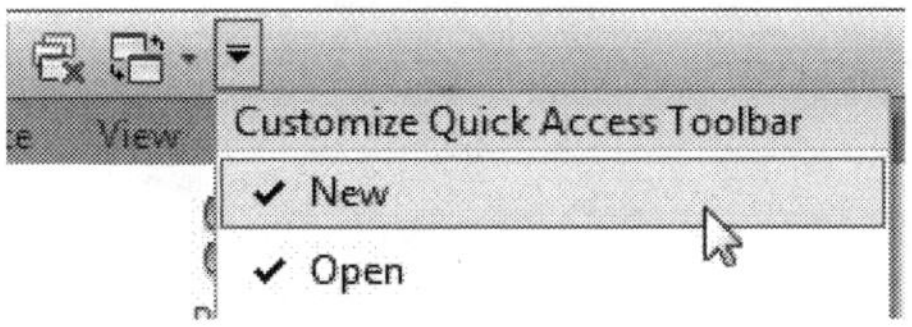

Figure 1–37

Saving Projects

Saving your project frequently is a good idea. In the Quick Access Toolbar or Application Menu click (Save), or press <Ctrl>+<S> to save your project. If the project has not yet been saved, the Save As dialog box opens, where you can specify a file location and name.

- To save an existing project with a new name, in the Application Menu, expand (Save As) and click (Project).
- If you have not saved in a set amount of time, the software opens the Project Not Saved Recently alert box, as shown in Figure 1–38. Select **Save the project**. If you want to set reminder intervals or not save at this time, select the other options.

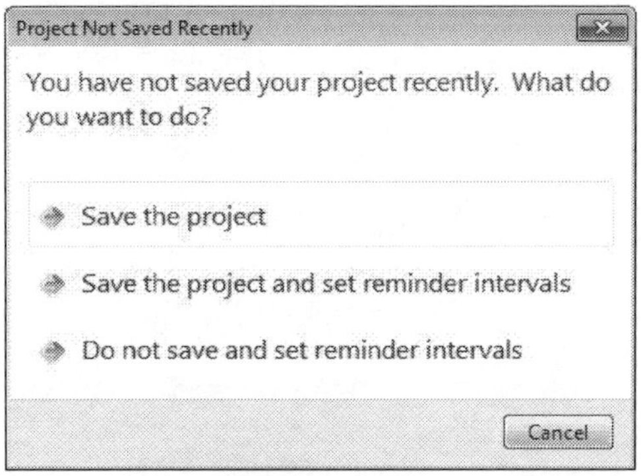

Figure 1–38

- You can set the *Save Reminder interval* to **15** or **30 minutes**, **1**, **2**, or **4 hours**, or to have **No reminders** display. In the Application Menu, click **Options** to open the Options dialog box. In the left pane, select **General** and set the interval as shown in Figure 1–39.

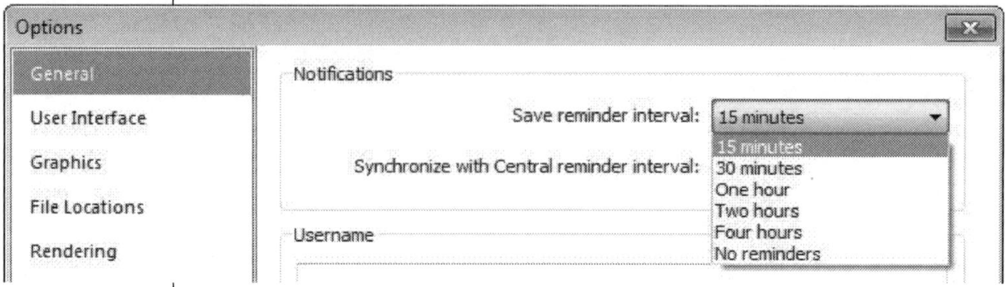

Figure 1–39

Saving Backup Copies

By default, the software saves a backup copy of a project file when you save the project. Backup copies are numbered incrementally (e.g., **My Project.0001.rvt**, **My Project.0002.rvt**, etc.) and are saved in the same folder as the original file. In the Save As dialog box, click **Options...** to control how many backup copies are saved. The default number is three backups. If you exceed this number, the software deletes the oldest backup file.

Hint: Saving Workset-Related Projects

If you use worksets in your project, you need to save the project locally and to the central file. It is recommended to save the local file frequently, just like any other file, and save to the central file every hour or so.

To synchronize your changes with the main file, in the Quick Access Toolbar expand (Synchronize and Modify Settings) and click (Synchronize Now). After you save to the central file, save the file locally again.

At the end of the day, or when you are finished with the current session, use (Synchronize and Modify Settings) to relinquish the files you have been working on to the central file.

1.4 Viewing Commands

Viewing commands are crucial to working efficiently in most drawing and modeling programs and the Autodesk Revit software is no exception. Once in a view, you can use the Zoom controls to navigate in it. You can zoom in and out and pan in any view. There are also special tools for viewing in 3D.

Zooming and Panning

Using The Mouse to Zoom and Pan

Use the mouse wheel (shown in Figure 1–40) as the main method of moving around the models.

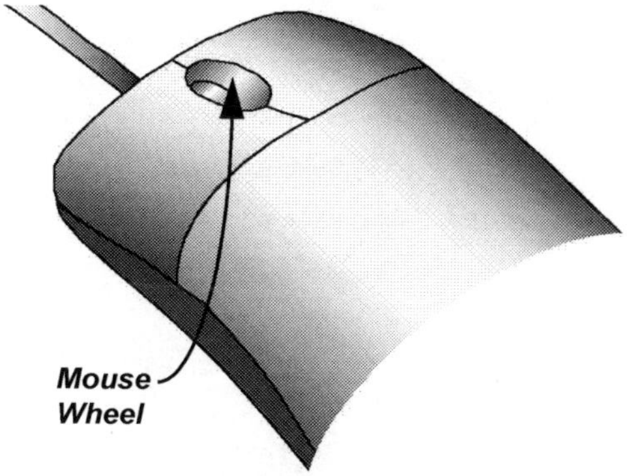

Figure 1–40

- Scroll the wheel on the mouse up to zoom in and down to zoom out.
- Hold the wheel and move the mouse to pan.
- Double-click on the wheel to zoom to the extents of the view.
- In a 3D view, hold <Shift> and the mouse wheel and move the mouse to rotate around the model.

- When you save a model and exit the software, the pan and zoom location of each view is remembered. This is especially important for complex models.

Zoom Controls

A number of additional zoom methods enable you to control the screen display. **Zoom** and **Pan** can be performed at any time while using other commands.

- You can access the **Zoom** commands in the Navigation Bar in the upper right corner of the view (as shown in Figure 1–41). You can also access them from most shortcut menus and by typing the shortcut commands.

 *(2D Wheel) provides cursor-specific access to* ***Zoom*** *and* ***Pan****.*

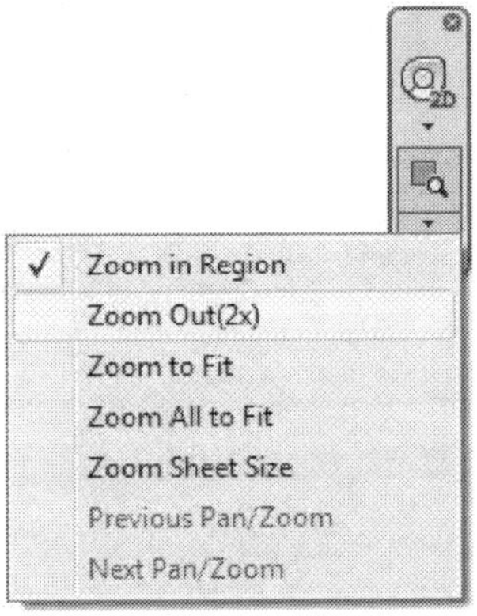

Figure 1–41

Zoom Commands

	**Zoom In Region (ZR)**	Zooms into a region that you define. Drag the cursor or select two points to define the rectangular area you want to zoom into. This is the default command.
	**Zoom Out(2x) (ZO)**	Zooms out to half the current magnification around the center of the elements.
	**Zoom To Fit (ZF or ZE)**	Zooms out so that the entire contents of the project only display on the screen in the current view.
	**Zoom All To Fit (ZA)**	Zooms out so that the entire contents of the project display on the screen in all open views.
	**Zoom Sheet Size (ZS)**	Zooms in or out in relation to the sheet size.
N/A	**Previous Pan/Zoom (ZP)**	Steps back one **Zoom** command.
N/A	**Next Pan/Zoom**	Steps forward one **Zoom** command if you have done a **Previous Pan/Zoom**.

Viewing in 3D

*There are two types of 3D views: isometric views created by the **3D View** command and perspective views created by the **Camera** command.*

Even if you started a project entirely in plan views, you can quickly create 3D views of the model, as shown in Figure 1–42.

Figure 1–42

Working in 3D views helps you visualize the project and position some of the elements correctly. You can create and modify elements in 3D views just as in plan views.

- Once you have created a 3D view, you can save it and easily return to it.

How To: Create and Save a 3D Isometric View

You can spin the view to a different angle using the mouse wheel or the middle button of a three-button mouse. Hold <Shift> as you press the wheel or middle button and drag the cursor.

1. In the Quick Access Toolbar or *View* tab>Create panel, click (Default 3D View). The default 3D Southeast isometric view opens, as shown in Figure 1–43.

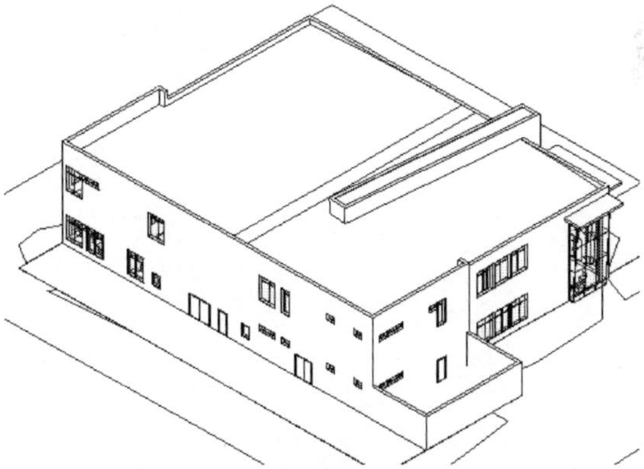

Figure 1–43

2. Modify the view to display the building from other directions.
3. In the Project Browser, right-click on the {3D} view and select **Rename...**

4. Type a new name in the Rename View dialog box, as shown in Figure 1–44, and click **OK**.

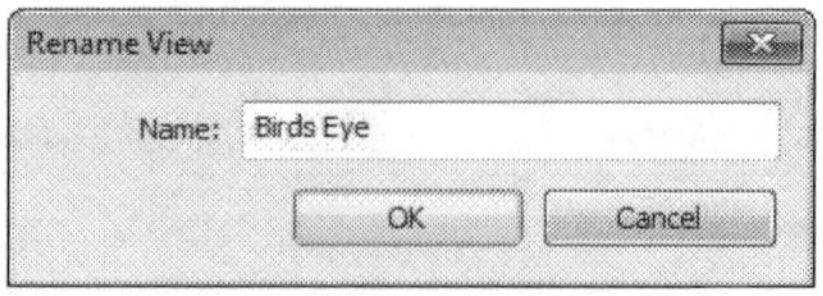

Figure 1–44

- When changes to the default 3D view are saved and you start another default 3D view, it displays the Southeast isometric view once again. If you modified the default 3D view but did not save it to a new name, the **Default 3D View** command opens the view in the last orientation you specified.

How To: Create a Perspective View

1. Switch to a Floor Plan view.
2. In the Quick Access Toolbar or *View* tab>Create panel, expand (Default 3D View) and click (Camera).
3. Place the camera on the view.
4. Point the camera in the direction in which you want it to shoot by placing the target on the view, as shown in Figure 1–45.

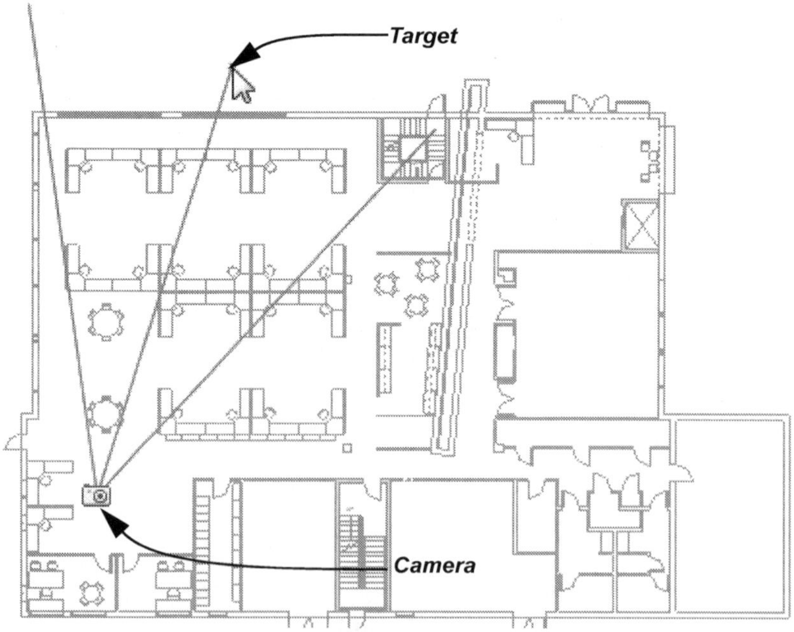

Figure 1–45

Use the round controls to modify the display size of the view and press <Shift> + the mouse wheel to change the view.

A new view is displayed, as shown in Figure 1–46.

Figure 1–46

5. In the Properties palette scroll down and adjust the *Eye Elevation* and *Target Elevation* as required.

- You can rename perspective views.
- If the view becomes distorted, reset the target so that it is centered in the boundary of the view (called the crop region).

  In the *Modify | Cameras* tab>Camera panel, click (Reset Target).
- You can further modify a view by adding shadows, as shown in Figure 1–47. In the View Control Bar, toggle (Shadows Off) and (Shadows On). Shadows display in any model view, not just in the 3D views.

Figure 1–47

Hint: Using the ViewCube

The ViewCube provides visual clues as to where you are in a 3D view. It helps you move around the model with quick access to specific views (such as top, front, and right), as well as corner and directional views, as shown in Figure 1–48.

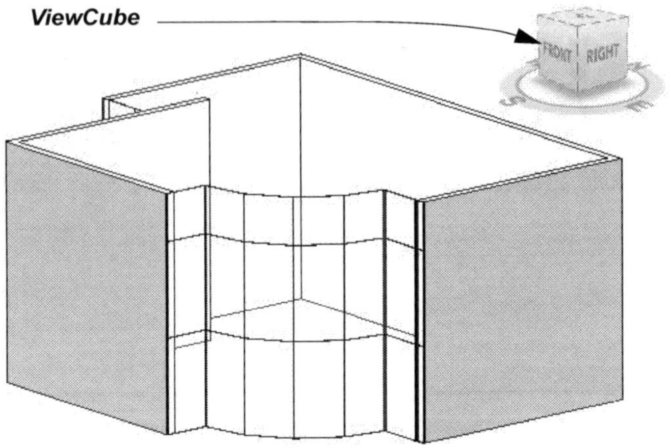

Figure 1–48

Move the cursor over any face of the ViewCube to highlight it. Once a face is highlighted, you can select it to reorient the model. You can also click and drag on the ViewCube to rotate the box, which rotates the model.

- (Home) displays when you hover the cursor over the ViewCube. Click it to return to the view defined as **Home**. To change the Home view, set the view as you want it, right-click on the ViewCube, and select **Set Current View as Home**.
- The ViewCube is available in isometric and perspective views.
- If you are in a camera view, you can switch between Perspective and Isometric mode. Right-click on the View Cube and click **Toggle to Parallel-3D View** or **Toggle to Perspective-3D View**. You can make more changes to the model in a parallel view.

Visual Styles

Any view can have a visual style applied. The **Visual Style** options found in the View Control Bar (as shown in Figure 1–49), specify the shading of the building model. These options apply to plan, elevation, section, and 3D views.

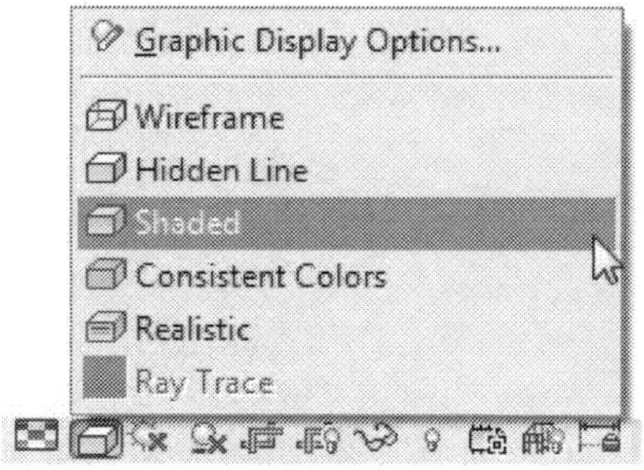

Figure 1–49

- (Wireframe) displays the lines and edges that make up elements, but hides the surfaces. This can be useful when you are dealing with complex intersections.
- (Hidden Line) displays the lines, edges, and surfaces of the elements, but it does not display any colors. This is the most common visual style to use while working on a design.
- (Shaded) and (Consistent Colors) give you a sense of the materials, including transparent glass. An example that uses Consistent Colors is shown in Figure 1–50.

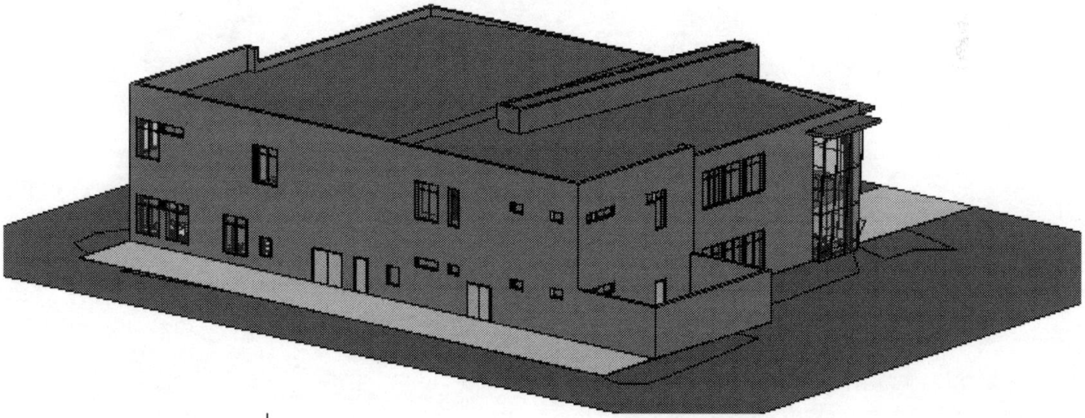

Figure 1–50

- (Realistic) displays what is shown when you render the view, including RPC (Rich Photorealistic Content) components and artificial lights. It takes a lot of computer power to execute this visual style. Therefore, it is better to use the other visual styles most of the time as you are working.

- (Ray Trace) is useful if you have created a 3D view that you want to render. It gradually moves from draft resolution to photorealistic. You can stop the process at any time.

Hint: Rendering

Rendering is a powerful tool which enables you to display a photorealistic view of the model you are working on, such as the example shown in Figure 1–51. This can be used to help clients and designers to understand a building's design in better detail.

Figure 1–51

- In the View Control Bar, click (Show Rendering Dialog) to set up the options. **Show Rendering Dialog** is only available in 3D views.

Practice 1a Review an Architectural Project

Practice Objectives

- Navigate the graphic user interface.
- Manipulate 2D and 3D views by zooming and panning.
- Create 3D Isometric and Perspective views.
- Set the Visual Style of a view.

Estimated time for completion: 15 minutes

In this practice you will open a project file and view each of the various areas in the interface. You will investigate elements, commands, and their options. You will also open views through the Project Browser and view the model in 3D, as shown in Figure 1–52.

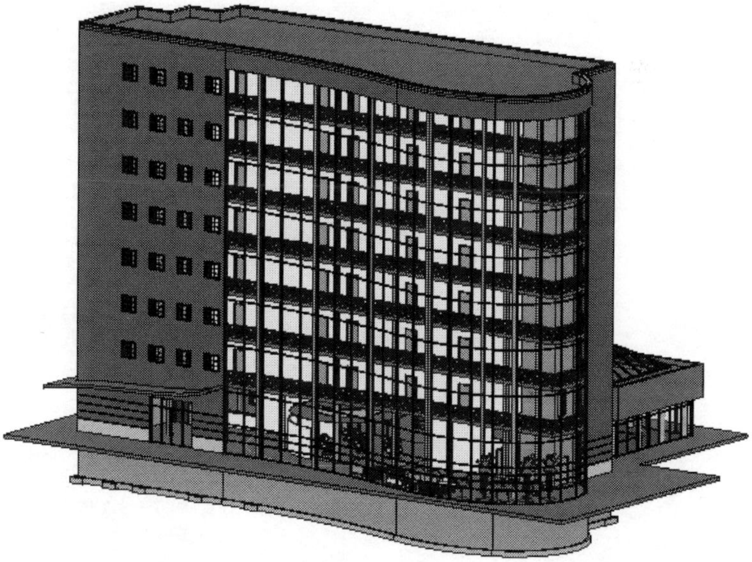

Figure 1–52

- This is a version of the main project you will work on throughout the student guide.

Task 1 - Explore the interface.

1. In the Application Menu, expand (Open) and click (Project).
2. In the Open dialog box, navigate to the practice files folder and select **Modern-Hotel-Final.rvt**.

3. Click **Open**. The 3D view of the modern hotel building opens in the view window.

If the Project Browser and Properties palette are docked over each other, use the Project Browser tab at the bottom to display it.

4. In the Project Browser, expand the *Floor Plans* node. Double-click on **Floor 1** to open it. This view is referred to as **Floor Plans: Floor 1**.

5. Take time to review the floor plan to get acquainted with it.

6. Review the various parts of the screen.

7. In the view window, hover the cursor over one of the doors. A tooltip displays describing the element, as shown in Figure 1–53.

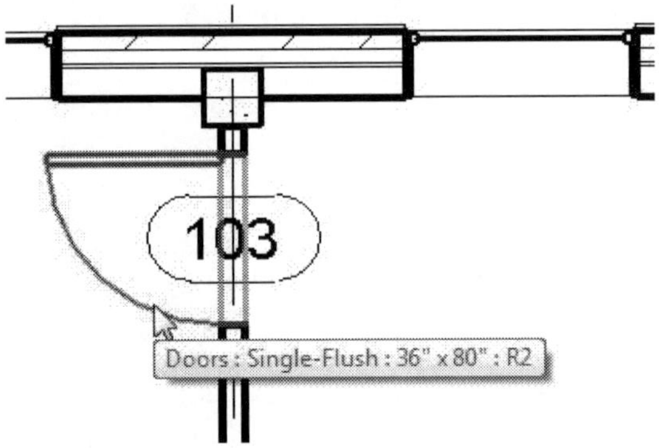

Figure 1–53

8. Hover the cursor over another element to display its description.

9. Select a door. The ribbon changes to the *Modify* | *Doors* tab.

10. Click in an empty space to release the selection.

11. Hold <Ctrl> and select several elements of different types. The ribbon changes to the *Modify* | *Multi-Select* tab.

12. Click in an empty space to release the selection set.

13. In the *Architecture* tab>Build panel, click (Wall). The ribbon changes to the *Modify* | *Place Wall* tab and at the end of the ribbon, the Draw panel is displayed. It contains tools that enable you to create walls. The rest of the ribbon displays the same tools that are found on the *Modify* tab.

14. In the Select panel, click (Modify) to return to the main ribbon.

15. In the *Architecture* tab>Build panel, click (Door). The ribbon changes to the *Modify | Place Door* tab and displays the options and tools you can use to create doors.

16. In the Select panel, click (Modify) to return to the main ribbon.

Task 2 - Look at views.

You might need to widen the Project Browser to display the full names of the views.

1. In the Project Browser, verify that the *Floor Plans* node is open. Double-click on the **Floor 1 - Furniture Plan** view.
2. The basic floor plan displays with the furniture, but without the annotations that were displayed in the **Floor 1** view.
3. Open the **Floor1 - Life Safety Plan** view by double-clicking on it.
4. The walls and furniture display, but the furniture is grayed out and red lines describing important life safety information display.

This view is referred to as ***Elevations (Building Elevation): East*** *view.*

5. In the Project Browser, scroll down and expand *Elevations (Building Elevation)*. Double-click on the **East** elevation to open the view.
6. Expand *Sections (Building Section)* and double-click on the **East-West Section** to open it.
7. At the bottom of the view window, in the View Control Bar, click (Visual Style) and select **Shaded**. The elements in the section are now easier to read.
8. In the Project Browser, scroll down to the *Sheets (all)* node and expand the node.

9. View several of the sheets. Some have views already applied, (e.g., **A2.3 - 2nd-8th Floor Plan (Typical)** as shown in Figure 1–54).

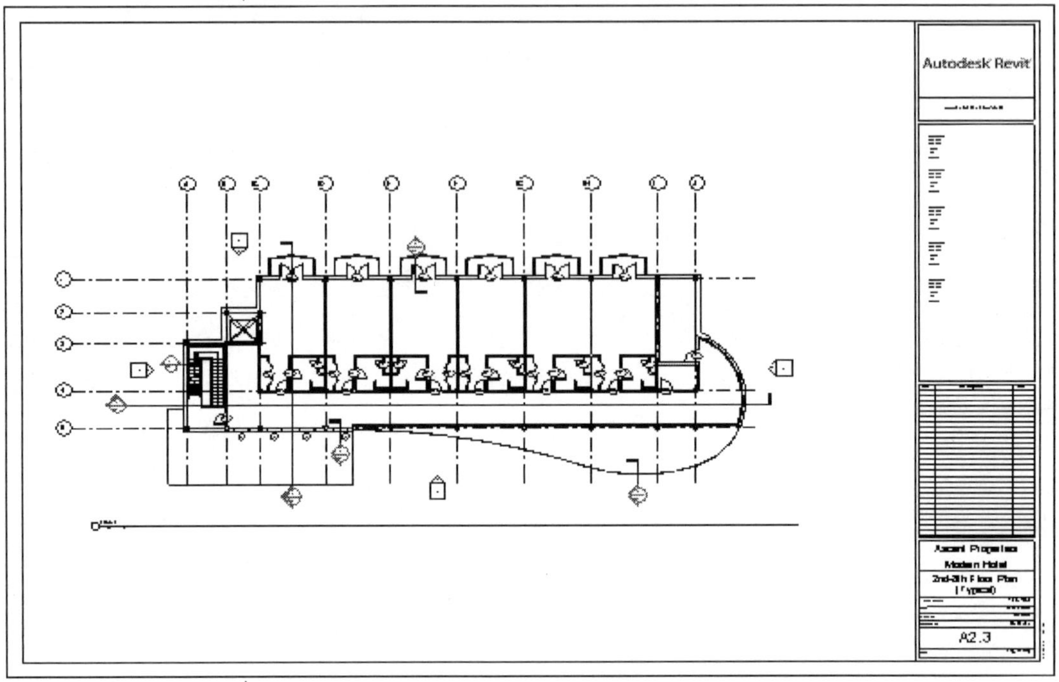

Figure 1–54

10. Which sheet displays the view that you just set to **Shaded**?

Task 3 - Practice viewing tools.

1. Return to the **Floor Plans: Floor 1** view.
2. In the Navigation Bar, click  and select **Zoom In Region** or type **ZR**. Zoom in on one of the stairs.
3. Pan to another part of the building by holding and dragging the middle mouse button or wheel. Alternatively, you can use the 2D Wheel in the Navigation Bar.
4. Double-click on the mouse wheel to zoom out to fit the extents of the view.

5. In the Quick Access Toolbar, click (Default 3D View) to open the default 3D view, as shown in Figure 1–55.

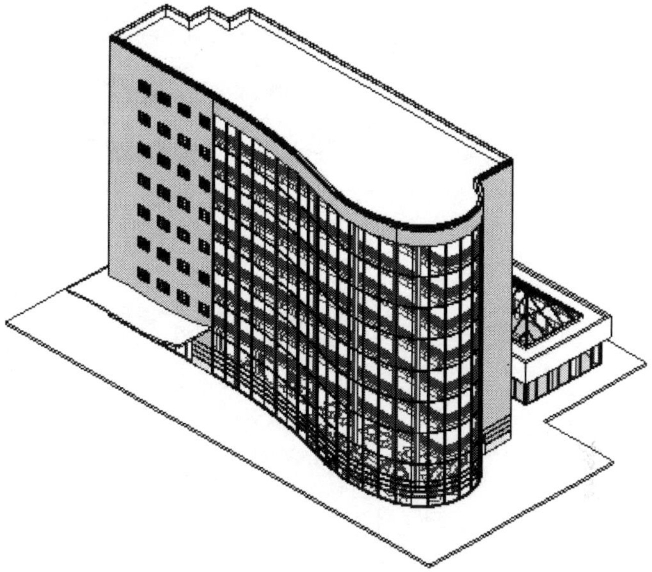

Figure 1–55

6. Hold <Shift> and use the middle mouse button or wheel to rotate the model in the 3D view.

7. In the View Control Bar, change the *Visual Style* to (Shaded). Then try (Consistent Colors). Which one works best when you view the back of the building?

8. Use the ViewCube to find a view that you want to use.

9. In the Project Browser, expand *3D Views* and right-click on the {3D} view and select **Rename...**. In the Rename View dialog box type in a useful name.

10. Review the other 3D views that have already been created.

11. Press <Ctrl>+<Tab> to cycle through the open views.

12. In the Quick Access Toolbar, expand (Switch Windows) and select the **Modern-Hotel-Final.rvt - Floor Plan: Floor 1** view.

13. In the Quick Access Toolbar, click (Close Hidden Windows). This closes all of the other windows except the one in which you are working.

14. In the Quick Access Toolbar, expand (Default 3D View) and click (Camera).

15. Click the first point near the Lobby room name and click the second point (target) outside the building, as shown in Figure 1–56.

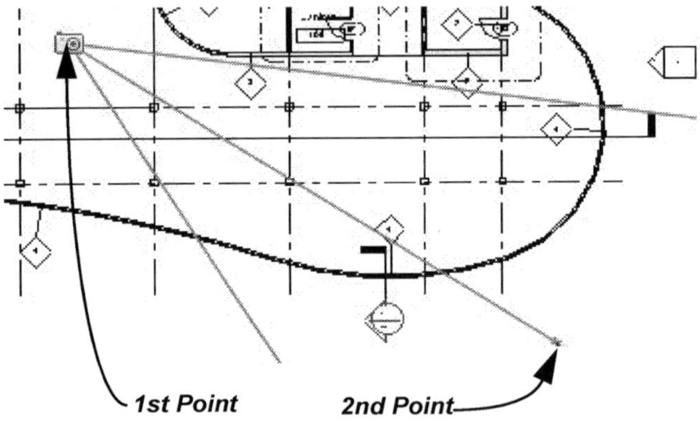

Figure 1–56

16. The furniture and planters display even though they did not display in the floor plan view.

This file is not set up to work with Raytrace.

17. In the View Control Bar, set the *Visual Style* to (Realistic).

18. In the Project Browser, right-click on the new camera view and select **Rename...** In the Rename View dialog box, type **Lobby Seating Area** and click **OK**.

19. In the Quick Access Toolbar, click (Save) to save the project.

20. In the Application Menu, click (Close). This closes the entire project.

Practice 1b Review an MEP Project

Practice Objectives

- Navigate the graphic user interface.
- Manipulate 2D and 3D views by zooming and panning.
- Create 3D Isometric and Perspective views.
- Set the Visual Style of a view.

Estimated time for completion: 15 minutes

In this practice you will open a project file, as shown in Figure 1–57 and display each of the various parts of the Autodesk Revit MEP interface. You will open views through the Project Browser, and switch between different views. You will also select elements and display the information about them in the Properties palette. Finally you will create and save 3D views.

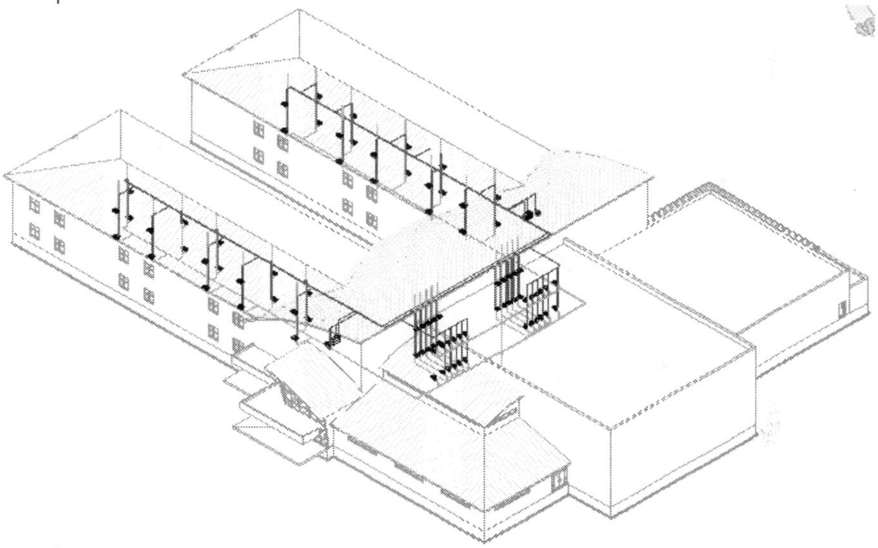

Figure 1–57

Task 1 - Open an Autodesk Revit MEP project and review it.

1. In the Application Menu, expand (Open) and click (Project).
2. In the Open dialog box, navigate to the practice files folder and select **MEP-Elementary-School- Review.rvt**.
3. Click **Open**. The project opens in the **3D Plumbing** view, as shown in Figure 1–57.

4. Close any other open projects and views.

5. In the Project Browser, expand Mechanical>HVAC>**Floor Plans**, as shown in Figure 1–58.

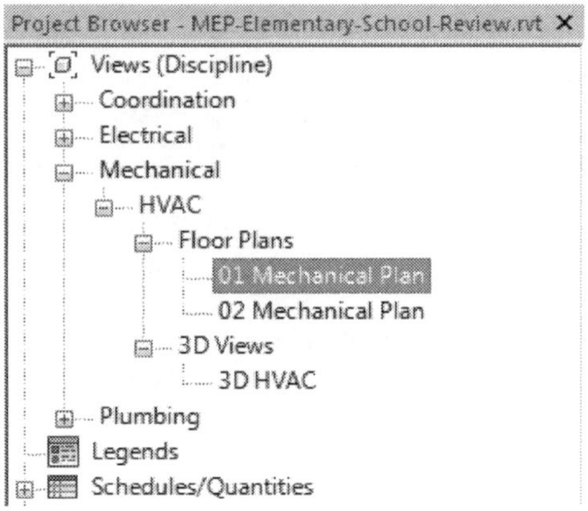

Figure 1–58

6. Double-click on **01 Mechanical Plan**. The applicable view opens as shown in Figure 1–59.

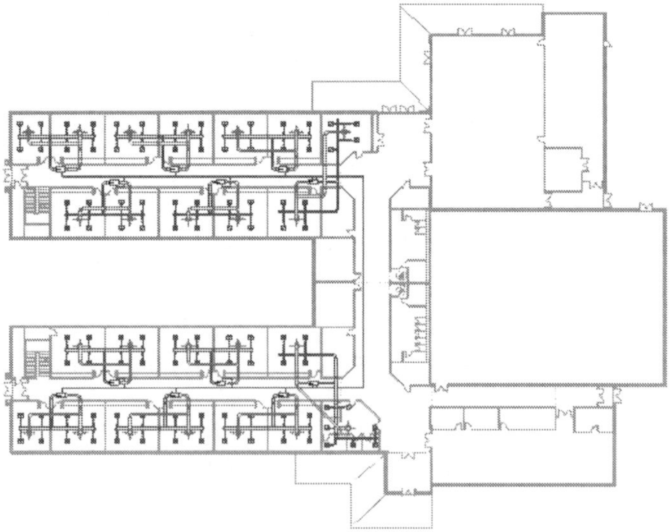

Figure 1–59

7. Use the scroll wheel to zoom and pan around the view.

8. Double-click on the scroll wheel or type **ZF** (Zoom to Fit) to return to the full view.

9. Expand Plumbing>Plumbing>**Floor Plans**. Double-click on the **01 Plumbing Plan** view to open it.

10. Expand Coordination>MEP>**Floor Plans**. Double-click on **01 Space Planning** to open this view.

11. All of the previous views are still open. In the Quick Access Toolbar (or *View* tab>Windows panel), expand (Switch Windows), as shown in Figure 1–60, and select one of the previous views to which to switch.

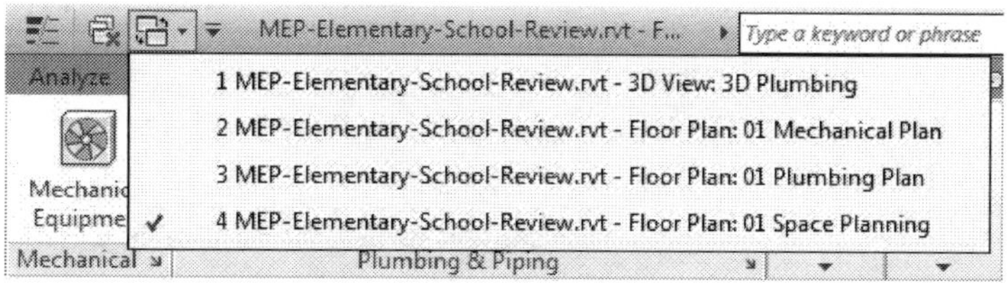

Figure 1–60

12. In the *View* tab>Windows panel, click (Tile) or type **WT** to display all of the open views on the screen at the same time.

13. Type **ZA** (Zoom All to Fit) to have the model display completely within each view window, as shown in Figure 1–61.

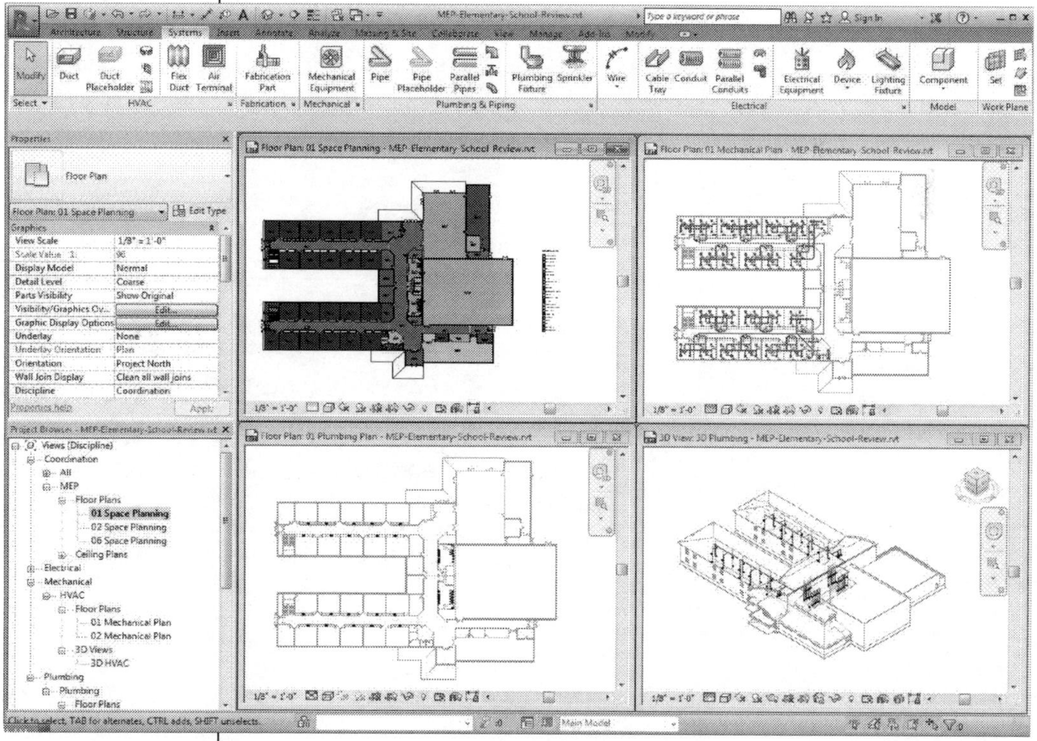

Figure 1–61

14. Click in the open **01 Mechanical Plan** view to make it active.

15. In the upper right corner, click (Maximize), as shown in Figure 1–62, so that this view fills the drawing area. Then use one of the zoom commands so that the model fills the view.

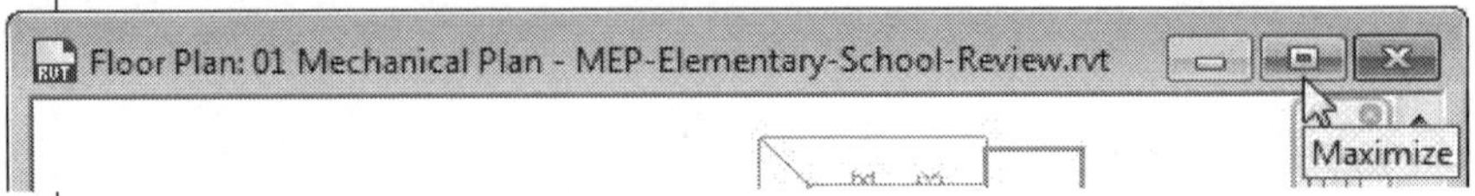

Figure 1–62

16. In the Quick Access Toolbar, click (Close Hidden Windows). Only the current active view is open.

Task 2 - Display the Element Properties.

1. In the **01 Mechanical Plan** view, hover over a duct without selecting it first. The duct highlights and a tooltip displays as shown in Figure 1–63. Information about the element also displays in the Status Bar but not in Properties.

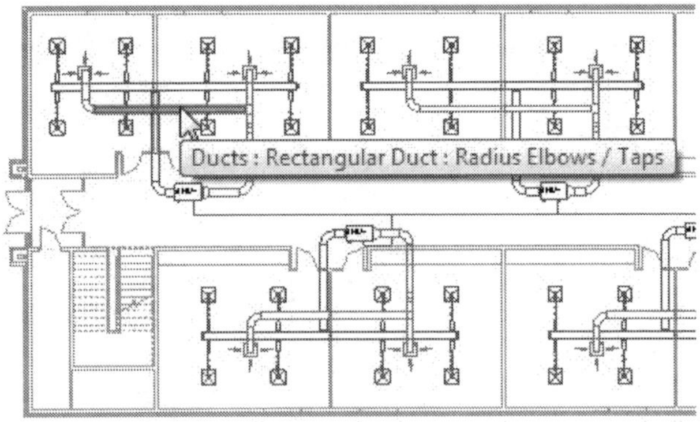

Figure 1–63

2. Click on the duct to select it. The selection color and tabs on the ribbon at the top of the screen change. Properties now displays information about this piece of ductwork, as shown in Figure 1–64.

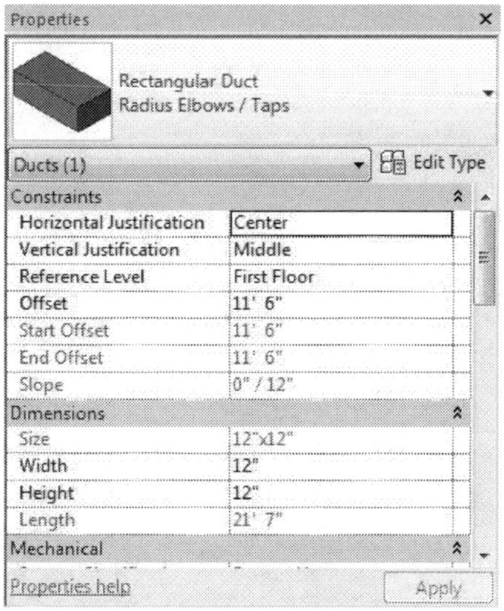

Figure 1–64

3. Hold <Ctrl> and in the view, select another, similar Duct element, as shown in Figure 1–65. Properties now displays that two ducts (Ducts(2)) are selected with the same information.

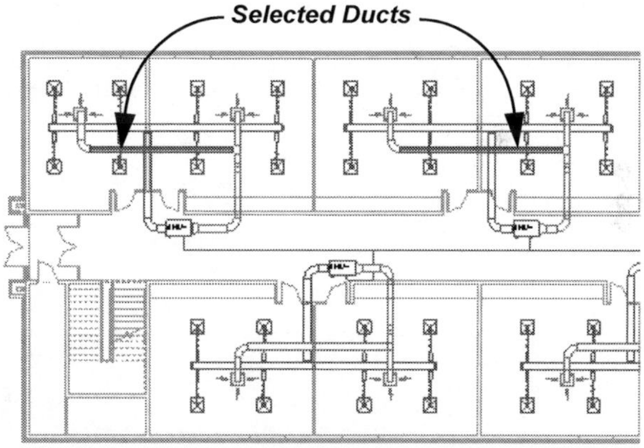

Figure 1–65

4. Hold <Ctrl> and select an air terminal. Properties now displays Common (3) in the Filter drop-down list, because the three selected elements are not of the same type. Therefore they do not share the same type of properties.

5. In Properties, expand the Filter drop-down list and select **Air Terminals**, as shown in Figure 1–66.

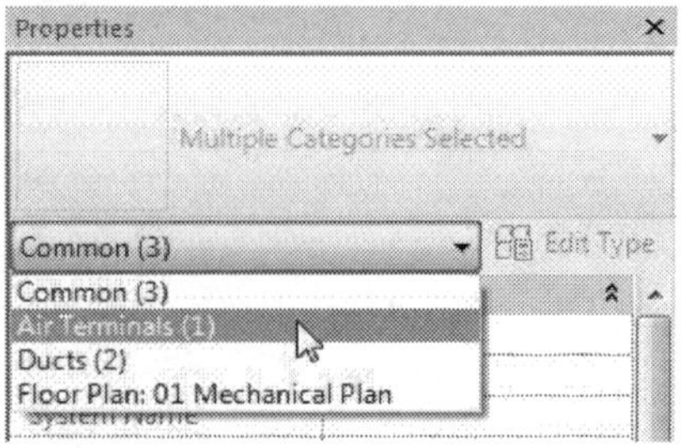

Figure 1–66

6. Only the Air Terminal properties are displayed, but the selection set has not changed. In the view they are all still selected.

7. End the command using one of the following methods:

    - In *Modify | Multi-Select* tab>Select panel, click (Modify).
    - Press <Esc> twice.
    - Click in the view window (without selecting an element).
    - Right-click in the view window and select **Cancel**.

Task 3 - Create 3D Views.

1. In the Quick Access Toolbar, click (Default 3D View).

2. A 3D Isometric view displays, as shown in Figure 1–67.

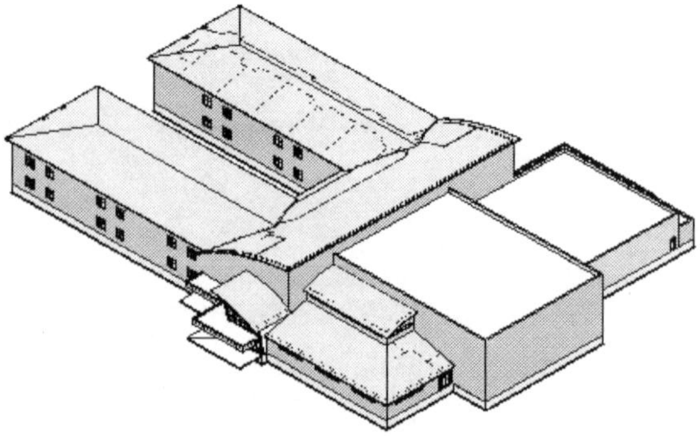

Figure 1–67

3. Press and hold <Shift> and press the middle mouse (scroll) button to orbit the view.

4. In the View Control Bar, select several different Visual Styles to see how they impact the view, as shown in Figure 1–68.

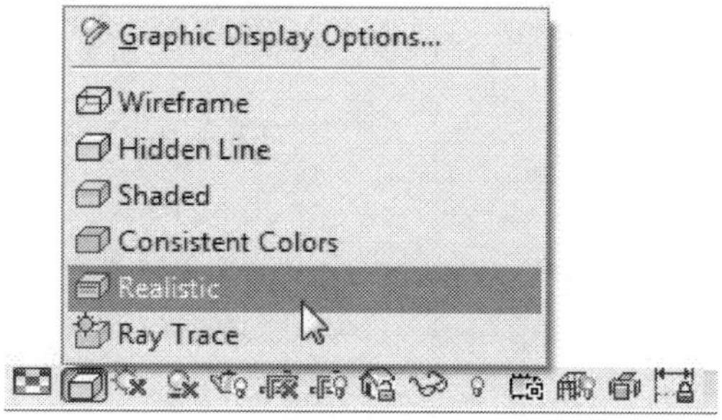

Figure 1–68

5. Select a view and visual style that you like. In the Project Browser, expand Coordination>All>**3D Views**, right-click on **{3D}** and select **Rename**.
6. Name the view **3D Exterior** and click **OK**.

Task 4 - Create a camera view.

1. Switch back to the **01 Mechanical Plan** view.
2. In the Quick Access Toolbar, expand  (Default 3D View) and click  (Camera).
3. Place the camera and select a point for the target similar to that shown in Figure 1–69.

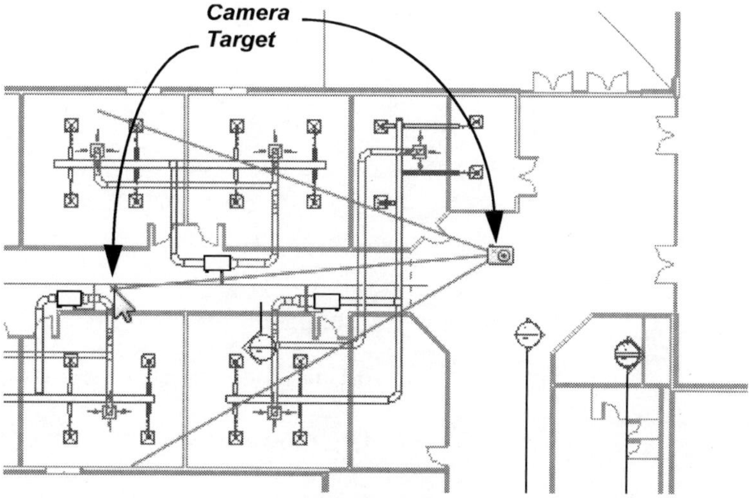

Figure 1–69

4. The new view displays. Use the controls on the outline of the view to resize the view.

5. Click inside the 3D view and use <Shift>+ mouse wheel to rotate around until you get a good view of the ductwork.

6. Set the Visual Style as required.

7. In the Project Browser, expand Mechanical>???>*3D Views* and select the new **3D View 1** as shown in Figure 1–70.

The new view displays in the ??? category because it has not been assigned a Sub-Discipline.

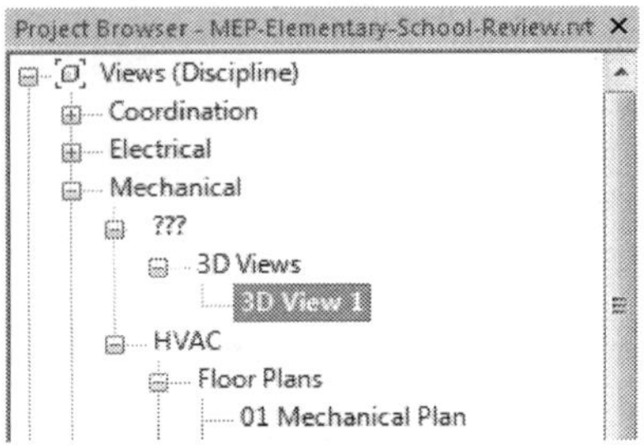

Figure 1–70

8. In Properties, in the *Graphics* area, expand Sub-Discipline and select **HVAC**, as shown in Figure 1–71.

9. Click **Apply**. The view moves to the correct sub-discipline group as shown in Figure 1–72. Rename the view as required.

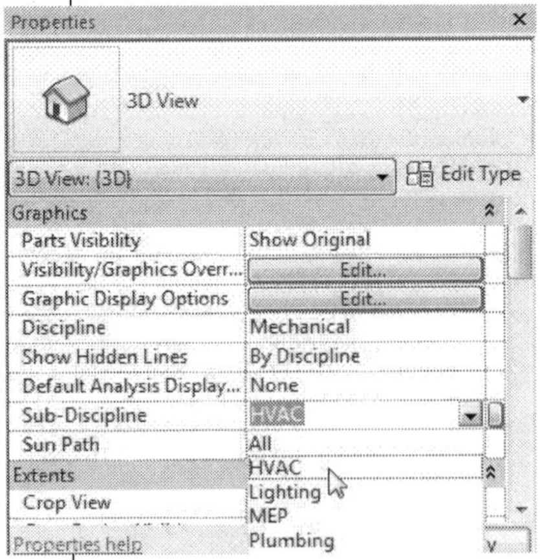

Figure 1–71

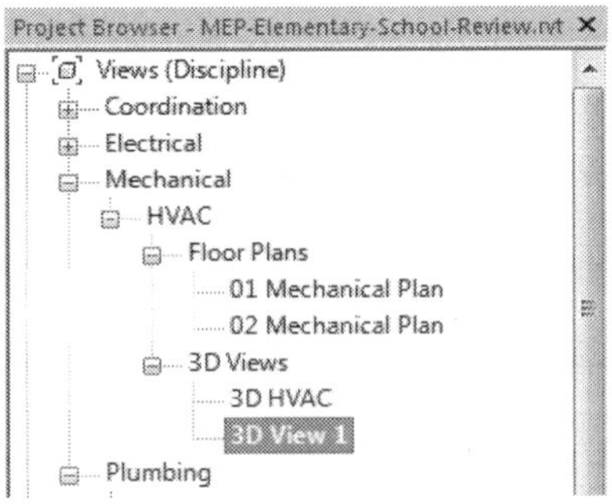

Figure 1–72

10. Save the project.

11. In the Application Menu, click  (Close).

Practice 1c Review a Structural Project

Practice Objectives

- Navigate the graphic user interface.
- Manipulate 2D and 3D views by zooming and panning.
- Create 3D Isometric and Perspective views.
- Set the Visual Style of a view.

Estimated time for completion: 15 minutes

In this practice you will open a project file and view each of the various areas in the interface. You will investigate elements, commands, and their options. You will also open views through the Project Browser and view the model in 3D, as shown in Figure 1–52.

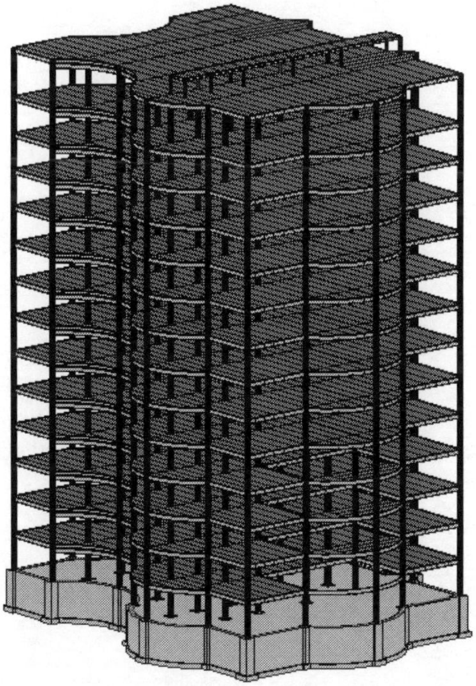

Figure 1–73

Task 1 - Explore the interface.

1. In the Application Menu, expand  (Open) and click  (Project).

2. In the Open dialog box, select **Syracuse-Suites.rvt**. It is found in your practice folder and is a version similar to the main project you will work on throughout the student guide.

3. Click **Open**. The 3D view of the building opens in the drawing window.

If the Project Browser and Properties palette are docked over each other, use the Project Browser tab at the bottom to display it.

4. In the Project Browser, double-click on the **Structural Plans: 00 GROUND FLOOR** view. It opens a plan with the Visual Style set to **Wireframe** so that the footings and foundation walls display, although there is a slab over them.

5. In the View Control toolbar, change the *Visual Style* to **Hidden Line**. The lines that are hidden in the view display as dashed, as shown in Figure 1–74.

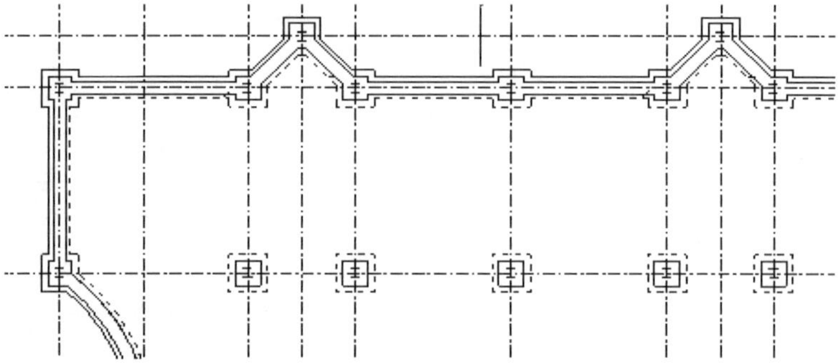

Figure 1–74

6. In the Project Browser, double-click on the **Structural Plans: T.O. FOOTING** view. The strip footings and spread footings display as continuous lines because they are not obscured by a slab, as shown in Figure 1–75.

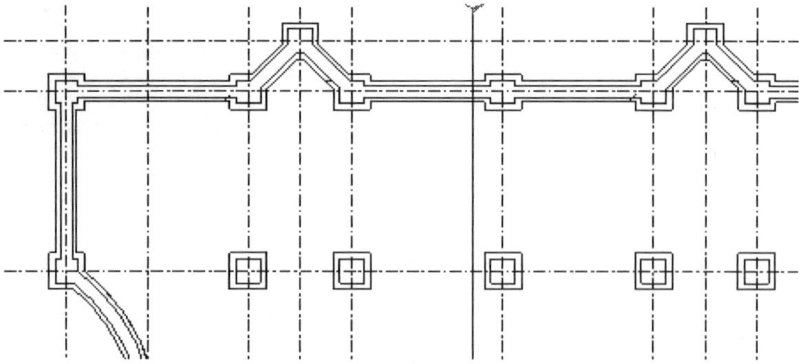

Figure 1–75

7. Zoom in on one corner of the building. The foundation walls are in-filled with the appropriate concrete hatch, as shown in Figure 1–76.

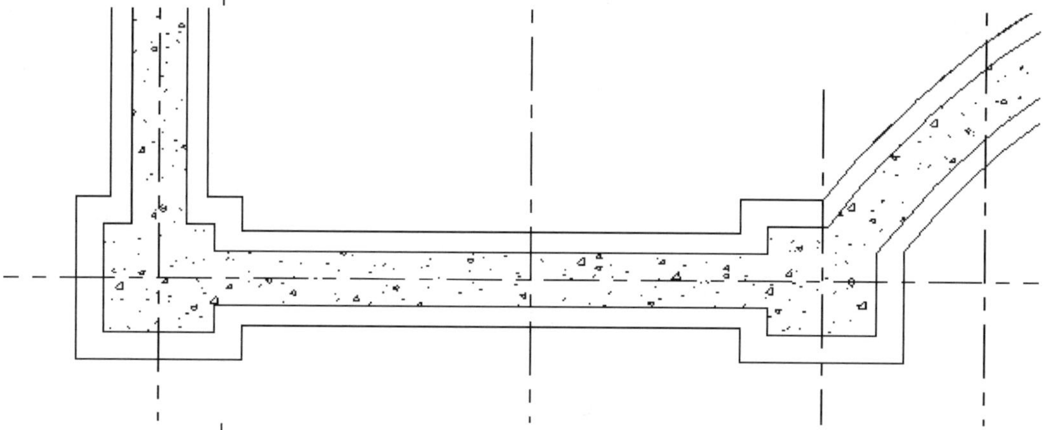

Figure 1–76

8. Double-click the mouse wheel or type **ZE** to zoom to the extents of the view. (**ZA** zooms to the extents of all of the opened view windows). Find the section marker that extends vertically along the model as shown in Figure 1–77.

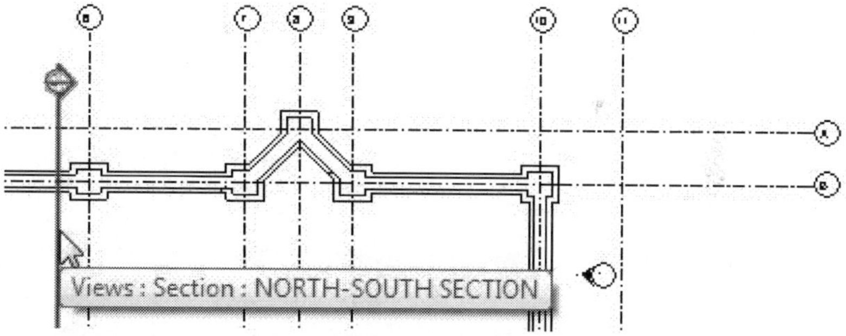

Figure 1–77

9. Double-click on the section head to open the **NORTH-SOUTH SECTION** view.

10. In the Project Browser, navigate to the *Sections (Building Section)* category. The **NORTH-SOUTH SECTION** view name is bold. You can navigate through your model by double-clicking on the element in the Project Browser, or by using the graphical view elements in the model.

11. In the section view, zoom in on the area in which the callout has been placed as shown in Figure 1–78. Double-click on the callout-head to open the **TYPICAL EDGE DETAIL** view.

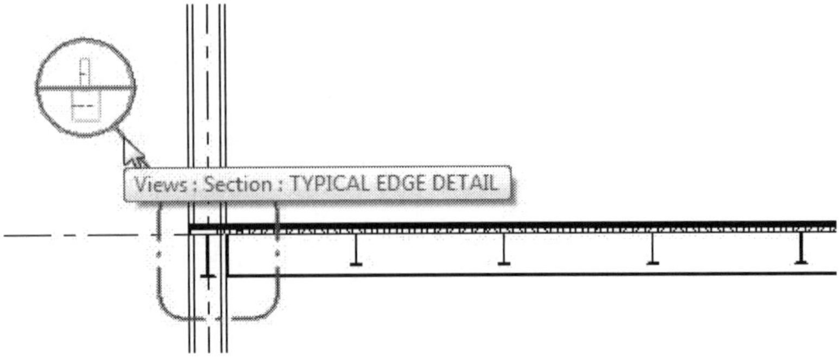

Figure 1–78

12. In the **TYPICAL EDGE DETAIL** view, select the floor, as shown in Figure 1–79.

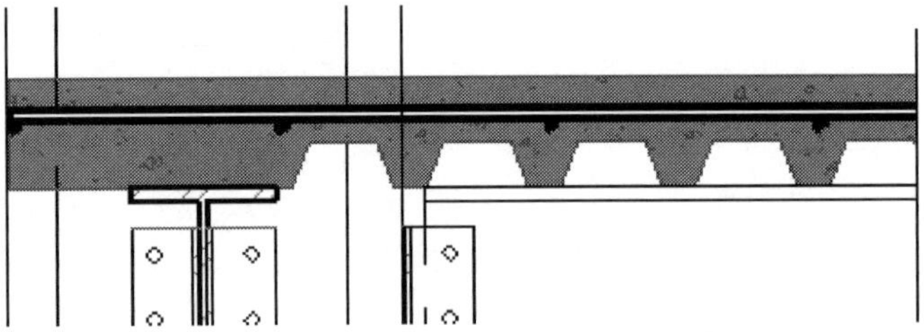

Figure 1–79

13. This is a full 3D floor element. You can edit it using the tools shown in the *Modify | Floors* contextual tab, as shown in Figure 1–80.

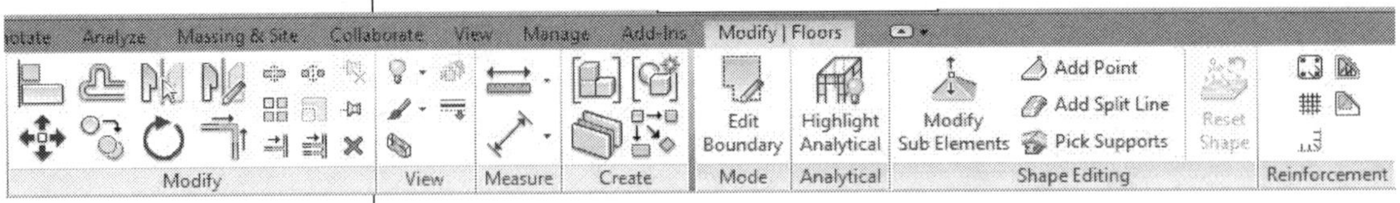

Figure 1–80

Any changes made here are applied to the selected element only.

14. The Properties palette displays the Instance Parameters for the element, as shown in Figure 1–81.

Figure 1–81

Any changes made here to the element are applied to all its other instances in the project.

15. In Properties, click (Edit Type) to access the Type Parameters in the Type Properties dialog box, as shown in Figure 1–82.

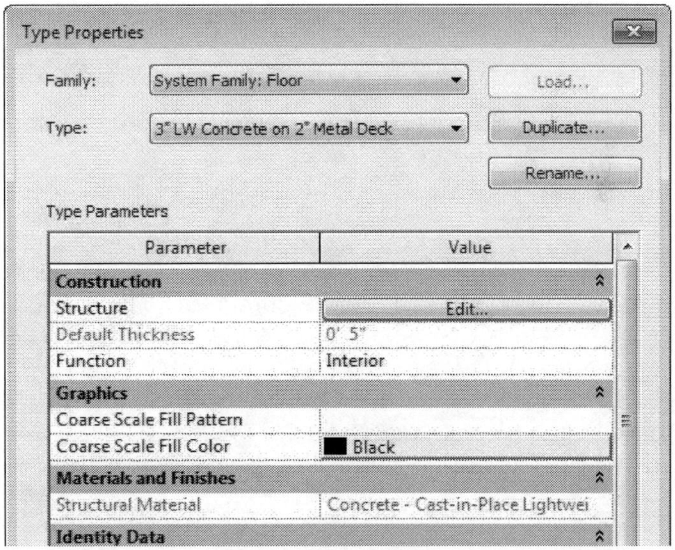

Figure 1–82

16. Click **Cancel** to close the Type Properties dialog box.

17. Press <Esc> or click in empty space to clear the selection.

18. Select one of the bolted connections. This is a detail component (2D element). The *Modify | Detail Items* contextual tab displays the modifying options specific to this element as shown in Figure 1–83.

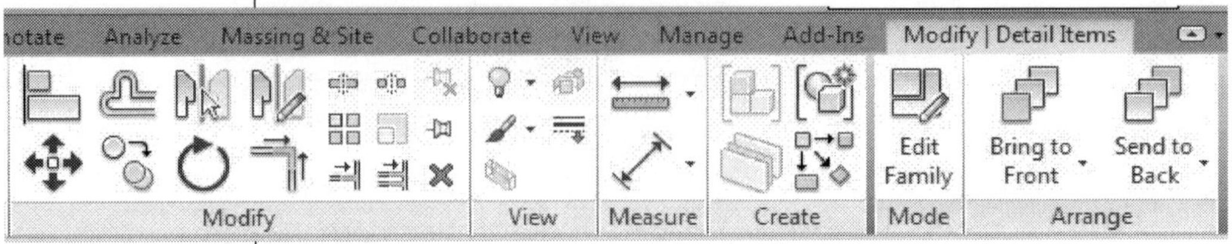

Figure 1–83

19. Press <Esc> to clear the selection.

Task 2 - Work with Multiple views and 3D views.

1. In the **Section: TYPICAL EGE DETAIL** view, double-click on the **01 FIRST FLOOR** datum mark, as shown in Figure 1–84. This opens the **Structural Plans: 01 FIRST FLOOR** view.

Figure 1–84

2. In the Quick Access Toolbar, expand  (Switch Windows). The growing list of opened windows displays as shown in Figure 1–85. This can quickly become a management issue once the model size increases.

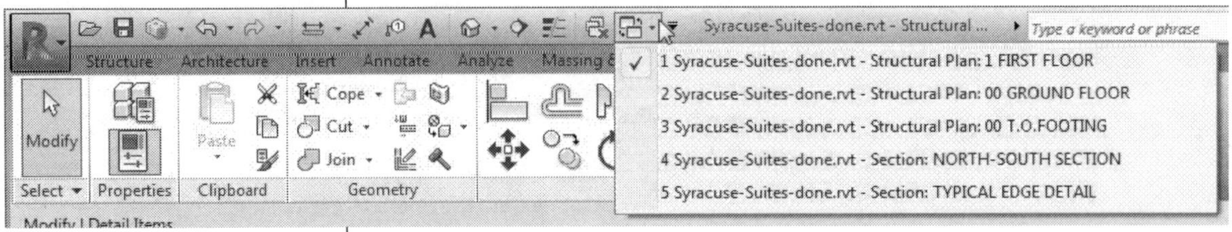

Figure 1–85

3. In the Quick Access Toolbar, click (Close Hidden Windows) so that only the current window remains open.

4. In the *View* tab>Create panel or the Quick Access Toolbar, click (3D View).

5. Type **WT** to tile the windows.

6. Type **ZA** to zoom extents in both windows, as shown in Figure 1–86. This view configuration is useful when placing elements in a model.

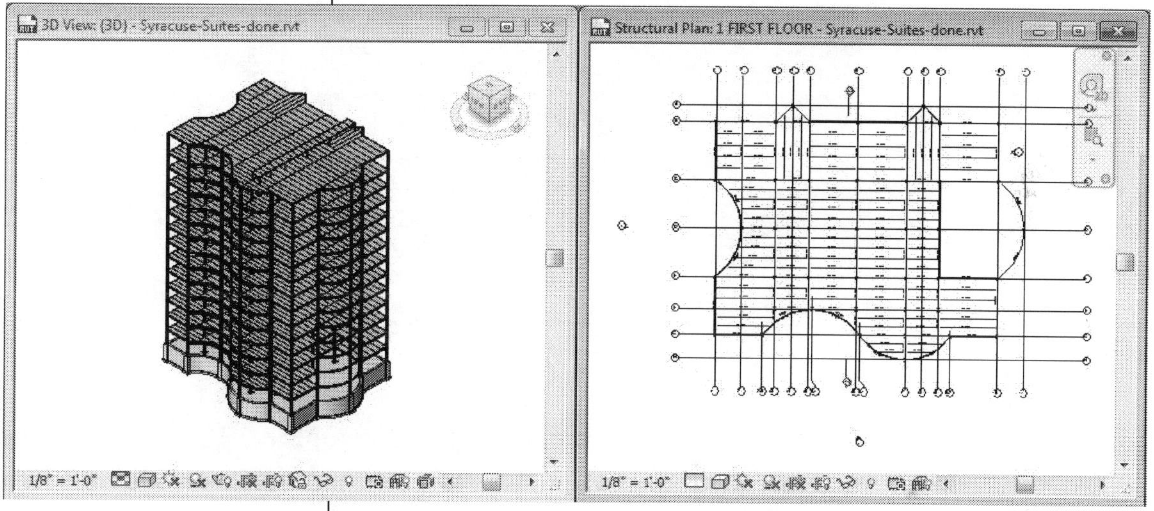

Figure 1–86

7. Click inside the 3D view window.

8. Press and hold <Shift> and then press and hold the wheel on the mouse. Move the mouse to dynamically view the 3D model. You can also navigate in 3D using the ViewCube in the upper right corner of the view.

9. In the upper right corner of the view, click (Close) to close the 3D view. (This also works when many views are open.)

10. Expand the Application Menu and click (Close) to exit the project. Do not save changes.

Chapter Review Questions

1. When you create a project in the Autodesk Revit software, do you work in 3D (as shown on the left in Figure 1–87) or 2D (as shown on the right in Figure 1–87)?

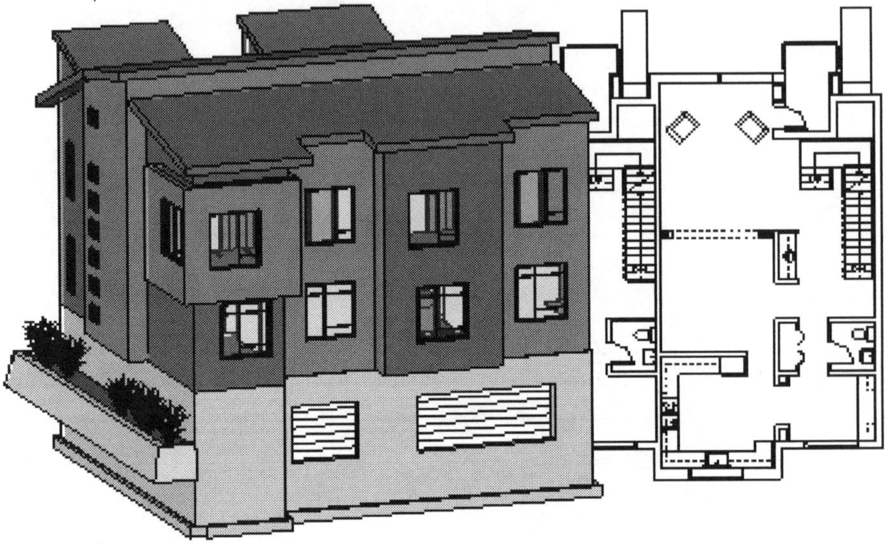

Figure 1–87

   a. You work in 2D in plan views and in 3D in non-plan views.
   b. You work in 3D almost all of the time, even when you are using what looks like a flat view.
   c. You work in 2D or 3D depending on how you toggle the 2D/3D control.
   d. You work in 2D in plan and section views and in 3D in isometric views.

2. What is the purpose of the Project Browser?
   a. It enables you to browse through the building project, similar to a walk through.
   b. It is the interface for managing all of the files that are required to create the complete architectural model of the building.
   c. It manages multiple Autodesk Revit projects as an alternative to using Windows Explorer.
   d. It is used to access and manage the views of the project.

3. Which part(s) of the interface changes according to the command you are using? (Select all that apply.)
    a. Ribbon
    b. View Control Bar
    c. Options Bar
    d. Properties Palette
4. The difference between Type Properties and Properties (the ribbon location is shown in Figure 1–88) is...

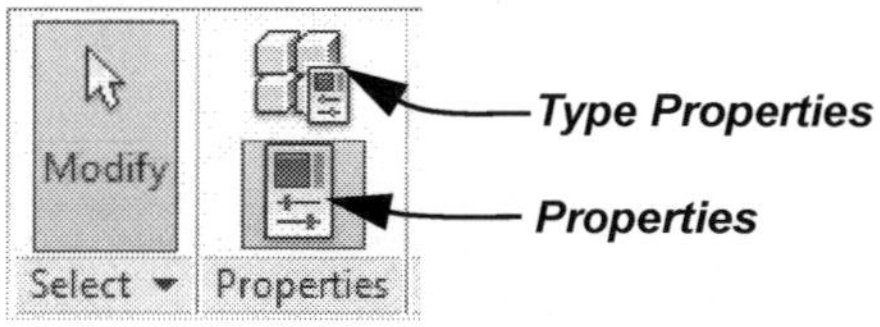

Figure 1–88

    a. Properties stores parameters that apply to the selected individual element(s). Type Properties stores parameters that impact every element of the same type in the project.
    b. Properties stores the location parameters of an element. Type Properties stores the size and identity parameters of an element.
    c. Properties only stores parameters of the view. Type Properties stores parameters of model components.
5. When you start a new project, how do you specify the base information in the new file?
    a. Transfer the base information from an existing project.
    b. Select the right template for the task.
    c. The Autodesk Revit software automatically extracts the base information from imported or linked file(s).
6. What is the main difference between a view made using  (Default 3D View) and a view made using  (Camera)?
    a. Use Default **3D View** for exterior views and **Camera** for interiors.
    b. **Default 3D View** creates a static image and a **Camera** view is live and always updated.
    c. **Default 3D View** is isometric and a **Camera** view is perspective.
    d. **Default 3D View** is used for the overall building and a **Camera** view is used for looking in tight spaces.

Command Summary

Button	Command	Location
General Tools		
	Modify	• **Ribbon:** All tabs>Select panel • **Shortcut:** MD
	New	• **Quick Access Toolbar** (Optional) • **Application Menu** • **Shortcut:** <Ctrl>+<N>
	Open	• **Quick Access Toolbar** • **Application Menu** • **Shortcut:** <Ctrl>+<O>
	Open Documents	• **Application Menu**
	Properties	• **Ribbon:** *Modify* tab>Properties panel • **Shortcut:** PP
	Recent Documents	• **Application Menu**
	Save	• **Quick Access Toolbar** • **Application Menu** • **Shortcut:** <Ctrl>+<S>
	Synchronize and Modify Settings	• **Quick Access Toolbar**
	Synchronize Now/	• **Quick Access Toolbar**>expand Synchronize and Modify Settings
	Type Properties	• **Ribbon:** *Modify* tab>Properties panel • **Properties palette**
Viewing Tools		
	Camera	• **Quick Access Toolbar**> Expand Default 3D View • **Ribbon:** *View* tab>Create panel> expand Default 3D View
	Default 3D View	• **Quick Access Toolbar** • **Ribbon:** *View* tab>Create panel
	Home	• **ViewCube**
N/A	**Next Pan/Zoom**	• **Navigation Bar** • **Shortcut Menu**
N/A	**Previous Pan/Zoom**	• **Navigation Bar** • **Shortcut Menu** • **Shortcut:** ZP

	Shadows On/Off	• **View Control Bar**
	Show Rendering Dialog/ Render	• **View Control Bar** • **Ribbon:** *View* tab>Graphics panel • **Shortcut:** RR
	Zoom All to Fit	• **Navigation Bar** • **Shortcut:** ZA
	Zoom in Region	• **Navigation Bar** • **Shortcut Menu** • **Shortcut:** ZR
	Zoom Out (2x)	• **Navigation Bar** • **Shortcut Menu** • **Shortcut:** ZO
	Zoom Sheet Size	• **Navigation Bar** • **Shortcut:** ZS
	Zoom to Fit	• **Navigation Bar** • **Shortcut Menu** • **Shortcut:** ZF, ZE
Visual Styles		
	Consistent Colors	• **View Control Bar**:
	Hidden Line	• **View Control Bar** • **Shortcut:** HL
	Ray Trace	• **View Control Bar**:
	Realistic	• **View Control Bar**
	Shaded	• **View Control Bar** • **Shortcut:** SD
	Wireframe	• **View Control Bar** • **Shortcut:** WF

Reviewing Projects

Basic sketching, selecting, and modifying tools are the foundation of working with all types of elements in the Autodesk® Revit® software. Using these tools with drawing aids helps you to place and modify elements to create accurate building models. You can also troubleshoot a project by reviewing warnings and running interference checks between disciplines.

Learning Objectives in this Chapter

- Sketch linear elements such as walls, beams, and pipes.
- Ease the placement of elements by incorporating drawing aids, such as alignment lines, temporary dimensions, and snaps.
- Place Reference Planes as temporary guide lines.
- Use techniques to select and filter groups of elements.
- Modify elements using a contextual tab, Properties, temporary dimensions, and controls.
- Work with errors and warnings in models.
- Run Interference Check to find out if there are problems within a model or between disciplines.

2.1 Using General Sketching Tools

When you start a command, the contextual tab on the ribbon, the Options Bar, and the Properties palette enable you to set up features for each new element you are placing in the project. As you are working, several features called *drawing aids* display, as shown in Figure 2–1. They help you to create designs quickly and accurately.

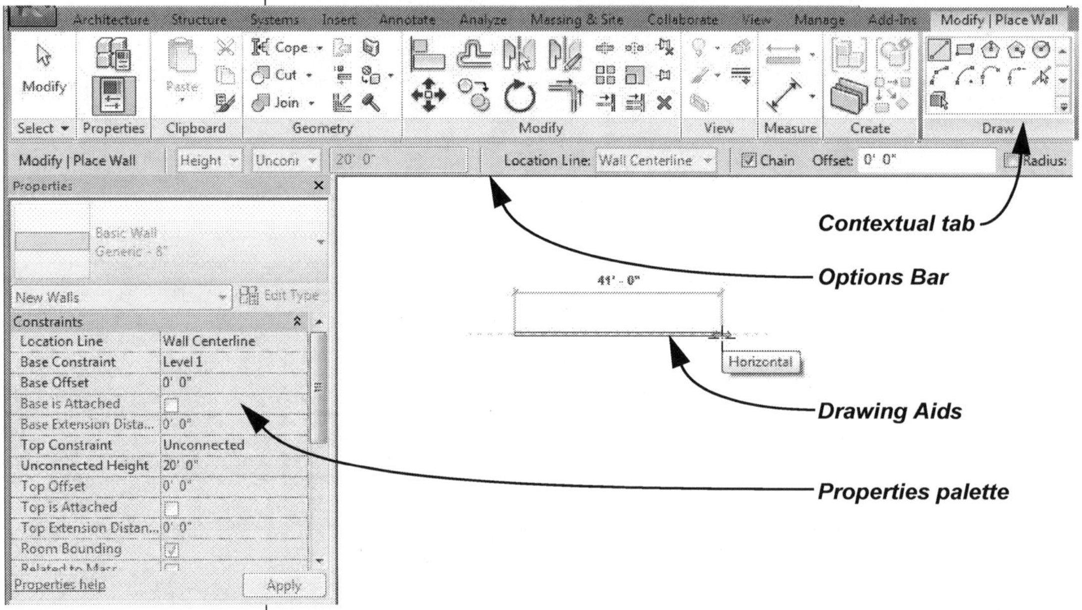

Figure 2–1

- in Autodesk Revit, you are most frequently creating 3D model elements rather than 2D sketches. These tools work with both 3D and 2D elements in the software.

Draw Tools

Many linear elements (such as walls, beams, ducts, pipes, and conduits) are modeled using the tools on the contextual tab on the *Draw* panel, as shown for walls in Figure 2–1. Other elements (such as floors, ceilings, roofs, and slabs) have boundaries that are sketched using many of the same tools. Draw tools are also used when you create details or schematic drawings.

Two methods are available:

The exact tools vary according to the element being modeled.

- *Draw* the element using a geometric form
- *Pick* an existing element (such as a line, face, or wall) as the basis for the new element's geometry and position.

How To: Create Linear Elements

1. Start the command you want to use.
2. In the contextual tab>Draw panel, as shown in Figure 2–2, select a drawing tool.
3. Select points to define the elements.

You can change from one Draw tool shape to another in the middle of a command.

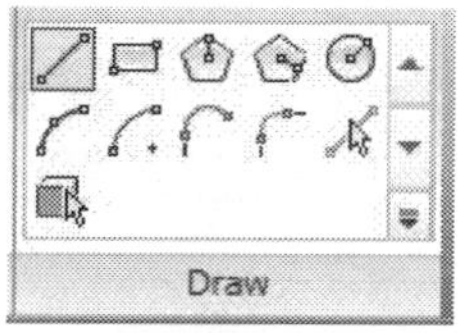

Figure 2–2

4. Finish the command using one of the standard methods:

- Click  (Modify).
- Press <Esc> twice.
- Right-click and select **Cancel** twice.
- Start another command.

Draw Options

When you are in Drawing mode, several options display in the Options Bar, as shown in Figure 2–3.

Different options display according to the type of element that is selected or the command that is active.

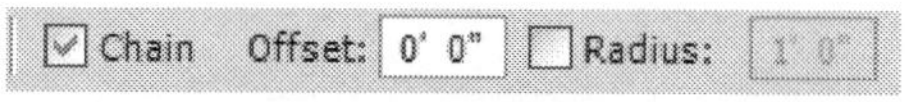

Figure 2–3

- **Chain:** Controls how many segments are created in one process. If this option is not selected, the **Line** and **Arc** tools only create one segment at a time. If it is selected, you can continue adding segments until you select the command again.
- **Offset:** Enables you to enter values so you can create linear elements at a specified distance from the selected points or element.
- **Radius:** Enables you to enter values when using a radial tool.

Draw Tools

	Line	Draws a straight line defined by the first and last points. If Chain is enabled, you can continue selecting end points for multiple segments.
	Rectangle	Draws a rectangle defined by two opposing corner points. You can adjust the dimensions after selecting both points.
	Inscribed Polygon	Draws a polygon inscribed in a hypothetical circle with the number of sides specified in the Options Bar.
	Circumscribed Polygon	Draws a polygon circumscribed around a hypothetical circle with the number of sides specified in the Options Bar.
	Circle	Draws a circle defined by a center point and radius.
	Start-End-Radius Arc	Draws a curve defined by a start, end, and radius of the arc. The outside dimension shown is the included angle of the arc. The inside dimension is the radius.
	Center-ends Arc	Draws a curve defined by a center, radius, and included angle. The selected point of the radius also defines the start point of the arc.
	Tangent End Arc	Draws a curve tangent to another element. Select an end point for the first point, but do not select the intersection of two or more elements. Then select a second point based on the included angle of the arc.
	Fillet Arc	Draws a curve defined by two other elements and a radius. Because it is difficult to select the correct radius by clicking, this command automatically moves to edit mode. Select the dimension and then modify the radius of the fillet.
	Spline	Draws a spline curve based on selected points. The curve does not actually touch the points (Model and Detail Lines only).
	Ellipse	Draws an ellipse from a primary and secondary axis (Model and Detail Lines only).
	Partial Ellipse	Draws only one side of the ellipse, like an arc. A partial ellipse also has a primary and secondary axis (Model and Detail Lines only).

Pick Tools

	**Pick Lines**	Use this option to select existing linear elements in the project. This is useful when you start the project from an imported 2D drawing.
	**Pick Face**	Use this option to select the face of a 3D massing element (walls and 3D views only).
	**Pick Walls**	Use this option to select an existing wall in the project to be the basis for a new sketch line (floors, ceilings, etc.).

Drawing Aids

As soon as you start sketching or placing elements, three drawing aids display, as shown in Figure 2–4:

- Alignment lines
- Temporary dimensions
- Snaps

These aids are available with most modeling and many modification commands.

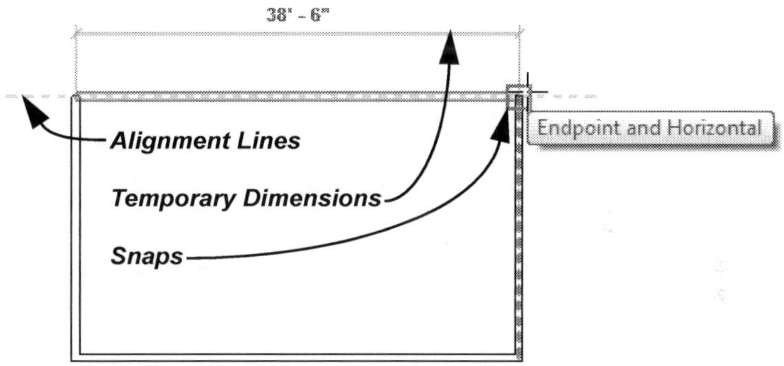

Figure 2–4

Alignment lines display as soon as you select your first point. They help keep lines horizontal, vertical, or at a specified angle. They also line up with the implied intersections of walls and other elements.

- Hold <Shift> to force the alignments to be orthogonal (90 degree angles only).

Temporary dimensions display to help place elements at the correct length, angle and location.

- You can type in the dimension and then move the cursor until you see the dimension you want, or you can place the element and then modify the dimension as required.
- The length and angle increments shown vary depending on how far in or out the view is zoomed.
- For Imperial measurements (feet and inches), the software uses a default of feet. For example, when you type **4** and press <Enter>, it assumes 4'-0". For a distance such as 4'-6", you can type any of the following: **4'-6"**, **4'6**, **4-6**, or **4 6** (the numbers separated by a space). To indicate distances less than one foot, type the inch mark (") after the distance, or enter **0**, a space, and then the distance.

Hint: Temporary Dimensions and Permanent Dimensions

Temporary dimensions disappear as soon as you finish adding elements. If you want to make them permanent, select the control shown in Figure 2–5.

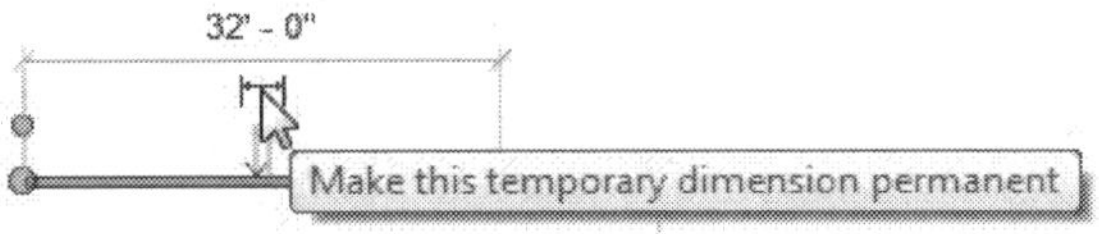

Figure 2–5

Snaps are key points that help you reference existing elements to exact points when modeling, as shown in Figure 2–6.

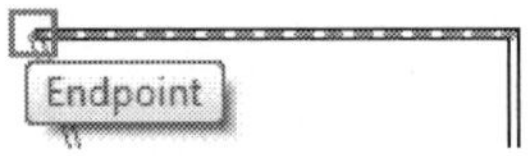

Figure 2–6

- When you move the cursor over an element, the snap symbol displays. Each snap location type displays with a different symbol.

Hint: Snap Settings and Overrides

In the *Manage* tab>Settings panel, click (Snaps) to open the Snaps dialog box, which is shown in Figure 2–7. The Snaps dialog box enables you to set which snap points are active, and set the dimension increments displayed for temporary dimensions (both linear and angular).

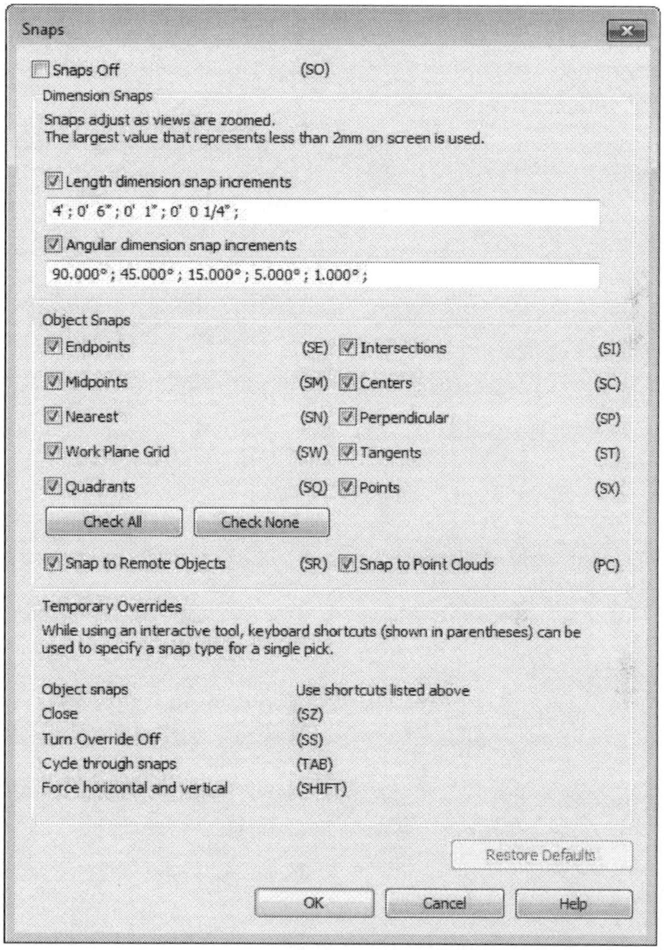

Figure 2–7

- Keyboard shortcuts for each snap can be used to override the automatic snapping. Temporary overrides only affect a single pick, but can be very helpful when there are snaps nearby other than the one you want to use.

Reference Planes

As you develop designs in the Autodesk Revit software, there are times when you need lines to help you define certain locations. You can sketch reference planes (displayed as dashed green lines) and snap to them whenever you need to line up elements. For the example shown in Figure 2–8, the lighting fixtures in the reflected ceiling plan are placed using reference planes.

- To insert a reference plane, in the *Architecture, Structure*, or *Systems* tab>Work Plane panel, click (Ref Plane) or type **RP**.

Reference planes do not display in 3D views.

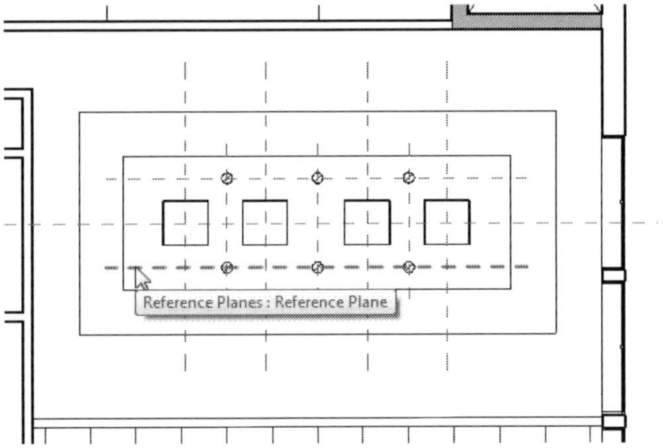

Figure 2–8

- Reference planes display in associated views because they are infinite planes, and not just lines.

Enhanced in **2017**

- You can name Reference planes by clicking on **<Click to name>** and typing in the text box, as shown in Figure 2–9.

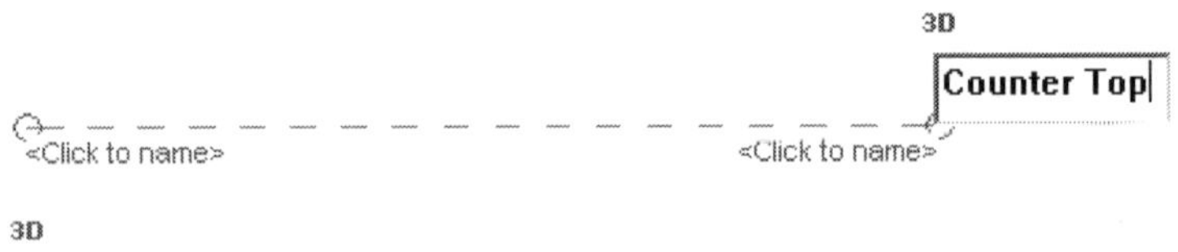

Figure 2–9

- If you sketch a reference pane in Sketch Mode (used with floors and similar elements), it does not display once the sketch is finished.
- Reference planes can have different line styles if they have been defined in the project. In Properties, select a style from the Subcategory list.

2.2 Editing Elements

Building design projects typically involve extensive changes to the model. The Autodesk Revit software was designed to make such changes quickly and efficiently. You can change an element using the following methods, as shown in Figure 2–10:

- Type Selector enables you to specify a different type. This is frequently used to change the size and/or style of the elements.
- Properties enables you to modify the information (parameters) associated with the selected elements.
- Temporary dimensions enable you to change the element's dimensions or position.
- The contextual tab in the ribbon contains the Modify commands and element-specific tools.
- Controls enable you to drag, flip, lock, and rotate the element.
- Shape handles (not shown) enable you to drag elements to modify their height or length.

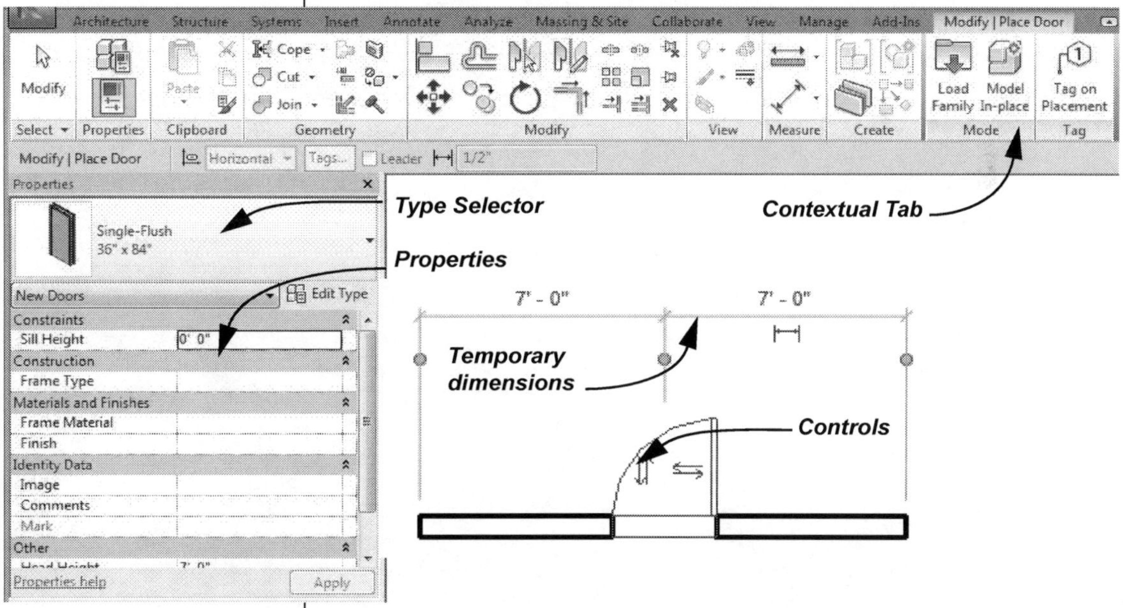

Figure 2–10

- To delete an element, select it and press <Delete>, right-click and select **Delete**, or in the Modify panel, click (Delete).

Working with Controls and Shape Handles

When you select an element, various controls and shape handles display depending on the element and view. For example, in plan view you can use controls to drag the ends of a wall and change its orientation. You can also drag the wall ends in a 3D view, and you can also use the arrow shape handles to change the height of the wall, as shown in Figure 2–11

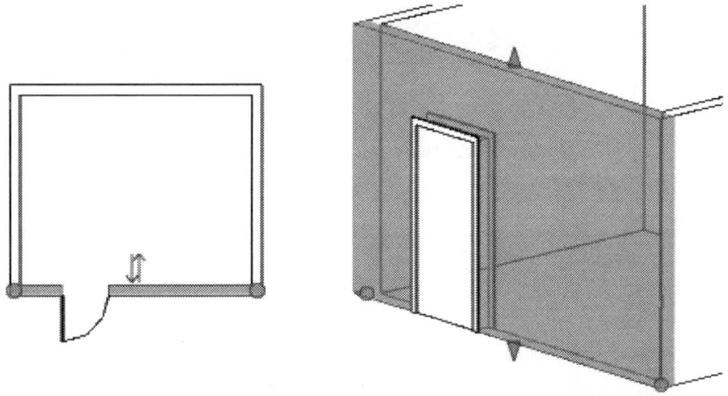

Figure 2–11

- If you hover the cursor over the control or shape handle, a tooltip displays showing its function.

Hint: Editing Temporary Dimensions

Temporary dimensions automatically link to the closest wall. To change this, drag the *Witness Line* control (as shown in Figure 2–12) to connect to a new reference. You can also click on the control to toggle between justifications in the wall.

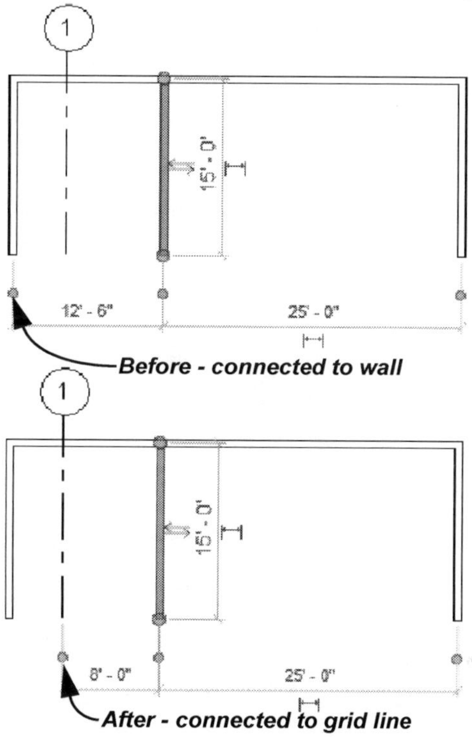

Figure 2–12

- The new location of a temporary dimension for an element is remembered as long as you are in the same session of the software.

Selecting Multiple Elements

- Once you have selected at least one element, hold <Ctrl> and select another item to add it to a selection set.
- To remove an element from a selection set, hold <Shift> and select the element.
- If you click and drag the cursor to *window* around elements, you have two selection options, as shown in Figure 2–13. If you drag from left to right, you only select the elements completely inside the window. If you drag from right to left, you select elements both inside and crossing the window.

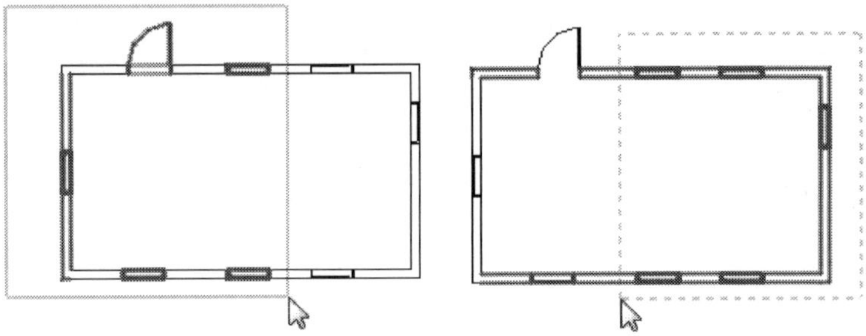

Window: Left to Right ***Crossing: Right to Left***

Figure 2–13

- If several elements are on or near each other, press <Tab> to cycle through them before you click. If there are elements that might be linked to each other, such as walls that are connected, pressing <Tab> selects the chain of elements.
- Press <Ctrl>+<Left Arrow> to reselect the previous selection set. You can also right-click in the view window with nothing selected and select **Select Previous**.
- To select all elements of a specific type, right-click on an element and select **Select All Instances>Visible in View** or **In Entire Project**, as shown in Figure 2–14.

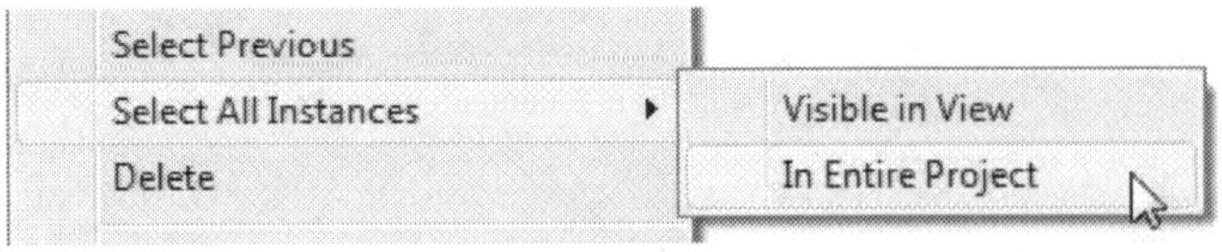

Figure 2–14

Hint: Measuring Tools

When modifying a model, it is useful to know the distance between elements. This can be done with temporary dimensions, or more frequently, by using the measuring tools found in the Quick Access Toolbar or on the *Modify* tab> Measure panel, as shown in Figure 2–15.

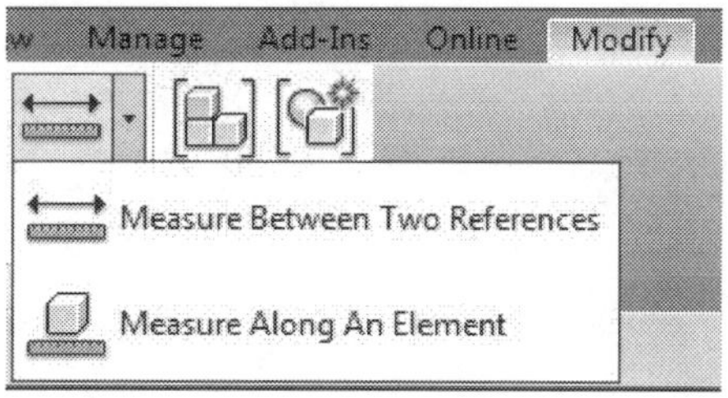

Figure 2–15

-  (Measure Between Two References) - Select two elements and the measurement displays.
-  (Measure Along An Element) - Select the edge of a linear element and the total length displays.

Filtering Selection Sets

When multiple element categories are selected, the *Multi-Select* contextual tab opens in the ribbon. This gives you access to all of the Modify tools, and the **Filter** command. The **Filter** command enables you to specify the types of elements to select. For example, you might only want to select columns, as shown in Figure 2–16.

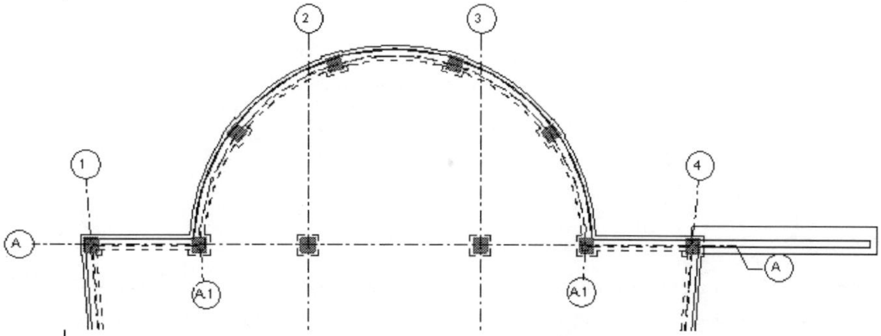

Figure 2–16

How To: Filter a Selection Set

The Filter dialog box displays all types of elements in the original selection.

1. Select everything in the required area.
2. in the *Modify* | *Multi-Select* tab>Selection panel, or in the Status Bar, click (Filter). The Filter dialog box opens, as shown in Figure 2–17.

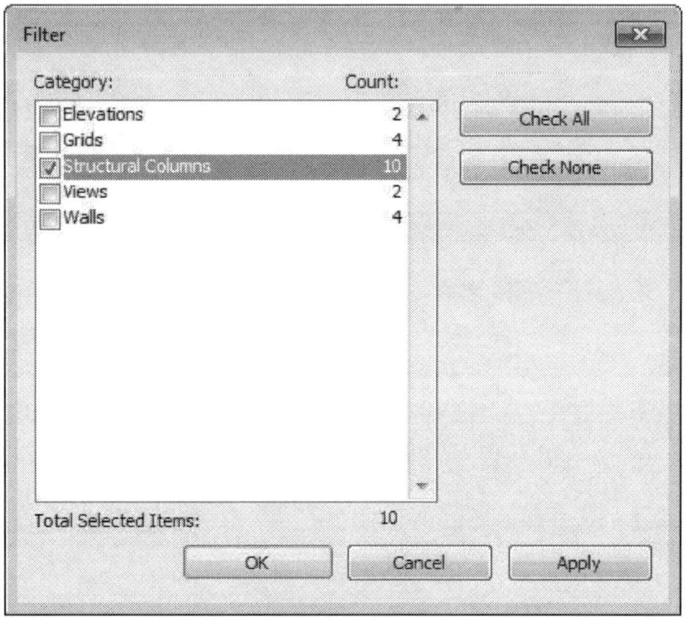

Figure 2–17

3. Click **Check None** to clear all of the options or **Check All** to select all of the options. You can also select or clear individual categories as required.
4. Click **OK**. The selection set is now limited to the elements you specified.

- The number of elements selected displays on the right end of the status bar and in the Properties palette.
- Clicking **Filter** in the Status Bar also opens the Filter dialog box.

Hint: Selection Options

You can control how the software selects specific elements in a project by toggling **Selection Options** on and off on the Status Bar, as shown in Figure 2–18. Alternatively, in any tab on the ribbon, expand the Select panel's title and select the option.

Figure 2–18

-  **Select links:** When toggled on, you can selected linked CAD drawings or Autodesk Revit models. When it is toggled off you cannot select them when using **Modify** or **Move**.

-  **Select underlay elements:** When toggled on, you can select underlay elements. When toggled off, you cannot select them when using **Modify** or **Move**.

-  **Select pinned elements:** When toggled on, you can selected pinned elements. When toggled off, you cannot select them when using **Modify** or **Move**.

-  **Select elements by face:** When toggled on you can select elements (such as the floors or walls in an elevation) by selecting the interior face or selecting an edge. When toggled off, you can only select elements by selecting an edge.

-  **Drag elements on selection:** When toggled on, you can hover over an element, select it, and drag it to a new location. When toggled off, the Crossing or Box select mode starts when you press and drag, even if you are on top of an element. Once elements have been selected they can still be dragged to a new location.

Practice 2a Sketch and Edit Architectural Elements

Estimated time for completion: 10 minutes

Practice Objective

- Use sketch tools and drawing aids.

In this practice you will use the **Wall** command along with sketching tools and drawing aids, such as temporary dimensions and snaps. You will use the **Modify** command and modify the walls using grips, temporary dimensions, the Type Selector, and Properties. You will add a door and modify it using temporary dimensions and controls. The completed model is shown in Figure 2–19.

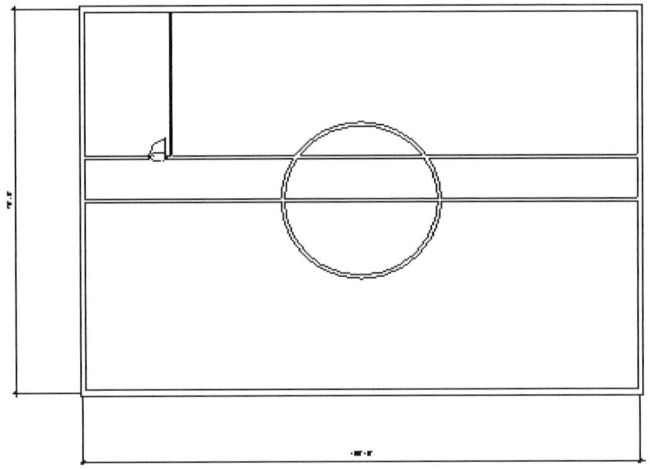

Figure 2–19

Task 1 - Draw and modify walls.

1. In the Application Menu, click (New)> (Project).
2. In the New Project dialog box, select **Architectural Template** in the Template file drop-down list, and click **OK**.
3. In the Quick Access Toolbar, click (Save). When prompted, name the project **Simple Building.rvt**.

4. In the *Architecture* tab>Build panel, click (Wall).
5. In the *Modify | Place Wall* tab>Draw panel, click (Rectangle) and sketch a rectangle approximately **100' x 70'**. You do not have to be precise because you can change the dimensions later.
6. Note that the dimensions are temporary. Select the vertical dimension text and type **70' 0"**, as shown in Figure 2–20. Press <Enter>.

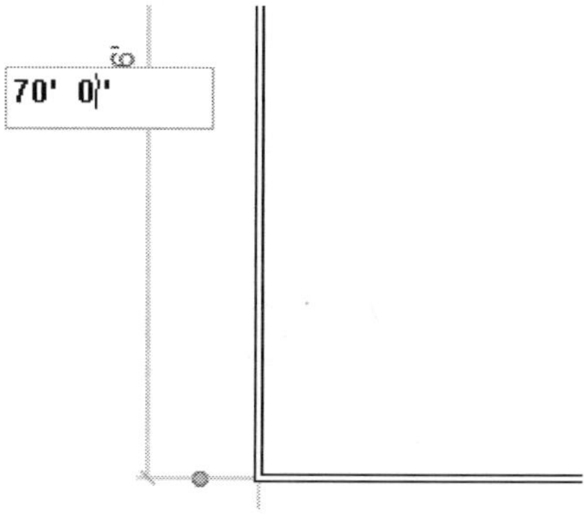

Figure 2–20

7. The dimensions are still displayed as temporary. Click the dimension controls of both the dimensions to make them permanent, as shown in Figure 2–21.

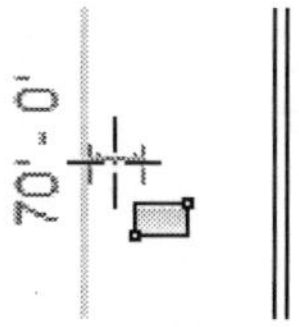

Figure 2–21

- You will change the horizontal wall dimension using the permanent dimension.

8. In the Select panel, click (Modify). You can also use one of the other methods to switch to **Modify:**
   - Type the shortcut **MD**.
   - Press <Esc> once or twice.
   - Right-click and select **Cancel**.

9. Select either vertical wall. The horizontal dimension becomes active (changes to blue). Click the dimension text and type **100' 0"**, as shown in Figure 2–22.

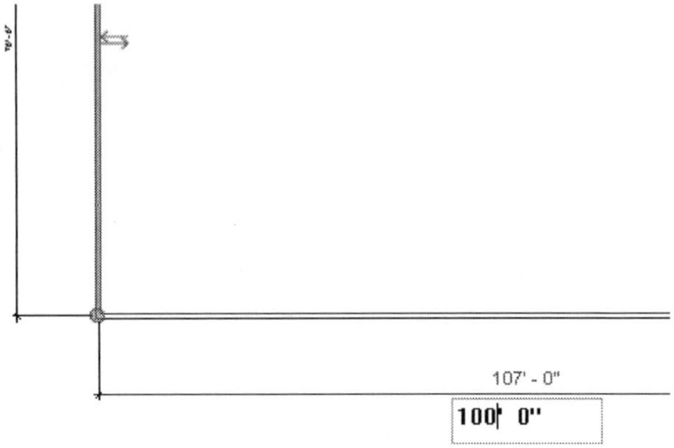

Figure 2–22

10. Click in an empty space to end the selection. You are still in the **Modify** command.

11. In the *Architecture* tab>Build panel, click (Wall). In the Draw panel, verify that (Line) is selected. Sketch a wall horizontally from midpoint to midpoint of the vertical walls.

12. Draw another horizontal wall **8'-0"** above the middle horizontal wall. You can use temporary dimensions or the *Offset* field to do this.

13. Draw a vertical wall exactly **16'-0"** from the left wall, as shown in Figure 2–23.

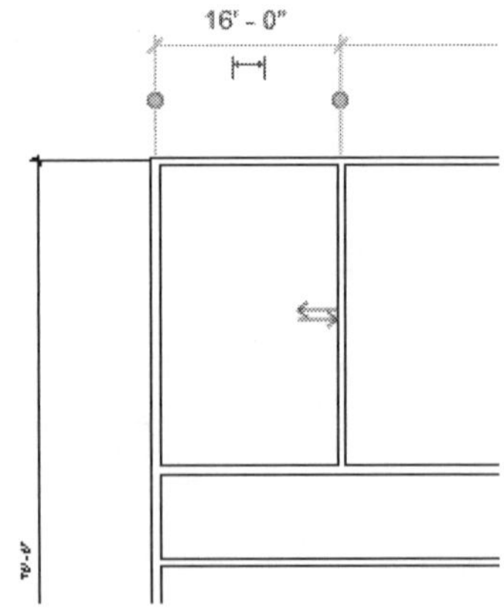

Figure 2–23

14. In the Draw panel, click (Circle) and sketch a **14'-0"** radius circular wall at the midpoint of the lower interior horizontal wall, as shown in Figure 2–24.

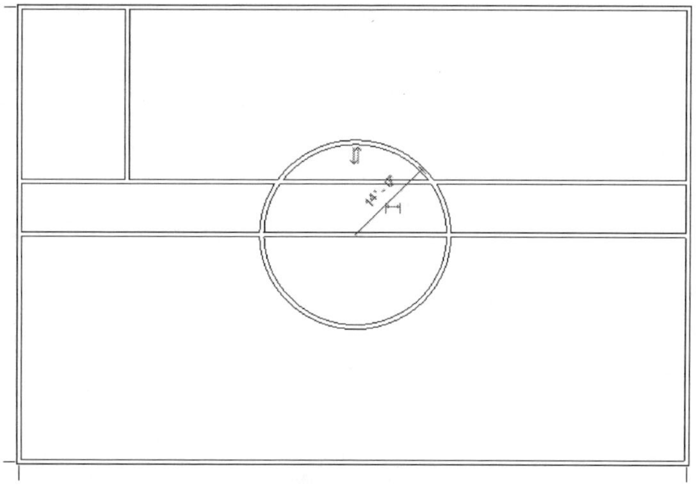

Figure 2–24

15. Click (Modify) to finish the command.

16. Hover the cursor over one of the outside walls, press <Tab> to highlight the chain of outside walls, and click to select the walls.

17. In the Type Selector, select **Basic Wall: Generic-12"**, as shown in Figure 2–25. The thickness of the outside walls change.

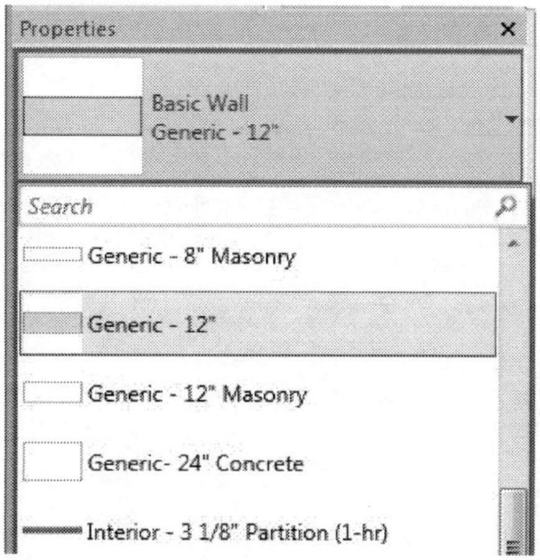

Figure 2–25

18. Click in empty space to release the selection.
19. Select the vertical interior wall. In the Type Selector, change the wall to one of the small interior partition styles.
20. Click in an empty space to release the selection.

Task 2 - Add and modify a door.

1. Zoom in on the room in the upper left corner.
2. In the *Architecture* tab>Build panel, click (Door).
3. In the *Modify* | *Place Door* tab>Tag panel, click (Tag on Placement) if it is not already selected.
4. Place a door anywhere along the wall in the hallway.
5. Click (Modify) to finish the command.
6. Select the door. Use temporary dimensions to move it so that it is **2'-6"** from the right interior vertical wall. If required, use controls to flip the door so that it swings into the room, as shown in Figure 2–26.

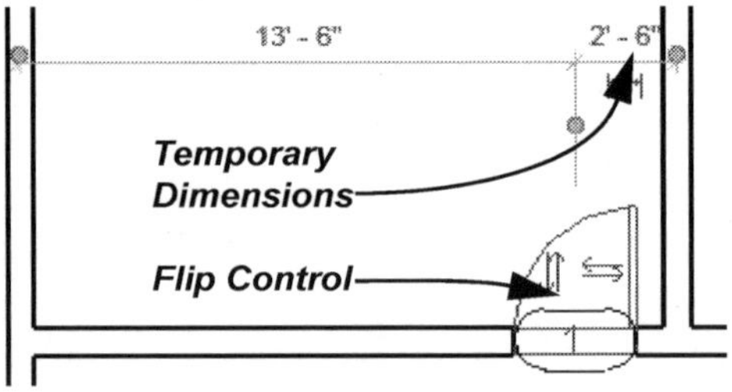

Figure 2–26

7. Type **ZE** to zoom out to the full view.
8. Save the project.

Practice 2b Select and Edit MEP Elements

Practice Objectives

- Use a variety of selection methods.
- Use temporary dimensions and connectors to modify the location of elements.

Estimated time for completion: 10 minutes

In this practice you will select lighting fixtures and change the type (as shown in Figure 2–27), as well as test a variety of selection methods and filters. You will then use connectors to modify the location of an air terminal and use **Create Similar** to add additional components. You will also modify the height of the air terminals in Properties.

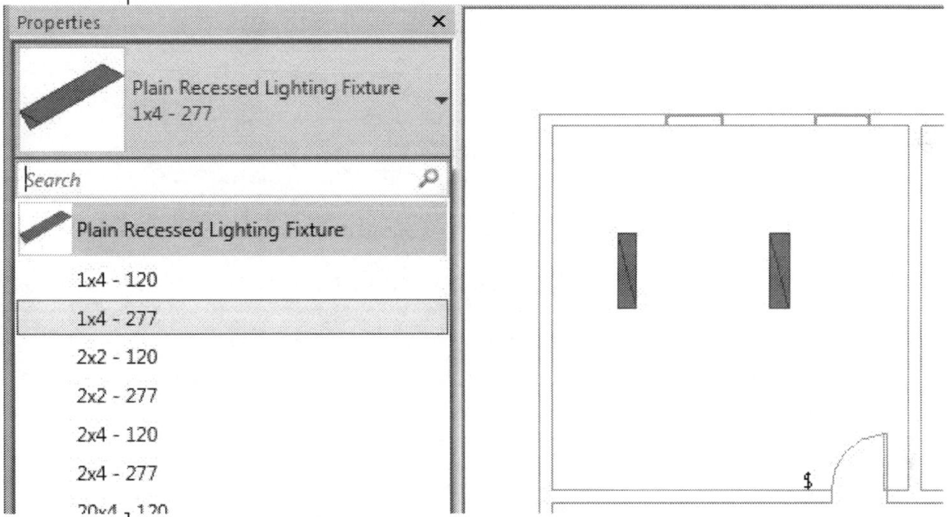

Figure 2–27

Task 1 - Use a variety of selection methods.

1. Open the project **Simple-Building-Edit.rvt**. It opens in the **1 - Lighting** view.
2. Select one of the light fixtures. The connectors and controls are displayed.
3. Hold <Ctrl> and select the other fixture. The connectors no longer display, but you can still modify the fixture type.

4. In the Type Selector, change the type to **Plain Recessed Lighting Fixture: 1x4 - 277**. Both fixtures change, as shown in Figure 2–28.

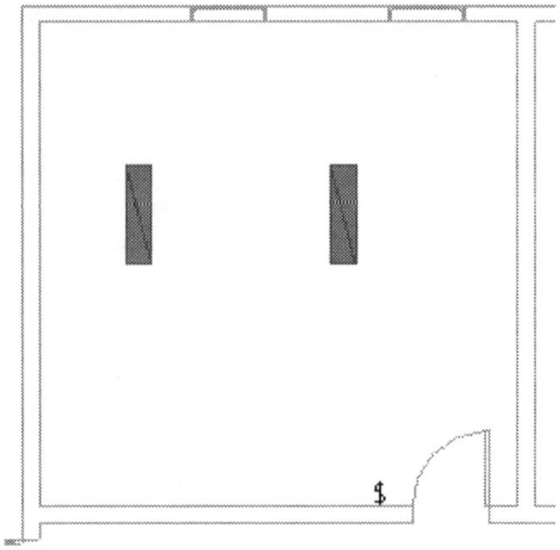

Figure 2–28

5. Click away from any elements to clear the selection.
6. Open the Mechical>HVAC>**Floor Plans>1 - Mech** view.
7. Draw a window from left to right around some of the elements, similar to that shown in Figure 2–29.

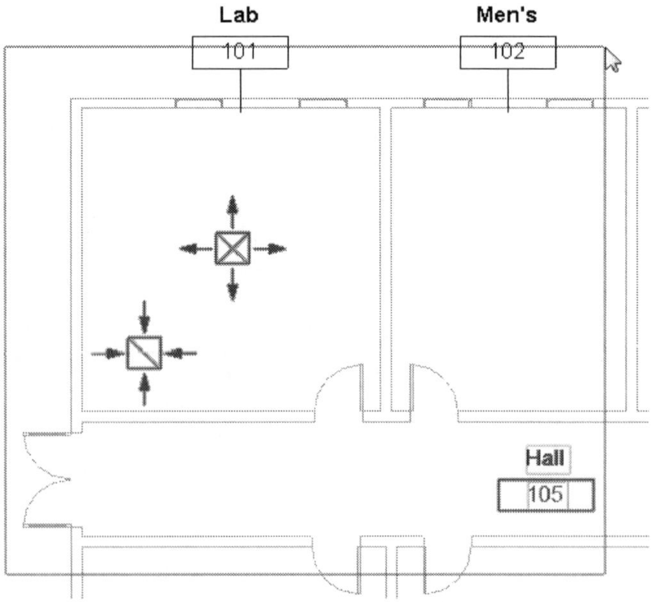

Figure 2–29

8. Note that only the elements completely inside the selection window are selected.

9. Click to clear the selection.

10. Draw a crossing window (i.e., from right to left) around the same area, as shown in Figure 2–30. Note that any elements that the window touches are included in the selection, including the linked architectural model.

You can also toggle (Select Links) in the Status Bar to keep the link from being selected.

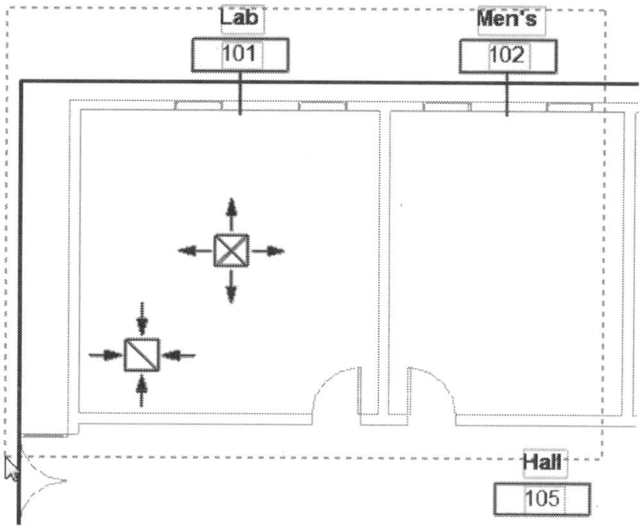

Figure 2–30

11. Hold <Shift> and select the edge of the architectural model. This removes the element from the selection set.

12. In the Status Bar, note the number of items that are selected and click (Filter).

13. In the Filter dialog box, view the categories and clear the check from **Air Terminals**.

14. Click **OK**. Only the room tags are still selected.

15. Press <Esc>. The elements are no longer selected.

16. Select one of the room tags. Right-click and select **Select All Instances>Visible in View**. All of the tags are selected.

17. Click (Modify). The elements are no longer selected.

- Remember these selection methods as you start working in the projects.

Task 2 - Modify elements using controls and properties.

1. Continue working in the **1 - Mech** view.
2. Select, click and drag the supply air terminal to a new location using the alignment lines referencing the return air terminal.
3. Right-click on the control and look at the variety of options you can use, as shown in Figure 2–31.

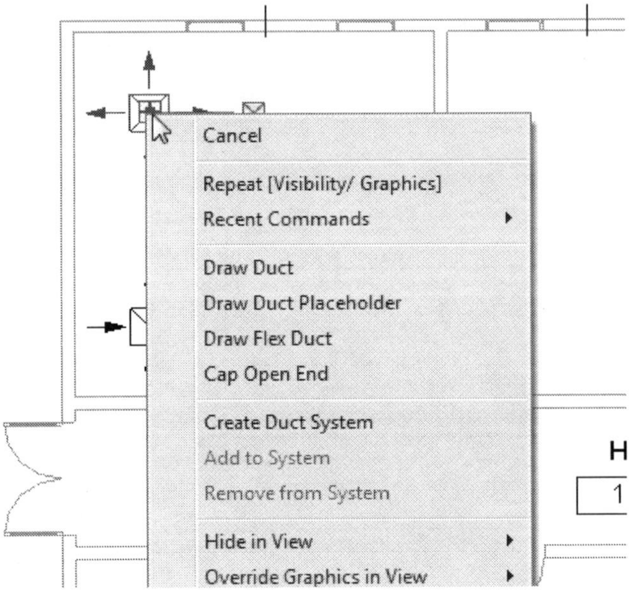

Figure 2–31

4. In the shortcut menu, select **Create Similar**. This starts the **Air Terminal** command using that type. Place two more air terminals in the same room, using alignment lines to place them.
5. Click (Modify) and select all three of the supply air terminals. Note the information in Properties. The *Offset* is set to **0'-0"** above **Level 1**.
6. Hold <Ctrl> and select the return air terminal. The *Level* and *Offset* are available to change, although two different types of components are selected.

7. Change the *Offset* to **8'-0"** and click **Apply**. The offset for all of the air terminals is updated, as shown in Figure 2–32.

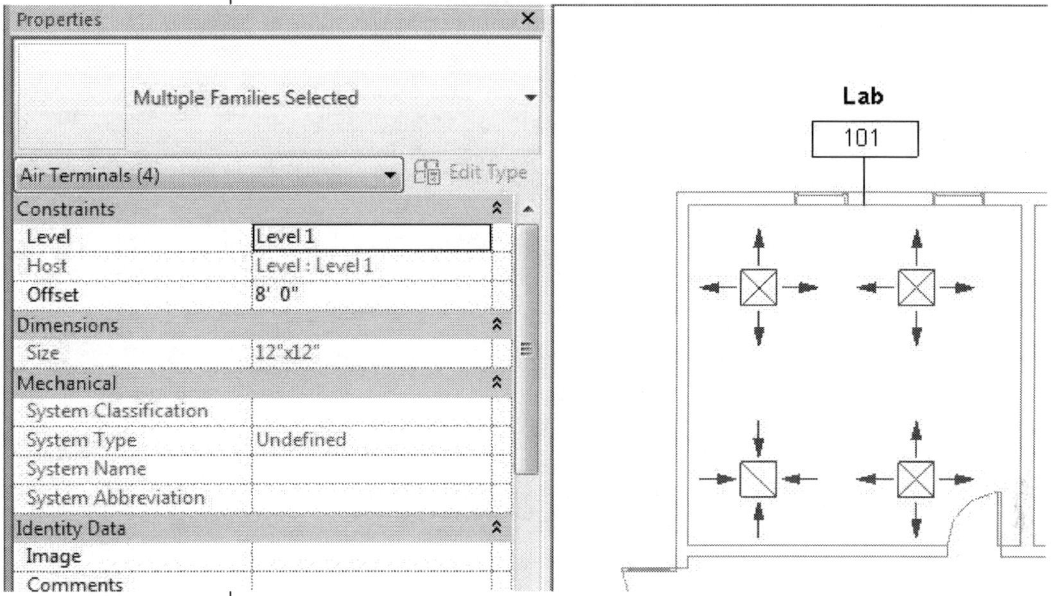

Figure 2–32

8. Click away from any elements to clear the selection.

9. Save the project.

Practice 2c

Select and Edit Structural Elements

Practice Objective

- Use sketch tools and drawing aids.

Estimated time for completion: 10 minutes

In this practice you will use a variety of ways to select elements, use the Filter dialog box to only select one type of element, select only elements of one type in the view, and use the Type Selector to change the type. You will then modify element locations using temporary dimensions as shown in Figure 2–33.

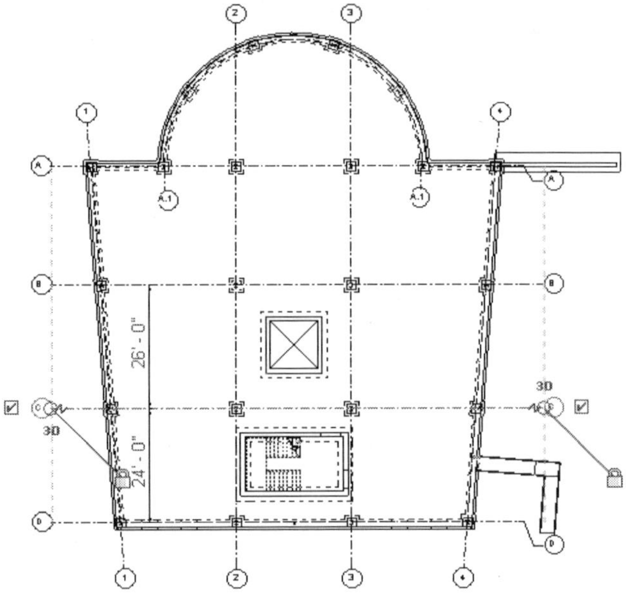

Figure 2–33

Task 1 - Select elements.

1. Open the project **Practice-Model-Select.rvt**.
2. Select a point just outside the upper left corner of the building.

3. Hold the mouse button and drag a window toward the lower right corner, as shown in Figure 2–34.

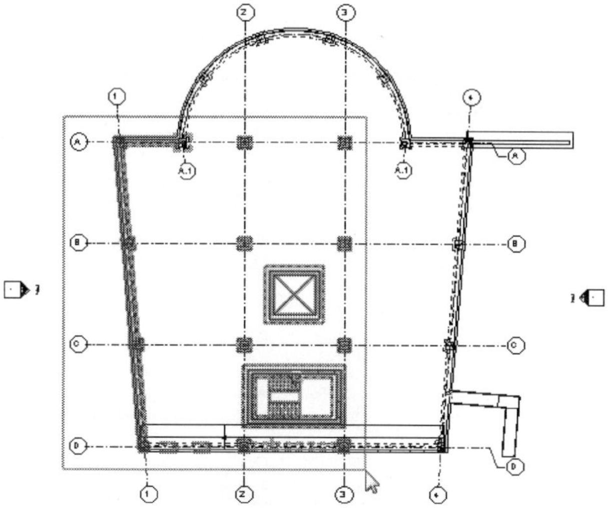

Figure 2–34

4. Select a second point. All of the elements inside the window are selected and those outside the window are not selected. Press <Esc>.

5. Select two points from just outside the upper right corner of the building to the lower left corner, as shown in Figure 2–35. All of the elements inside and touching the window are selected.

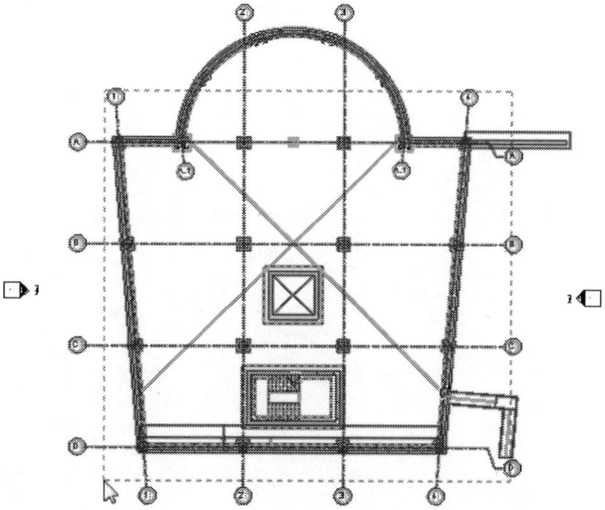

Figure 2–35

The numbers here and in the next steps might be slightly different depending on your selection set.

6. In the Status Bar, click  (Filter).
7. In the Filter dialog box shown in Figure 2–36, review the selected element categories.

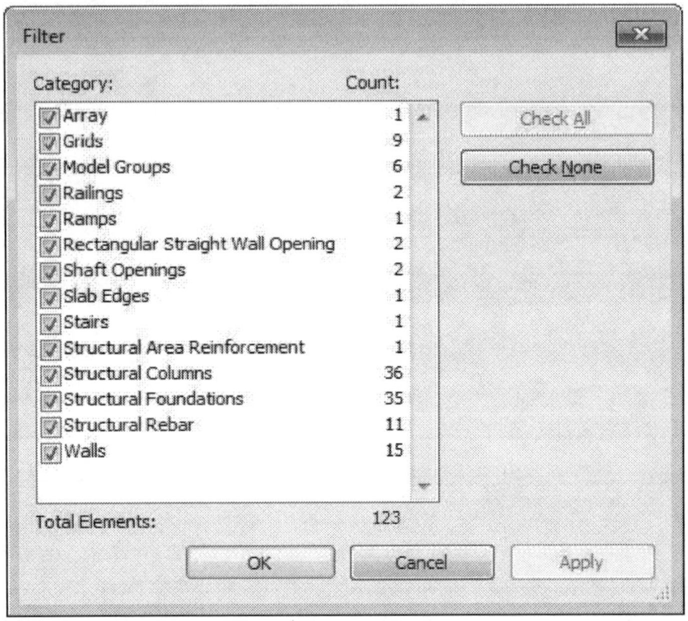

Figure 2–36

8. Click **Check None**.
9. Select only the Structural Columns category and click **OK**.
10. The total number of Structural Columns in the selection set displays in the Status Bar as shown in Figure 2–37.

Figure 2–37

11. In Properties, the display indicates that multiple Families are selected.
12. Click in empty space to clear the selection.

13. Zoom in on the lower left corner of the building and select one Structural Column as shown in Figure 2–38.

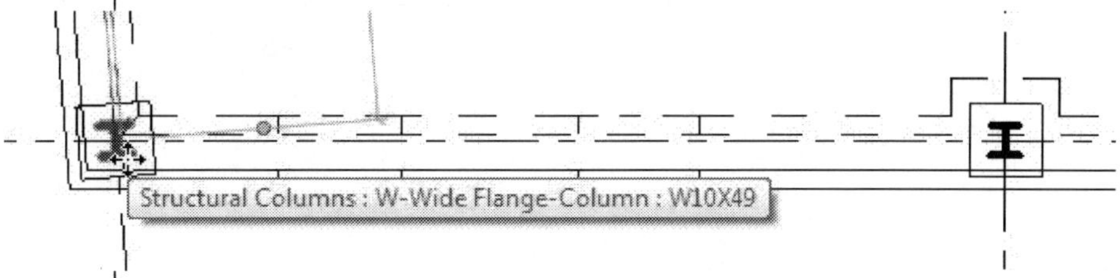

Figure 2–38

14. In the Type Selector, the column name and type are displayed as shown in Figure 2–39.

Figure 2–39

15. In the view, right-click, expand **Select All Instances**, and select **Visible in View** as shown in Figure 2–40.

Figure 2–40

16. The total number of this type of column displays in the Status Bar by Filter and in Properties.

17. In the Type Selector, select **W-Wide Flange-Column: W12x40**, as shown in Figure 2–41.

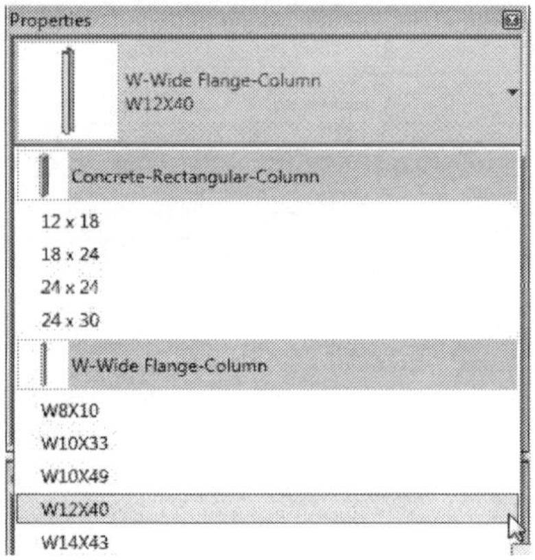

Figure 2–41

18. The view regenerates and the selected columns are updated to the new type. Press <Esc> to release the selection set.

Task 2 - Using temporary dimensions.

1. Zoom out to see the entire building.
2. Select Grid C.
3. If the temporary dimensions are not displayed, in the Options Bar, click **Activate Dimensions**.
4. The temporary dimensions are automatically connected to the closest structural elements.
5. Use the **Move Witness Line** controls on the temporary dimensions and move them to the nearest grid lines as shown in Figure 2–42.

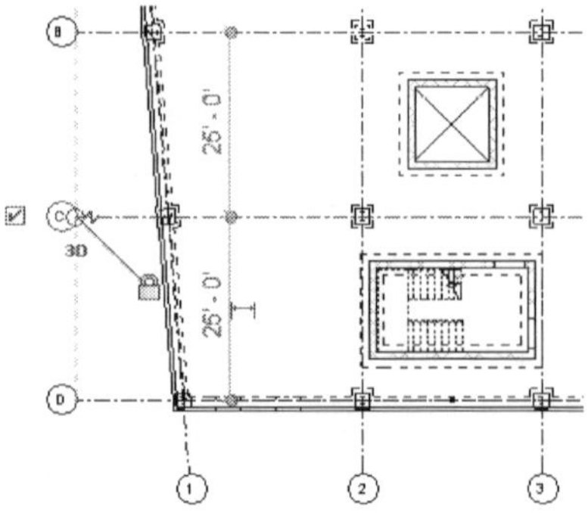

Figure 2–42

6. Click (Make this temporary dimension line permanent).

7. Click in empty space to release the selection. The new dimensions are now part of the view.

8. Select Grid C again.

9. Click **Activate Dimensions**, if required.

10. Select the lower dimension text and change it to **24'-0"** as shown in Figure 2–43. Press <Enter>.

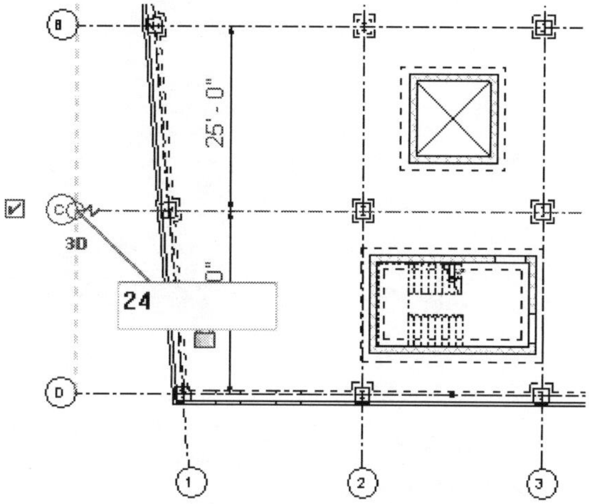

Figure 2–43

11. The model regenerates and the percentage of completion is displayed in the Status Bar as shown in Figure 2–44. This change is being made to the grid and throughout the model, wherever elements touch the grid.

Figure 2–44

12. Save and close the project.

2.3 Troubleshooting

The Autodesk Revit software provides you with many options for troubleshooting while you are working. Two that are most helpful for project managers are reviewing warnings (such as that shown in Figure 2–45), and Interference Checking if you are working with other disciplines.

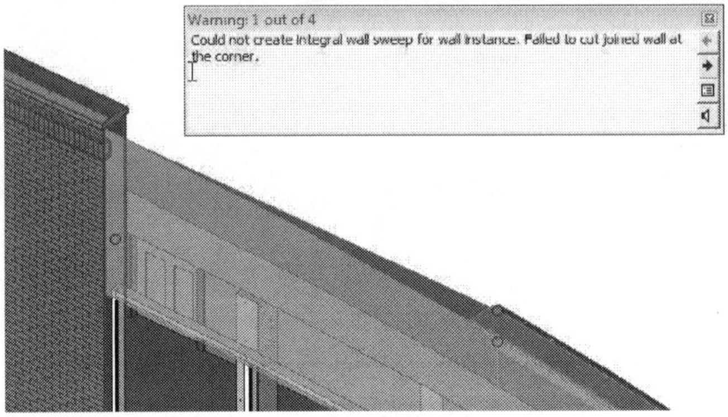

Figure 2–45

Reviewing Warnings

Because the Autodesk Revit software works with smart elements that know how other elements relate to them, you can easily check whether there are any problems with the connections. There are two types of error alerts. Those that you cannot ignore (as shown in Figure 2–46), and those that can be ignored but need to be dealt with at a later time.

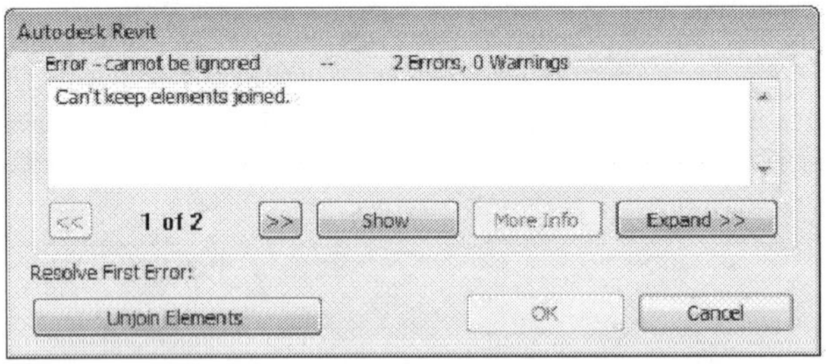

Figure 2–46

When errors that cannot be ignored display you must take action. They force you to stop and fix the situation. In some cases you can resolve the error if it gives you an option, in other cases you have to cancel and try again.

Warnings (such as the one shown in Figure 2–47), display when something is wrong, but you can keep on working. In many cases you can close the dialog box and fix the issue or wait and do it later.

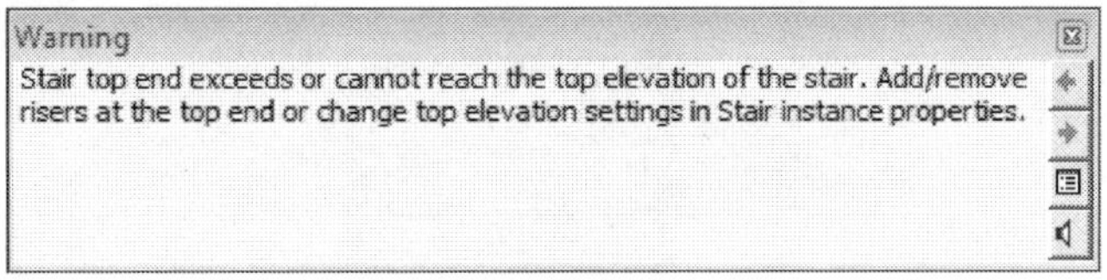

Figure 2–47

- Click (Expand Warning Dialog) to open the dialog box as shown in Figure 2–48. You can expand each node in the box and select elements to show or delete.

*If there are a lot of warnings to review, you can click **Export...** and save an HTML report to review separately.*

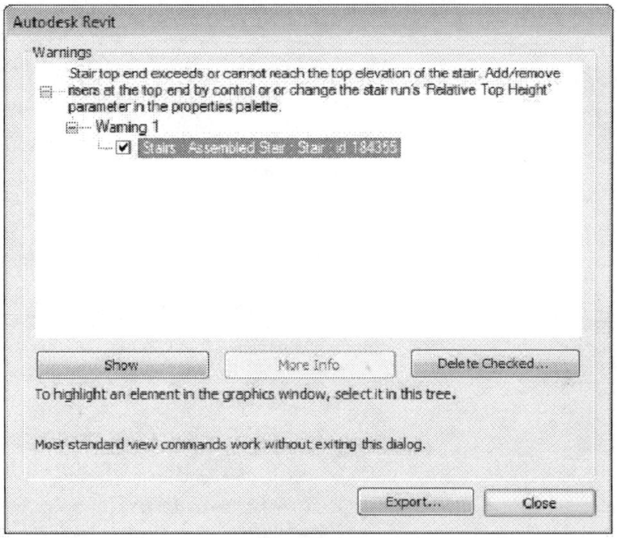

Figure 2–48

- Sometimes issues that create warnings are dealt with as you continue working on a project. If numerous warnings have been ignored you might want to check the project and deal with each of the warnings individually.
- When you select an element for which there has been a warning, (Show Related Warnings) displays in the Ribbon. It opens a dialog box in which you can review the warning(s) related to the selected element. You can also display a list of all of the warnings in the project by clicking (Review Warnings) in the *Manage* tab>Inquiry panel.

Interference Checking

Interference Checking can be used when there are potential overlaps between disciplines, such as the structural column and stair shown in Figure 2–49.

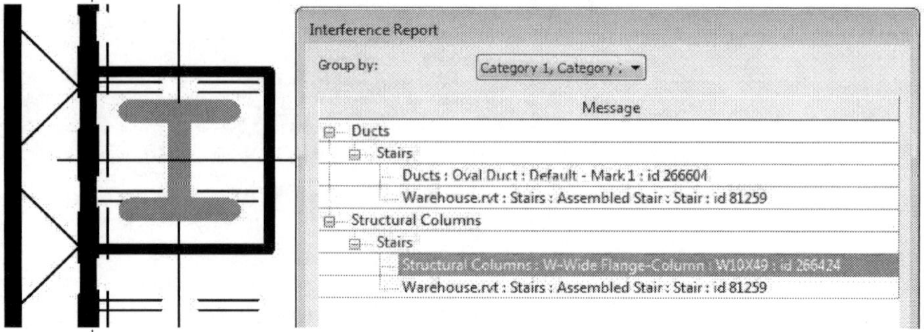

Figure 2–49

- Typical items to check include structural elements against architectural columns, walls, door or window openings, floors and roofs, specialty equipment and floors, and any elements in a linked file with the host file.
- For more complex projects and those that include files from other software, the Navisworks software provides a much more powerful solution than this basic interference checking.

How To: Run an Interference Check

1. In the *Collaborate* tab>Coordinate panel, expand  (Interference Check) and click  (Run Interference Check).
   - To filter out unneeded elements, select the elements first and then run the interference check.
2. In the Interference Check dialog box, as shown in Figure 2–50, in the *Categories From* drop-down list, select the projects that you want to compare. This can be the same project or any linked projects.

Select only the categories that you need to review. In a large project, selecting all categories can take a very long time to process.

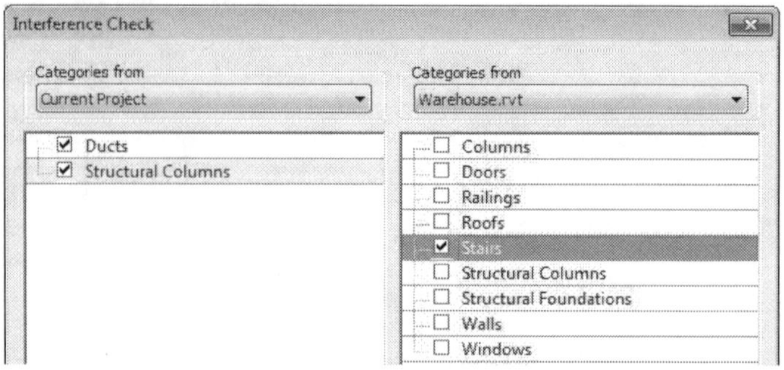

Figure 2–50

3. Select the element types that you want to compare.
4. Click **OK**.
5. If there are interferences, the Interference Report dialog box opens as shown in Figure 2–51.

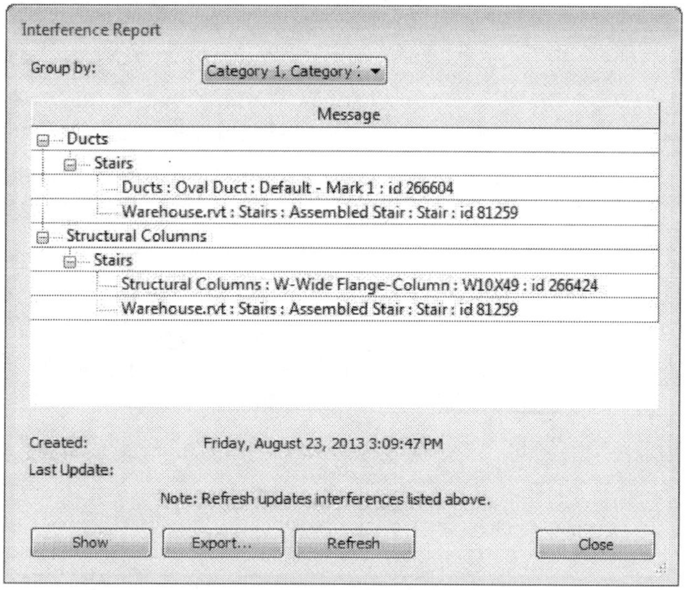

Figure 2–51

6. To see the elements that are interfering, select an element in the list and click **Show**.
7. If you need to create a report that can be viewed by other users, click **Export...**. This creates an HTML file listing the conflicts.
8. The dialog box can remain open while you make changes or you can click **Close** and then expand  (Interference Check) and click  (Show Last Report) to see the report again.
9. In the Interference Report dialog box, click **Refresh** to display any changes.
10. Refreshing the report only reviews the elements selected when the report was first run. If you need to select other elements, run a new report.

Chapter Review Questions

1. What is the purpose of an alignment line?
   a. Displays when the new element you are placing or modeling is aligned with the grid system.
   b. Indicates that the new element you are placing or modeling is aligned with an existing object.
   c. Displays when the new element you are placing or modeling is aligned with a selected tracking point.
   d. Indicates that the new element is aligned with true north rather than project north.
2. When you are modeling (not editing) a linear element, how do you edit the temporary dimension, as that shown in Figure 2–52?

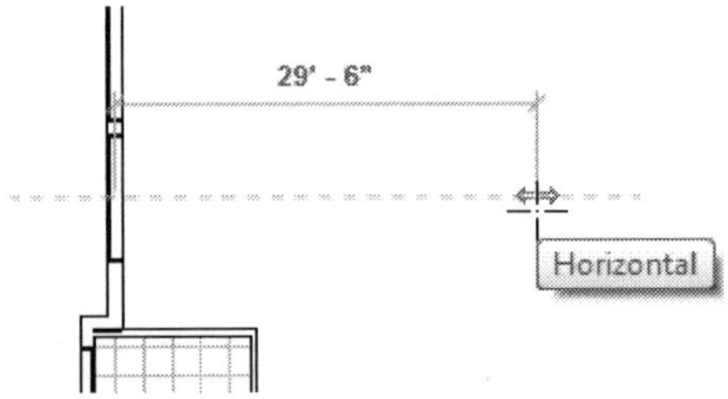

Figure 2–52

   a. Select the temporary dimension and enter a new value.
   b. Type a new value and press <Enter>.
   c. Type a new value in the Distance/Length box in the Options Bar and press <Enter>.
3. How do you select all door types, but no other elements in a view?
   a. In the Project Browser, select the *Door* category.
   b. Select one door, right-click and select **Select All Instances>Visible in View**.
   c. Select all of the objects in the view and use (Filter) to clear the other categories.
   d. Select one door, and click (Select Multiple) in the ribbon.

Command Summary

Button	Command	Location
Draw Tools		
	**Center-ends Arc**	• **Ribbon:** *Modify | (various linear elements)* tab>Draw panel
	**Circle**	• **Ribbon:** *Modify | (various linear elements)* tab>Draw panel
	**Circumscribed Polygon**	• **Ribbon:** *Modify | (various linear elements)* tab>Draw panel
	**Ellipse**	• **Ribbon:** *Modify | Place Lines, Place Detail Lines, and various boundary sketches*>Draw panel
	**Ellipse Arc**	• **Ribbon:** *Modify | Place Lines, Place Detail Lines, and various boundary sketches*>Draw panel
	**Fillet Arc**	• **Ribbon:** *Modify | (various linear elements)* tab>Draw panel
	**Inscribed Polygon**	• **Ribbon:** *Modify | (various linear elements)* tab>Draw panel
	**Line**	• **Ribbon:** *Modify | (various linear elements)* tab>Draw panel
	**Pick Faces**	• **Ribbon:** *Modify | Place Wall*> Draw panel
	**Pick Lines**	• **Ribbon:** *Modify | (various linear elements)* tab>Draw panel
	**Pick Walls**	• **Ribbon:** *Modify | (various boundary sketches)*>Draw panel
	**Rectangle**	• **Ribbon:** *Modify | (various linear elements)* tab>Draw panel
	**Spline**	• **Ribbon:** *Modify | Place Lines, Place Detail Lines, and various boundary sketches*>Draw panel
	**Start-End-Radius Arc**	• **Ribbon:** *Modify | (various linear elements)* tab>Draw panel
	**Tangent End Arc**	• **Ribbon:** *Modify | (various linear elements)* tab>Draw panel
Select Tools		
	**Drag elements on selection**	• **Ribbon:** All tabs>Expanded Select panel • **Status Bar**
	**Filter**	• **Ribbon:** *Modify | Multi-Select* tab> Filter panel • **Status Bar**

	**Select Elements By Face**	• **Ribbon:** All tabs>Expanded Select panel • **Status Bar**
	**Select Links**	• **Ribbon:** All tabs>Expanded Select panel • **Status Bar**
	**Select Pinned Elements**	• **Ribbon:** All tabs>Expanded Select panel • **Status Bar**
	**Select Underlay Elements**	• **Ribbon:** All tabs>Expanded Select panel • **Status Bar**
Additional Tools		
	**Measure Between Two References**	• **Ribbon:** *Modify* tab>Measure panel • **Quick Access Toolbar**
	**Measure Along An Element**	• **Ribbon:** *Modify* tab>Measure panel> Expand Measure • **Quick Access Toolbar**>Expand Measure
	**Reference Plane**	• **Ribbon:** *Architecture/Structure/Systems* tab> Work Plane panel
	**Interference Check**	• **Ribbon:** *Collaborate* tab>Coordinate panel>Interference Check
	**Properties**	• **Ribbon:** *Modify* tab>Properties panel> Properties • **Shortcut:** PP
	**Review Warnings**	• **Ribbon:** *Manage* tab>Inquiry panel> Review Warnings

Working in a Model

Views are the cornerstone of working with Autodesk® Revit® models as they enable you to see the model in both 2D and 3D. As you are working, you can duplicate and change views to display different information based on the same view of the model. Accurate schedules and views (callouts, elevations, and sections) are important tools for reviewing and creating construction documents.

Learning Objectives in this Chapter

- Change the way elements display in different views to show required information and set views for construction documents.
- Duplicate views so that you can modify the display as you are creating the model and for construction documents.
- Create callout views of parts of plans, sections, or elevations for detailing.
- Add building and interior elevations that can be used to demonstrate how a building will be built.
- Create building and wall sections to help you create the model and to include in construction documents.
- Modify schedule content including the instance and type properties of related elements.
- Add schedules to sheets as part of the construction documents.

3.1 Setting the View Display

Views are a powerful tool as they enable you to create multiple versions of a model without having to recreate building elements. For example, you can have views that are specifically used for working on the model, while other views are annotated and used for construction documents. Different disciplines can have different views that show only the features they require, as shown in Figure 3–1.

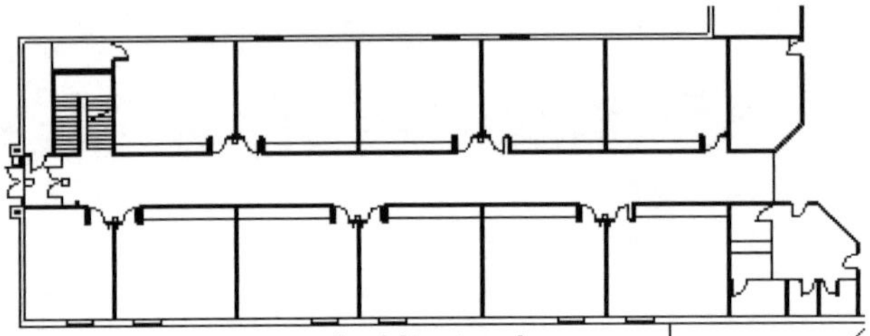

Architectural

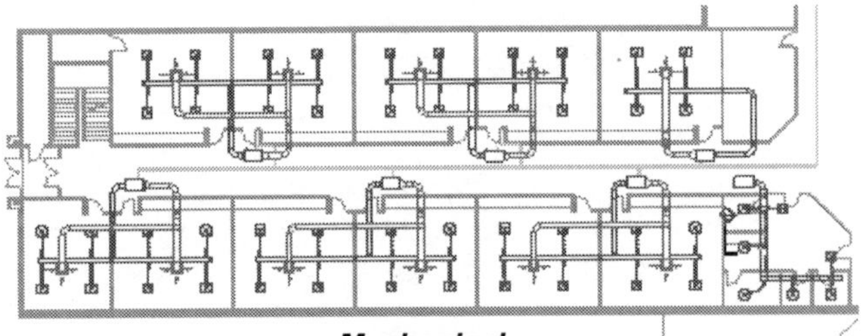

Mechanical

Figure 3–1

The view display can be modified in the following locations:

- View Control Bar
- Properties
- Shortcut menu
- Visibility/Graphic Overrides dialog box

Hiding and Overriding Graphics

Two common ways to customize a view are to:

- Hide individual elements or categories
- Modify how graphics display for elements or categories (e.g., altering lineweight, color, or pattern)

An element is an individual item such as one wall in a view, while a category includes all instances of a selected element, such as all walls in a view.

In the example shown in Figure 3–2, a Furniture Plan has been created by toggling off the structural grids category, and then graying out all of the walls and columns.

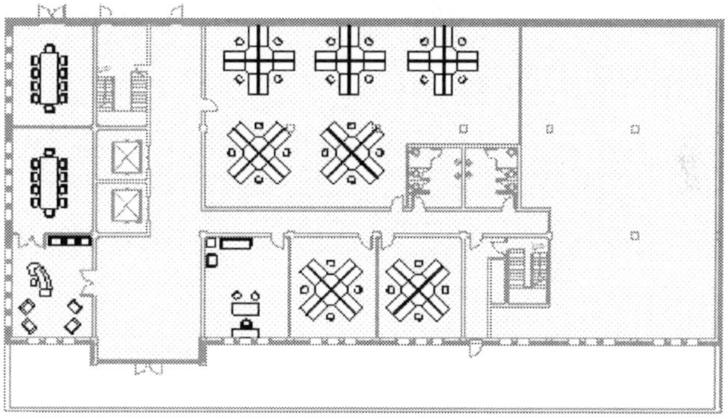

Figure 3–2

How To: Hide Elements or Categories in a view

1. Select the elements or categories you want to hide.
2. Right-click and select **Hide in View>Elements** or **Hide in View>Category**, as shown in Figure 3–3.
3. The elements or categories are hidden in current view only.

A quick way to hide entire categories is to select an element(s) and type ***VH****.*

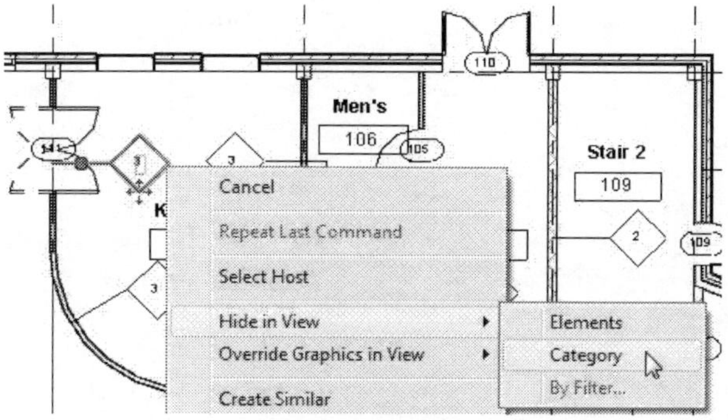

Figure 3–3

How To: Override Graphics of Elements or Categories in a View

The exact options in the dialog box vary depending on the type of elements selected.

1. Select the element(s) you want to modify.
2. Right-click and select **Override Graphics in View>By Element** or **By Category**. The View-Specific Element (or Category) Graphics dialog box opens, as shown in Figure 3–4.

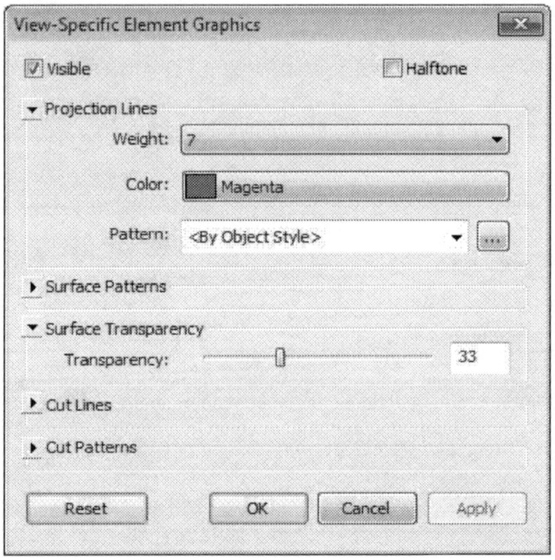

Figure 3–4

3. Select the changes you want to make and click **OK**.

View-Specific Options

- Clearing the **Visible** option is the same as hiding the elements or categories.
- Selecting the **Halftone** option grays out the elements or categories.
- The options for Projection Lines, Surface Patterns, Cut Lines, and Cut Patterns include **Weight**, **Color**, and **Pattern**, as shown in Figure 3–4.
- **Surface Transparency** can be set by moving the slider bar, as shown in Figure 3–5.

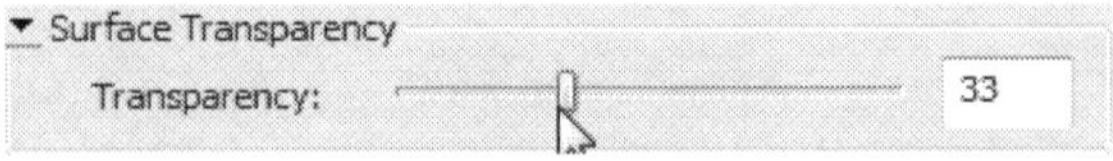

Figure 3–5

- The View-Specific Category dialog box includes **Open the Visibility Graphics dialog...**, which opens the full dialog box of options.

The Visibility/Graphic Overrides dialog box

The options in the Visibility/Graphic Overrides dialog box (shown in Figure 3–6) control how every category and sub-category of elements is displayed per view.

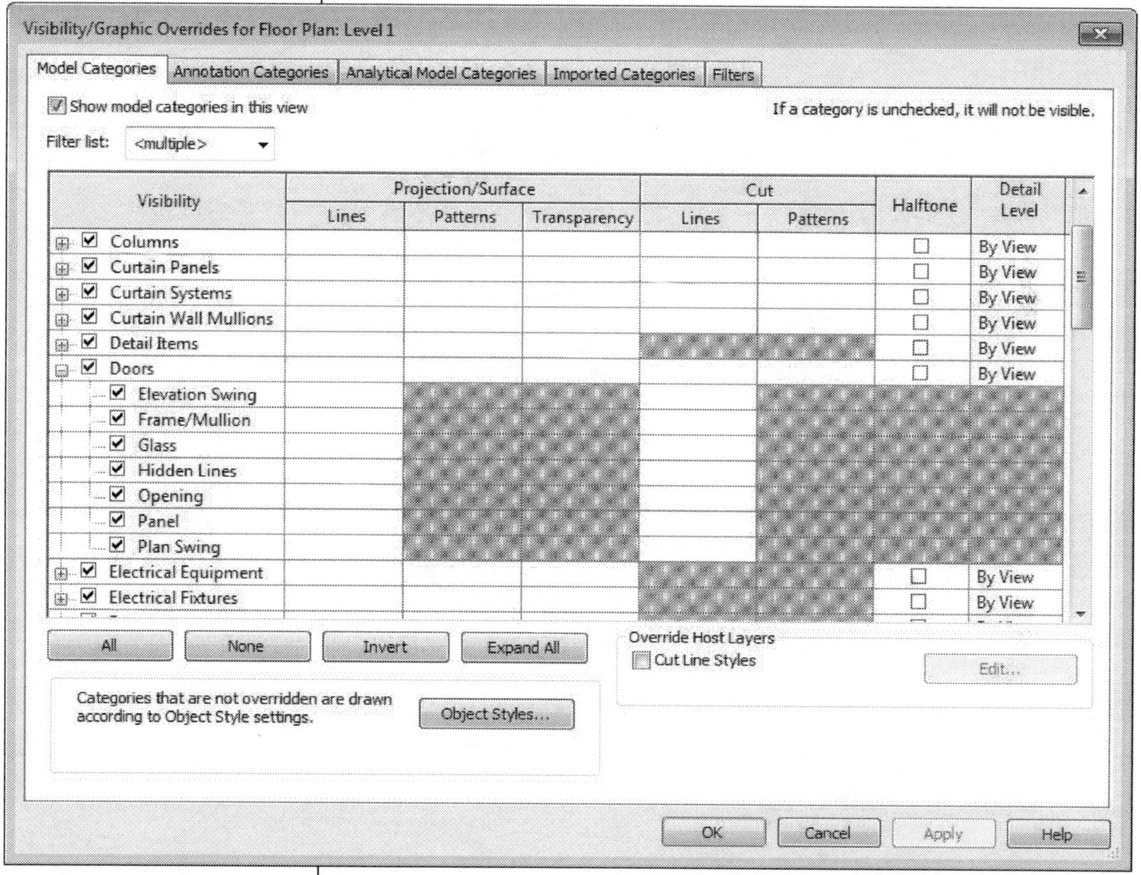

Figure 3–6

To open the Visibility/Graphic Overrides dialog box, type **VV** or **VG**. It is also available in Properties: in the *Graphics* area, beside *Visibility/Graphic Overrides*, click **Edit...**.

- The Visibility/Graphic Overrides are divided into *Model*, *Annotation*, *Analytical Model*, *Imported,* and *Filters* categories.
- Other categories might be available if specific data has been included in the project, including *Design Options*, *Linked Files*, and *Worksets*.
- To limit the number of categories showing in the dialog box select a discipline from the *Filter list,* as shown in Figure 3–7

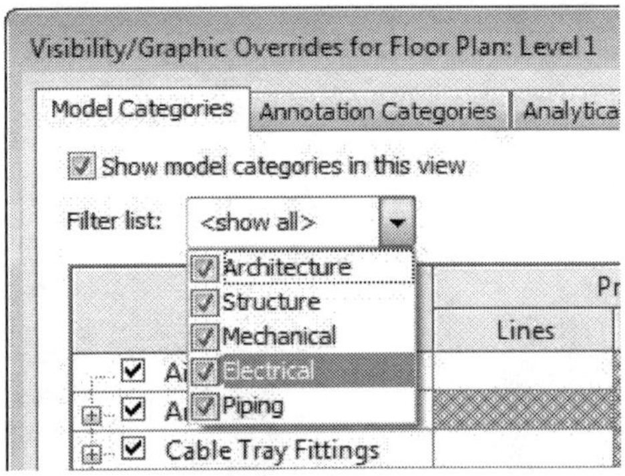

Figure 3–7

- To help you select categories, use the **All**, **None**, and **Invert** buttons. The **Expand All** button displays all of the sub-categories.

Hint: Restoring Hidden Elements or Categories

If you have hidden categories, you can display them using the Visibility/Graphic Overrides dialog box. To display hidden elements, however, you must temporarily reveal the elements first.

1. In the View Control Bar, click (Reveal Hidden Elements). The border and all hidden elements are displayed in magenta, while visible elements in the view are grayed out, as shown in Figure 3–8.

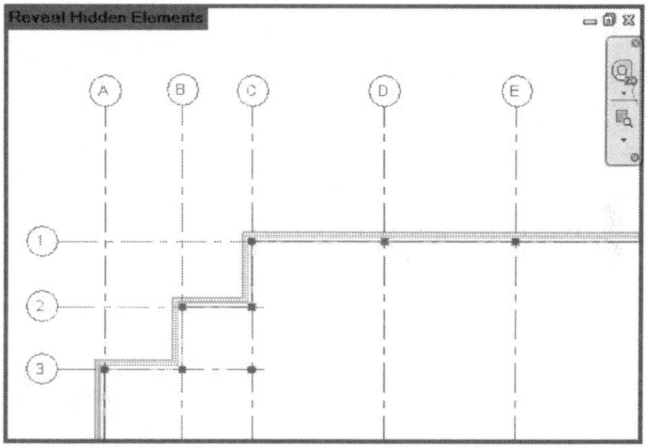

Figure 3–8

2. Select the hidden elements you want to restore, right-click, and select **Unhide in View>Elements** or **Unhide in View>Category**. Alternatively, in the *Modify* | contextual tab>Reveal Hidden Elements panel, click (Unhide Element) or (Unhide Category).
3. When you are finished, in the View Control Bar, click (Close Reveal Hidden Elements) or, in the *Modify* | contextual tab>Reveal Hidden Elements panel, click (Toggle Reveal Hidden Elements Mode).

View Properties

The most basic properties of a view are accessed using the View Control Bar, shown in Figure 3–9. These include the *Scale*, *Detail Level*, and *Visual Style* options. Additional options include temporary overrides and other advanced settings.

Figure 3–9

Other modifications to views are available in Properties, as shown in Figure 3–10. These properties include *Underlays*, *View Range*, and *Crop Regions*.

The options in Properties vary according to the type of view. A plan view has different properties than a 3D view.

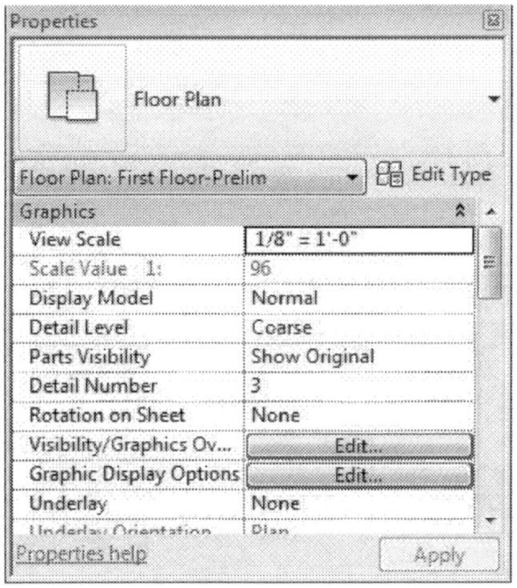

Figure 3–10

Setting an Underlay

Setting an *Underlay* is helpful if you need to display elements on a different level, such as the basement plan shown with an underlay of the first floor plan in Figure 3–11. You can then use the elements to trace over or even copy to the current level of the view.

Underlays are only available in Floor Plan and Ceiling Plan views.

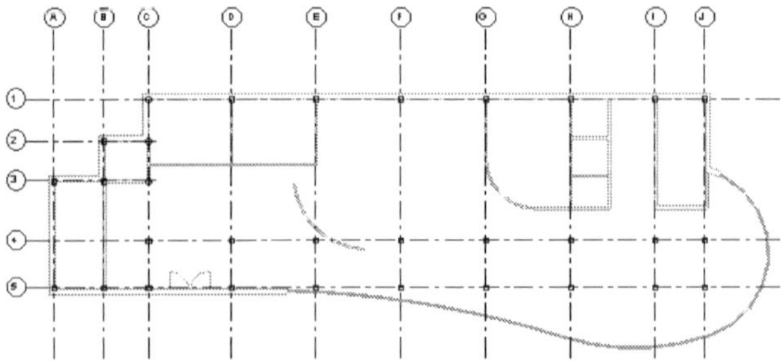

Figure 3–11

Enhanced in 2017

In Properties in the *Underlay* area, specify the *Range: Base Level* and the *Range: Top Level*. You can also specify the Underlay Orientation to **Look down** or **Look up** as shown in Figure 3–12.

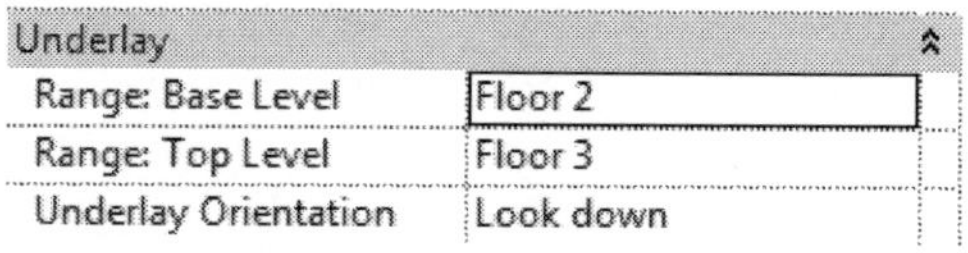

Figure 3–12

- To prevent moving elements in the underlay by mistake, in the Select panel, expand the panel title, and clear **Select underlay elements**. You can also toggle this on/off using  (Select Underlay Elements) in the Status Bar.

How To: Set the View Range

Enhanced in 2017

1. In Properties, in the *Extents* area, beside *View Range*, select **Edit...** or type **VR**.
2. In the View Range dialog box, as shown in Figure 3–13, modify the Levels and Offsets for the *Primary Range* and *View Depth*.
   - Click **Show>>** to display the Sample View Range graphics and key to the various options.
3. Click **OK**.

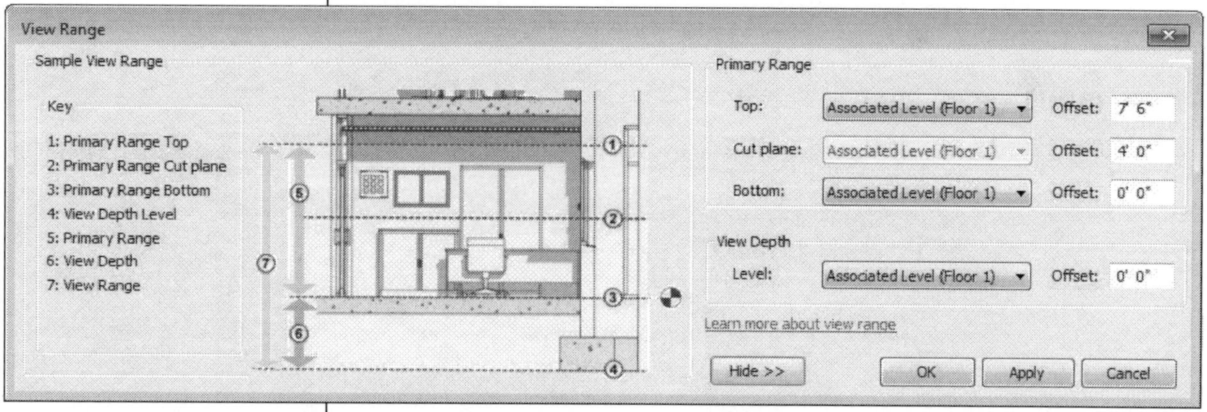

Figure 3–13

- If the settings used cannot be represented graphically, a warning displays stating the inconsistency.
- A Reflected Ceiling Plan (RCP) is created as if the ceiling is reflected by a mirror on the floor so that the ceiling is the same orientation as the floor plan. The cutline is placed just below the ceiling to ensure that any windows and doors below do not display

Hint: Depth Clipping and Far Clipping

Depth Clipping, shown in Figure 3–14, is a viewing option which sets how sloped walls are displayed if the *View Range* of a plan is set to a limited view.

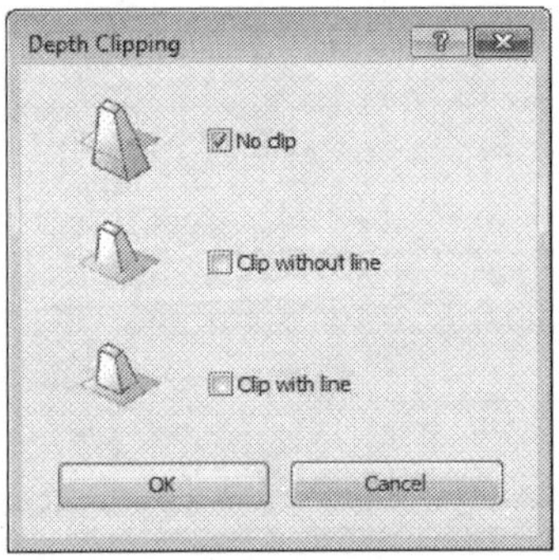

Figure 3–14

Far Clipping (shown in Figure 3–15) is available for section and elevation views.

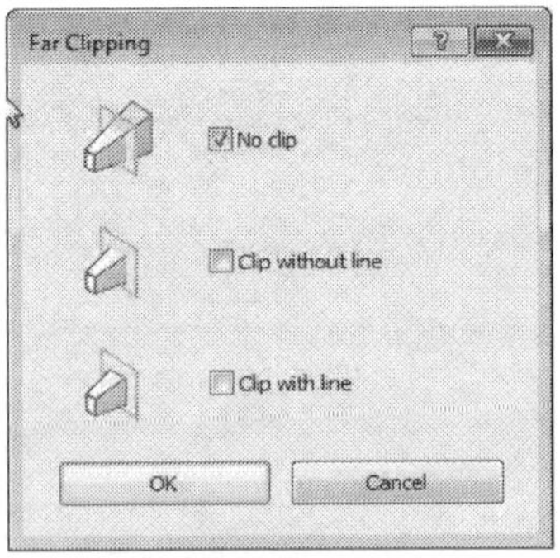

Figure 3–15

New in **2017**

- An additional Graphic Display Option enables you to specify *Depth Cueing*, so that items that are in the distance will be made lighter.

Crop Regions

Plans, sections, and elevations can all be modified by changing how much of the model is displayed in a view. One way to do this is to set the Crop Region. If there are dimensions, tags, or text near the required crop region, you can also use the Annotation Crop Region to include these, as shown in Figure 3–16.

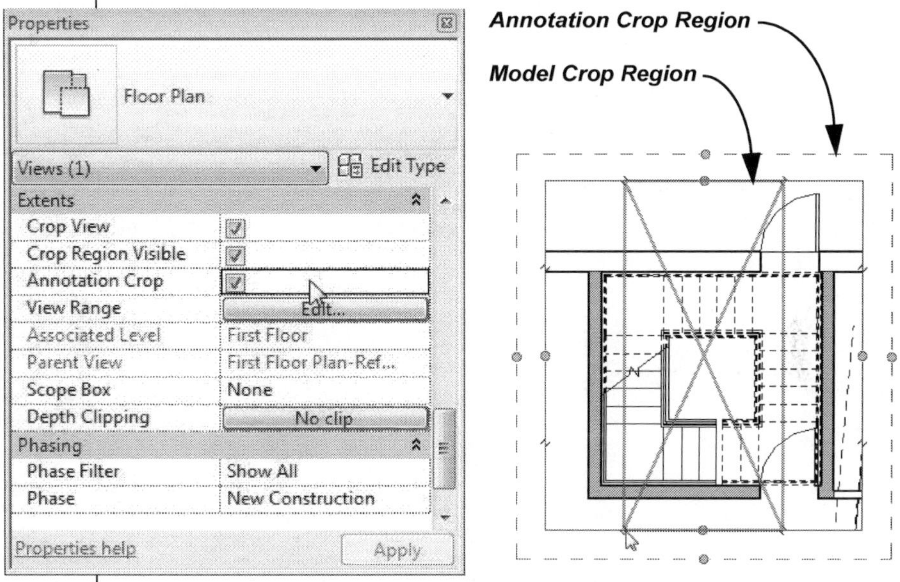

Figure 3–16

Zoom out if you do not see the crop region when you set it to be displayed.

- The crop region must be displayed to modify the size of the view. In the View Control Bar, click (Show Crop Region) Alternatively, in Properties, in the *Extents* area, select **Crop Region Visible**. **Annotation Crop** is also available in this area.

- Resize the crop region using the control on each side of the region.

Breaking the crop region is typically used with sections or details.

- Click (Break Line) control to split the view into two regions, horizontally or vertically. Each part of the view can then be modified in size to display what is required and be moved independently.

- It is a best practice to hide a crop region before placing a view on a sheet. In the View Control Bar, click (Hide Crop Region).

Hint: Applying View Templates

A powerful way to use views effectively is to set up a view and then save it as a View Template. To apply a View Template, right-click on a view in the Project Browser and select **Apply View Template Properties....** Then, in the Apply View Template dialog box, select a *Name* in the list (as shown in Figure 3–17) and click **OK**.

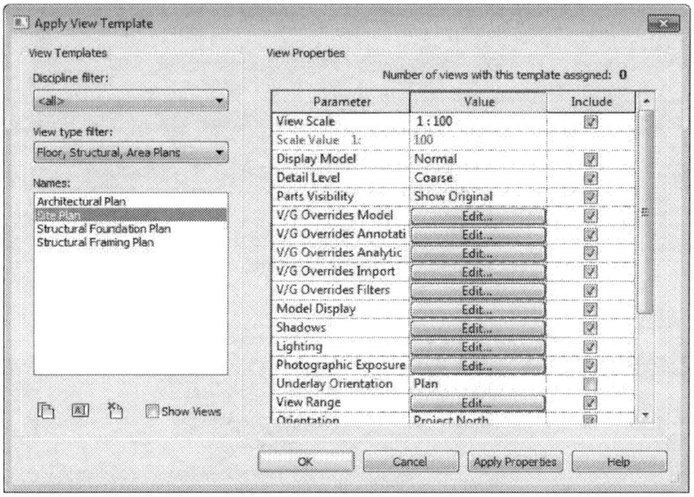

Figure 3–17

- View Templates can be preset in Properties so that changes cannot be made to the view.
- In the View Control Bar use  (Temporary View Properties) to temporarily apply a view template to a view.

3.2 Duplicating Views

Once you have created a model, you do not have to recreate the elements at different scales or copy them so that they can be used on more than one sheet. Instead, you can duplicate the required views and modify them to suit your needs.

Duplication Types

Duplicate creates a copy of the view that only includes the building elements, as shown in Figure 3–18. Annotation and detailing are not copied into the new view. Building model elements automatically change in all views, but view-specific changes made to the new view are not reflected in the original view.

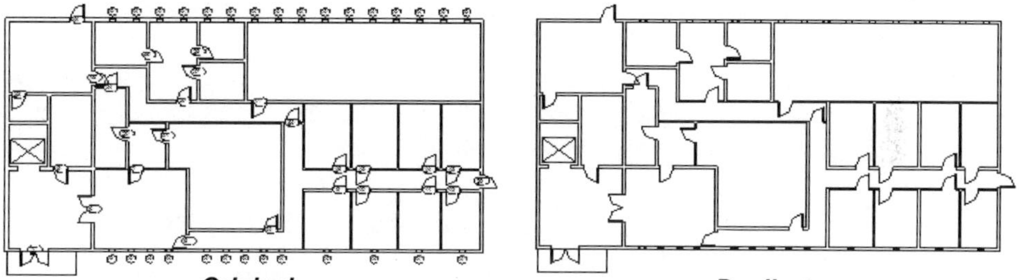

Original *Duplicate*

Figure 3–18

Duplicate with Detailing creates a copy of the view and includes all annotation and detail elements (such as tags), as shown in Figure 3–19. Any annotation or view-specific elements created in the new view are not reflected in the original view.

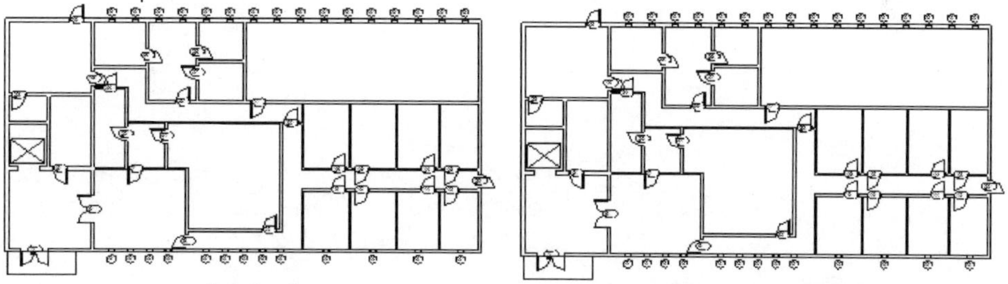

Original *Duplicate with Detailing*

Figure 3–19

Duplicate as a Dependent creates a copy of the view and links it to the original (parent) view, as shown in the Project Browser in Figure 3–20. View-specific changes made to the overall view, such as changing the *Scale*, are also reflected in the dependent (child) views and vice-versa.

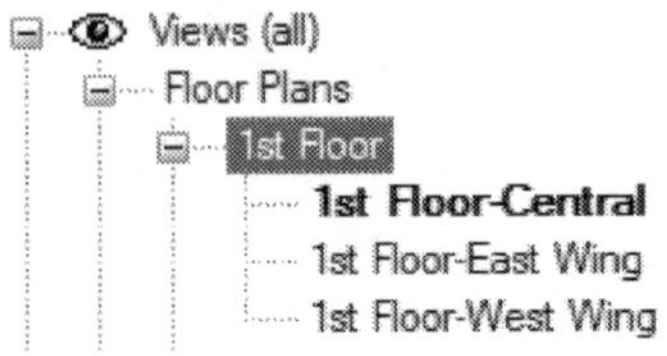

Figure 3–20

- Use dependent views when the building model is so large that you need to split the building onto separate sheets, while ensuring that the views are all same scale.
- If you want to separate a dependent view from the original view, right-click on the dependent view and select **Convert to independent view**.

How To: Create Duplicate Views

1. Open the view you want to duplicate.
2. In the *View* tab>Create panel, expand **Duplicate View** and select the type of duplicate view you want to create, as shown in Figure 3–21.

Most types of views can be duplicated.

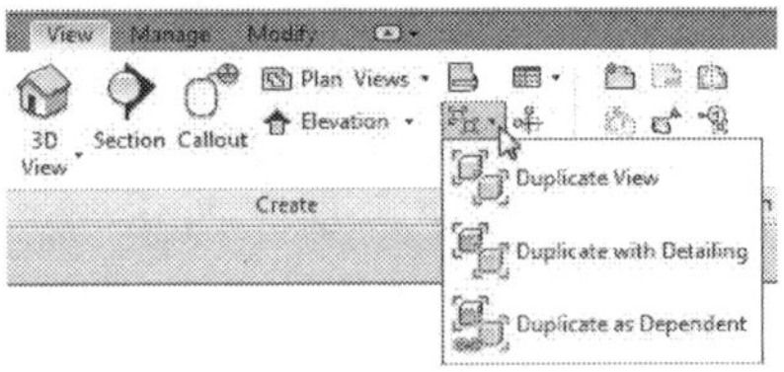

Figure 3–21

- Alternatively, you can right-click on a view in the Project Browser and select the type of duplicate that you want to use, as shown in Figure 3–22.

Figure 3–22

*You can also press <F2> to start the **Rename** command.*

- To rename a view, right-click on the new view in the Project Browser and select **Rename**. In the Rename View dialog box, type in the new name, as shown in Figure 3–23.

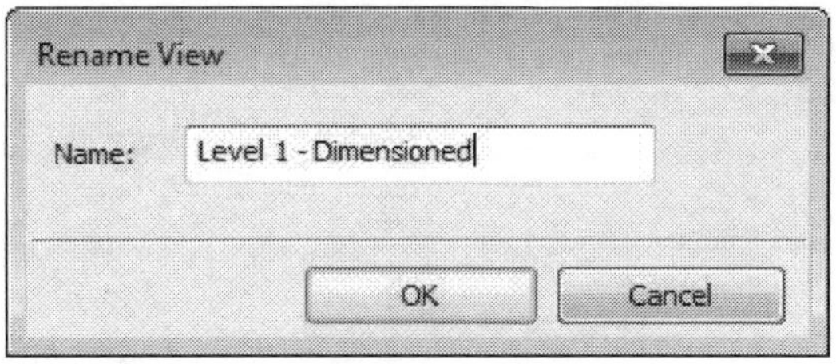

Figure 3–23

Practice 3a

Duplicate Views in an Architectural Project

Estimated time for completion: 10 minutes

Practice Objectives

- Duplicate views.
- Modify crop regions.
- Change the visibility and graphic display of elements in views.

In this practice you will duplicate views and then modify them by changing the scale and crop region, hiding some elements, and changing some elements to halftone to prepare them to be used in construction documents. The finished views of the second floor are shown in Figure 3–24.

The model used in this practice is that of the completed building.

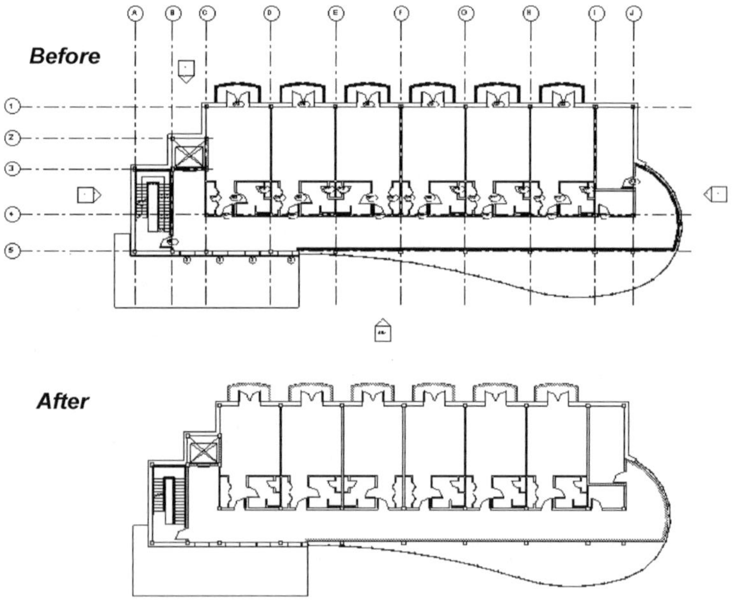

Figure 3–24

Task 1 - Duplicate and modify the first floor plan view.

1. Open the project **Modern-Hotel-Display.rvt**.
2. Open the **Floor Plans: Floor 1** view. This view includes a variety of tags.
3. In the Project Browser, right-click on the **Floor Plans: Floor 1** view and select **Duplicate View>Duplicate with Detailing**. This creates a view with all of the tags.

4. Right-click on the new view and rename it to **Floor 1 - Reference**. You will use this view later to place callouts and sections.

5. In the Project Browser, right-click on the **Floor Plans: Floor 1** view and select **Duplicate View>Duplicate**. This creates a view without all of the tags, but includes the grids and elevation markers.

6. Right-click on the new view and rename it to **Floor 1 - Overall**.

7. In the View Control Bar, change the *Scale* to **1/16"=1'-0"**. All of the annotations become larger, as they need to plot correctly at this scale.

8. In the View Control Bar, click (Show Crop Region).

9. Select the crop region and drag the control on the top until the pool house displays, as shown in Figure 3–25.

10. Select one of the vertical grid lines and drag them so they are above the poolhouse.

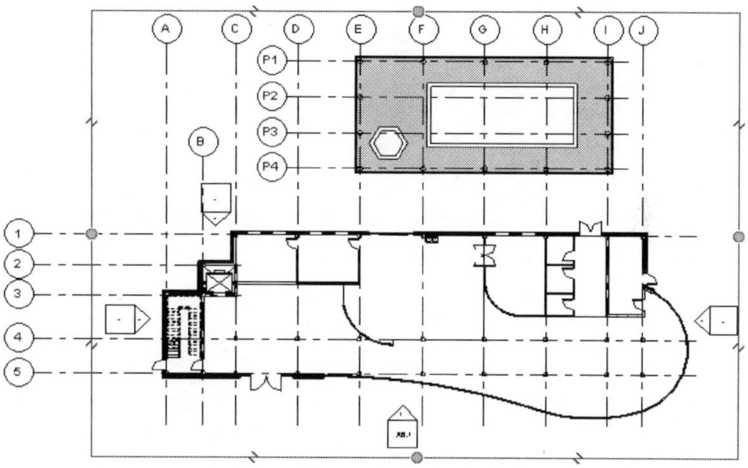

Figure 3–25

11. In the View Control Bar, click (Hide Crop Region).

12. Zoom out to display the entire view. (Hint: Use the shortcuts **ZF** or **ZE**, or double-click the mouse wheel.)

13. Save the project.

Task 2 - Duplicate and modify a second floor plan view.

1. Open the **Floor Plans: Floor 2** view.
2. In the Project Browser, right-click on the same view and select **Duplicate View>Duplicate**. This creates a new view without any annotation.
3. Rename this view to **Typical Guest Room Floor Plan**.
4. Select one of the grids and type **VH** (Hide in View Category).
5. Toggle on the crop region and bring it in close to the building on all sides. If any of the elevation markers still display, hide them.
6. Toggle off the crop region.
7. Select one of the railings along the balconies. Right-click and select **Select All Instances>Visible in View**. The railings are selected as shown in Figure 3–26.

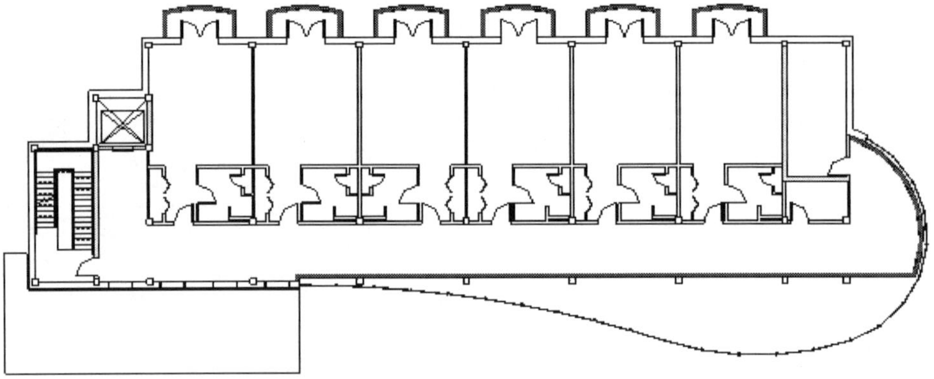

Figure 3–26

8. Right-click again and select **Override Graphics in View > By Element...**
9. In the View-Specific Element Graphics dialog box select **Halftone** and click **OK**.
10. Click in the view to release the selection. The railings are now gray and not as prominent.
11. Close any other projects that are opened.

12. In the Quick Access Toolbar, click (Close Hidden Windows). Only the Typical Guest Room Floor Plan view should be open.

13. Open the **Floor Plans: Floor 2** view again.

14. Type **WT** to tile the two windows and then type **ZA** so the model displays fully in the view so that you can see the differences in the views.

15. Save the project.

Practice 3b Duplicate Views in a MEP Project

Practice Objectives

- Duplicate a view.
- Apply view filters.
- Modify the view display using the Visibility/Graphic Overrides dialog box.

Estimated time for completion: 5 minutes

In this practice you will change a 3D plumbing view that displays sanitary systems to also display the hot and cold water systems, as shown in Figure 3–27. You will also duplicate a 3D view and apply supply and return system filters to create a 3D HVAC view and toggle off some additional elements.

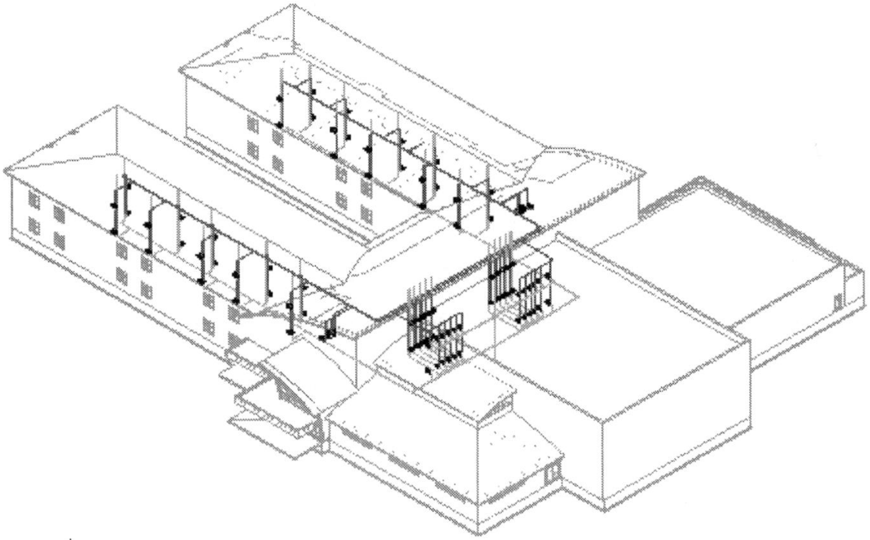

Figure 3–27

Task 1 - Apply view filters.

1. Open the project **MEP-Elementary-School-Views.rvt**. Note that you are in the 3D Plumbing view that displays only the sanitary piping.
2. Type **VV** to open the Visibility/Graphic Overrides dialog box.
3. In the dialog box, select the *Filters* tab.

4. In the *Visibility* column, select **Domestic Cold Water** and **Domestic Hot Water,** as shown in Figure 3–28. Click **OK**.

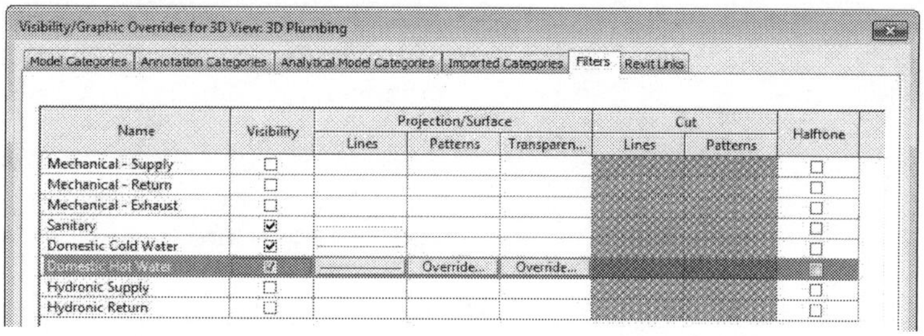

Figure 3–28

5. The rest of the plumbing system elements display as shown in Figure 3–27.

6. Save the project.

Task 2 - Duplicate and modify a view.

1. In the Project Browser, right-click on the **3D Plumbing** view and select **Duplicate View>Duplicate**.

2. Right-click on the new view name and select **Rename**.

3. In the Rename View dialog box type **3D HVAC** and then click **OK**.

4. The 3D HVAC view is still in the **Plumbing** sub-category of the Project Browser. In Properties, change the *Discipline* to **Mechanical** and the *Sub-Discipline* to **HVAC**, as shown in Figure 3–29.

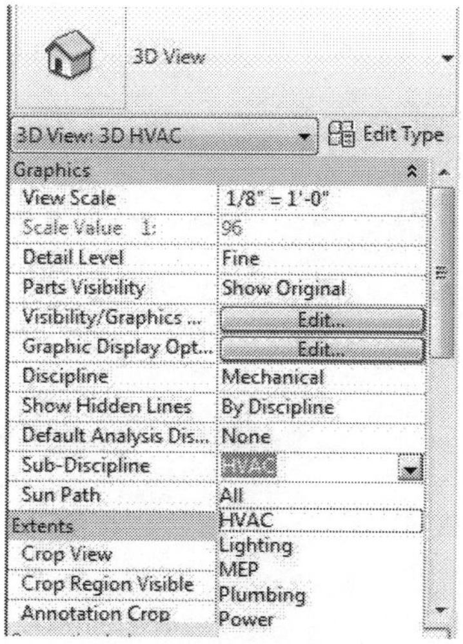

Figure 3–29

5. Open the Visibility/Graphic Overrides dialog box and set the filters to display only **Mechanical - Supply** and **Mechanical - Return**. Click **OK**.
6. The ductwork now displays, but the plumbing fixtures still display.
7. Select one of the plumbing fixtures and type **VH** (for Hide category in view). Now only the HVAC systems display, as shown in Figure 3–30.

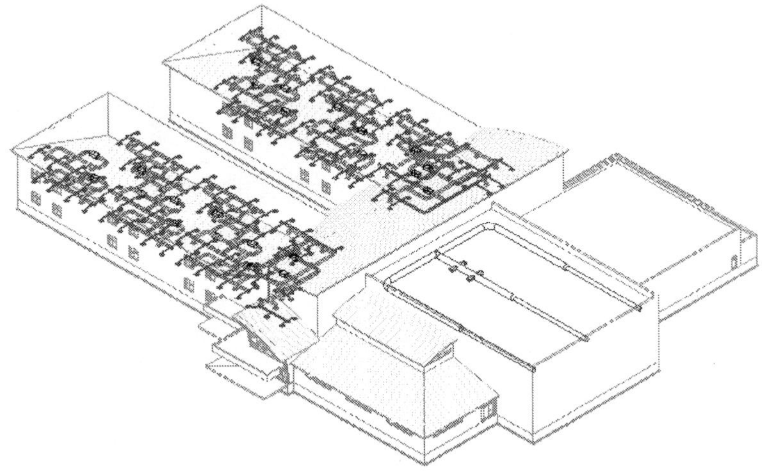

Figure 3–30

8. Save the project.

Practice 3c Duplicate Views in a Structural Project

Practice Objectives

- Duplicate views.
- Change the view template.

Estimated time for completion: 10 minutes

In this practice you will create an analytical view by duplicating a view and then applying an analytical view template that sets the view display, as shown in Figure 3–31.

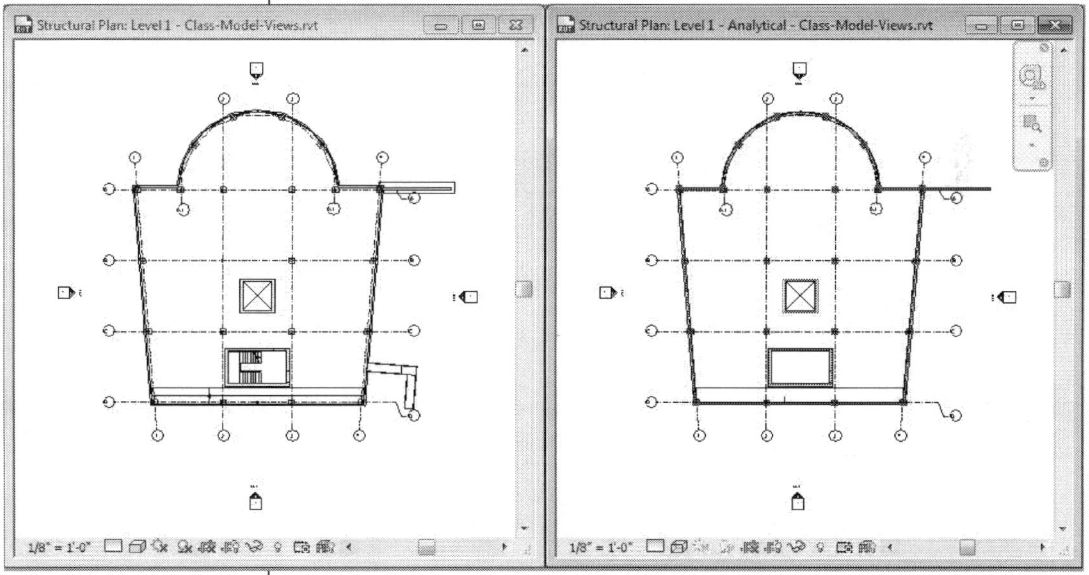

Figure 3–31

Task 1 - Duplicate views.

1. Open the project **Practice-Model-Views.rvt**.
2. Open the **Structural Plans**: **Level 2** view.
3. Open the **Structural Plans: Level 2 - Analytical** view to see the difference between the two views.
4. Close both of the **Level 2** views.

5. Right-click on **Level 1** and select **Duplicate View> Duplicate**.

6. In the Project Browser, right-click on the copy and rename it **Level 1 - Analytical**.

7. Verify that only the two **Level 1** views are open and tile them (Hint: type **WT**.)

8. Zoom each view so that you can see the entire building. (Hint: type **ZA**.)

9. In the Project Browser, select the new **Level 1 - Analytical** view. Right-click and select **Apply Template Properties...**

10. In the Apply View Template dialog box, in the *Names* area select **Structural Analytical Stick** and click **OK**. The new view displays with analytical indicators, as shown on the right in Figure 3–32.

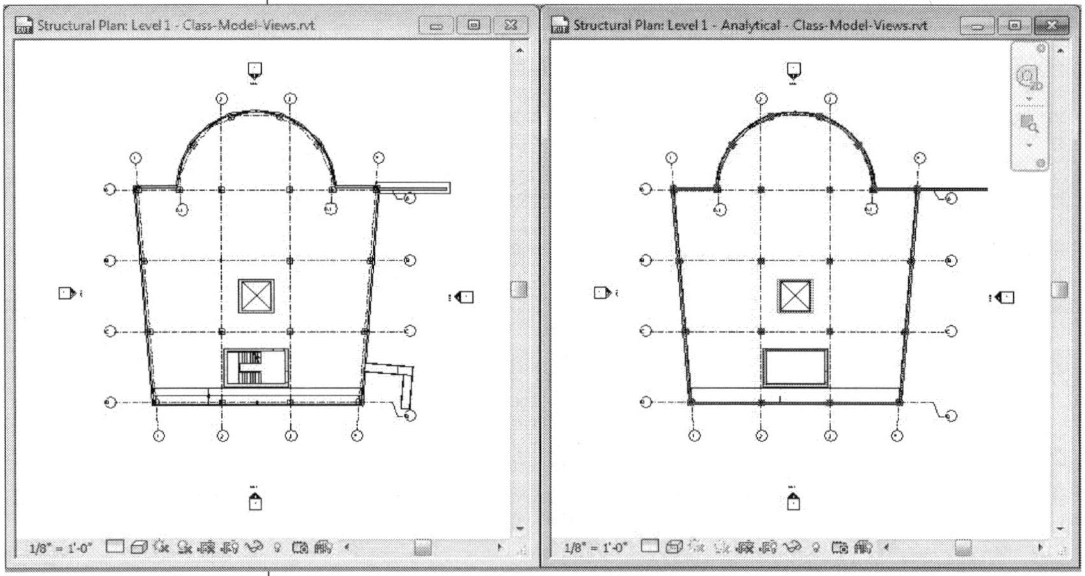

Figure 3–32

11. Close the analytical view and maximize the **Level 1** view window.

12. Save the project.

3.3 Adding Callout Views

Callouts are details of plan, elevation, or section views. When you place a callout in a view, as shown in Figure 3–33, it automatically creates a new view clipped to the boundary of the callout, as shown in Figure 3–34. If you change the size of the callout box in the original view, it automatically updates the callout view and vice-versa. You can create rectangular or sketched callout boundaries.

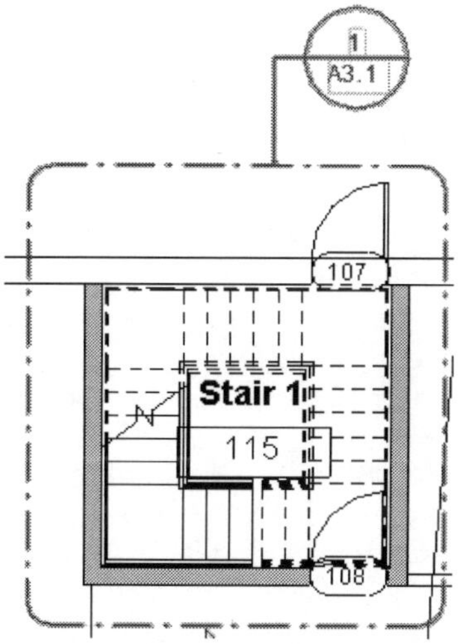

Callout in a view

Figure 3–33

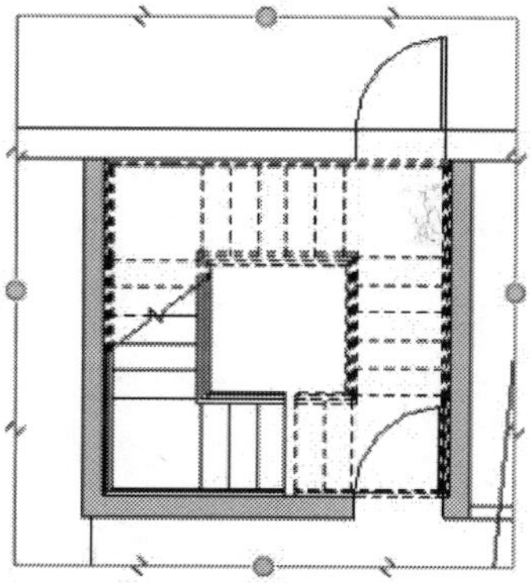

Callout view

Figure 3–34

How To: Create a Rectangular Callout

1. In the *View tab>Create panel,* click  **(Callout)**.
2. Select points for two opposite corners to define the callout box around the area you want to detail.
3. Select the callout and use the shape handles to modify the location of the bubble and any other edges that might need changing.
4. In the Project Browser, rename the callout.

How To: Create a Sketched Callout

1. In the *View tab>Create panel,* expand (Callout), and click (Sketch).
2. Sketch the shape of the callout using the tools in the *Modify | Edit Profile* tab>Draw panel, as shown in Figure 3–35.

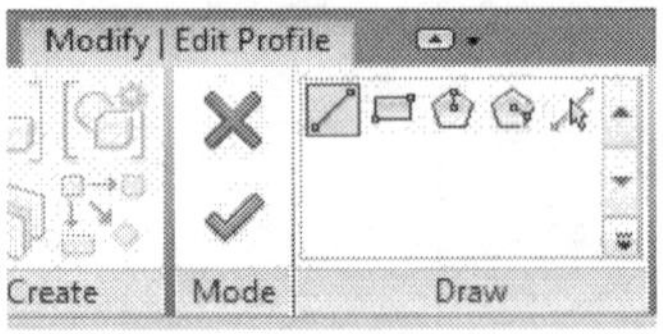

Figure 3–35

3. Click (Finish) to complete the boundary.
4. Select the callout and use the shape handles to modify the location of the bubble and any other edges that might need to be changed.
5. In the Project Browser, rename the callout

- To open the callout view, double-click on its name in the Project Browser or double-click on the callout bubble (verify that the callout itself is not selected before you double-click on it).

Modifying Callouts

The callout bubble displays numbers when the view is placed on a sheet.

In the original view where the callout is created, you can use the shape handles to modify the callout boundary and bubble location, as shown in Figure 3–36.

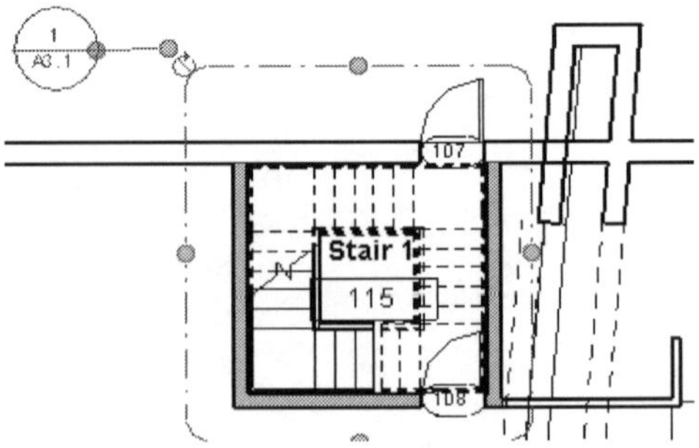

Figure 3–36

- You can rotate the callout box by dragging the (Rotate) control or by right-clicking on edge of callout and selecting **Rotate**.

In the callout view, you can modify the crop region with shape handles and view breaks, as shown in Figure 3–37.

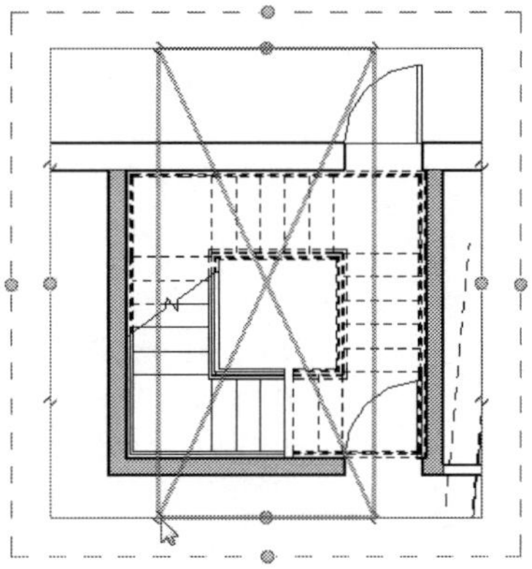

Figure 3–37

- If you want to edit the crop region to reshape the boundary of the view, select the crop region and, in the *Modify* | *Floor Plan* tab>Mode panel, click (Edit Crop).
- If you want to return a modified crop region to the original rectangular configuration, click (Reset Crop).
- You can also resize the crop region and the annotation crop region using the Crop Region Size dialog box as shown in Figure 3–38. In the *Modify* | *Floor Plan* tab>Crop panel, click (Size Crop) to open the dialog box.

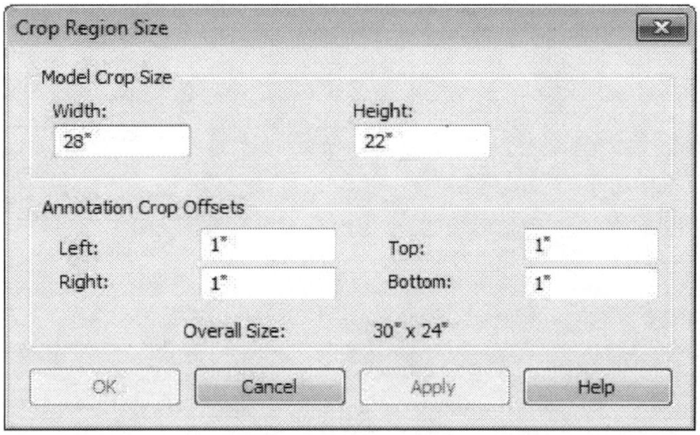

Figure 3–38

Practice 3d

Add Callout Views in an Architectural Project

Practice Objectives

- Create callouts.
- Override visibility and graphic styles in views.

Estimated time for completion: 10 minutes

In this practice you will create callout views of a guest room and make modifications to the visibility graphics so that one does not display the furniture and the other one does, as shown in Figure 3–39. You will also add callout views for other areas that need enlarged plans.

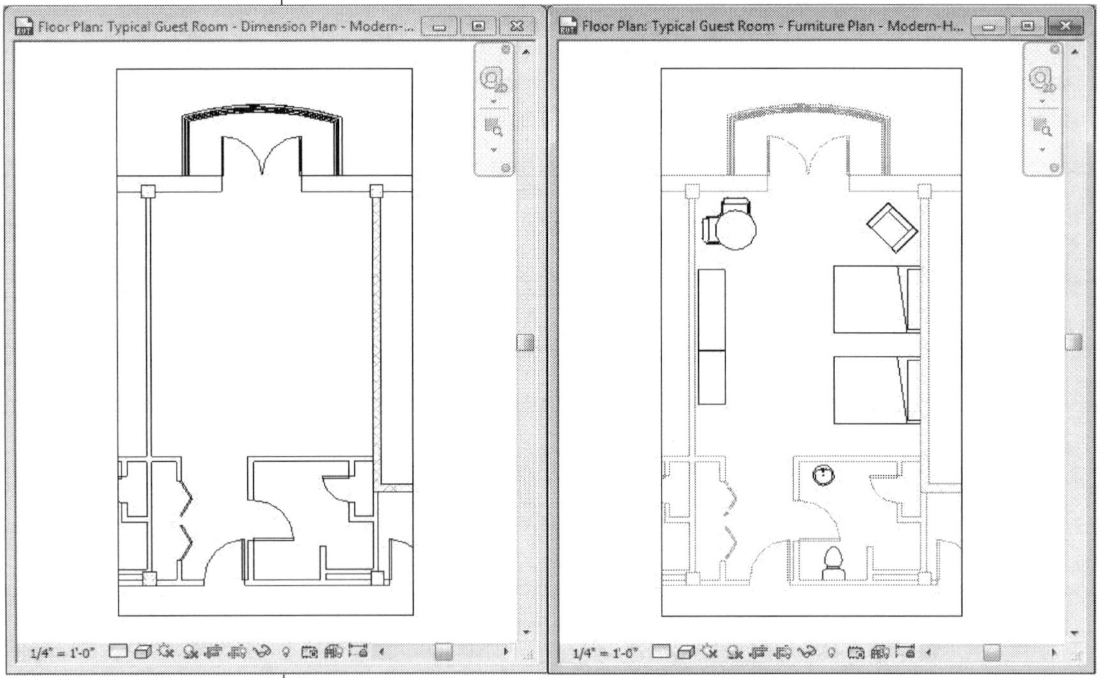

Figure 3–39

Task 1 - Add callout views.

1. Open the project **Modern-Hotel-Callouts.rvt**.
2. Open the **Floor Plans: Typical Guest Room Floor Plan** view (if it is not already open).
3. In the *View* tab>Create panel, click  (Callout).
4. Place a callout around the guest room with furniture, as shown in Figure 3–40. Move the bubble as required.

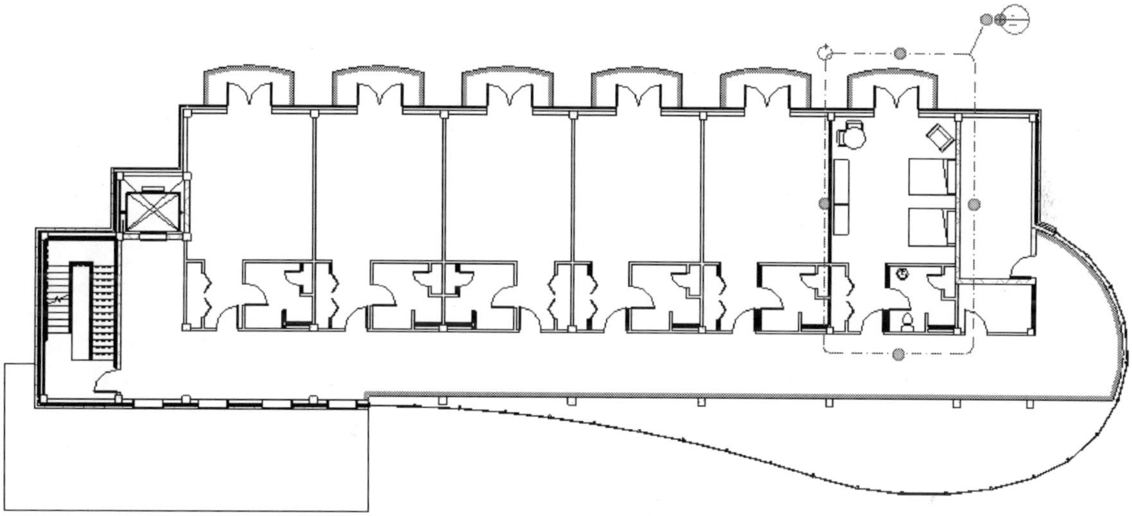

Figure 3–40

5. Click in empty space to release the selection.
6. Double-click on the callout view bubble to display the view. It is automatically scaled up to **1/4"= 1'-0"** as it is a partial plan view.
7. Rename the view to **Typical Guest Room - Dimension Plan**.

8. Duplicate the callout view and rename it to **Typical Guest Room - Furniture Plan**.

9. Close all other views except the Dimension and Furniture Plans.

10. Type **WT** to tile the windows and **ZA** to zoom out in both of them, as shown in Figure 3–41.

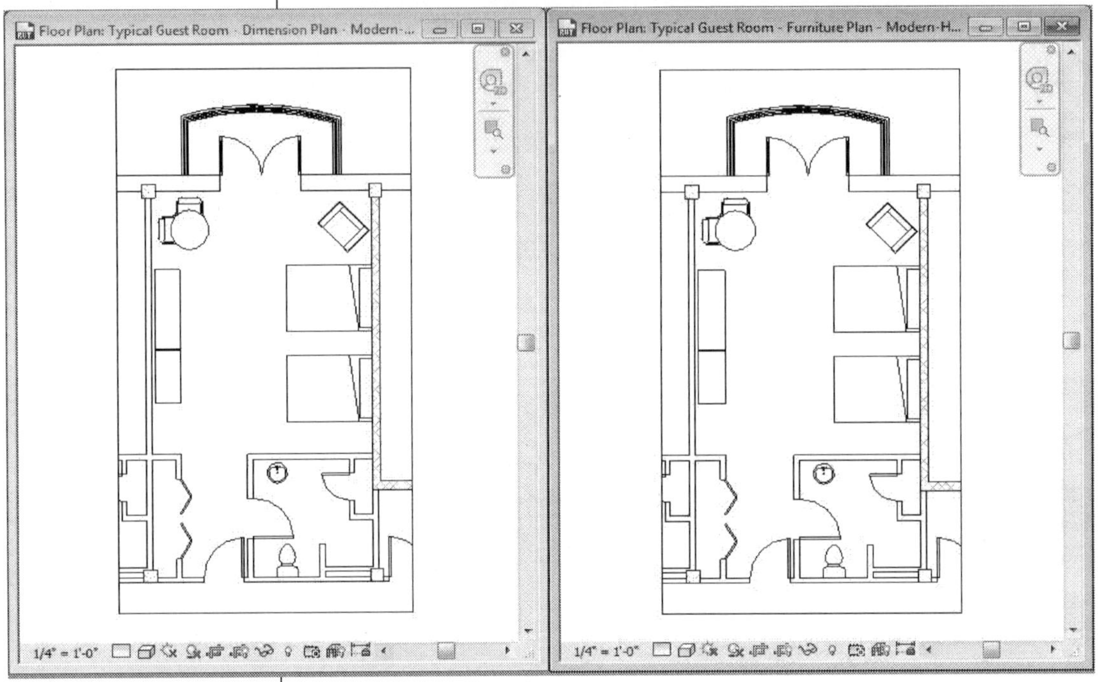

Figure 3–41

11. Save the project.

Task 2 - Override graphics in views.

1. Click in the **Floor Plans: Typical Guest Room - Dimension Plan** view.

2. Open the Visibility/Graphic Overrides dialog box by typing **VV**.

3. In the dialog box, set the *Filter list* to **Architecture** (by clearing the checkmarks for the other options). In the *Visibility* column, clear **Casework**, **Furniture**, **Furniture Systems**, as shown in Figure 3–42 and **Plumbing Fixtures** (not shown).

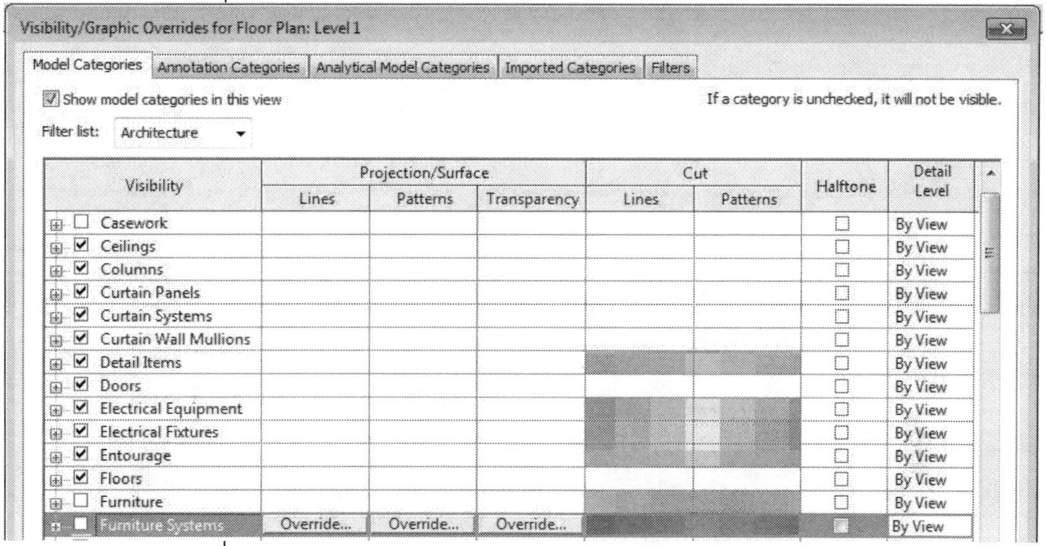

Figure 3–42

4. Click **OK**. The furniture is removed from the room.

5. Click in the **Floor Plans: Typical Guest Room - Furniture Plan** view.

6. Reopen the Visibility/Graphic Overrides dialog box. Below the table, click **All** and place a checkmark in one of the *Halftone* columns. All of the elements are set to halftone.

7. Click **None** to clear all categories.

8. In the *Halftone* column, clear the **Casework**, **Furniture**, **Furniture Systems**, and **Plumbing Fixtures** categories.

9. Click **Apply** to set the changes without exiting the dialog box.

10. In the *Annotation Categories* tab, clear **Show annotation categories in this view**. No annotations elements will display in this view.

11. Click **OK** to close the dialog box. The view should display with all existing elements in halftone, as shown in Figure 3–43.

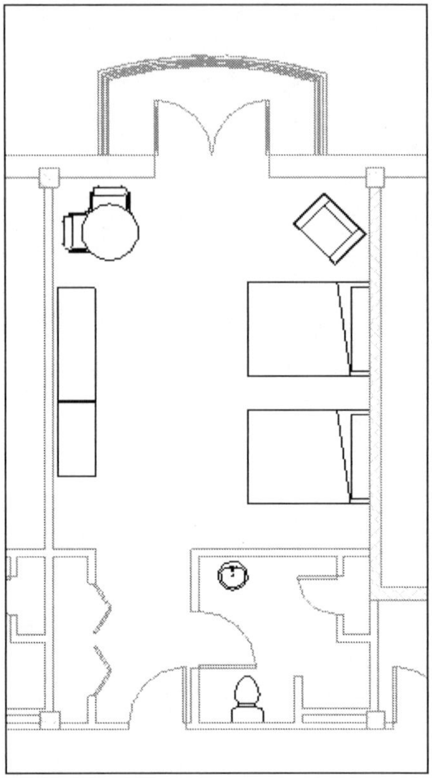

Figure 3–43

12. Save the project.

Task 3 - Additional Callouts

1. Open the **Floor Plans: Floor 1 - Reference** view.
2. In the *View* tab>Create panel, click  (Callout) and add callouts to the stairs and restrooms. Name the views as shown in Figure 3–44.

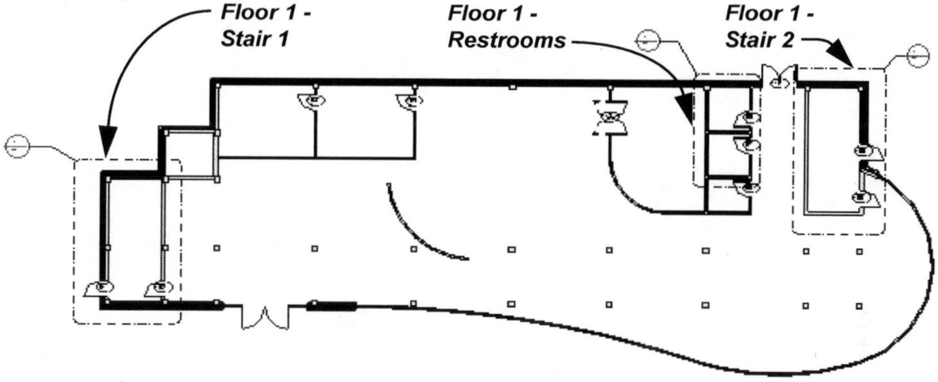

Figure 3–44

- The view has been simplified for clarity.

3. Save the project.

Practice 3e Add Callout Views in a MEP Project

Estimated time for completion: 5minutes

Practice Objective

- Create callouts.

In this practice you will create a callout view of one wing of the building. In the new callout view, you will then create an additional callout view of the electrical room, as shown in Figure 3–45.

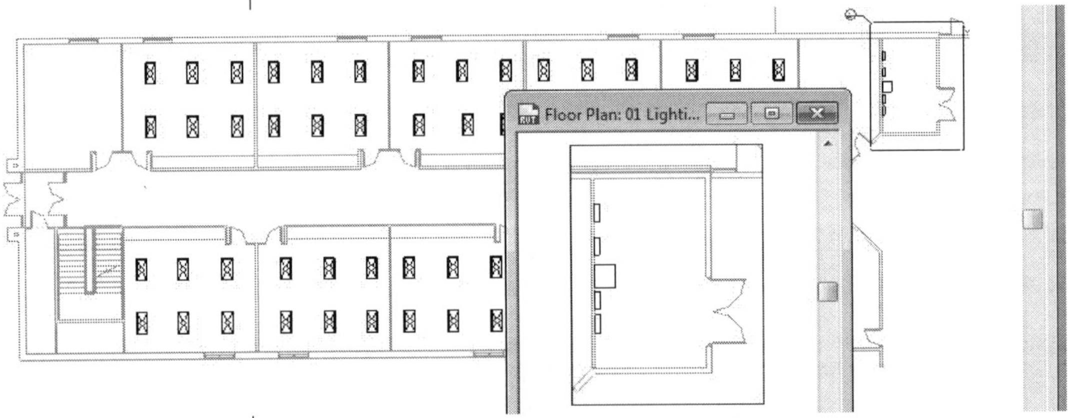

Figure 3–45

Task 1 - Add callout views.

1. Open the project **MEP-Elementary-School-Callout.rvt**.
2. Open the Electrical>Lighting>Floor Plans>**01 Lighting Plan** view.
3. In the *View* tab>Create panel, expand (Callout) and select (Sketch).

4. Sketch a boundary similar to that shown in Figure 3–46.

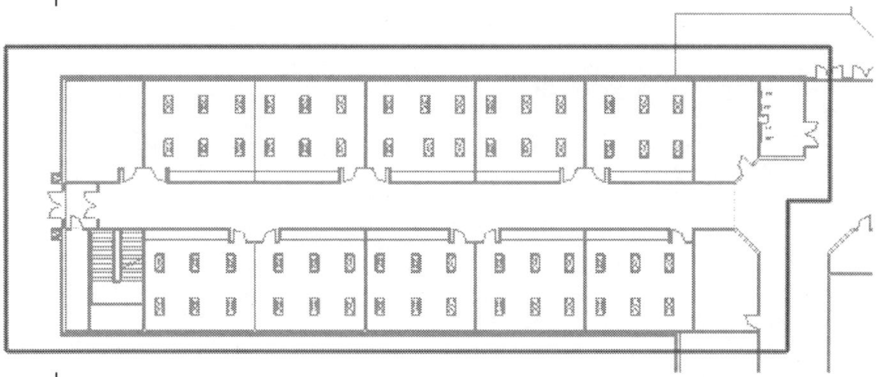

Figure 3–46

5. Click (Finish Edit Mode). Use the controls to move the bubble as shown in Figure 3–47.

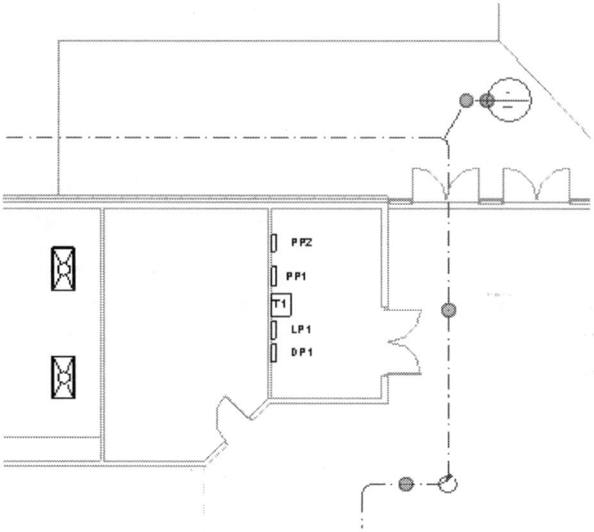

Figure 3–47

6. In the Project Browser, double-click on the new callout view to open it. Rename the callout **01 Lighting Plan-Area A**.

7. In the View Control Bar, click (Hide Crop Region).

8. In the *View* tab>Create panel, click (Callout).

9. Draw a callout box around the electrical room and move the bubble as shown in Figure 3–48.

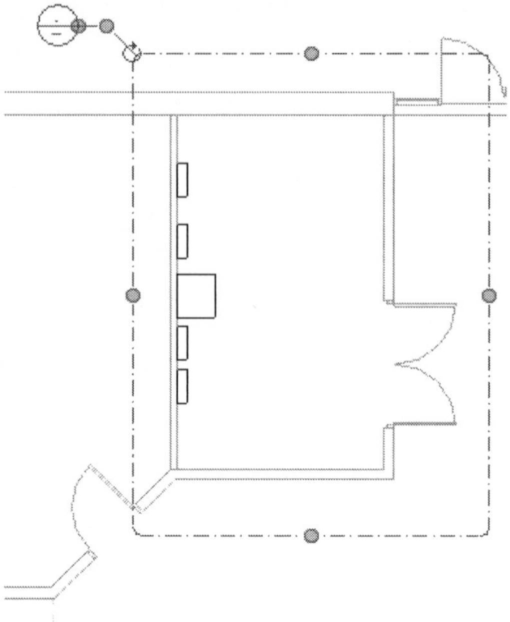

Figure 3–48

10. In the Project Browser, rename the new callout **01 Lighting Plan - Electrical Room**.

11. Reopen the **01 Lighting Plan** view. The larger callout displays, but the callout in the larger callout does not.

12. Save the project.

Practice 3f

Add Callout Views in a Structural Project

Estimated time for completion: 5 minutes

Practice Objective

- Create callouts.

In this practice you will create a callout view of the elevator pit walls, as shown in Figure 3–49.

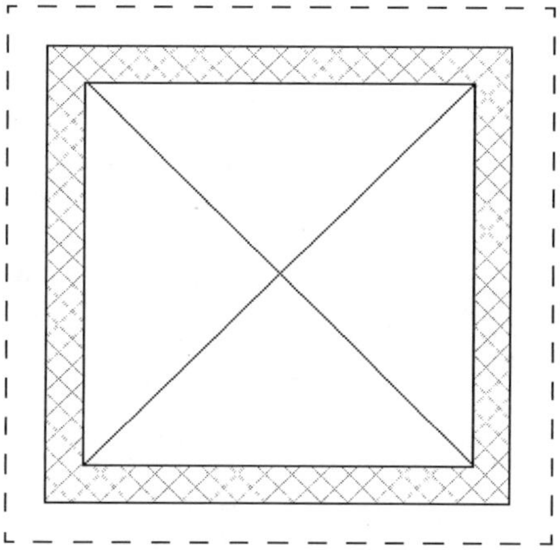

Figure 3–49

Task 1 - Add a callout view.

1. Open the project **Practice-Model-Callouts.rvt**.
2. Ensure that you are in the **Structural Plans: Level 1** view.
3. In the View Control Bar, check the *Scale* and *Detail Level* of the view, as shown in Figure 3–50.

Figure 3–50

4. In the *View* tab>Create panel, click  (Callout).
5. In the Type Selector, select **Detail View: Detail.**

6. Draw a callout box around the elevator pit walls, as shown in Figure 3–51. Move the callout bubble as required.

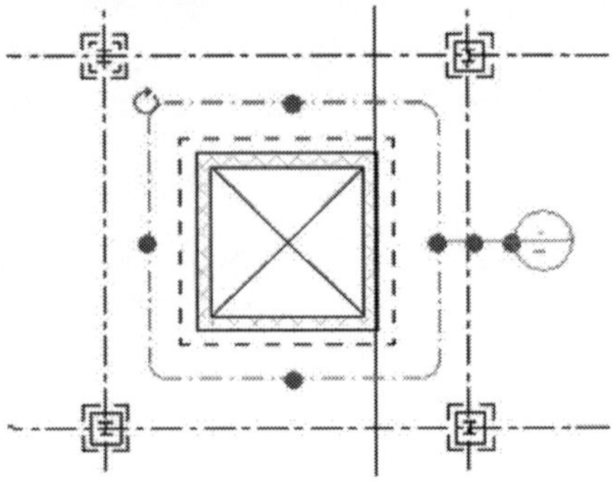

Figure 3–51

7. In the Project Browser, in the *Structural Plans* area, rename *Level 1- Callout* as **Elevator Pit Enlarged Plan**.

8. Open the view to display the callout.

9. In the View Control Bar, set the *Scale* to **1/4"=1'-0"** and the *Detail Level* to **Fine**.

10. In the View Control Bar, click (Hide Crop Region).

11. Return to the **Level 1** view.

12. Save the project.

3.4 Elevations and Sections

Elevations and sections are critical elements of construction documents and can assist you as you are working on a model. Any changes made in one of these views (such as the section in Figure 3–52), changes the entire model and any changes made to the project model are also displayed in the elevations and sections.

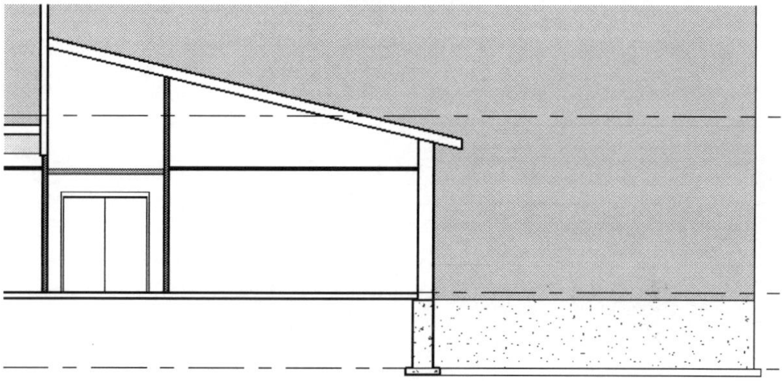

Figure 3–52

- In the Project Browser, elevations are separated by elevation type and sections are separated by section type, as shown in Figure 3–53.

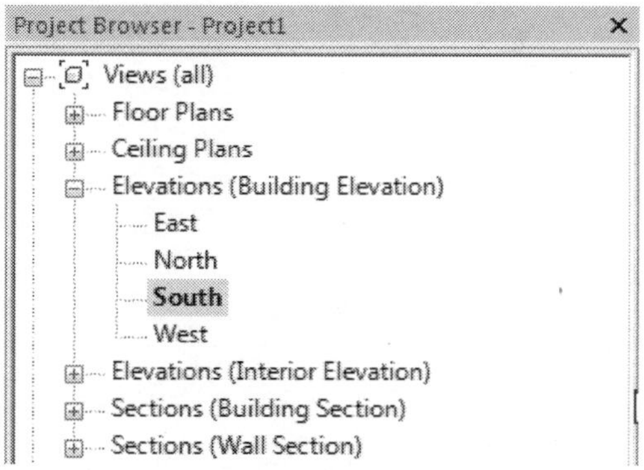

Figure 3–53

- To open an elevation or section view, double-click on the marker arrow or on its name in the Project Browser.

- To give the elevation or section a new name, right-click on it in the Project Browser and select **Rename...**

Elevations

Elevations are *face-on* views of the interiors and exteriors of a building. Four Exterior Elevation views are defined in the default template: **North**, **South**, **East**, and **West**. You can create additional building elevation views at other angles or interior elevation views, such as the Kitchen elevation shown in Figure 3–54.

When you add an elevation or section to a sheet, the detail number and sheet number are automatically added to the view title.

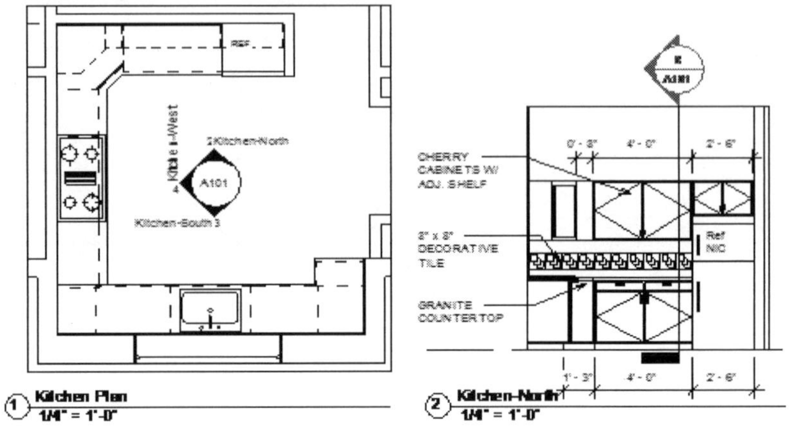

Figure 3–54

- Elevations must be created in plan views.

Structural only

- A framing elevation is set up to only capture the framing elements that are behind other model elements in an elevation of a single area in a building.
  - By default, the framing elevation snaps and sets its extents along the grid lines by using **Attach to Grid** in the Options Bar.
  - The most common use for a framing elevation is to generate braced frames and shear wall elevations.

How To: Create an Elevation

The software remembers the last elevation type used, so you can click the top button if you want to use the same elevation command.

1. In the *View* tab>Create panel, expand (Elevation) and click (Elevation).
2. In the Type Selector, select the elevation type. Two types come with the templates: **Building Elevation** and **Interior Elevation**.
3. Move the cursor near one of the walls that defines the elevation. The marker follows the angle of the wall.
4. Click to place the marker.

- The length, width, and height of an elevation are defined by the wall(s) and ceiling/floor at which the elevation marker is pointing.
- When creating interior elevations, ensure that the floor or ceiling above is in place before creating the elevation or you will need to modify the elevation crop region so that the elevation markers do not show on all floors.

How To: Create Framing Elevations

1. Open a plan view.
2. In the *View* tab>Create panel, expand (Elevation) and click (Framing Elevation).
3. Hover the cursor over a grid line to display an elevation element, as shown in Figure 3–55. Click to add the marker.

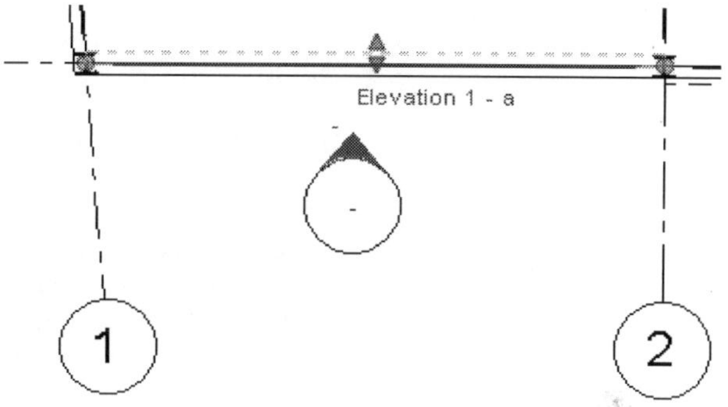

Figure 3–55

4. Click (Modify) and select the marker. The extents focus on the bracing bay only. You can use the round segment handles to expand the length of the elevation, as required.

- Framing Elevations are found in the Project Browser in the *Elevations (Framing Elevation)* area.

Sections

Sections can be created in plan, elevation, and other section views.

Sections are slices through a model. You can create a section through an entire building, as shown in Figure 3–56, or through one wall for a detail.

Figure 3–56

How To: Create a Section

1. In the *View* tab>Create panel or in the Quick Access Toolbar, click  (Section).
2. In the Type Selector, select **Section: Building Section** or **Section: Wall Section.** If you want a section in a Drafting view select **Detail View: Detail.**
3. In the view, select a point where you want to locate the bubble and arrowhead.
4. Select the other end point that describes the section.
5. The shape controls display. You can flip the arrow and change the size of the cutting plane, as well as the location of the bubble and flag.

Hint: Selection Box

You can modify a 3D view to display parts of a building, as shown in Figure 3–57.

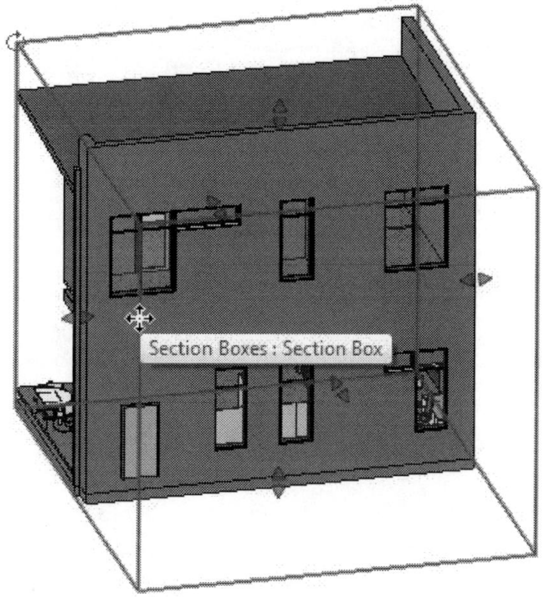

Figure 3–57

1. In a 3D view, select the elements you want to isolate. In the example shown in Figure 3–57, the front wall was selected.
2. In the *Modify* tab>View panel, click (Selection Box) or type **BX**.
3. The view is limited to a box around the selected item(s).
4. Use the controls of the Section Box to modify the size of the box to show exactly what you want.

- To toggle off a section box and restore the full model, in the view's Properties, in the *Extents* area, clear the check from **Section Box**.

Modifying Elevations and Sections

There are two parts to modifying elevations and sections:

- To modify the view (as shown in Figure 3–58), use the controls to modify the size or create view breaks.
- To modify the markers (as shown in Figure 3–59), use the controls to change the length and depth of elevations and sections. There are other specific type options as well.

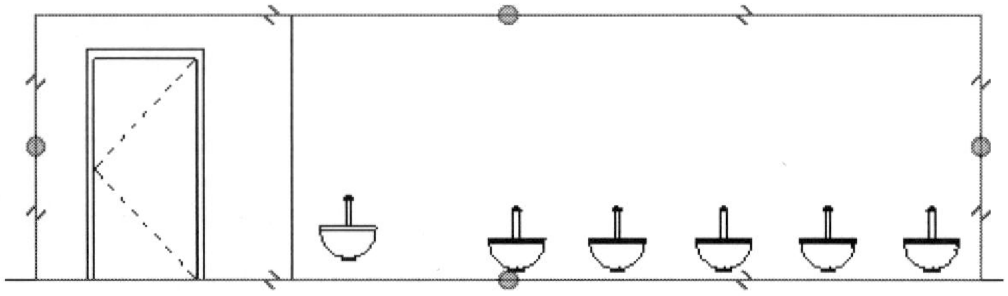

Figure 3–58

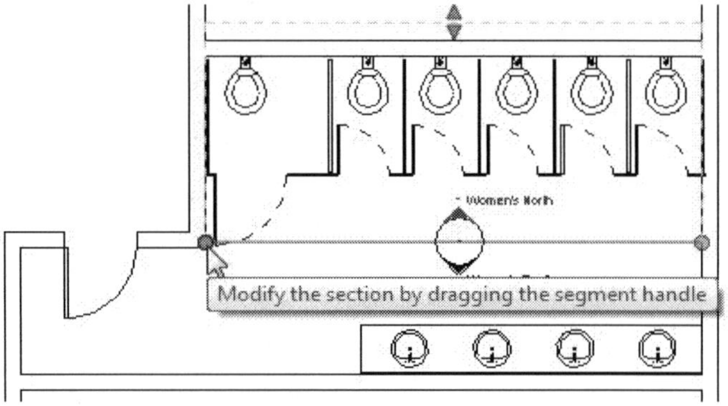

Figure 3–59

Modifying Elevation Markers

When you modify elevation markers, you can specify the length and depth of the clip plane, as shown in Figure 3–60.

- Select the arrowhead of the elevation marker (not the circle portion) to display the clip plane.
- Drag the round shape handles to lengthen or shorten the elevation.
- Drag the (Arrow) controls to adjust the depth of the elevation.

To display additional interior elevations from one marker, select the circle portion (not the arrowhead) and place a checkmark in the directions that you want to display, as shown in Figure 3–60.

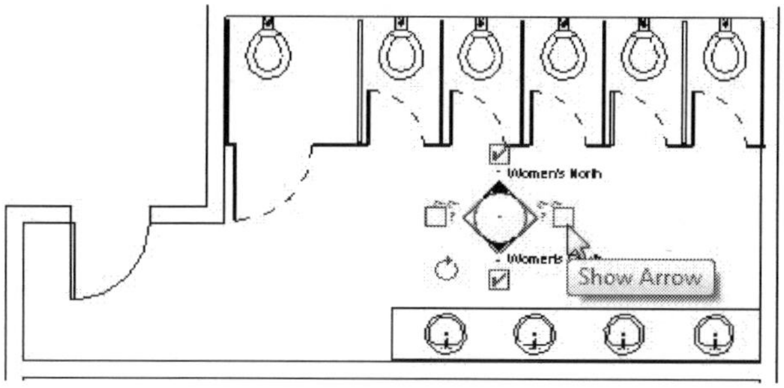

Figure 3–60

- Use the (Rotate) control to angle the marker (i.e., for a room with angled walls).

Modifying Section Markers

When you modify section markers, various shape handles and controls enable you to modify a section, as shown in Figure 3–61.

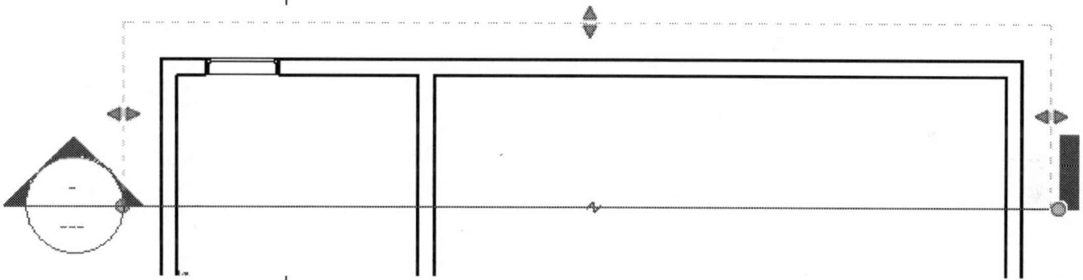

Figure 3–61

- Drag the (Arrow) controls to change the length and depth of the cut plane.
- Drag the circular controls at either end of the section line to change the location of the arrow or flag without changing the cut boundary.
- Click (Flip) to change the direction of the arrowhead, which also flips the entire section.

- Click (Cycle Section Head/Tail) to switch between an arrowhead, flag, or nothing on each end of the section.
- Click (Gaps in Segments) to create an opening in section lines, as shown in Figure 3–62. Select it again to restore the full section cut.

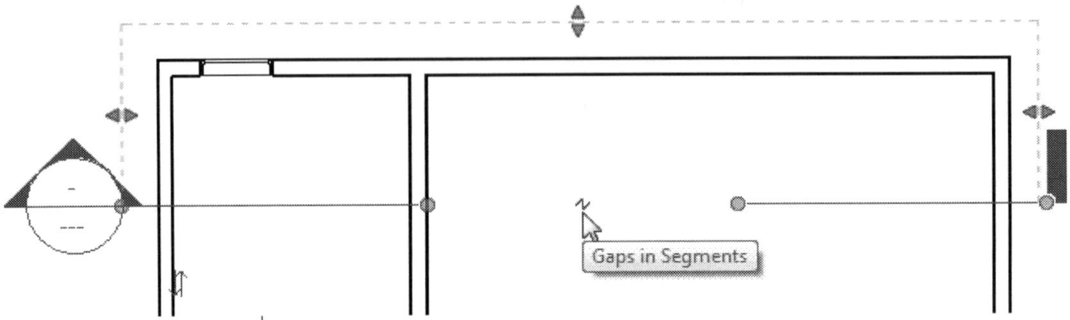

Figure 3–62

How To: Add a Jog to a Section Line

1. Select the section line you want to modify.
2. In the *Modify* | *Views* tab> Section panel, click (Split Segment).
3. Select the point along the line where you want to create the split, as shown in Figure 3–63.
4. Specify the location of the split line, as shown in Figure 3–64.

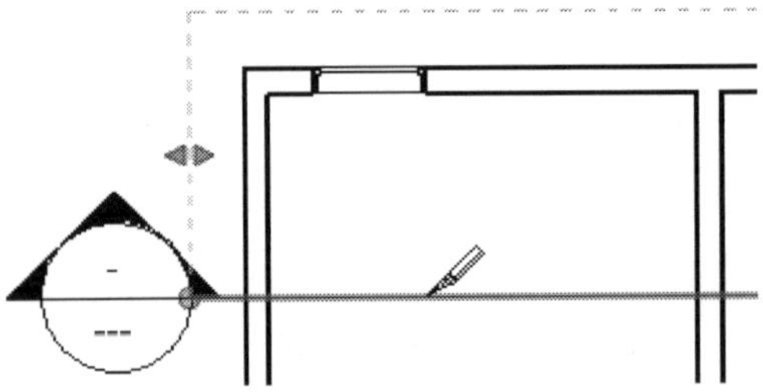

Figure 3–63

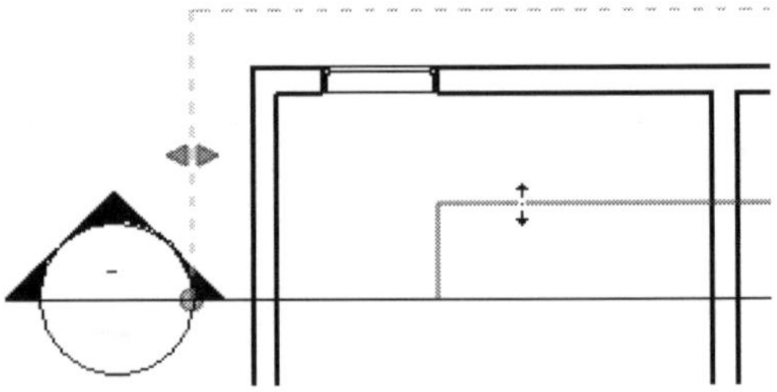

Figure 3–64

- If you need to adjust the location of any segment on the section line, modify it and drag the shape handles along each segment of the line, as shown in Figure 3–65.

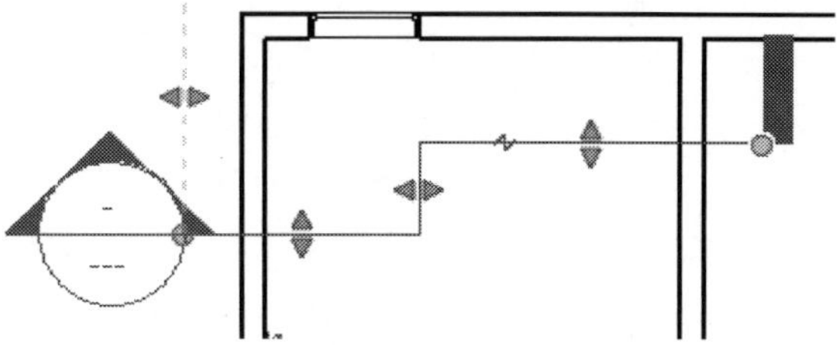

Figure 3–65

- To bring a split section line back into place, use a shape handle to drag the jogged line until it is at the same level with the rest of the line.

Hint: Using Thin Lines

The software automatically applies line weights to views, as shown for a section on the left in Figure 3–66. If a line weight seems heavy or obscures your work on the elements, toggle off the line weights. In the Quick Access Toolbar or in the *View* tab>Graphics panel, click (Thin Lines) or type **TL**. The lines display with the same weight, as shown on the right in Figure 3–66.

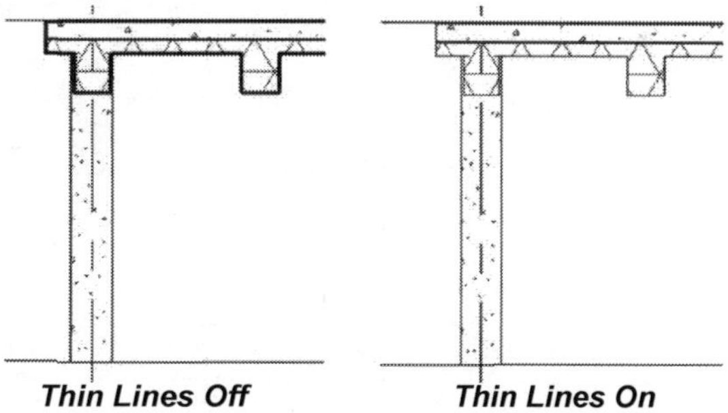

Thin Lines Off ***Thin Lines On***

Figure 3–66

- The Thin Line setting is remembered until you change it, even if you shut down and restart the software.

Practice 3g

Create Elevations and Sections in an Architectural Project

Estimated time for completion: 20 minutes

Practice Objectives

- Create exterior and interior elevations.
- Add building sections and wall sections.

In this practice you will create exterior elevations of the poolhouse and interior elevations of the restrooms. You will also add building sections, as shown in Figure 3–67, and several wall sections to the project.

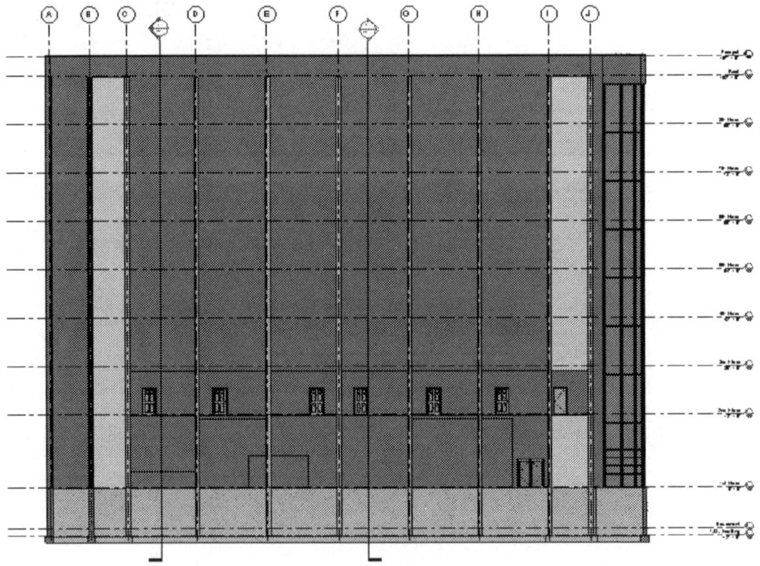

Figure 3–67

Task 1 - Add exterior elevations.

1. Open the project **Modern-Hotel-Elevations.rvt**.
2. Open the **Floor Plans: Floor 1 Overall** view.
3. In the View Control Bar, click (Show Crop Region).
4. Ensure that there is enough space above the pool house to add an elevation mark at this scale, if not, move the crop region up.

5. In the *View* tab>Create panel, expand (Elevation) and click (Elevation). In the Type Selector, select **Elevation: Building Elevation**.

6. Place an elevation marker outside of the pool building, as shown in Figure 3–68.

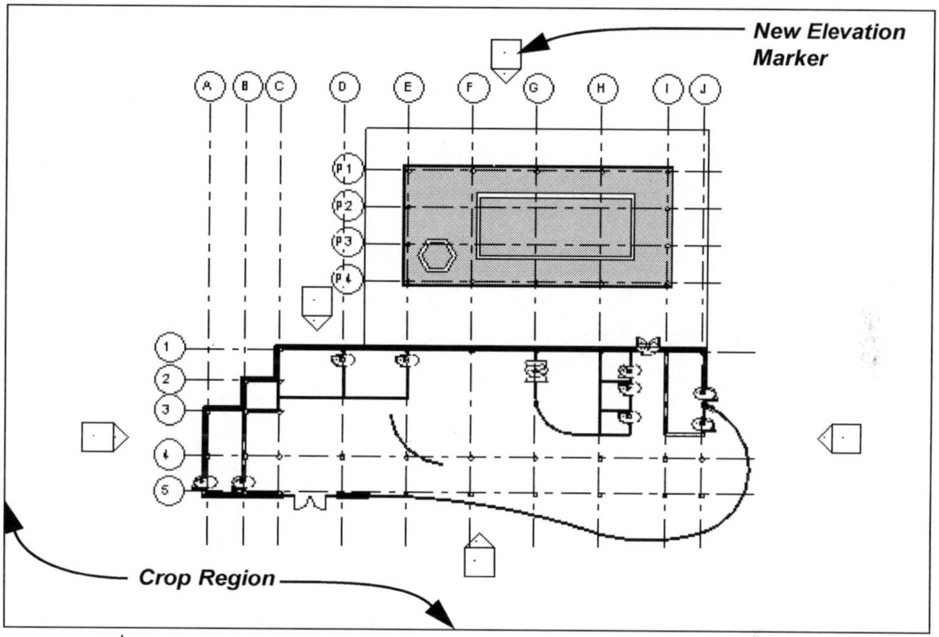

Figure 3–68

7. Click (Modify) and select the pointed side of the new elevation marker.

8. Change the length and depth of the elevation boundaries so only the poolhouse is displayed, as shown in Figure 3–69.

Grids are hidden to clarify the view.

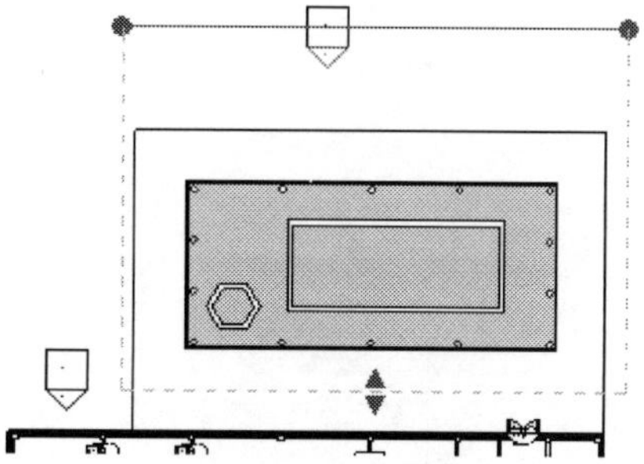

Figure 3–69

9. Double-click on the pointed side of the elevation marker to open the elevation view.

10. Change the crop region so that the height is up to **Floor 3** and the bottom is just below the floor line. Bring the sides in close to the pool building.

11. Hide the grids and levels so that the elevation is similar to that shown in Figure 3–70.

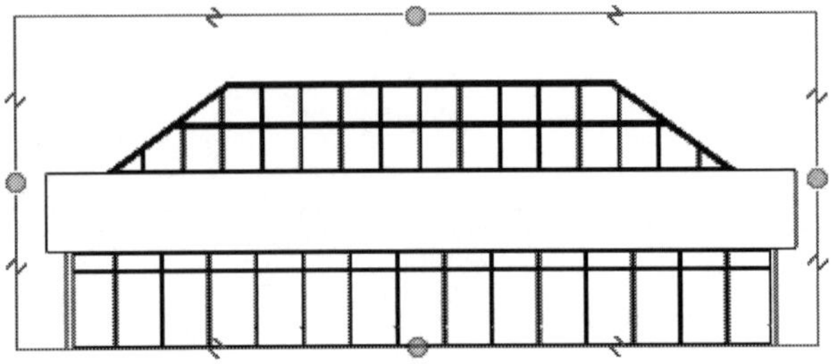

Figure 3–70

12. Hide the crop region.

In this project, North is considered the top of the project.

13. In the Project Browser, in the *Elevations (Building Elevation)* area) rename the elevation (Elevation 1 -a if you selected this direction first) as **Pool-North**.

14. Return to the **Floor Plans: Floor 1 Overall** view.

15. Add elevation markers to the other sides of the poolhouse.

16. Open the new elevations. Resize and rename them as required.

17. Save the project.

Task 2 - Add interior elevations.

1. Open the **Floor Plans: Floor 1 - Restrooms** view.
2. Select the floor that shows the floor drain slopes and hide it.
3. In the *View* tab>Create panel, click (Elevation).
4. In the Type Selector, select **Elevation: Interior Elevation**.

5. Place an elevation in one of the restrooms and then in the other restroom.

6. Click (Modify and select the circle part of one of the elevation markers and check each of the boxes, as shown in Figure 3–71. This places an elevation in each direction.

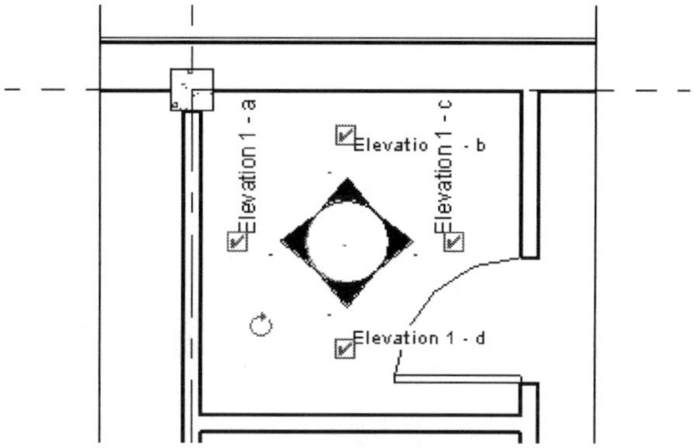

Figure 3–71

7. Repeat for the other restroom.

8. In the Project Browser, under *Elevations (Interior Elevation)*, as shown in Figure 3–72, rename the top restroom elevations as **Men's Restroom-North**, **South**, **East**, **West** and the bottom restroom elevations as **Women's Restroom-North**, **South**, **East**, **West**.

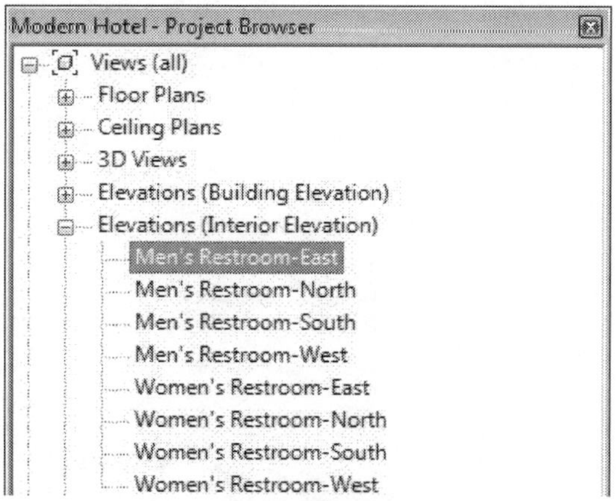

Figure 3–72

Doing this keeps these markers from showing up in other plans at larger scales.

9. Select all of the elevation marker arrows (not the circles) and, in Properties, set the *Hide at scales coarser than* to **1/4"=1'-0"**, as shown in Figure 3–73.

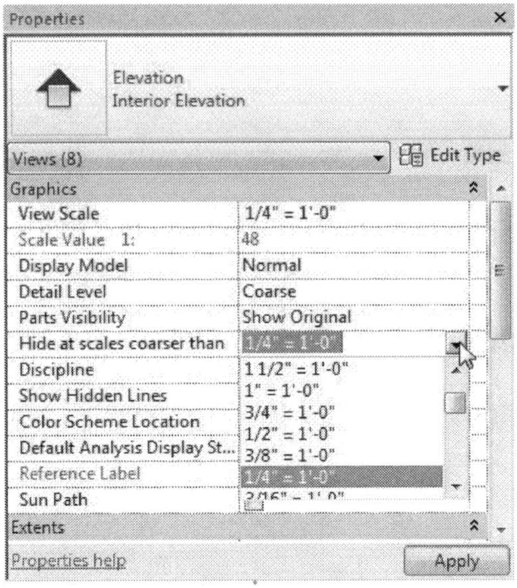

Figure 3–73

10. Open one of the elevations facing the door (**Men's Restroom-East**). The interior elevation should automatically stop at the boundaries of the walls and ceiling.

11. If the elevation is not bounded as expected, move the crop region so that it is tight against the walls, as shown in Figure 3–74

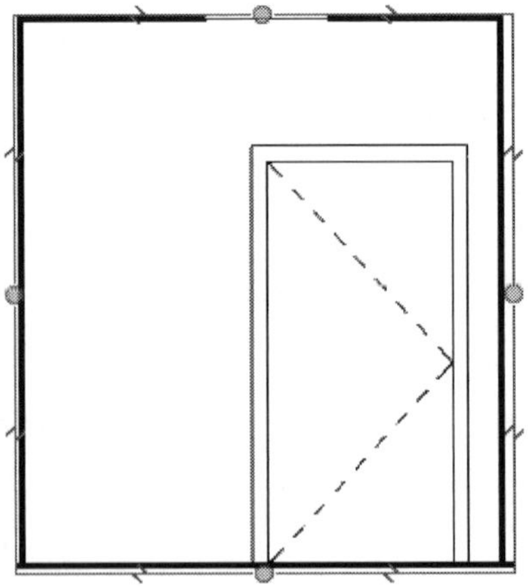

Figure 3–74

12. Save the project.

Task 3 - Clean up a view and add building sections.

1. Select and hide the elevation markers facing the poolhouse. (Do not hide the category as that would also hide the markers you do want to display.)
2. In the *View* tab>Create panel, click (Section).
3. In the Type Selector, select **Section: Building Section**.
4. Draw a horizontal section and a vertical section through the building, as shown in Figure 3–75.

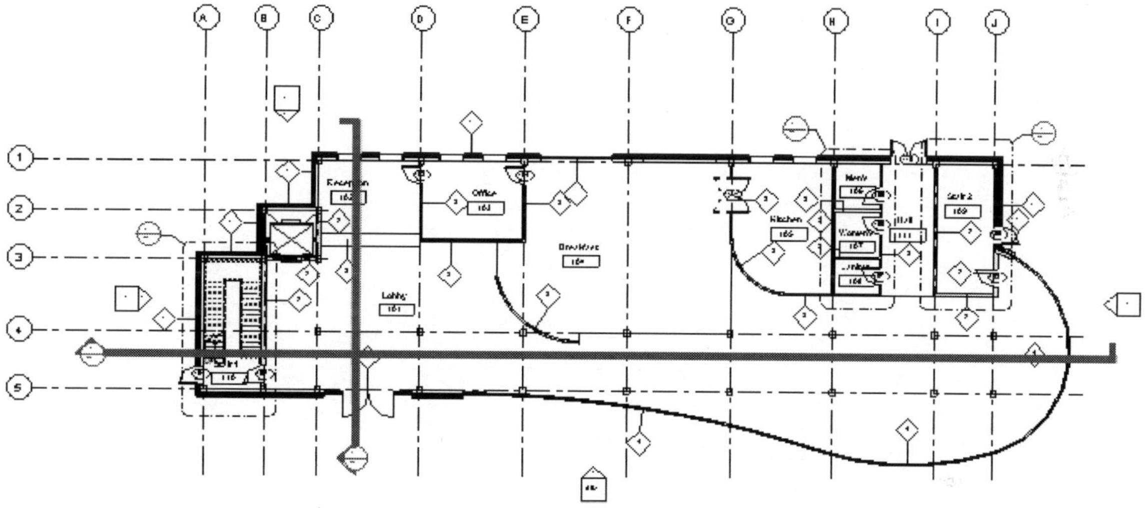

Figure 3–75

5. In the Project Browser, under *Sections*, rename them to **East-West Section** and **North-South Section**.
6. View each of the building sections.

Task 4 - Add wall sections.

*You are using the **Floor 2** view to place the wall sections, as you want to ensure they go through certain features, such as doors and windows.*

1. Open the **Floor Plans: Floor 2** view.
2. Hide by element, the elevation markers facing the poolhouse.
3. In the *View* tab>Create panel, click (Section). In the Type Selector, select **Section: Wall Section**.

4. Draw four wall sections, as shown in Figure 3–76. Ensure that the front wall section passes through a window and the back wall section passes through a door.

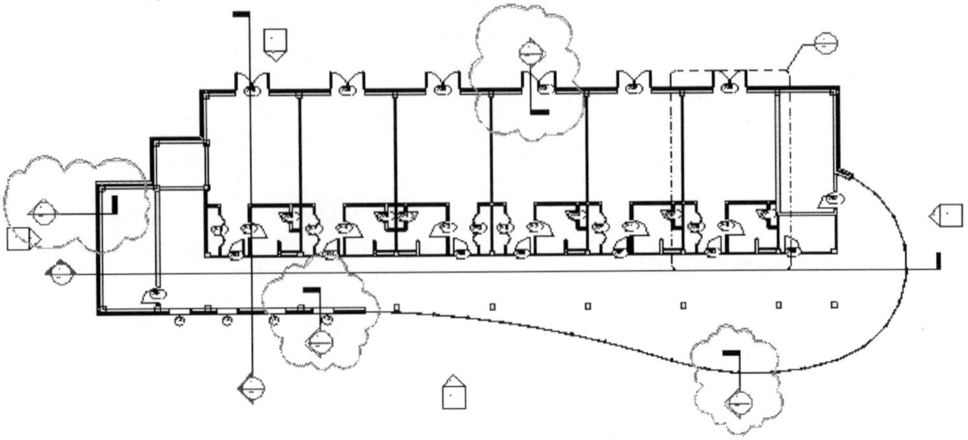

Figure 3–76

5. Move any annotation elements so they do not interfere with the section cut.
6. View each of the wall sections.
7. Save the project.

Practice 3h Create Elevations and Sections in a MEP Project

Practice Objectives

- Create interior elevations.
- Add building sections.

Estimated time for completion: 10 minutes

In this practice you will create interior elevations, as shown in Figure 3–77. You will also add several building sections.

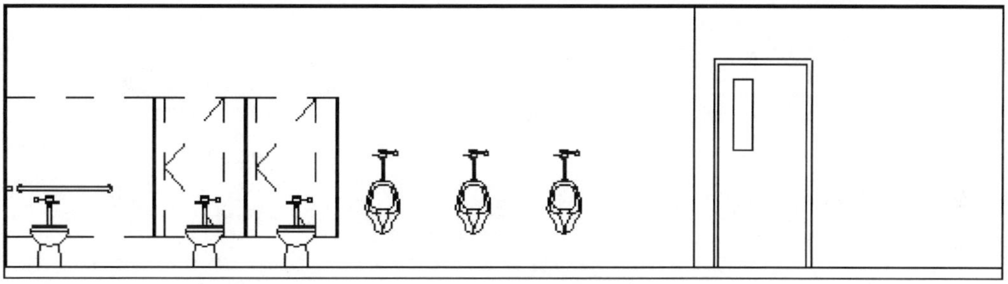

Figure 3–77

Task 1 - Add interior elevations.

1. Open the project **MEP-Elementary-School-Elevations.rvt**.
2. Open the Plumbing>Plumbing>Floor Plans>**01 Plumbing Plan** view.
3. Zoom in on the restrooms near the gym.
4. In the *View* tab>Create panel, click (Elevation).
5. In the Type Selector, select **Elevation: Interior Elevation**.
6. Place an elevation facing the wall of sinks in one of the restrooms.
7. Click (Modify).

8. Select the circle part of the elevation marker and check the box on the opposite side, as shown in Figure 3–78.

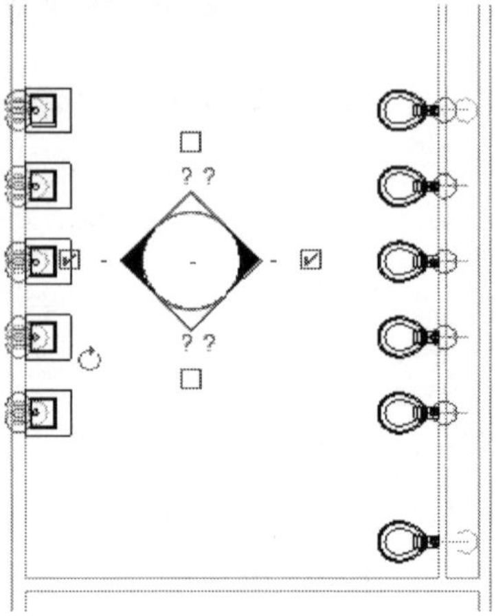

Figure 3–78

9. Press <Esc> to release the selection.

10. Select one of the arrows and zoom out to see the full length and depth of the section.

11. Drag the ends back to the restroom and modify the depth as required as shown in Figure 3–79.

The elevation does not reflect the size of the room automatically because it cannot read the location of the walls in the linked model.

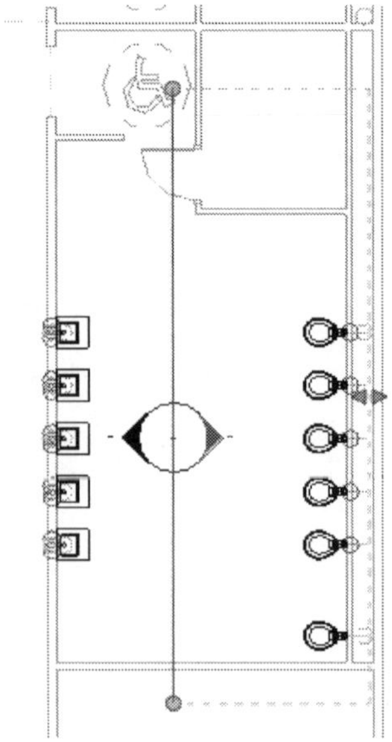

Figure 3–79

12. Repeat with the other direction.

Task 2 - Modify Elevation Views.

1. Double-click on the arrow pointing toward the water closets to open the corresponding view. The elevation cannot find the ceiling of the linked model so it selects the extents of the building model, as shown in Figure 3–80.

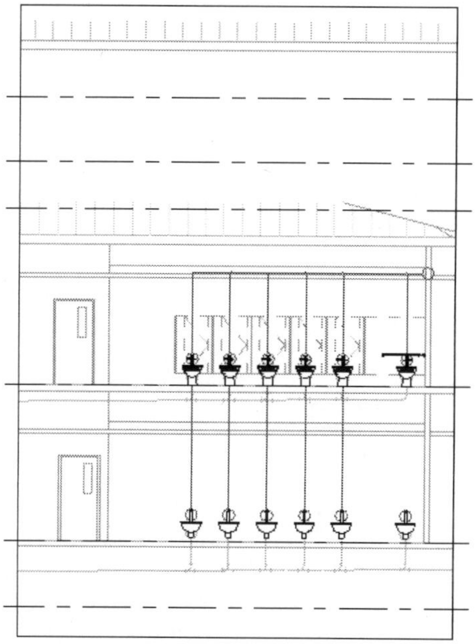

Figure 3–80

2. Select the crop region and resize the view so that only the lower floor restroom is displayed.
3. Type **VG** and toggle off the Grids category.
4. Return to plan view and open the arrow in the other direction. Repeat the process of resizing the crop region as shown in Figure 3–81.

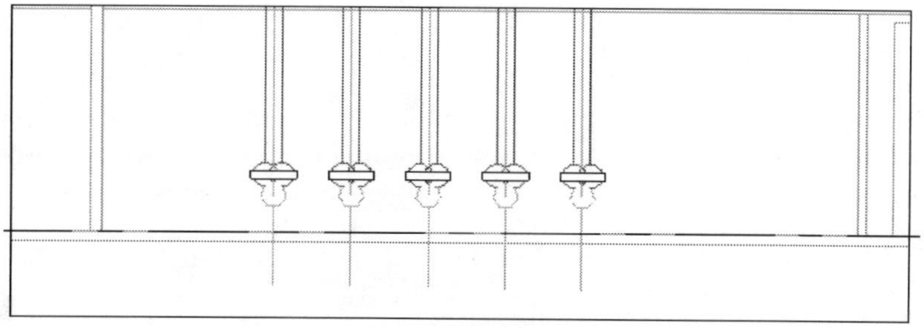

Figure 3–81

5. Return to plan view.
6. Select the entire elevation marker (the circle and both arrows).
7. Hold <Ctrl> and drag a copy of the marker up to the other restroom.
8. Open each of the new elevation views and modify the crop regions as required. The example in Figure 3–82 was lengthened to display the full sanitary line.

By setting up one elevation and then copying it to a location, you can save some steps.

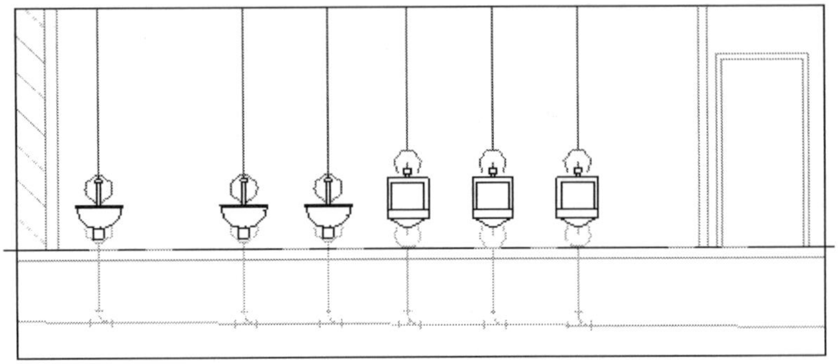

Figure 3–82

9. In the Project Browser expand Plumbing>???>**Elevations (Interior Elevation)**. Note that the four new elevations have generic names and are in an unknown sub-category, as shown in Figure 3–83.

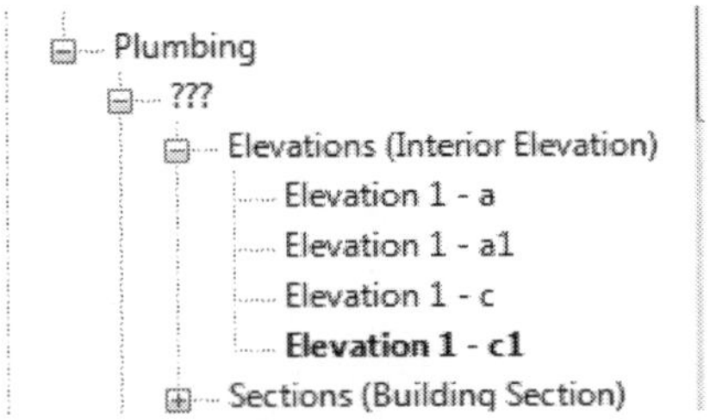

Figure 3–83

10. Right-click on the open elevation and give it a new title. For example, the elevation in Figure 3–82 would be **01 Men's East Elevation**.
11. Once you have finished renaming each of the elevations, hold <Ctrl> and select each of the new elevations.
12. In Properties, change the *Sub-Discipline* to **Plumbing**.

13. In the Project Browser, note that the elevations are now in the Plumbing sub-category, as shown in Figure 3–84.

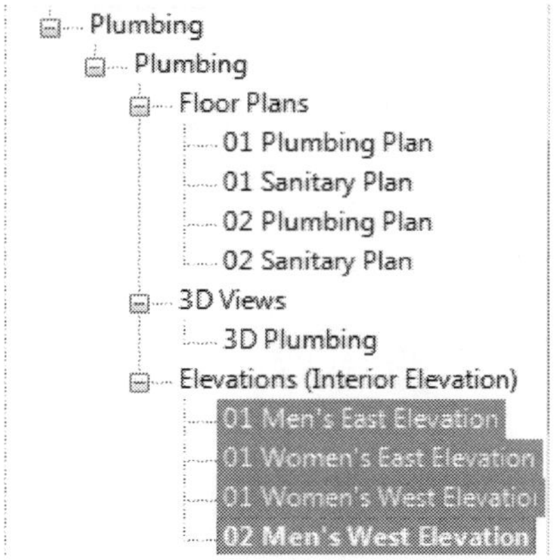

Figure 3–84

14. Save the project.

Task 3 - Add building sections.

1. Open the Mechanical>HVAC>**FloorPlans 01 Mechanical Plan** view.
2. In the *View* tab>Create panel, click (Section).
3. In the Type Selector, select **Elevation: Building Section**.
4. Draw a section through the north wing, as shown in Figure 3–85.

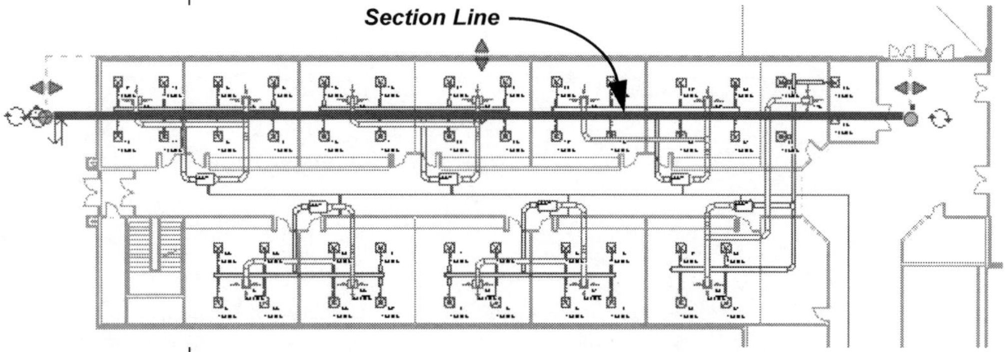

Figure 3–85

5. Press <Esc> and then double-click on the arrow of the section marker to open the section view.

6. Select one of the level lines and then type **VH** to toggle them off.

7. Expand the crop region so that the first floor and the full height of the roof is displayed, as shown in Figure 3–86.

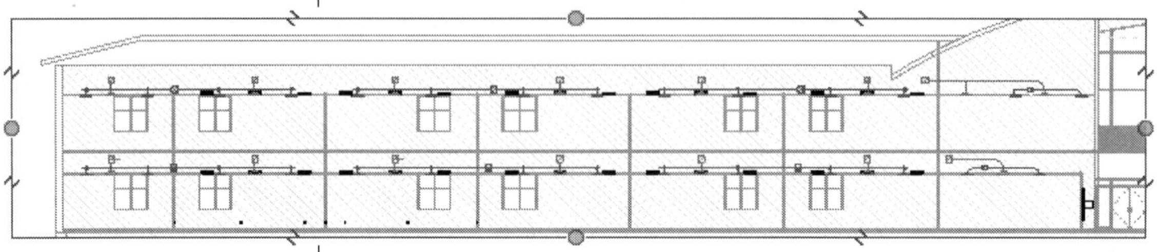

Figure 3–86

8. In the plan view, draw several other sections and review the section views.

9. In the Project Browser, under the *Sections* group, rename the sections as required.

10. Save the project.

Practice 3i

Create Elevations and Sections in a Structural Project

Estimated time for completion: 15 minutes

Practice Objectives

- Add building sections and wall sections.
- Add a framing elevation

In this practice you will add a Building Section and a Wall Section to an existing project. You will also add a Framing Elevation as shown in Figure 3–87.

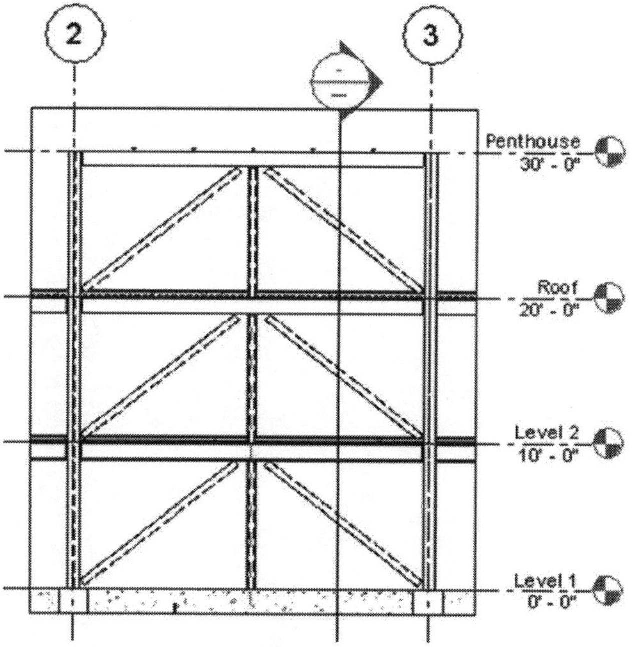

Figure 3–87

Task 1 - Create sections.

1. Open the project **Practice-Model-Sections.rvt**.
2. In the Project Browser, open the **Structural Plans: Level 1** view.
3. In the *View* tab>Create panel or in the Quick Access Toolbar, click (Section).

4. Place a vertical section offset slightly from the middle. Change the width of the section using the controls as shown in Figure 3–88.

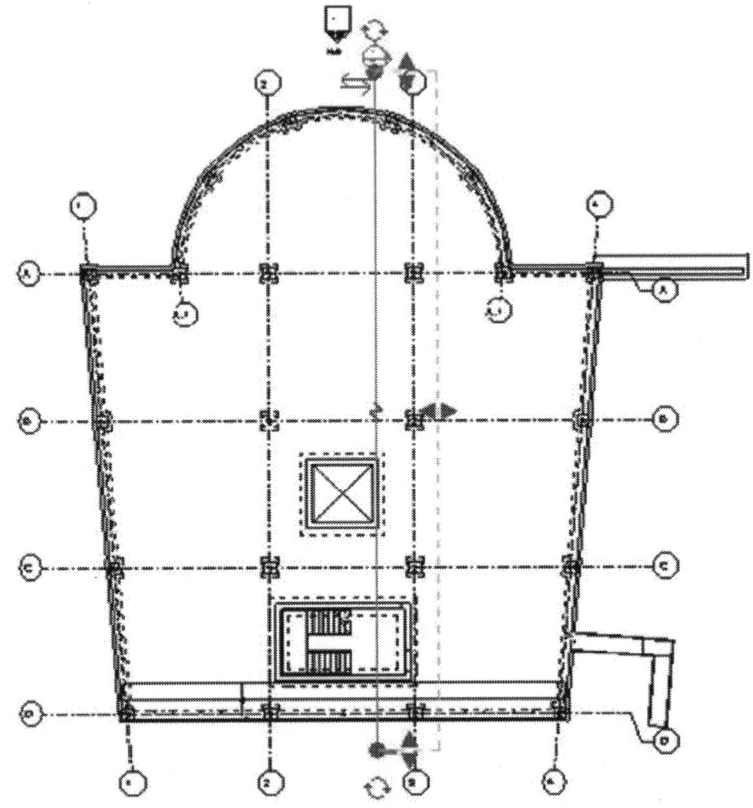

Figure 3–88

5. In the Project Browser, expand *Sections (Building Section)*. Right-click on the new section and rename it **Building Section**, as shown in Figure 3–89.

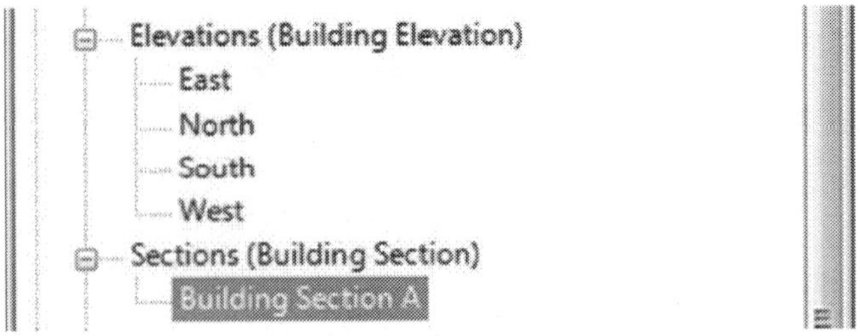

Figure 3–89

6. Open the new section by double-clicking on its name in the Project Browser. The entire Building displays as shown in Figure 3–90.

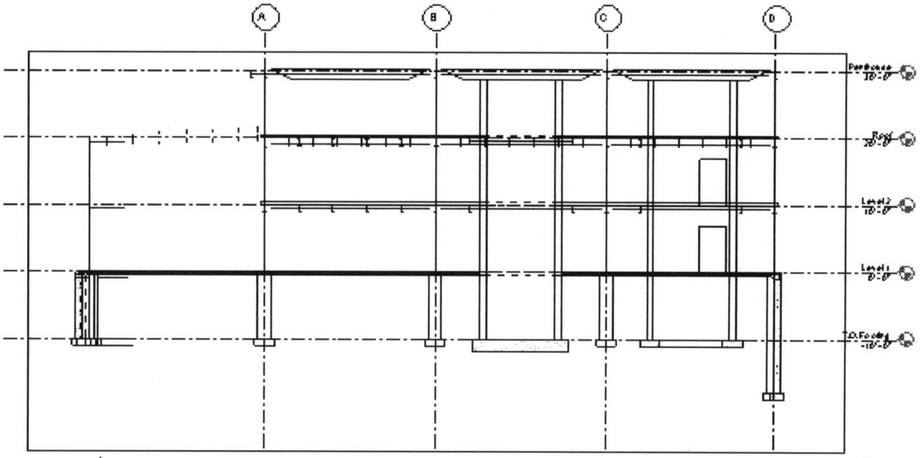

Figure 3–90

7. Select the crop region and use the controls to shorten the section so that the curved walls to the left do not display, as shown in Figure 3–91.

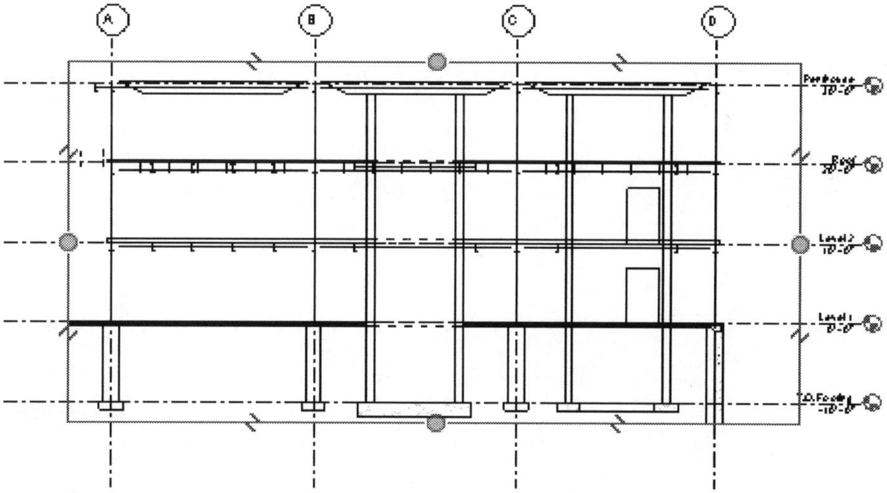

Figure 3–91

8. Return to the Level 1 view. The boundary of the section has changed as shown on the left in Figure 3–92. Use the circular control to move the section head down as shown on the right in Figure 3–92.

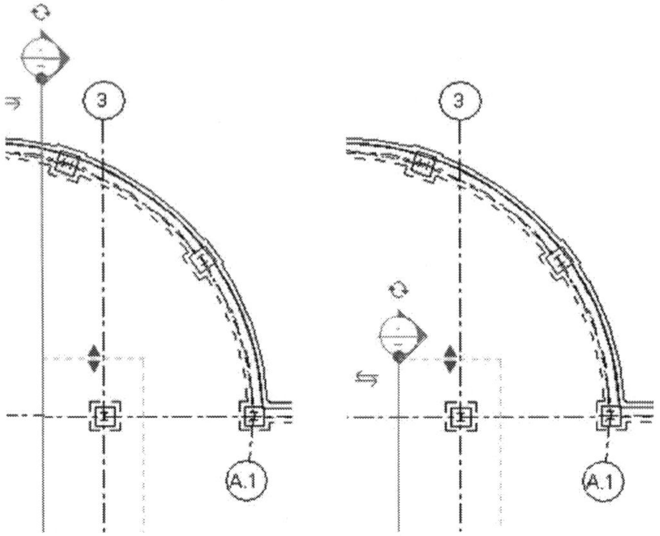

Boundary changed ***Section head moved***

Figure 3–92

9. Start the **Section** command again.

10. In the Type Selector, select **Section: Wall Section**.

11. Draw a short section through the wall as shown in Figure 3–93. Modify the section boundary so that it does not touch anything other than the wall.

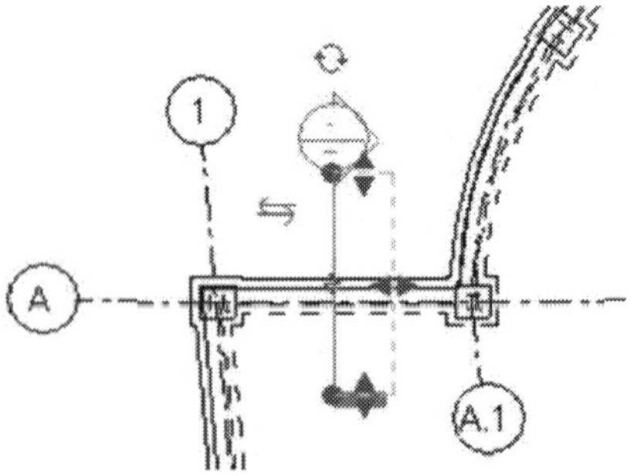

Figure 3–93

12. In the Project Browser, expand *Sections (Wall Section)* and rename the section as **Foundation Section**.

13. Open the new section view.

14. In the View Control Bar, change the *Scale* to **1/2"=1'-0"**.

15. By default, the section expands the entire height of the project. Use the controls to resize the section so that only the foundation displays as shown in Figure 3–94.

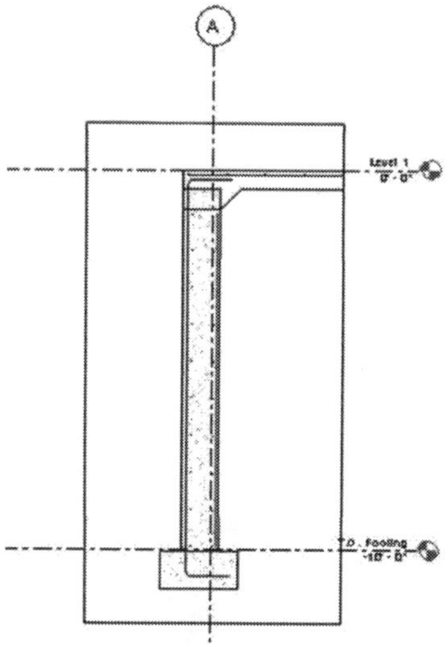

Figure 3–94

Task 2 - Add a framing elevation.

1. Open the **Structural Plans: Level 1** view.

2. Zoom in on the south wall of the building between columns 2 and 3.

3. In the *View* tab>Create panel, expand (Elevation) and click (Framing Elevation).

4. Hover the cursor over Grid D as shown in Figure 3–95. Pick a point when the elevation marker is on the outside of the building.

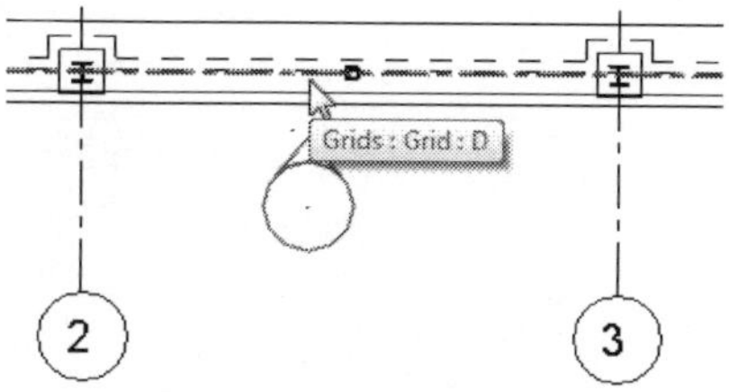

Figure 3–95

5. In the Project Browser, in the *Elevations (Framing Elevation)* area, rename the view as **Typical Bracing**.
6. Click on the pointer of the elevation marker. Expand the length of the elevation so that it is just on each side of the columns as shown in Figure 3–96.

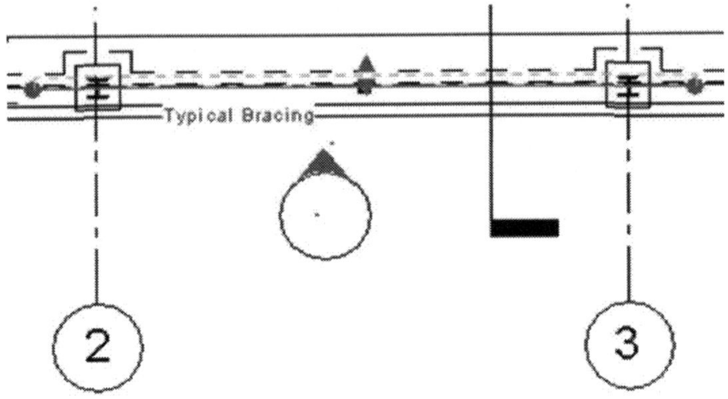

Figure 3–96

7. Open the framing elevation.
8. In the View Control Bar, change the *Detail Level* to  (Fine).
9. Modify the size of the elevation to only display the bracing as shown in Figure 3–97.

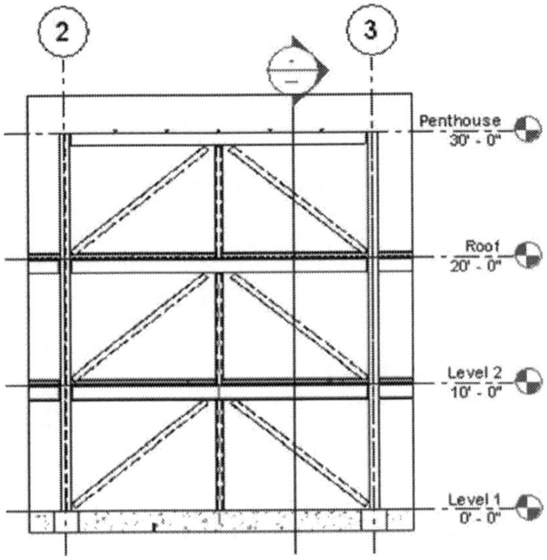

Figure 3–97

10. Return to the **Structural Plans: Level 1** view.

11. Zoom out to display the entire building.

12. In the Quick Access Toolbar, click (Close Hidden Windows).

13. Save the project.

3.5 Working with Schedules

Schedules extract information from a project and display it in table form. Each schedule is stored as a separate view and can be placed on sheets, as shown in Figure 3–98. Any changes you make to the project elements that affect the schedules are automatically updated in both views and sheets.

Schedules are typically included in project templates. Ask your BIM Manager for more information about your company's schedules.

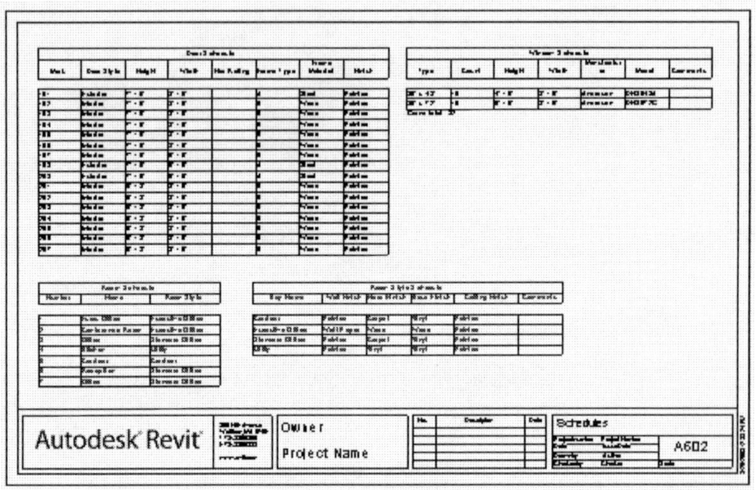

Figure 3–98

How To: Work with Schedules

1. In the Project Browser, expand the *Schedules/Quantities* area, as shown in Figure 3–99, and double-click on the schedule you want to open.

Figure 3–99

2. Schedules are automatically filled out with the information stored in the instance and type parameters of related elements that are added to the model.
3. Fill out additional information in either the schedule or Properties.
4. Drag and drop the schedule onto a sheet.

Modifying Schedules

If you change a Type Property in the schedule, it applies to all elements of that type. If you change an Instance Property, it only applies to that one element.

Information in schedules is bi-directional:

- If you make changes to elements, the schedule automatically updates.
- If you change information in the cells of the schedule, it automatically updates the elements in the project.

How To: Modify Schedule Cells

1. Open the schedule view.
2. Select the cell you want to change. Some cells have drop-down lists, as shown in Figure 3–100. Others have edit fields.

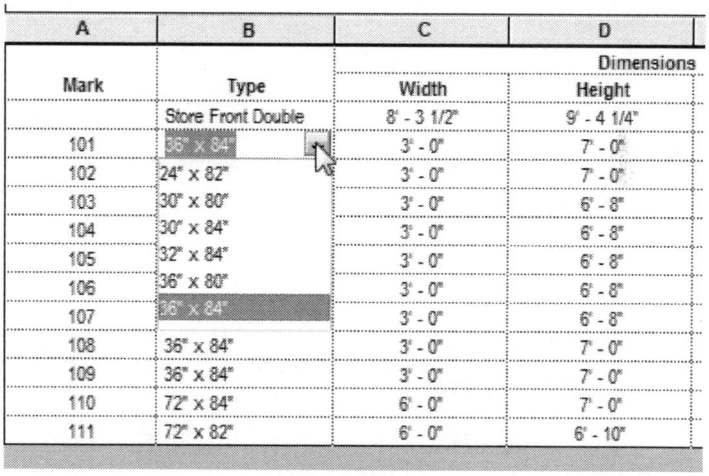

A	B	C	D
		Dimensions	
Mark	Type	Width	Height
	Store Front Double	8' - 3 1/2"	9' - 4 1/4"
101	36" x 84"	3' - 0"	7' - 0"
102	24" x 82"	3' - 0"	7' - 0"
103	30" x 80"	3' - 0"	6' - 8"
104	30" x 84"	3' - 0"	6' - 8"
105	32" x 84"	3' - 0"	6' - 8"
106	36" x 80"	3' - 0"	6' - 8"
107	36" x 84"	3' - 0"	6' - 8"
108	36" x 84"	3' - 0"	7' - 0"
109	36" x 84"	3' - 0"	7' - 0"
110	72" x 84"	6' - 0"	7' - 0"
111	72" x 82"	6' - 0"	6' - 10"

Figure 3–100

3. Add the new information. The change is reflected in the schedule, on the sheet, and in the elements of the project.

- If you change a Type Property, an alert box opens, as shown in Figure 3–101.

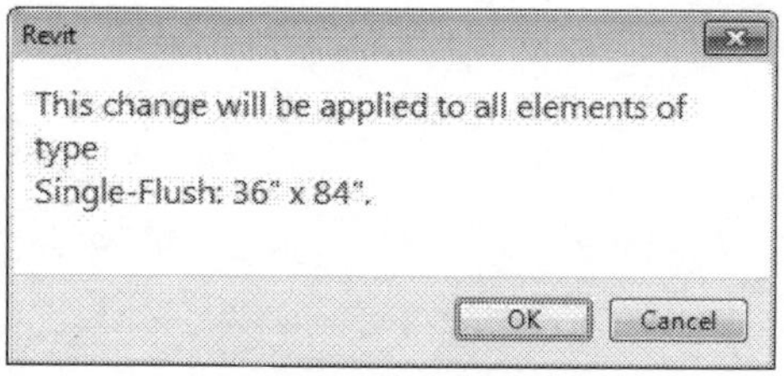

Figure 3–101

- When you select an element in a schedule, in the *Modify Schedule/Quantities* tab>Element panel, you can click  (Highlight in Model). This opens a close-up view of the element with the Show Element(s) in View dialog box, as shown in Figure 3–102. Click **Show** to display more views of the element. Click **Close** to finish the command.

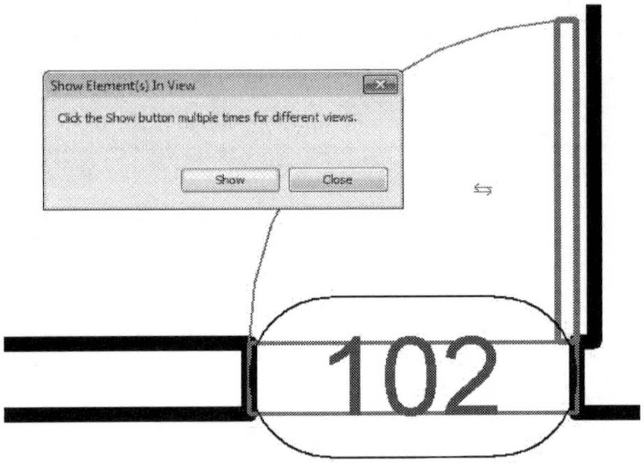

Figure 3–102

Modifying a Schedule on a Sheet

Once you have placed a schedule on a sheet, you can manipulate it to fit the information into the available space. Select the schedule to display the controls that enable you to modify it, as shown in Figure 3–103.

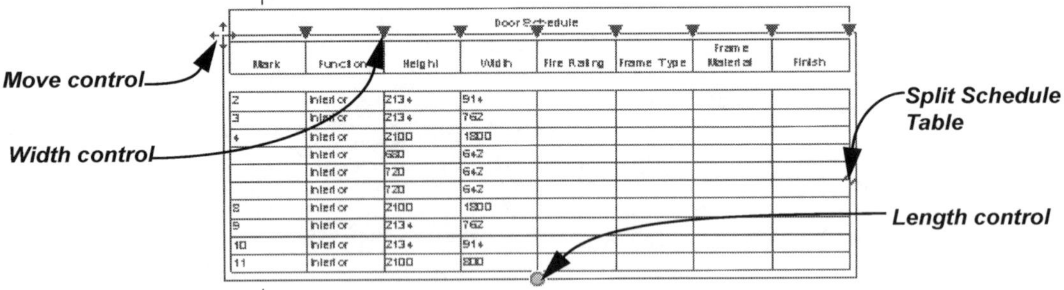

Figure 3–103

- The blue triangles modify the width of each column.
- The break mark splits the schedule into two parts.

- In a split schedule you can use the arrows in the upper left corner to move that portion of the schedule table. The control at the bottom of the first table changes the length of the table and impacts any connected splits, as shown in Figure 3–104.

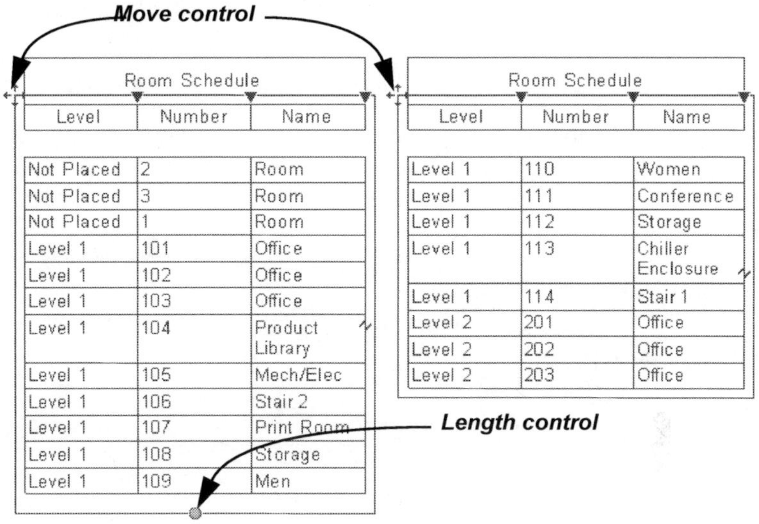

Figure 3–104

- To unsplit a schedule, drag the Move control from the side of the schedule that you want to unsplit back to the original column.

Practice 3j

Work with Schedules in an Architectural Project

Practice Objectives

- Update schedule information.
- Add a schedule to a sheet.

Estimated time for completion: 10 minutes

In this practice you will add information to a door schedule and to elements that are connected to the schedule. You will then place the schedule on a sheet, as shown in Figure 3–105.

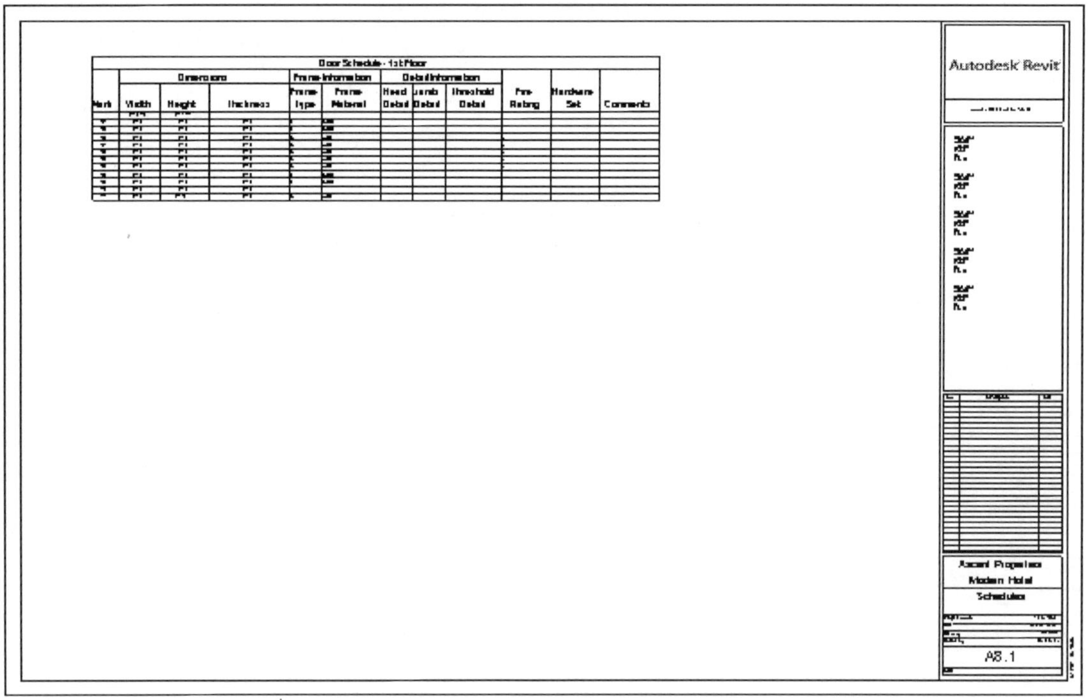

Figure 3–105

Task 1 - Fill in schedules.

1. Open the project **Modern-Hotel-Schedules.rvt**.
2. In the Project Browser, expand *Schedules/Quantities*. Four schedules have been added to this project.

3. Double-click on **Door Schedule - 1st Floor** to open it. The existing doors in the project are already populated with some of the basic information included with the door, as shown in Figure 3–106.

<Door Schedule - 1st Floor>

A	B	C	D	E	F	G	H	I	J
	Dimensions			Frame Information		Detail Information			
Mark	Width	Height	Thickness	Frame Type	Frame Material	Head Detail	Jamb Detail	Threshold Detail	Fire Rating
101	3' - 0"	7' - 0"	0' - 2"						A
102	3' - 0"	7' - 0"	0' - 2"						A
103	3' - 0"	6' - 8"	0' - 2"						B
104	3' - 0"	6' - 8"	0' - 2"						B
105	3' - 0"	6' - 8"	0' - 2"						B
106	3' - 0"	6' - 8"	0' - 2"						B
107	3' - 0"	6' - 8"	0' - 2"						B
108	3' - 0"	7' - 0"	0' - 2"						A
109	3' - 0"	7' - 0"	0' - 2"						A
110	6' - 0"	7' - 0"	0' - 2"						D
111	6' - 0"	6' - 6"	0' - 2"						

Figure 3–106

4. Select Mark **101**.

5. In the *Modify Schedules/Quantities* tab>Element panel, click (Highlight in Model).

6. In the Show Element(s) In View dialog box click **Show** until you see a plan view of the door, as shown in Figure 3–107. Then, click **Close**.

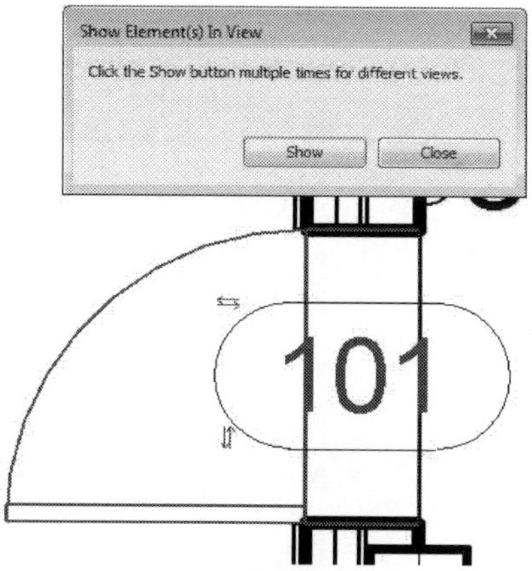

Figure 3–107

7. The door is still selected. In Properties, set the following:
   - *Frame Type:* **A**
   - *Frame Material:* **Steel**
   - *Finish:* **Coated**

8. Click (Edit Type).
9. In the Type Properties dialog box, in the *Identity Data* area, set the *Fire Rating* to **A**.
10. Click **OK** to finish.
11. Return to the Door Schedule. (Press <Ctrl>+<Tab> to switch between open windows.)
12. Note that the *Frame Type* and *Frame Material* display for one door and the matching exterior doors also have a fire rating.
13. Use the drop-down list and change the options for the matching doors, as shown in Figure 3–108.

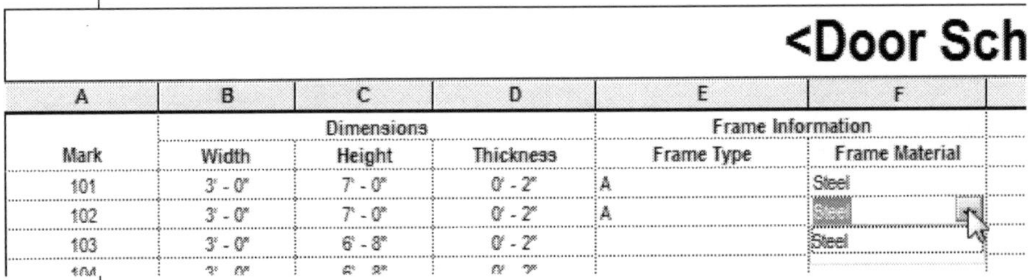

<Door Sch

A	B	C	D	E	F
	Dimensions			Frame Information	
Mark	Width	Height	Thickness	Frame Type	Frame Material
101	3' - 0"	7' - 0"	0' - 2"	A	Steel
102	3' - 0"	7' - 0"	0' - 2"	A	Steel
103	3' - 0"	6' - 8"	0' - 2"		Steel

Figure 3–108

14. In the Door Schedule view, specify the *Fire Rating* for some other doors in the schedule. When you change the fire rating, you are prompted to change all elements of that type. Click **OK**.
15. Open the **Floor Plans: Floor 1** view and zoom out if required.
16. Select the door to the office, then right-click and select **Select All Instances>In Entire Project**.
17. Look at the Status Bar beside (Filter) and note that more doors have been selected than are in the current view.
18. In Properties, set the *Frame Type* and *Frame Material* for these doors.

No visual changes to the door display because these are just text properties.

19. Press <Esc> to clear the selection when you are finished.
20. Switch back to the schedule view to see the additions. Not all of the doors are showing because the schedule has been limited to the 1st floor doors.
21. Save the project.

Task 2 - Add schedules to a sheet.

Note that your schedule might look different than the one shown in the image.

1. In the Project Browser, open the sheet **A8.1 - Schedules**.
2. Drag and drop the **Door Schedule - 1st Floor** view onto the sheet, as shown in Figure 3–109.

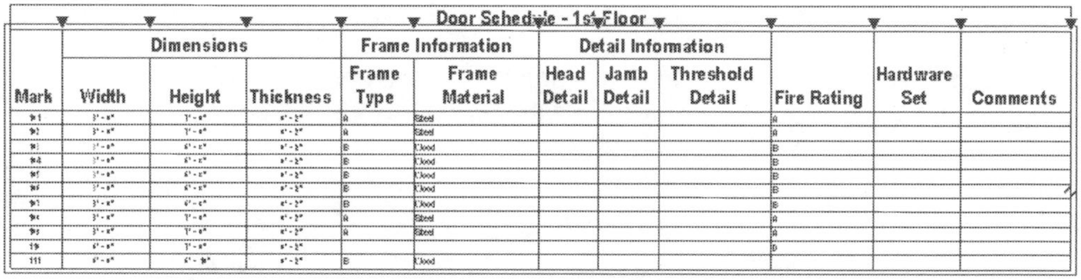

Figure 3–109

3. Zoom in and use the arrows at the top to modify the width of the columns so that the titles display correctly.
4. Click in empty space on the sheet to finish placing the schedule.
5. Switch back to the **Floor Plans: Floor 1** view and select the double-swing door at the kitchen.
6. In the Type Selector, change the size to **72" x 82"**. In Properties, add a Frame Type, Frame Material, and Finish.
7. Return to the Door Schedule sheet. The information is automatically populated, as shown in Figure 3–110.

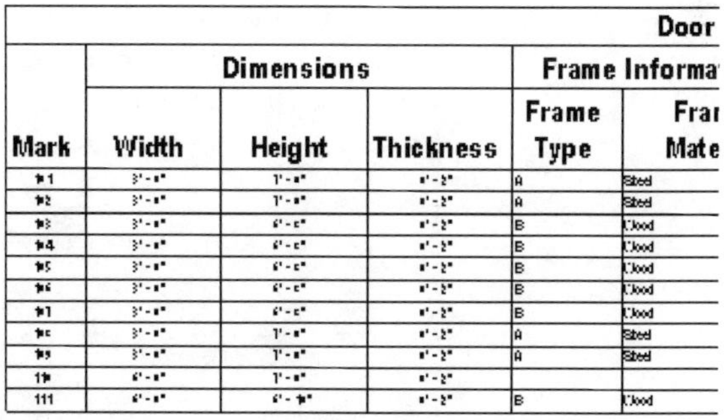

Figure 3–110

8. Return to the 3D view.
9. In the Quick Access Toolbar, click  (Close Hidden Windows.
10. Save the project.

Practice 3k

Work with Schedules in a MEP Project

Estimated time for completion: 10 minutes

Practice Objectives

- Update schedule information.
- Add a schedule to a sheet.

In this practice you will update a schedule and place it on a sheet., as shown in Figure 3–111.

MECHANICAL EQUIPMENT SCHEDULE					
Type Mark	Mark	Space: Name	Manufacturer	Model	Comments
AHU-1	1	CORRIDOR	ME Unlimited	AHU-24-M	
AHU-1	2	CORRIDOR	ME Unlimited	AHU-24-M	
AHU-1	3	CORRIDOR	ME Unlimited	AHU-24-M	
AHU-1	4	CORRIDOR	ME Unlimited	AHU-24-M	
AHU-1	5	CORRIDOR	ME Unlimited	AHU-24-M	
AHU-1	6	CORRIDOR	ME Unlimited	AHU-24-M	
AHU-1	7	CORRIDOR	ME Unlimited	AHU-24-M	
AHU-1	8	CORRIDOR	ME Unlimited	AHU-24-M	
AHU-3	9	CORRIDOR	ME Unlimited	AHU-36-L	
AHU-1	10	CORRIDOR	ME Unlimited	AHU-24-M	
AHU-1	11	CORRIDOR	ME Unlimited	AHU-24-M	
AHU-1	12	CORRIDOR	ME Unlimited	AHU-24-M	
AHU-2	13	CORRIDOR	ME Unlimited	AHU-12-S	
HW-1	14	STORAGE	ME Unlimited	HWH-10-M	
HW-1	15	STORAGE	ME Unlimited	HWH-10-M	
HW-1	16	JNTR.	ME Unlimited	HWH-10-M	
HW-1	17	JNTR.	ME Unlimited	HWH-10-M	

Figure 3–111

Task 1 - Fill in schedules.

1. Open the project **MEP-Elementary-School-Schedules.rvt**.
2. In the Project Browser, expand *Schedules/Quantities* and open **MECHANICAL EQUIPMENT SCHEDULE**. The schedule is already populated with some information, as shown in Figure 3–112.

<MECHANICAL EQUIPMENT SCHEDULE>					
A	B	C	D	E	F
Type Mark	Mark	Space: Name	Manufacturer	Model	Comments
AHU-1	1	CORRIDOR			
AHU-1	2	CORRIDOR			
AHU-1	3	CORRIDOR			
AHU-1	4	CORRIDOR			
AHU-1	5	CORRIDOR			
AHU-1	6	CORRIDOR			
AHU-1	7	CORRIDOR			

Figure 3–112

3. Several Type Marks are empty. Click in one of the empty *Type Mark* cells. In the *Modify Schedules/Quantities* tab> Element panel, click (Highlight in Model).
4. If an alert box displays about no open views, click **OK** to search and open a view.
5. In the view that comes up, click **Close** in the Show Element(s) in View dialog box.
6. Zoom out so that you can see the elements (i.e., a hot water heater) in context.
7. In Properties, click (Edit Type).
8. In the Type Properties dialog box, in the *Identity Data* area, set the *Type Mark* to **HW-1**.
9. Click **OK** to finish.
10. Return to the Mechanical Equipment Schedule (press <Ctrl>+<Tab> to switch between open windows).
11. All of the hot water heaters in the project now have a *Type Mark* set, as shown in Figure 3–113.

<MECHANICAL EQUIPMENT SCHEDULE>					
A	B	C	D	E	F
Type Mark	Mark	Space: Name	Manufacturer	Model	Comments
AHU-1	1	CORRIDOR			
AHU-1	2	CORRIDOR			
AHU-1	3	CORRIDOR			
AHU-1	4	CORRIDOR			
AHU-1	5	CORRIDOR			
AHU-1	6	CORRIDOR			
AHU-1	7	CORRIDOR			
AHU-1	8	CORRIDOR			
AHU-1	9	CORRIDOR			
AHU-1	10	CORRIDOR			
AHU-1	11	CORRIDOR			
AHU-1	12	CORRIDOR			
HW-1	49	STORAGE			
HW-1	50	STORAGE			
HW-1	51	JNTR.			
HW-1	52	JNTR.			
AHU-1	53	CORRIDOR			

Figure 3–113

12. In the *Mark* column you can see that the numbers are out of sequence. The numbering of hot water heaters and one air handling unit (AHU-1) is incorrect, starting at 49.

13. Change the *Mark* of the incorrectly numbered AHU-1 to **13**.

14. Modify the *Mark* of the hot water heaters to match the sequence.

15. In the schedule view, change the name of the Manufacturer of one of the AHUs. An alert displays warning that changing this changes all of the elements of this type, as shown in Figure 3–114. Click **OK**.

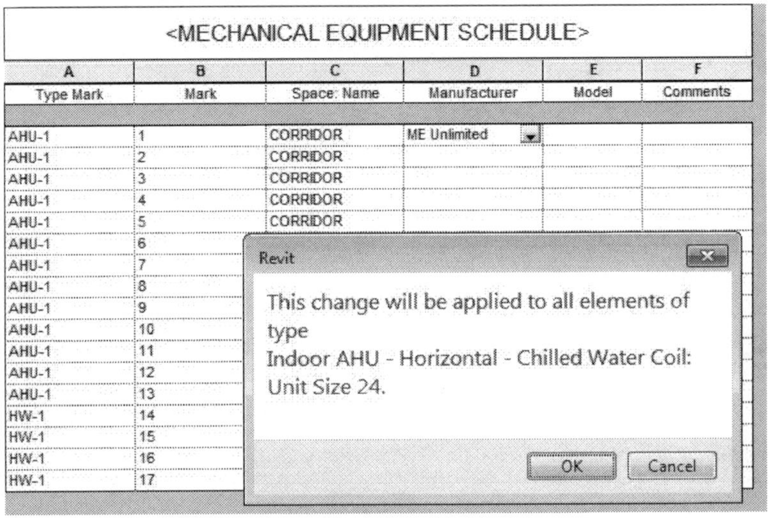

Figure 3–114

16. Open the Mechanical>HVAC>Floor Plans>**01 Mechanical** view and zoom in on the office area.

17. Select the AHU that is connected to the Office duct system. In the Type Selector, change it to **Indoor AHU - Horizontal - Chilled Water Coil: Unit Size 12**.

18. While it is still selected, edit the type and set the *Type Mark* to **AHU-2**.

19. Switch back to the schedule view to see the change.

20. In the *Manufacturer* column, use the drop-down list to select the same *Manufacturer* for the modified AHU, as shown in Figure 3–115.

<MECHANICAL EQUIPMENT SCHEDULE>					
A	B	C	D	E	F
Type Mark	Mark	Space: Name	Manufacturer	Model	Comments
AHU-1	1	CORRIDOR	ME Unlimited		
AHU-1	2	CORRIDOR	ME Unlimited		
AHU-1	3	CORRIDOR	ME Unlimited		
AHU-1	4	CORRIDOR	ME Unlimited		
AHU-1	5	CORRIDOR	ME Unlimited		
AHU-1	6	CORRIDOR	ME Unlimited		
AHU-1	7	CORRIDOR	ME Unlimited		
AHU-1	8	CORRIDOR	ME Unlimited		
AHU-1	9	CORRIDOR	ME Unlimited		
AHU-1	10	CORRIDOR	ME Unlimited		
AHU-1	11	CORRIDOR	ME Unlimited		
AHU-1	12	CORRIDOR	ME Unlimited		
AHU-2	13	CORRIDOR			
HW-1	14	STORAGE	ME Unlimited		
HW-1	15	STORAGE			
HW-1	16	JNTR.			
HW-1	17	JNTR.			

Figure 3–115

21. Fill in the other information.

22. Save the project.

Task 2 - Add schedules to a sheet.

1. In the Project Browser, right-click on Sheets (all) and select **New Sheet**. Select the E-sized title block and click **OK**.

2. In the Project Browser, right-click on the new sheet (which is bold) and select Rename. In the Sheet Title dialog box, set the *Number* to **M-801** and the *Name* to **Schedules** and click **OK**.

3. Drag and drop the **MECHANICALEQUIPMENT SCHEDULE** view onto the sheet, as shown in Figure 3–116.

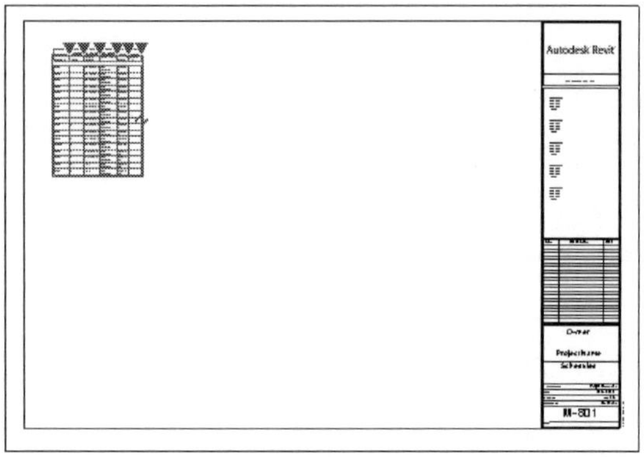

Figure 3–116

4. Zoom in and use the arrows at the top to modify the width of the columns so that the titles display correctly.

5. Click in empty space on the sheet to finish placing the schedule.

6. Switch back to the Mechanical>HVAC>Floor Plans> **01 Mechanical** view and select one of the Classroom AHUs.

7. In the Type Selector, change the size to **Unit Size 36**. In Type Properties add the *Model*, *Manufacturer*, and *Type Mark*.

8. Return to the Schedule sheet. The information is automatically populated.

9. Save the project.

Practice 3I

Work with Schedules in a Structural Project

Estimated time for completion: 10 minutes

Practice Objectives

- Update schedule information.
- Add a schedule to a sheet.

In this practice you will add Type Mark information to a structural elements schedule and the elements that are connected to that schedule. You will then place the schedule on a sheet and add elements in the project. The final information displays as shown in Figure 3–117.

Structural Elements Schedule		
Type Mark	Family and Type	Count
Structural Columns		
P-1	Concrete-Rectangular-Column: 24 x 24	43
	W-Wide Flange-Column: W8X10	2
	W-Wide Flange-Column: W10X33	41
Structural Foundations		
	Footing-Rectangular: 14'x14'x2'-0"	2
	Footing-Rectangular: 36" x 36" x 12"	43
	Foundation Slab: 6" Foundation Slab	1
W-1	Wall Foundation: Bearing Footing - 24" x 12"	17
W-2	Wall Foundation: Bearing Footing - 36" x 12"	4
Structural Framing		
	HSS-Hollow Structural Section: HSS6X6X.500	28
	K-Series Bar Joist-Rod Web: 14K6	16
	K-Series Bar Joist-Rod Web: 16K7	100
	W-Wide Flange: W12X26	1558
	W-Wide Flange: W14X30	1023

Figure 3–117

Task 1 - Fill in schedules.

1. Open the project **Syracuse-Suites-Schedules.rvt.**
2. Open the 3D Views: **3D Foundation** view. This view only displays the foundation elements, including concrete piers, footings, walls, and wall footings.
3. In the Project Browser, expand *Schedules/Quantities*. Note that four schedules have been added to this project.

4. Double-click on **Structural Elements Schedule** to open it. The existing structural elements in the project populate the schedule, as shown in Figure 3–118.

A	B	C
<Structural Elements Schedule>		
Type Mark	Family and Type	Count
Structural Columns		
P-1	Concrete-Rectangular-Column: 24 x 24	42
	W-Wide Flange-Column: W8X10	2
	W-Wide Flange-Column: W10X33	41
Structural Foundations		
	Footing-Rectangular: 14'x14'x2'-0"	2
	Footing-Rectangular: 36" x 36" x 12"	42
	Foundation Slab: 6" Foundation Slab	1
	Wall Foundation: Bearing Footing - 24" x 12"	17
	Wall Foundation: Bearing Footing - 36" x 12"	4
Structural Framing		
	HSS-Hollow Structural Section: HSS6X6X.500	28
	K-Series Bar Joist-Rod Web: 14K6	16
	K-Series Bar Joist-Rod Web: 16K7	100
	W-Wide Flange: W12X26	1558
	W-Wide Flange: W14X30	1023

Figure 3–118

5. Note that only the *Concrete* columns have a **Type Mark**.

6. In the *Type Mark* column beside **Wall Foundation: Bearing Footing - 24" x 12"**, type **W-1.**

7. The warning dialog box shown in Figure 3–119 displays because the element is a type parameter; therefore, you are alerted before you make any changes. Click **OK**.

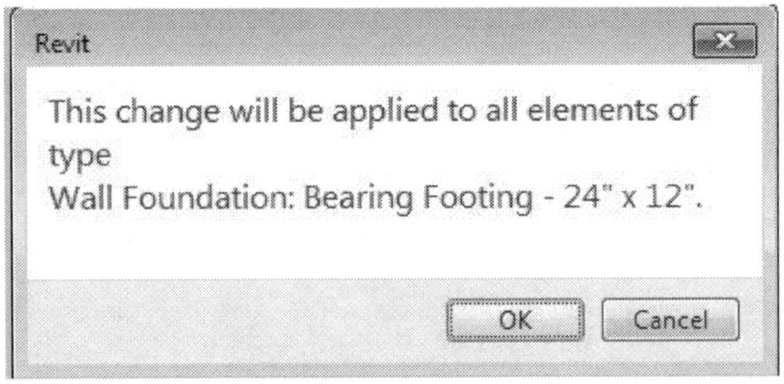

Figure 3–119

8. Select **Wall Foundation: Bearing Footing - 36" x 12"**. In the *Modify | Schedule/Quantities* tab>Element panel, click (Highlight in Model).

9. In the Show Element(s) in View dialog box, click **Show** until you see a foundation element displayed in the **3D Foundations** view, as shown in Figure 3–120. Click **Close**.

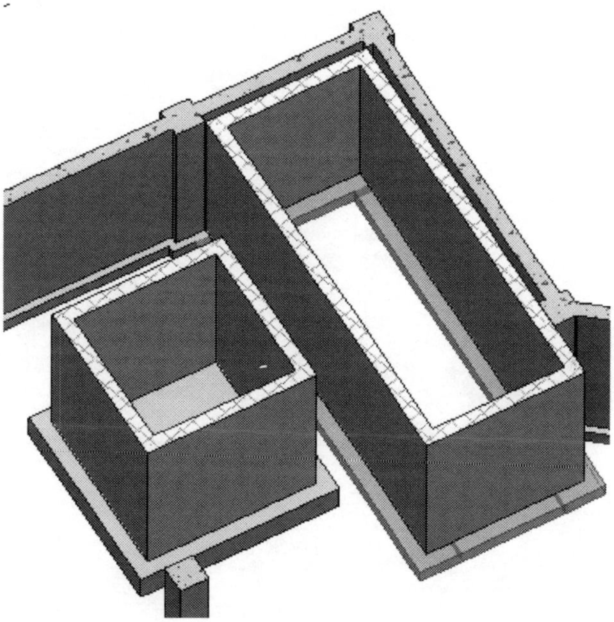

Figure 3–120

10. With the elements highlighted, in Properties, click (Edit Type).

11. In the Type Properties dialog box, in the *Identity Data* area, set the *Type Mark* to **W-2**.

12. Click **OK** to finish.

Remember that you can press <Ctrl>+<Tab> to switch between open windows, as required.

13. Return to the **Structural Elements Schedule** view, as shown in Figure 3–121. The **Type Mark** is now applied.

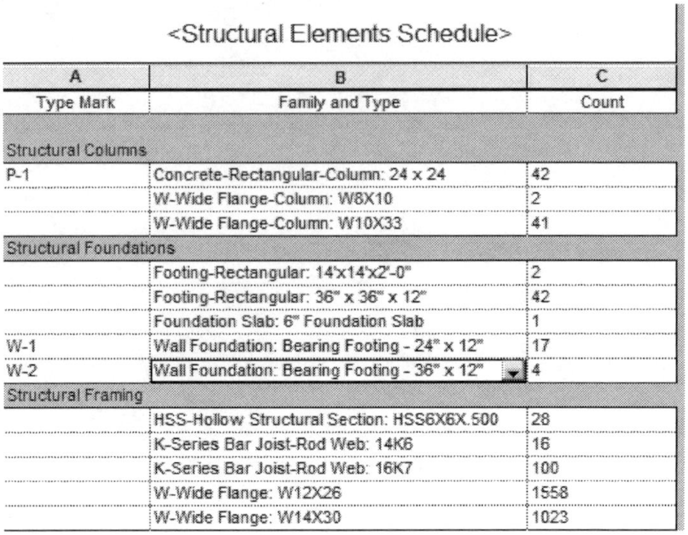

<Structural Elements Schedule>

A	B	C
Type Mark	Family and Type	Count
Structural Columns		
P-1	Concrete-Rectangular-Column: 24 x 24	42
	W-Wide Flange-Column: W8X10	2
	W-Wide Flange-Column: W10X33	41
Structural Foundations		
	Footing-Rectangular: 14'x14'x2'-0"	2
	Footing-Rectangular: 36" x 36" x 12"	42
	Foundation Slab: 6" Foundation Slab	1
W-1	Wall Foundation: Bearing Footing - 24" x 12"	17
W-2	Wall Foundation: Bearing Footing - 36" x 12"	4
Structural Framing		
	HSS-Hollow Structural Section: HSS6X6X.500	28
	K-Series Bar Joist-Rod Web: 14K6	16
	K-Series Bar Joist-Rod Web: 16K7	100
	W-Wide Flange: W12X26	1558
	W-Wide Flange: W14X30	1023

Figure 3–121

14. Open the other schedules and review the information.

15. Save the project.

Task 2 - Add schedules to a sheet.

1. In the Project Browser, open the sheet **S8.1 - Schedules**.

2. Drag and drop the **Structural Elements Schedule** view onto the sheet, as shown in Figure 3–122.

Your schedule may look different then the one shown in Figure 3–109.

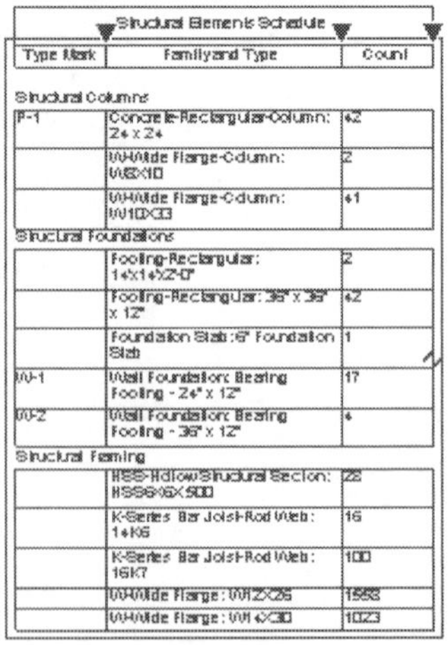

Figure 3–122

3. Zoom in and use the arrows at the top of the schedule to modify the width of the columns to ensure that the titles display correctly.

4. In the schedule, note the number of Concrete Columns and their related footings.

5. Open the **00 T.O. Footing** view.

6. Zoom in and copy a concrete column and its footing to a nearby grid location that does not have an existing column, similar to that shown in Figure 3–123.

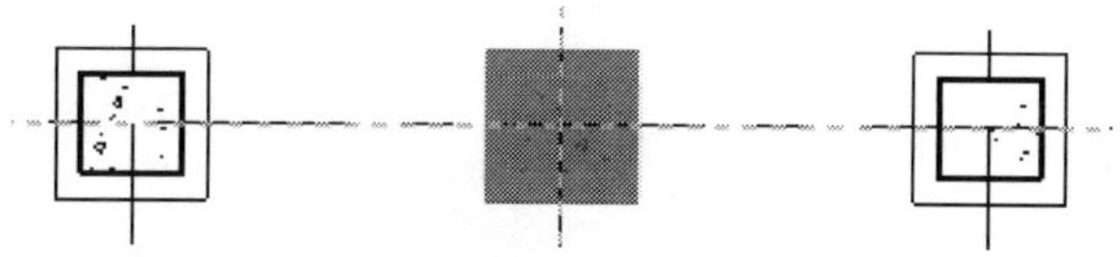

Figure 3–123

7. Switch back to the sheet view. Note that the numbers in the schedule have automatically updated to include the new column.

8. Switch to the **Structural Elements Schedule** view. Note that these column numbers have also been updated.

9. Save the project.

Chapter Review Questions

1. Which of the following commands shown in Figure 3–124, creates a view that results in an independent view displaying the same model geometry and containing a copy of the annotation?

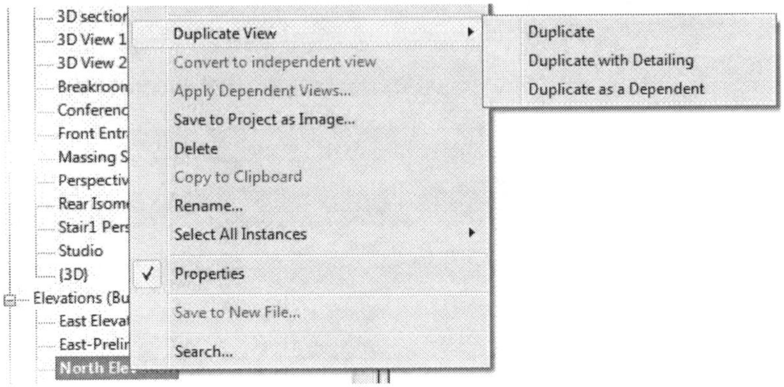

Figure 3–124

   a. Duplicate
   b. Duplicate with Detailing
   c. Duplicate as a Dependent

2. Which of the following is true about the Visibility Graphic Overrides dialog box?
   a. Changes made in the dialog box only affect the current view.
   b. It can only be used to toggle categories on and off.
   c. It can be used to toggle individual elements on and off.
   d. It can be used to change the color of individual elements.

3. The purpose of callouts is to create a...
   a. Boundary around part of the model that needs revising, similar to a revision cloud.
   b. View of part of the model for export to the AutoCAD® software for further detailing.
   c. View of part of the model that is linked to the main view from which it is taken.
   d. 2D view of part of the model.

4. You placed dimensions in a view and some of them display and others do not (as shown on the left in Figure 3–125) but you were expecting the view to display as shown on the right in Figure 3–125. To display the missing dimensions you need to modify the...

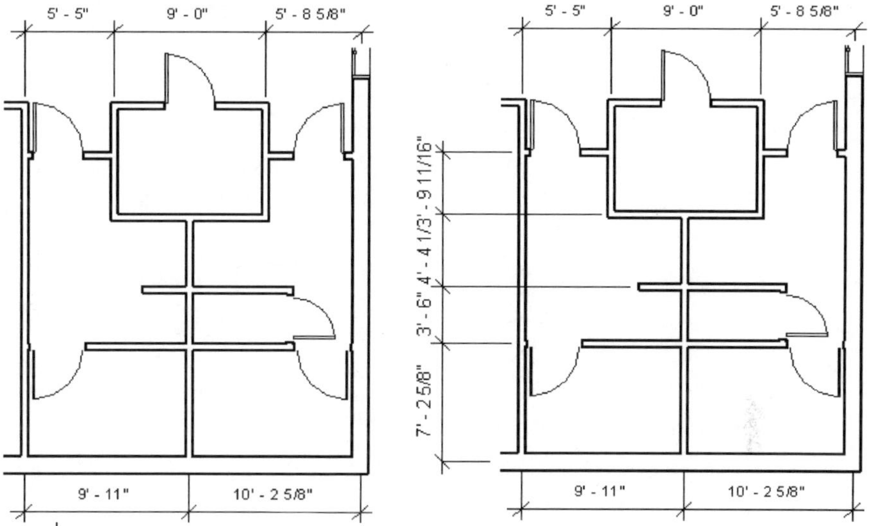

Figure 3–125

a. Dimension Settings
b. Dimension Type
c. Visibility Graphic Overrides
d. Annotation Crop Region

5. How do you create multiple interior elevations in one room?
   a. Using the **Interior Elevation** command, place the elevation marker.
   b. Using the **Elevation** command, place the first marker, select it and select the appropriate Show Arrow boxes.
   c. Using the **Interior Elevation** command, place an elevation marker for each wall of the room you want to display.
   d. Using the **Elevation** command, select a Multiple Elevation marker type, and place the elevation marker.

6. How do you create a jog in a building section, such as that shown in Figure 3–126?

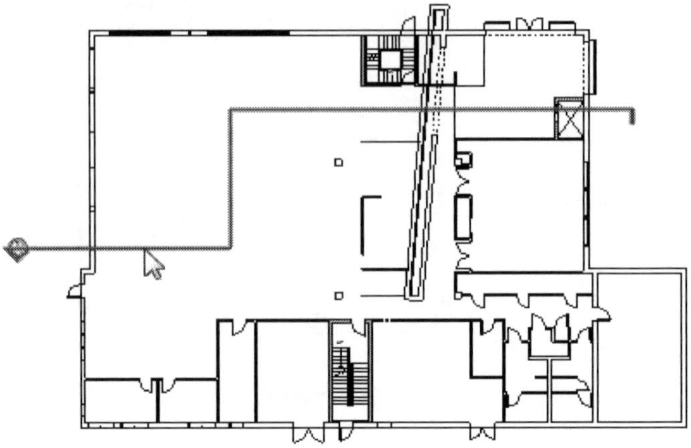

Figure 3–126

   a. Use the **Split Element** tool in the *Modify* tab>Modify panel.

   b. Select the building section and then click **Split Segment** in the contextual tab.

   c. Select the building section and click the blue control in the middle of the section line.

   d. Draw two separate sections, and use the **Section Jog** tool to combine them into a jogged section.

7. What happens when you delete a door in an Autodesk Revit model, as shown in Figure 3–127?

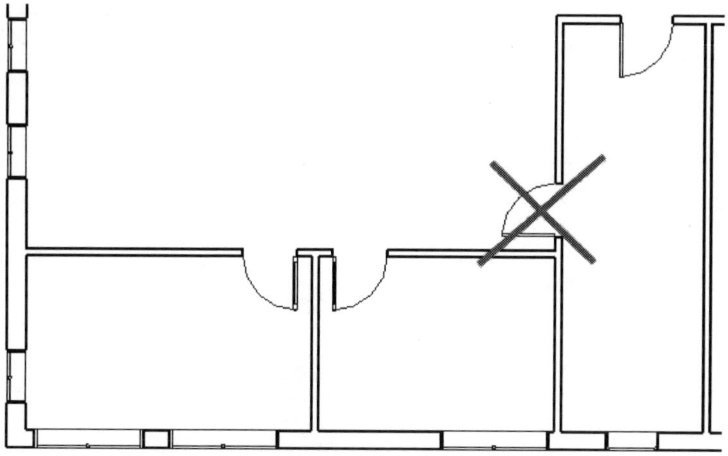

Figure 3–127

   a. You must delete the door on the sheet.
   b. You must delete the door from the schedule.
   c. The door is removed from the model, but not from the schedule.
   d. The door is removed from the model and the schedule.

8. In a schedule, if you change type information (such as a Type Mark) all instances of that type update with the new information.
   a. True
   b. False

Command Summary

Button	Command	Location
Views		
	**Elevation**	• **Ribbon:** *View* tab>Create panel> expand Elevation
	**Callout: Rectangle**	• **Ribbon:** *View* tab>Create panel> expand Callout
	**Callout: Sketch**	• **Ribbon:** *View* tab>Create panel> expand Callout
	**Duplicate**	• **Ribbon:** *View* tab>Create panel> expand Duplicate View • **Right-click:** (*on a view in the Project Browser*) expand Duplicate View
	**Duplicate as Dependent**	• **Ribbon:** *View* tab>Create panel> expand Duplicate View • **Right-click:** (*on a view in the Project Browser*) expand Duplicate View
	**Duplicate with Detailing**	• **Ribbon:** *View* tab>Create panel> expand Duplicate View • **Right-click:** (*on a view in the Project Browser*) Duplicate View
	**Section**	• **Ribbon:** *View* tab>Create panel • **Quick Access Toolbar**
	**Split Segment**	• **Ribbon:** (*when the elevation or section marker is selected*) *Modify | Views* tab> Section panel
Crop Views		
	**Crop View**	• **View Control Bar** • **View Properties:** Crop View (*check*)
	**Do Not Crop View**	• **View Control Bar** • **View Properties:** Crop View (*clear*)
	**Edit Crop**	• **Ribbon:** (*when the crop region of a callout, elevation, or section view is selected*) *Modify | Views* tab>Mode panel
	**Hide Crop Region**	• **View Control Bar** • **View Properties:** Crop Region Visible (*clear*)
	**Reset Crop**	• **Ribbon:** *(when the crop region of a callout, elevation or section view is selected) Modify | Views* tab>Mode panel
	**Show Crop Region**	• **View Control Bar** • **View Properties:** Crop Region Visible (*check*)

	**Size Crop**	• **Ribbon:** (*when the crop region of a callout, elevation or section view is selected*) *Modify* | *Views* tab>Mode panel
View Display		
	**Hide in View**	• **Ribbon:** *Modify* tab>View Graphics panel>Hide>Elements *or* By Category • **Right-click:** *(when an element is selected)* Hide in View>Elements *or* Category
	**Override Graphics in View**	• **Ribbon:** *Modify* tab>View Graphics panel>Hide>Elements *or* By Category • **Right-click:** *(when an element is selected)* Override Graphics in View>By Element *or* By Category • **Shortcut:** *(category only)* VV or VG
	**Reveal Hidden Elements**	• **View Control Bar**
	**Temporary Hide/Isolate**	• **View Control Bar**
	**Temporary View Properties**	• **View Control Bar**

Printing and Sharing

The accurate creation of construction documents in the Autodesk® Revit® software ensures that the design is correctly communicated to downstream users. Construction documents are created primarily in special views call sheets. Knowing how to select titleblocks, assign titleblock information, place views, and print the sheets are essential steps in the construction documentation process. You can also export Autodesk Revit projects so they can be used in vector-based programs for collaboration with clients or team members using other CAD programs.

Learning Objectives in this Chapter

- Add Sheets with titleblocks and views of a project.
- Enter the titleblock information for individual sheets and for an entire project.
- Place and organize views on sheets.
- Print sheets using the default Print dialog box.
- Export Autodesk Revit projects to other file formats, including CAD formats and DWF files.

4.1 Setting Up Sheets

While you are modeling a project, the foundations of the working drawings are already in progress. Any view (such as a floor plan, section, callout, or schedule) can be placed on a sheet, as shown in Figure 4–1.

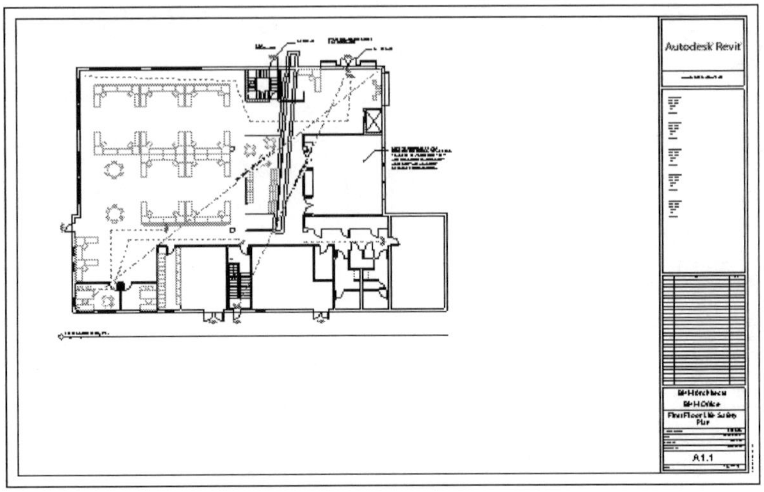

Figure 4–1

- Company templates can be created with standard sheets using the company (or project) titleblock and related views already placed on the sheet.
- The sheet size is based on the selected title block family.
- Sheets are listed in the *Sheets* area in the Project Browser.
- Most information on sheets is included in the views. You can add general notes and other non-model elements directly to the sheet.

How To: Set Up Sheets

1. In the Project Browser, right-click on the *Sheets* area header and select **New Sheet...** or in the *View* tab>Sheet Composition panel, click  (Sheet).

2. In the New Sheet dialog box, select a titleblock from the list as shown in Figure 4–2. Alternatively, if there is a list of placeholder sheets, select one or more from the list.

*Click **Load...** to load a sheet from the Library.*

Hold <Ctrl> to select multiple placeholder sheets.

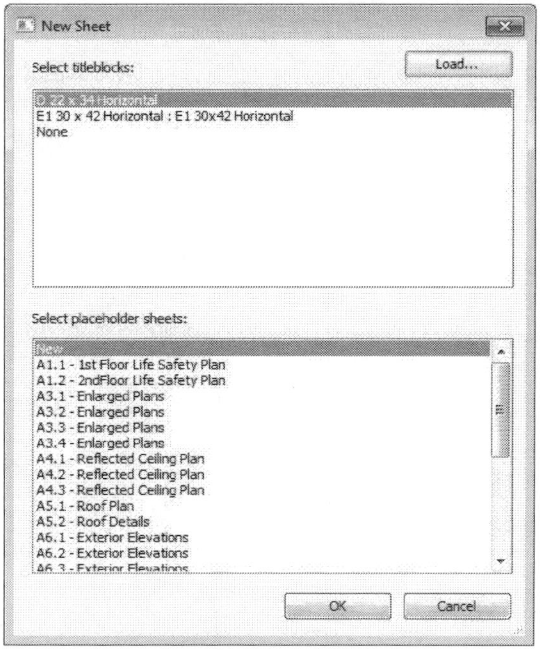

Figure 4–2

3. Click **OK**. A new sheet is created using the preferred title block.
4. Fill out the information in the title block as required.
5. Add views to the sheet.

- When you create sheets, the next sheet is incremented numerically.
- When you change the *Sheet Name* and/or *Number* in the title block, it automatically changes the name and number of the sheet in the Project Browser.
- The plot stamp on the side of the sheet automatically updates according to the current date and time. The format of the display uses the regional settings of your computer.
- The Scale is automatically entered when a view is inserted onto a sheet. If a sheet has multiple views with different scales, the scale displays **As Indicated.**

Sheet (Title Block) Properties

Each new sheet includes a title block. You can change the title block information in Properties, as shown in Figure 4–3 or by selecting any blue label you want to edit (Sheet Name, Sheet Number, Drawn by, etc.), as shown in Figure 4–4.

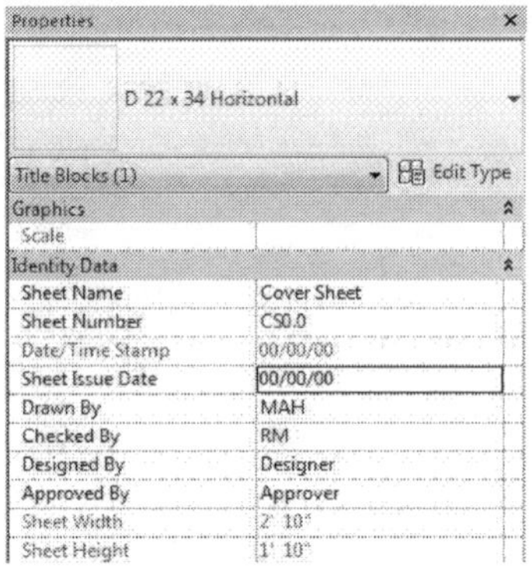

Figure 4–3

Figure 4–4

Properties that apply to all sheets can be entered in the Project Properties dialog box (as shown in Figure 4–5). In the *Manage* tab>Settings panel, click  (Project Information).

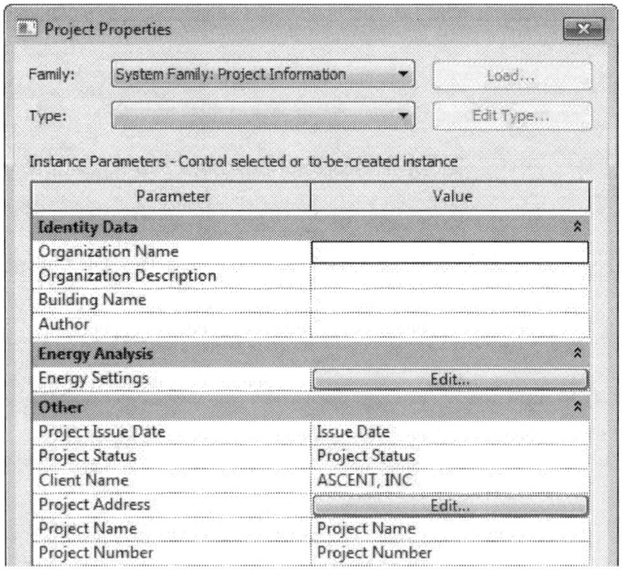

Figure 4–5

4.2 Placing and Modifying Views on Sheets

The process of adding views to a sheet is simple. Drag and drop a view from the Project Browser onto the sheet. The new view on the sheet is displayed at the scale specified in the original view. The view title displays the name, number, and scale of the view, as shown in Figure 4–6.

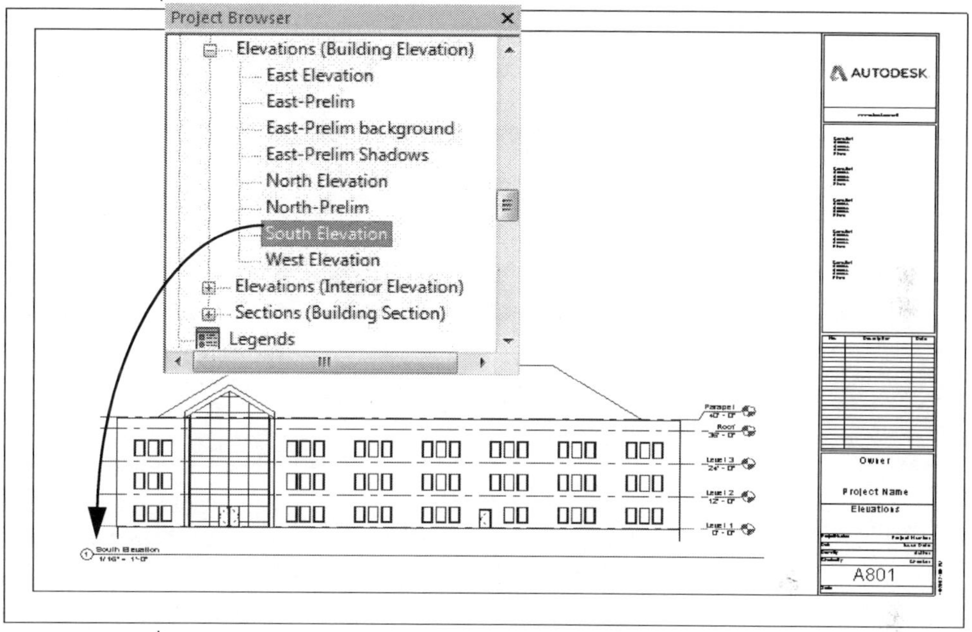

Figure 4–6

How To: Place Views on Sheets

Alignment lines from existing views display to help you place additional views.

1. Set up the view as you want it to display on the sheet, including the scale and visibility of elements.
2. Create or open the sheet where you want to place the view.
3. Select the view in the Project Browser, and drag and drop it onto the sheet.
4. The center of the view is attached to the cursor. Click to place it on the sheet.

Placing Views on Sheets

- Views can only be placed on a sheet once. However, you can duplicate the view and place that copy on a sheet.
- Views on a sheet are associative. They automatically update to reflect changes to the project.
- Each view on a sheet is listed under the sheet name in the Project Browser, as shown in Figure 4–7.

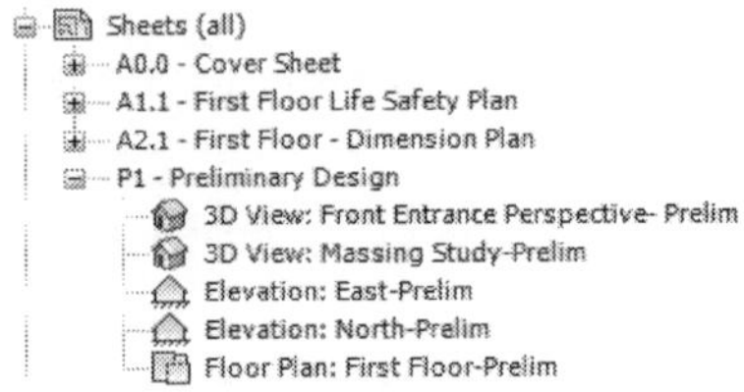

Figure 4–7

- You can also use two other methods to place views on sheets:
  - In the Project Browser, right-click on the sheet name and select **Add View...**
  - In the *View* tab>Sheet Composition panel click (Place View).

  Then, in the Views dialog box (shown in Figure 4–8), select the view you want to use and click **Add View to Sheet.**

This method lists only those views which have not yet been placed on a sheet.

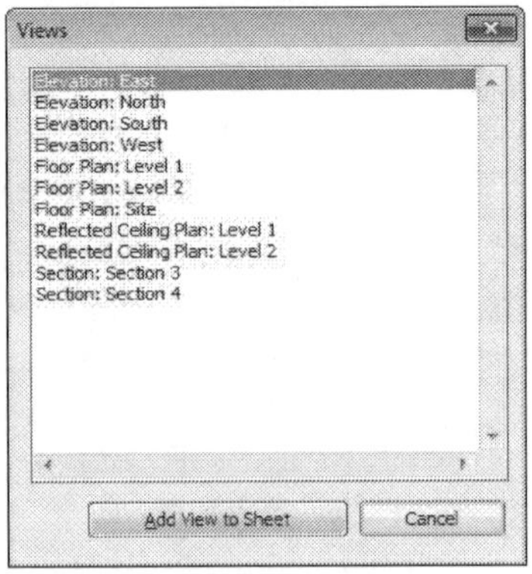

Figure 4–8

- To remove a view from a sheet, select it and press <Delete>. Alternatively, in the Project Browser, expand the individual sheet information to show the views, right-click on the view name and select **Remove From Sheet**.

Hint: Setting up the Project Browser

To view and change the Project Browser's types, select the top level node of the Project Browser (which is set to *Views (all)* by default) and select the type you want to use from the Type Selector. For example, you can set the Browser to only display views that are not on sheets, as shown in Figure 4–9.

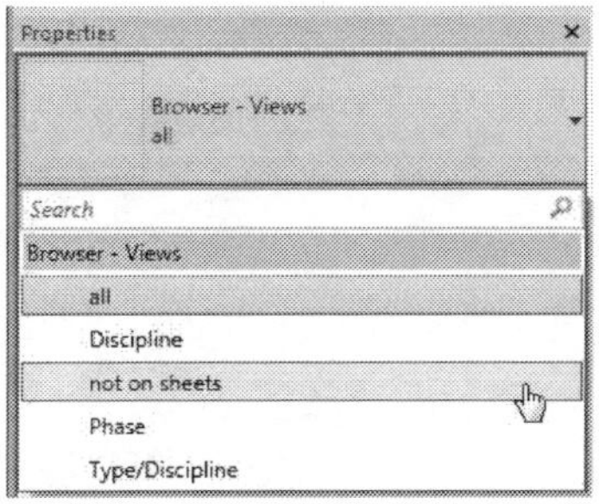

Figure 4–9

Moving Views and View Titles

*You can also use the **Move** command or the arrow keys to move a view.*

- To move a view on a sheet, select the edge of the view and drag it to a new location. The view title moves with the view.
- To move only the view title, select the title and drag it to the new location.
- To modify the length of the line under the title name, select the edge of the view and drag the controls, as shown in Figure 4–10.

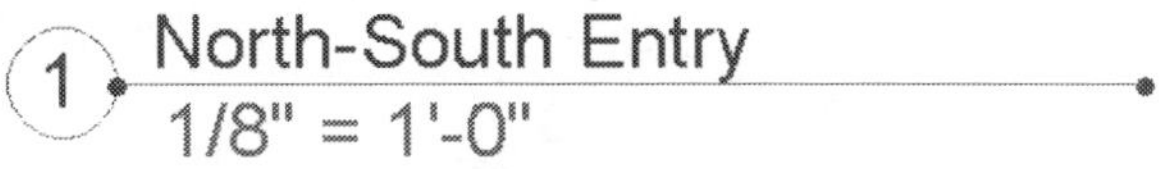

Figure 4–10

- To change the title of a view on a sheet without changing its name in the Project Browser, in Properties, in the *Identity Data* area, type a new title for the *Title on Sheet* parameter, as shown in Figure 4–11.

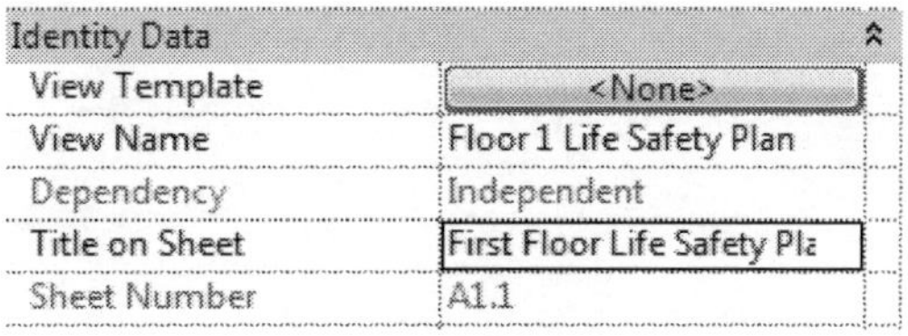

Figure 4–11

Rotating Views

- When creating a vertical sheet, you can rotate the view on the sheet by 90 degrees. Select the view and set the direction of rotation in the Rotation on Sheet drop-down list in the Options Bar, as shown in Figure 4–12.

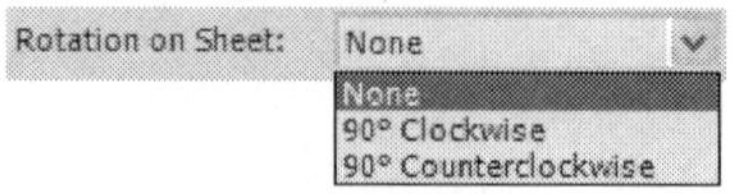

Figure 4–12

- To rotate a view to an angle other than 90 degrees, open the view, toggle on and select the crop region and use the **Rotate** command to change the angle.

Working Inside Views

To make small changes to a view while working on a sheet:

- Double-click *inside* the view to activate it.
- Double-click *outside* the view to deactivate it.

Only elements in the viewport are available for modification. The rest of the sheet is grayed out, as shown in Figure 4–13.

Only use this method for small changes. Significant changes should be made directly in the view.

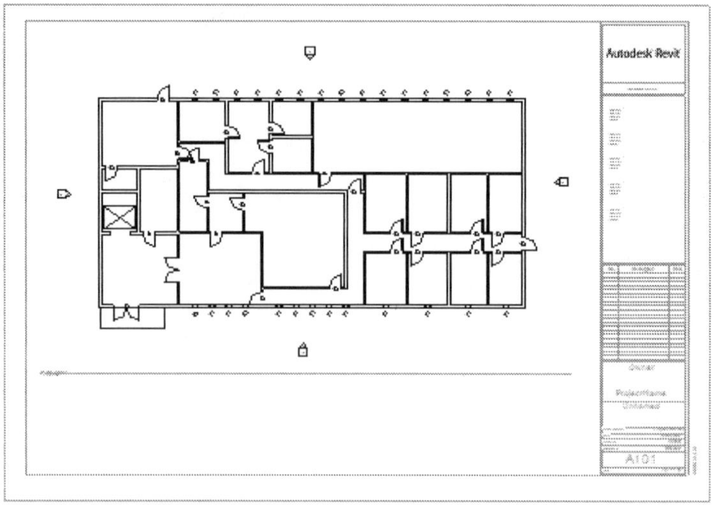

Figure 4–13

- You can activate and deactivate views by right-clicking on the edge of the view or by using the tools found on the *Modify | Viewports* and *Views* tab>Sheet Composition panel.
- Changes you make to elements when a view is activated also display in the original view.
- If you are unsure which sheet a view is on, right-click on the view in the Project Browser and select **Open Sheet**. This item is grayed out if the view has not been placed on a sheet and is not available for schedules and legends which can be placed on more than one sheet.

Resizing Views on Sheets

Each view displays the extents of the model or the elements contained in the crop region. If the view does not fit on a sheet (as shown in Figure 4–14), you might need to crop the view or move the elevation markers closer to the building.

If the extents of the view change dramatically based on a scale change or a crop region, it is easier to delete the view on the sheet and drag it over again.

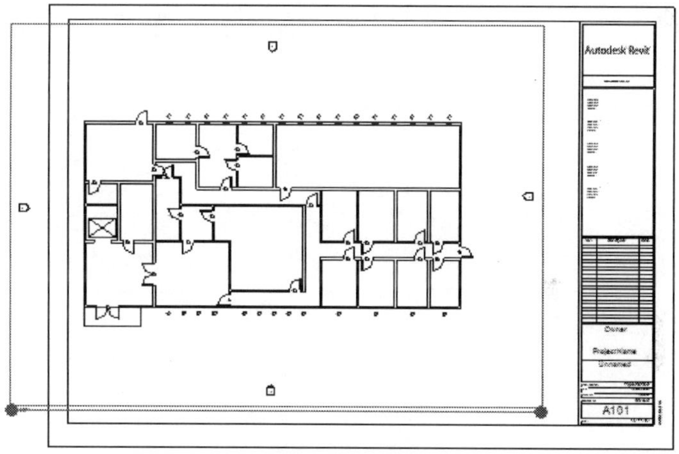

Figure 4–14

Hint: Add an Image to a Sheet

Company logos and renderings saved to image files (such as .JPG and .PNG) can be added directly on a sheet or in a view.

1. In the *Insert* tab>Import panel, click (Image).
2. In the Import Image dialog box, select and open the image file. The extents of the image display as shown in Figure 4–15.

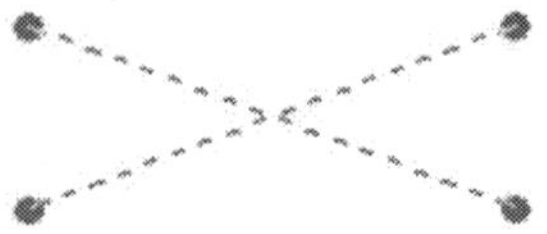

Figure 4–15

3. Place the image where you want it.
4. The image is displayed. Pick one of the grips and extend it to modify the size of the image.

- In Properties, you can adjust the height and width and also set the *Draw Layer* to either **Background** or **Foreground**, as shown in Figure 4–16.

Dimensions	
Width	1' 5 185/256"
Height	1' 1 41/64"
Horizontal Scale	1.000000
Vertical Scale	1.000000
Lock Proportions	☑
Other	
Draw Layer	Background

Figure 4–16

- You can select more than one image at a time and move them as a group to the background or foreground.

Practice 4a Work with Sheets in an Architectural Project

Practice Objectives

- Set up project properties.
- Create sheets individually.
- Modify views to prepare them to be placed on sheets.
- Place views on sheets.

Estimated time for completion: 20 minutes

In this practice you will complete the project information, add new sheets and use existing sheets. You will fill in title block information and then add views to sheets, such as the Wall Sections sheet shown in Figure 4–17. Complete as many sheets as you have time for.

- This practice follows the steps for working with a full set of construction documents. The process is the same for half- or full-size documentation sheets.

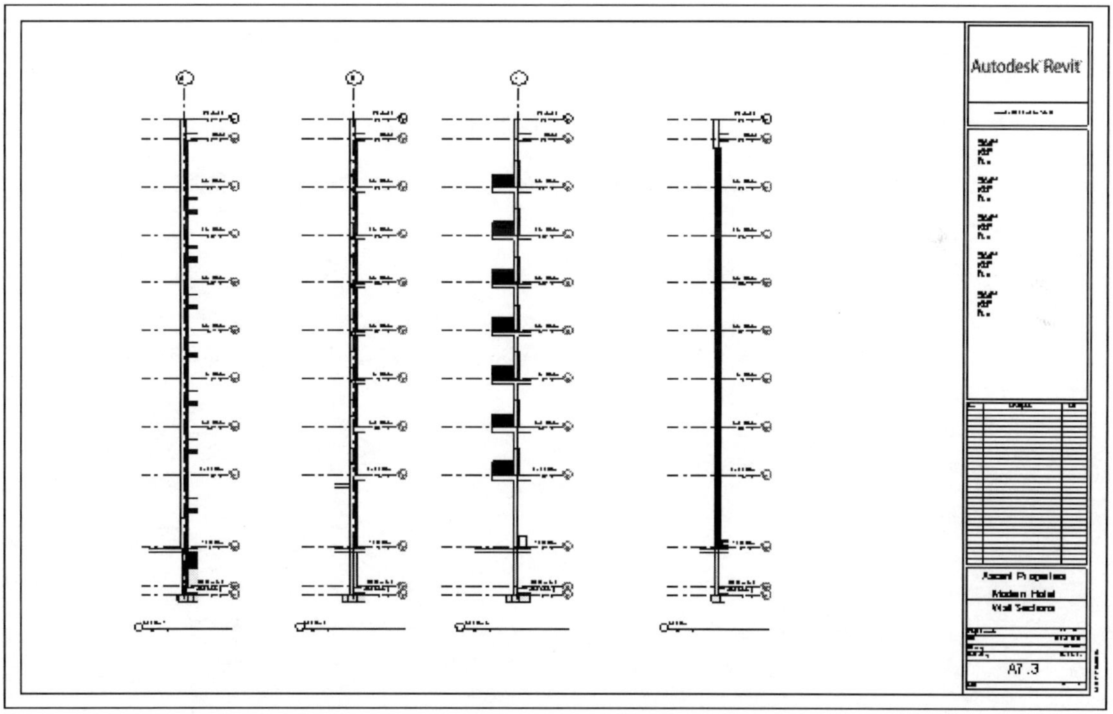

Figure 4–17

Task 1 - Complete the project information.

1. Open the project **Modern-Hotel-Sheets.rvt**.
2. In the *Manage* tab>Settings panel, click (Project Information).
3. In the Project Properties dialog box, in the *Other* area, set the following parameters:

These properties are used across the entire sheet set and do not need to be entered on each sheet.

   - *Project Issue Date:* **Issue Date**
   - *Project Status:* **Design Development**
   - *Client Name:* **Ascent Properties**
   - *Project Address:* Click **Edit...** and enter your address
   - *Project Name:* **Modern Hotel**
   - *Project Number:* **1234-567**
4. Click **OK**.
5. Save the project.

Task 2 - Create a Cover Sheet and Floor Plan Sheets.

1. In the *View* tab>Sheet Composition panel, click (Sheet).
2. In the New Sheet dialog box, select the **D 22 x 34 Horizontal** titleblock.
3. Click **OK**.
4. Zoom in on the lower right corner of the title block. The Project Properties filled out earlier are automatically added to the sheet.

5. Continue filling out the title block, as shown in Figure 4–18.

Figure 4–18

6. In the Project Browser, expand the **3D Views** node. Drag and drop the **Exterior Front Perspective** view on to the sheet, as shown in Figure 4–19. There are two items that are not required on the cover sheet, the viewport title and crop region.

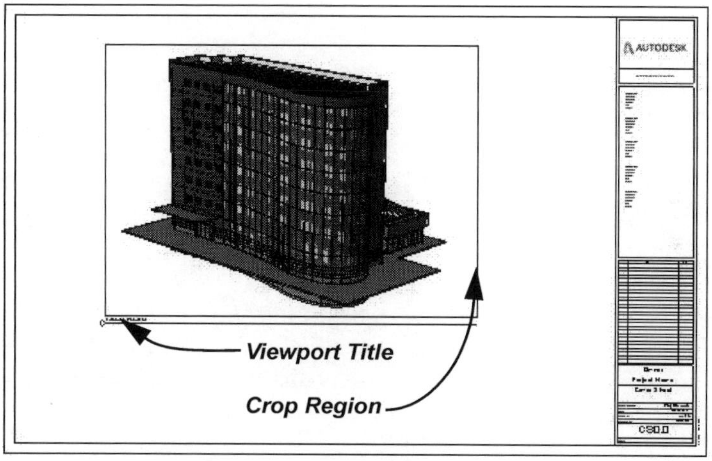

Figure 4–19

7. Select the edge of the viewport. In the Type Selector select **Viewport: No Title**.

8. Double-click inside the viewport, the title block grays out and you can modify the actual view.

9. In Properties, in the *Extents* area, clear the check from **Crop Region Visible**. (This could also be done in the View Control Bar.)

10. Double-click outside the viewport to return to the sheet.

11. In the Sheet Composition panel, click (Sheet). Using the D-sized title block, create the following new sheets:

Sheet Number and Name	View
A2.1: Ground Floor Plan	Floor 1
A2.2: Upper Floor Plan (Typical)	Typical Guest Room Floor Plan
A2.3: Roof Plan	Roof

12. Save the project.

Task 3 - Set up and add views to sheets.

1. Duplicate (no detailing) the **Floor Plans: Floor 1** and **Floor 2** views and name them **Floor 1 - Life Safety Plan** and **Floor 2-8 - Life Safety Plan**.

2. Open the new views and do the following:

    - Hide all elements except the actual building elements.
    - Toggle on the crop region and ensure it is tight up against the building.
    - Toggle the crop region off.

The crop region defines the extent of the view on the sheet.

3. Open the sheet **A1.1 - Floor 1 - Life Safety Plan**.

4. In the Project Browser, right click on that sheet and select **Add View...**.

5. In the Views dialog box scroll down and select **Floor Plan: Floor 1 - Life Safety Plan**, as shown in Figure 4–20. Click **Add View to Sheet** and place the view on the sheet.

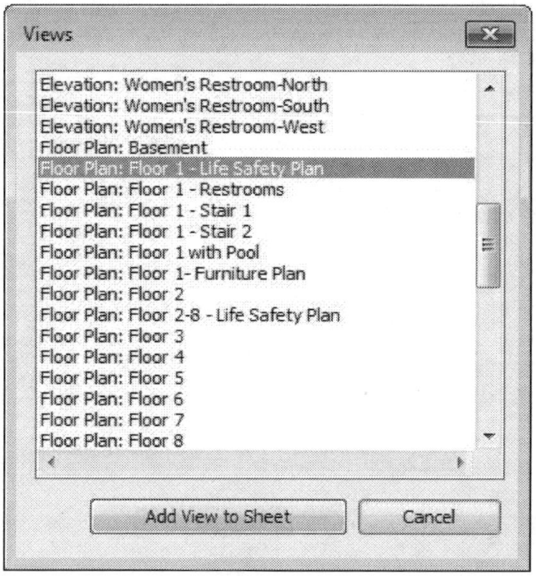

Figure 4–20

6. Repeat the process for the other floor and rename sheet **Floor 2 - Life Safety Plan** as **Floor 2-8 - Life Safety Plan**.
   - The **Floor 1 - Life Safety Plan** is no longer available because it has already been added to a sheet.
7. Repeat the process of adding views to sheets using the views you have available.
   - Modify crop regions and hide unnecessary elements in the views, as shown in Figure 4–21. Toggle off crop regions after you have modified them.

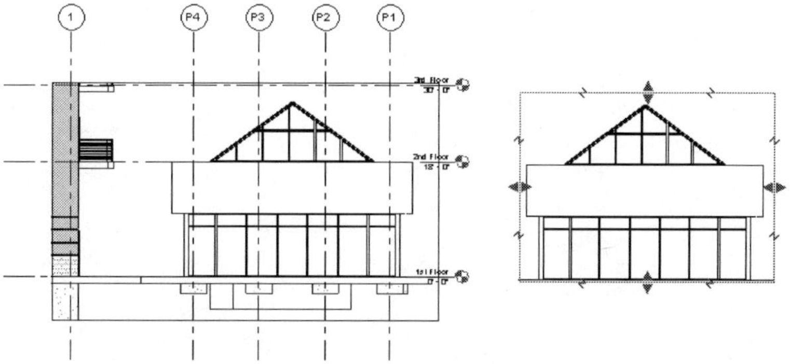

Figure 4–21

   - Verify the scale of a view in Properties before placing it on a sheet.

- Use alignment lines to help place multiple views on one sheet, as shown in Figure 4–22.

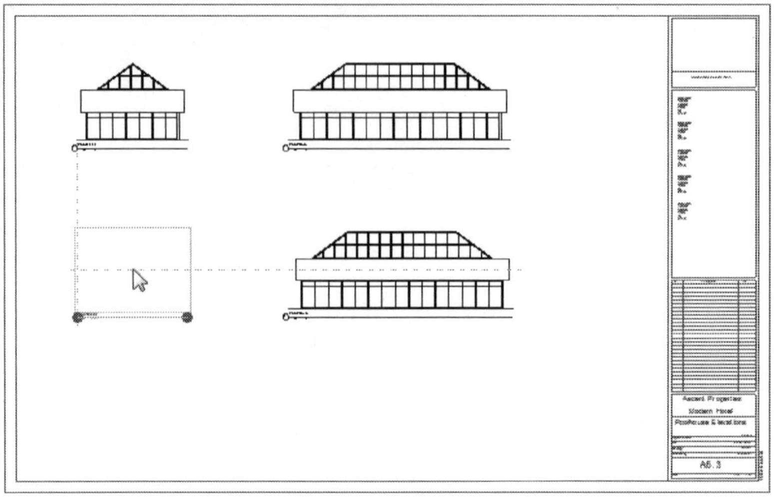

Figure 4–22

- Change the view title, if required, to more accurately describe what is on the sheet.
- To make minor changes to a view once it is on a sheet, double-click inside the viewport to activate the view. To return to the sheet, double-click outside the viewport to deactivate the view.

8. Once you have added callout, section, or elevation views to sheets, switch back to the **Floor Plans: Floor 1** view. Zoom in on one of the markers. Note that it has now been automatically assigned a detail and sheet number, as shown in Figure 4–23.

Your numbers might not exactly match the numbers in the example.

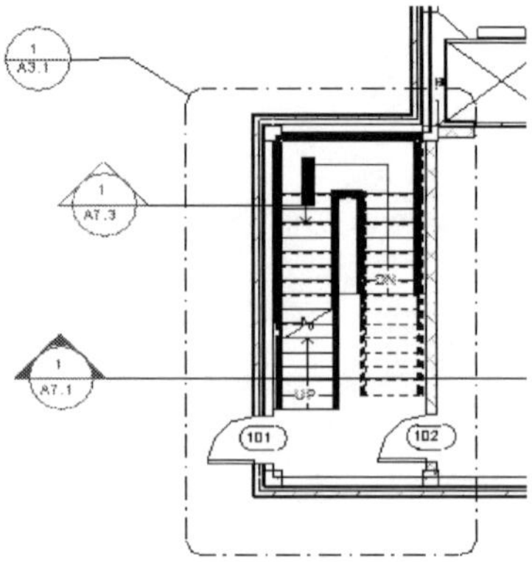

Figure 4–23

9. Save the project.

Practice 4b

Work with Sheets in a MEP Project

Practice Objectives

- Set up project properties.
- Create sheets individually.
- Modify views to prepare them to be placed on sheets.
- Place views on sheets.

Estimated time for completion: 20 minutes

In this practice you will complete the project information, add new sheets and use existing sheets. You will fill in title block information and then add views to sheets, such as the Lighting Plan sheet shown in Figure 4–24. Complete as many sheets as you have time for.

- This practice follows the steps for working with a full set of construction documents. The process is the same for half- or full-size documentation sheets.

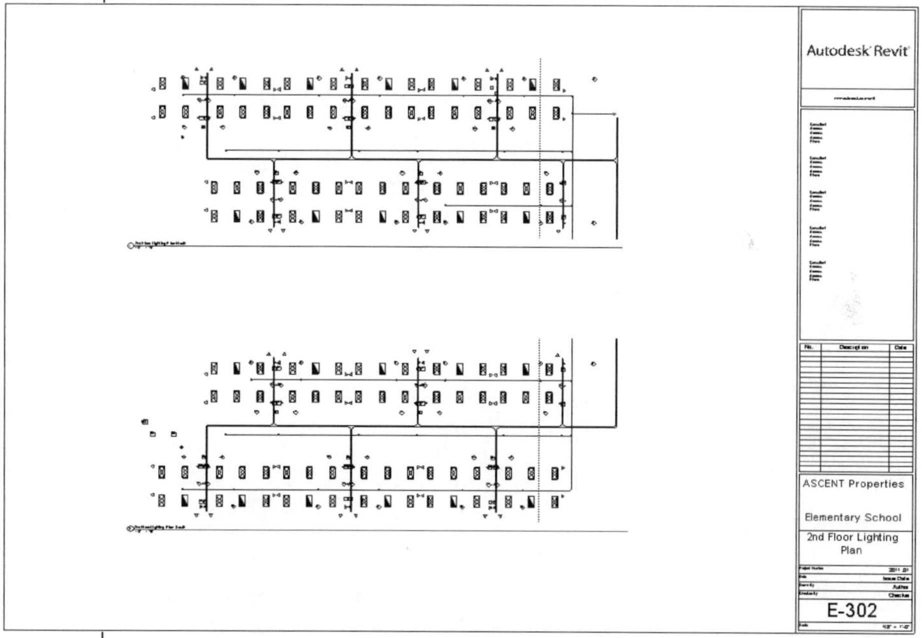

Figure 4–24

Task 1 - Complete the project information.

1. Open the project **MEP-Elementary-School-Documents.rvt**.

2. In the *Manage* tab>Settings panel, click (Project Information).

3. In the Project Properties dialog box, add the following values, as shown in Figure 4–25.

    - *Client Name:* **School District ABC**
    - *Project Name:* **Elementary School**
    - *Project Number:* **1234.56**

These values are added automatically to any sheet you create.

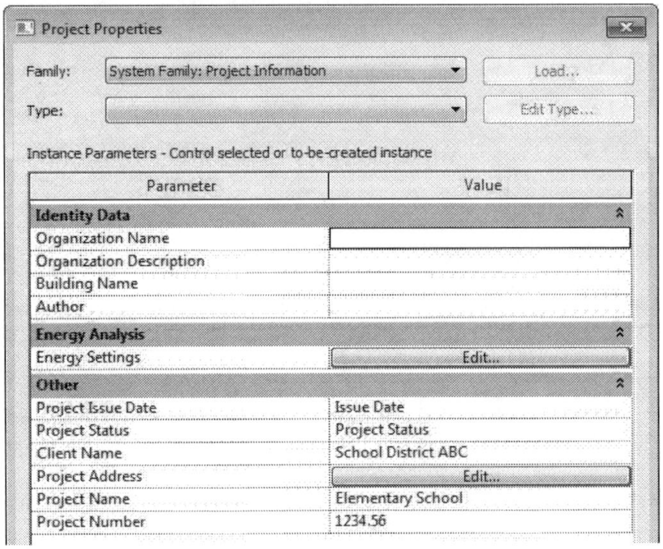

Figure 4–25

4. Click **OK**.

5. In the Project Browser, expand the *Sheets (all)* area and open **M-101 - 01 Mechanical Schematic**. There is already a view placed on the sheet.

6. Zoom in on the title block and review the contents. The Project Parameters that you added are automatically applied to the sheet, as shown in Figure 4–26.

*The Scale is automatically entered when a view is inserted onto a sheet. If a sheet has multiple scales, the scale reads **As Indicated**.*

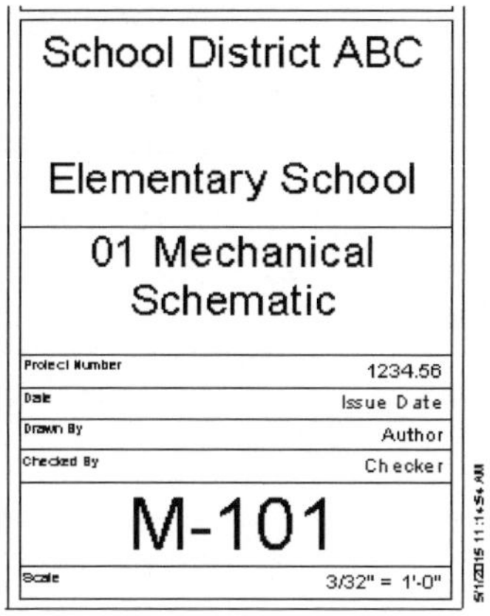

Figure 4–26

7. Set *Drawn by* to your initials. Leave the *Checked by* and *Issue Date* parameters as is.
8. Open another sheet. The project parameter values are repeated but note that the *Drawn By* value is not added because it is a by sheet parameter.
9. Review the other existing Mechanical sheets and save the project.

Task 2 - Add Sheets.

1. In the *View* tab>Sheet Composition panel, click (Sheet).
2. In the New Sheet dialog box, select the titleblock **E1 30 x42 Horizontal** and click **OK**.
3. In the Project Browser, select the new sheet, right-click, and select **Rename**.
4. In the Sheet Title dialog box, set *Number* as **C-101**, *Name* as **Cover Sheet**, and click **OK**. The titleblock updates as shown in Figure 4–27.

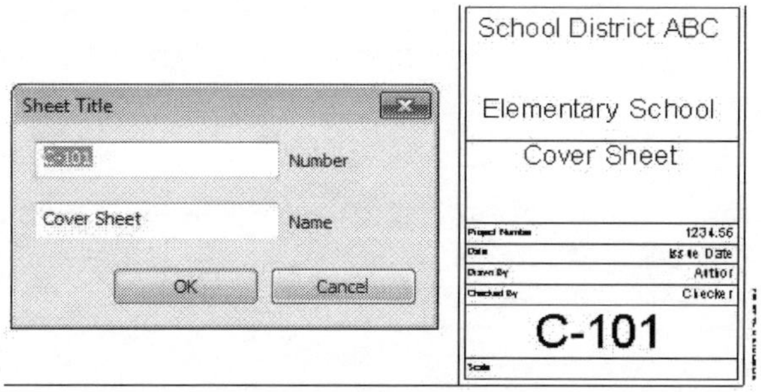

Figure 4–27

5. In the Project Browser, right-click on Sheets (all) and select **New Sheet....**

6. Using the same title block, create the following sheets:

You can change the sheet number and name in the titleblock or by renaming it in the Project Browser.

- E-301 - 1st Floor Lighting Plan
- E-302 - 2nd Floor Lighting Plan
- E-303 - Power Panel Plan Detail
- P-509 - Plumbing 3D

7. In the Project Browser, in the *Sheets (all)* area, note that these new sheets, the other sheets that you created, and the M-# sheets that were already created for you are displayed.

8. Save the project.

Task 3 - Set up and add views to sheets.

1. In the Project Browser, in the Electrical>Lighting>Floor Plans, right click on the **02 Lighting Plan** view and using **Duplicate as Dependent** create two copies. Name them as **02 Lighting Plan - North** and **02 Lighting Plan - South**.

2. Open the **02 Lighting Plan - North** view, display the crop region, and resize it to fit the north classroom wing, as shown in Figure 4–28.

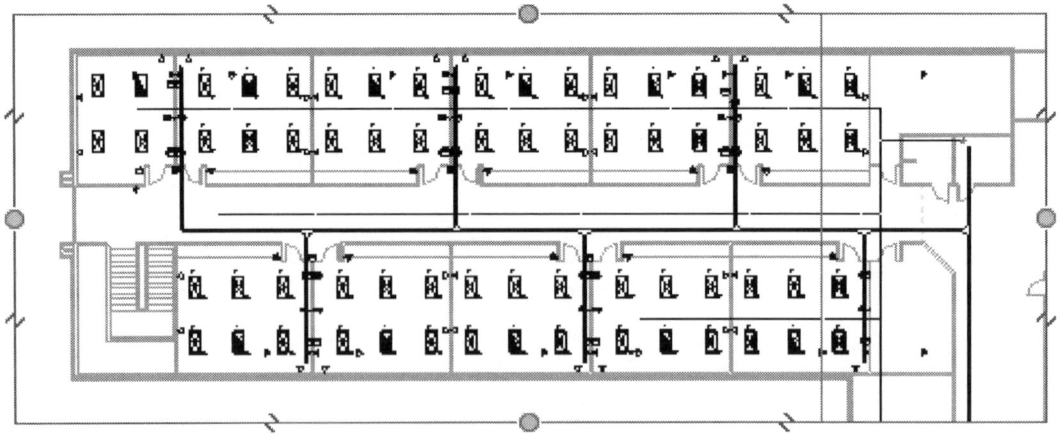

Figure 4–28

3. Toggle the crop region off.
4. Repeat the steps with the **02 Lighting Plan - South** view.
5. Open the sheet **E-302 - 2nd Floor Lighting Plan** and drag and drop the **2nd Floor Lighting Plan North** and **South** views you just created onto it.
6. Open the **E-303 - Power Panel Plan Detail** sheet and drag and drop the **Power Panel Callout** view onto it.
7. Switch to the **01Power Plan** view. Zoom in on the callout marker by the power panels. Note that it has now been automatically assigned a detail and sheet number, as shown in Figure 4–29.

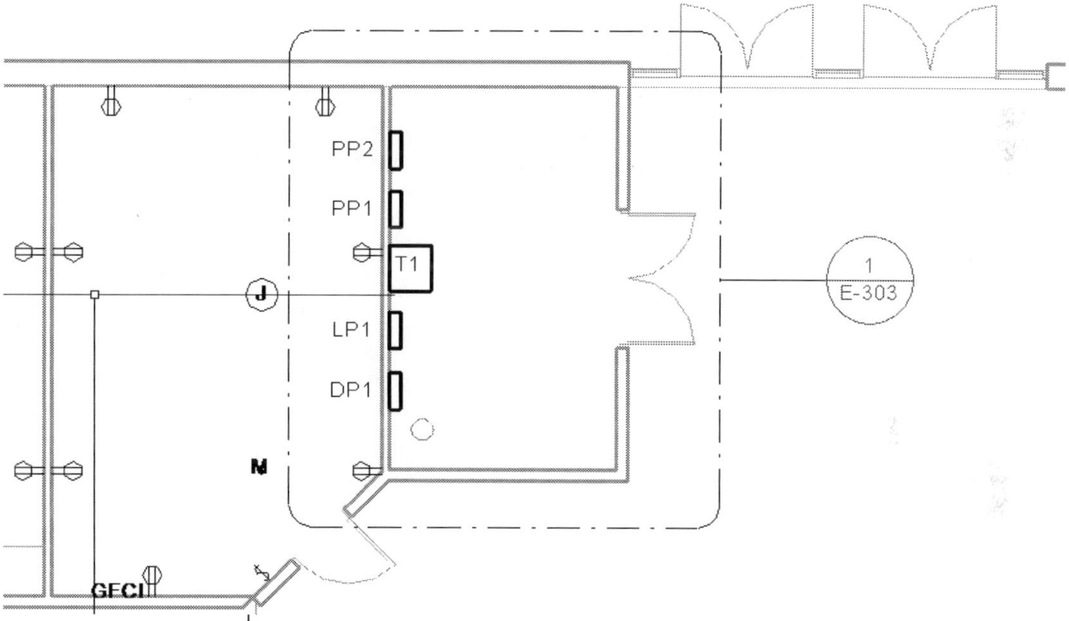

Figure 4–29

8. Repeat the process of adding views and schedules to sheets using the views and schedules you have available.

    - Modify crop regions and hide unnecessary elements in the views. Toggle off crop regions after you have modified them.
    - Verify the scale of a view in Properties before placing it on a sheet.
    - Use alignment lines to help place multiple views on one sheet.
    - Change the view title if required, to more accurately describe what is on the sheet.
    - To make minor changes to a view once it is on a sheet, right-click on the view and select **Activate View.** To return to the sheet, right-click on the view and select **Deactivate View**.
    - To make larger changes to a view on a sheet, return to the original view.
    - If you modify the size of a view that is already placed on a sheet, delete the view from the sheet and replace it with the updated view.

9. Save the project.

Practice 4c Work with Sheets in a Structural Project

Practice Objectives

- Set up project properties.
- Create sheets.
- Place views on sheets.

Estimated time for completion: 15 minutes

In this practice you will complete project information, create a cover sheet, and add views to the sheet. You will then create a foundation plan sheet, as shown in Figure 4–30, and as many other sheets as time permits, modifying the scales as required.

- This practice follows the steps for working with a full set of construction documents. The process is the same for half- or full-size documentation sheets.

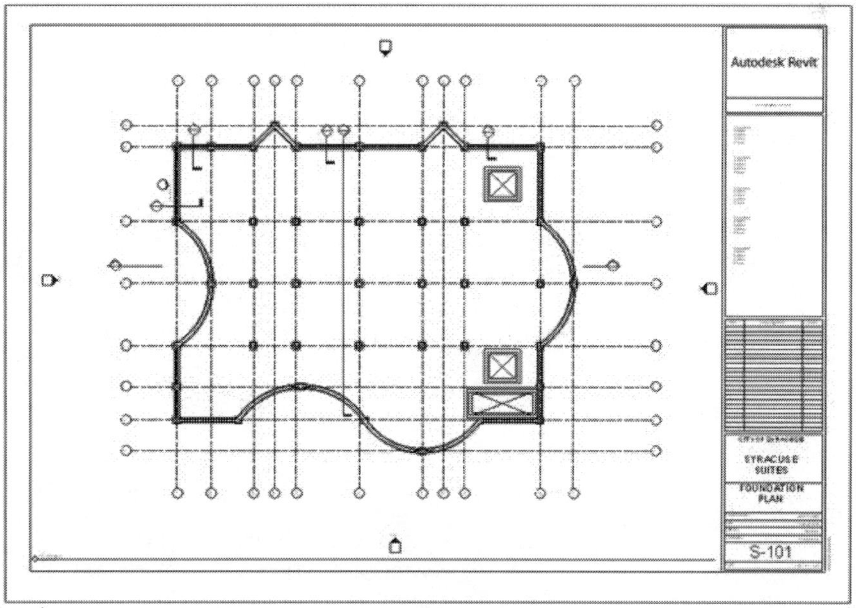

Figure 4–30

Task 1 - Complete the project information.

1. Open the project **Syracuse-Suites-Sheets.rvt**.
2. In the *Manage* tab>Setting panel, click (Project Information).

These properties are used across the entire sheet set and do not need to be entered on each sheet.

3. In the Project Properties dialog box set the following parameters (or use your own information based on your company standards):
   - *Project Issue Date:* current date
   - *Project Status:* **Design Development**
   - *Client Name:* **CITY OF SYRACUSE**
   - *Project Address:* **1234 Clinton St. Syracuse, NY 13066** click **Edit...**
   - *Project Name:* **SYRACUSE SUITES**
   - *Project Number:* **1234-567**
4. Click **OK**.
5. Save the project.

Task 2 - Create a cover sheet.

1. In the Project Browser, right-click on *Sheets (all)* and select **New Sheet**, as shown in Figure 4–31, or in the *View* tab> Sheet Composition panel, click (New Sheet).

Some sheets already exist in the project.

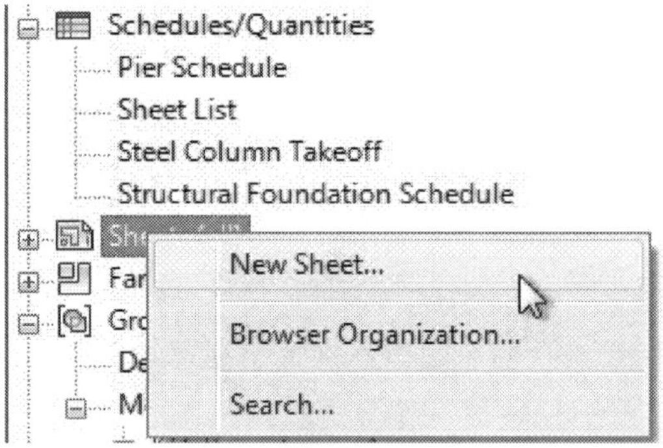

Figure 4–31

2. In the New Sheet dialog box, *Select Titleblocks* area, select **Syracuse Suites Cover Sheet: E1 30x42 Horizontal** and click **OK**.
3. In the Project Browser, *Sheets* category, right-click on new sheet and select **Rename**.

4. In the Sheet Title dialog box, set *Number* to **S-000** and *Name* to **COVER SHEET**, as shown in Figure 4–32.

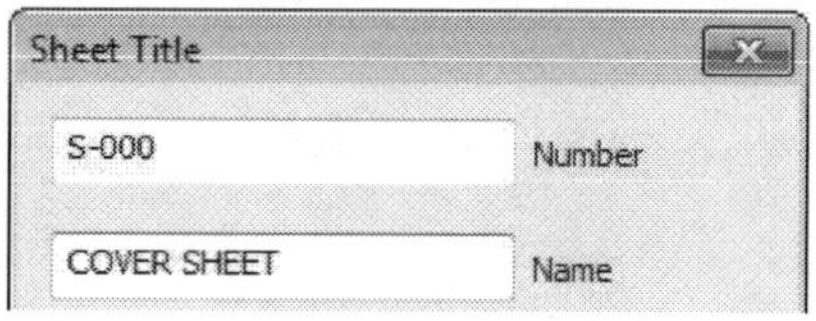

Figure 4–32

5. In the Project Browser, expand **3D Views**.
6. Select the **Isometric** view and drag it to the coversheet.
7. Delete the view because it is too large.
8. Open the **Isometric** view and set the *Scale* to **1/16"=1'-0"**.
9. Switch to the cover sheet and place the view on the sheet.
10. In the *Legends* category, add the Symbol Legend to the sheet as shown in Figure 4–33.

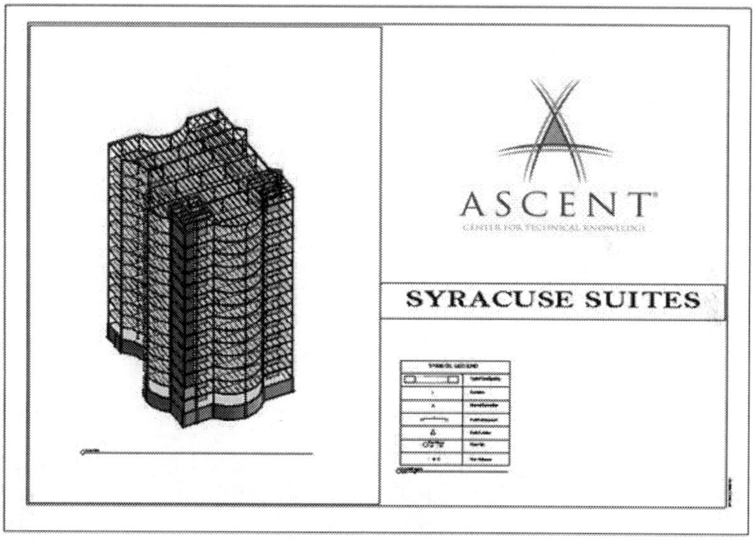

Figure 4–33

Task 3 - Create additional sheets.

1. In the *View* tab>Sheet Composition panel, click (Sheet).
2. In the New Sheet dialog box, select the titleblock **Syracuse Suites E1: 30x42 Horizontal** and click **OK**.

3. In the Project Browser, right-click on **S-001 – Unnamed** and rename it as **S-201: FOUNDATION PLAN**, as shown in Figure 4–34.

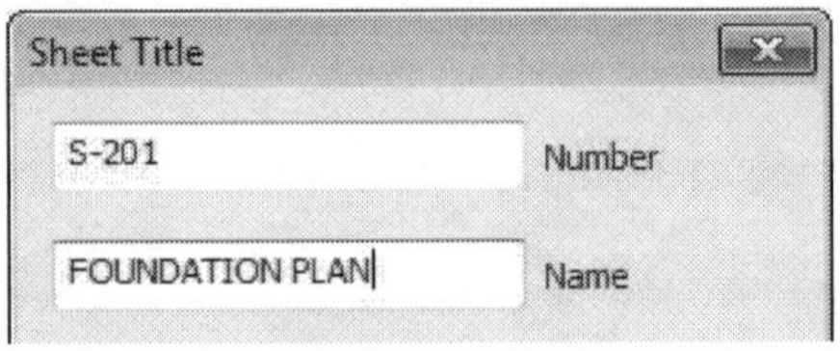

Figure 4–34

4. Click **OK**.

5. In the Project Browser, find the **T.O. FOOTING** structural plan view and drag it onto the sheet, centering it in the view as shown in Figure 4–35.

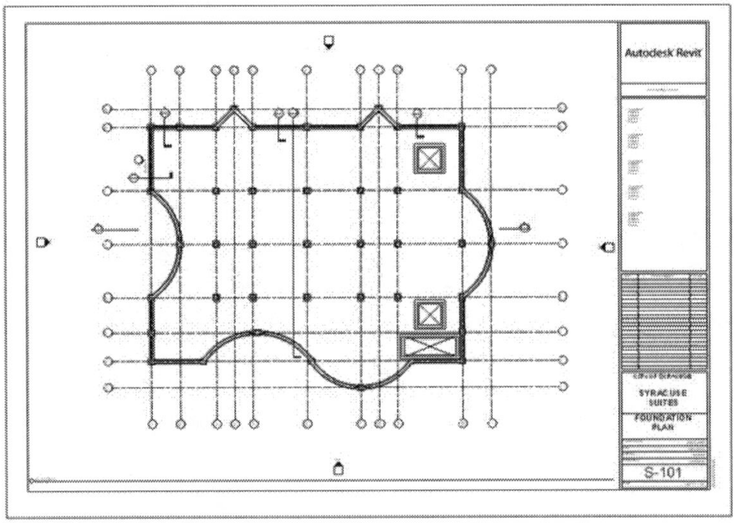

Figure 4–35

6. Several sheets already exist in the project. Place the Structural Plans: **00GROUND FLOOR PLAN** view on the sheet **S-202-Ground Floor Plan.**

7. Zoom in to see the title of the view. It displays as **00 GROUND FLOOR PLAN**, as shown in Figure 4–36.

Figure 4–36

8. In the Project Browser, select the view and scroll down to the *Identity Data* section. Change the *Title on Sheet* to **GROUND FLOOR - STRUCTURAL PLAN**, as shown in Figure 4–37.

Identity Data	
View Template	<None>
View Name	00 GROUND FLOOR PLAN
Dependency	Independent
Title on Sheet	GROUND FLOOR - STRUCTURAL PLAN
Sheet Number	S-202
Sheet Name	Ground Floor Plan

Figure 4–37

9. Click **Apply**.The title changes on the sheet, as shown in Figure 4–38.

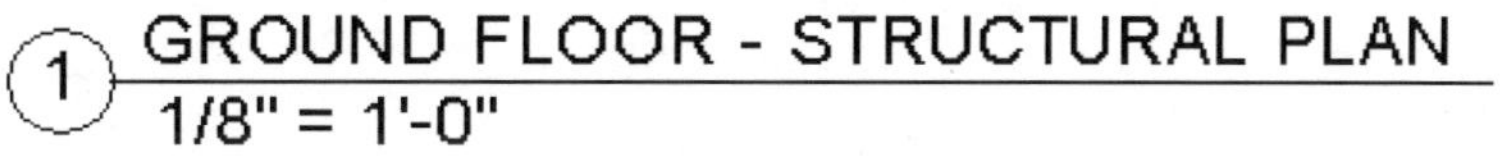

Figure 4–38

10. (Optional) Add views to the other sheets.
    - If any views do not fit on the sheet, change the scale.

11. When the sheets have been created, browse through them separately and note that all of the tags are filled out, as shown in Figure 4–39. This enables you to verify whether the tags point to the sheets correctly. If a tag does not display detail and sheet numbers, the view has not been dragged onto a sheet.

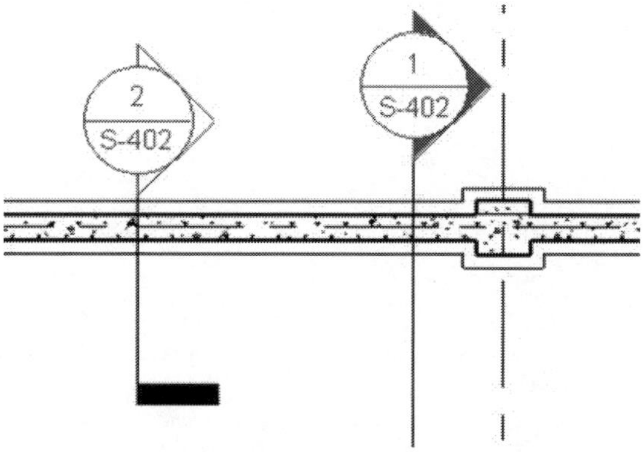

Figure 4–39

12. Save the project.

4.3 Printing Sheets

With the **Print** command, you can print individual sheets or a list of selected sheets. You can also print an individual view or a portion of a view for check prints or presentations. To open the Print dialog box (shown in Figure 4–40), in the Application Menu, click  (Print).

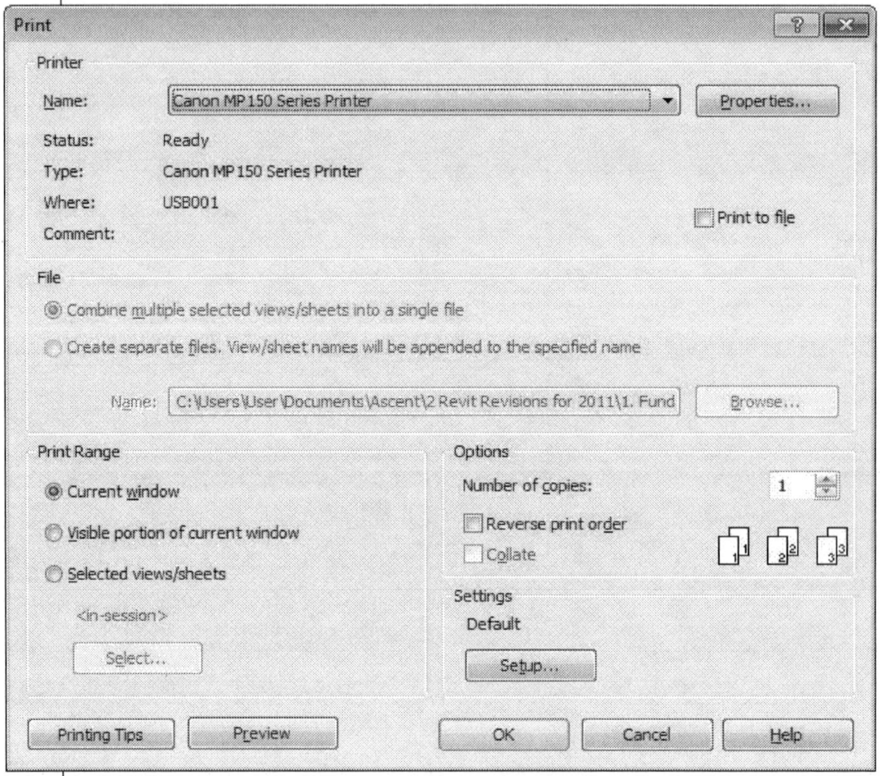

Figure 4–40

Printing Options

The Print dialog box is divided into the following areas: *Printer*, *File*, *Print Range, Options*, and *Settings*. Modify them as required to produce the plot you want.

- **Printing Tips**: Opens Autodesk WikiHelp online, in which you can find help with troubleshooting printing issues.
- **Preview**: Opens a preview of the print output so that you can see what is going to be printed.

Printer

Select from the list of available printers, as shown in Figure 4–41. Click **Properties...** to adjust the properties of the selected printer. The options vary according to the printer. Select **Print to file** to print to a file rather than directly to a printer. You can create .PLT or .PRN files.

You must have a .PDF print driver installed on your system to print to PDF.

Figure 4–41

File

The *File* area is only available if the **Print to file** option has been selected in the *Printer* area or if you are printing to an electronic-only type of printer. You can create one file or multiple files depending on the type of printer you are using, as shown in Figure 4–42. Click **Browse...** to select the file location and name.

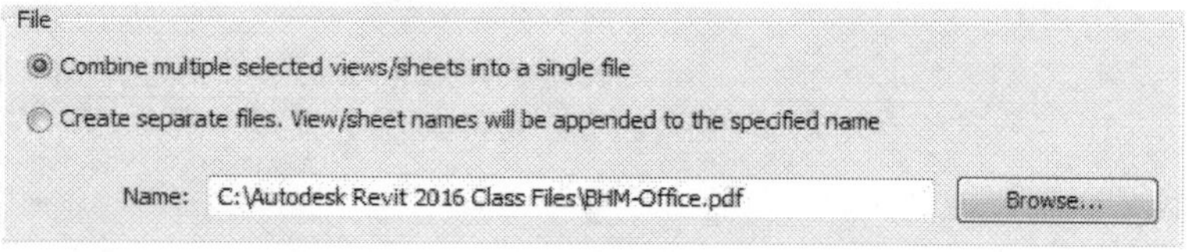

Figure 4–42

Print Range

The *Print Range* area enables you to print individual views/sheets or sets of views/sheets, as shown in Figure 4–43.

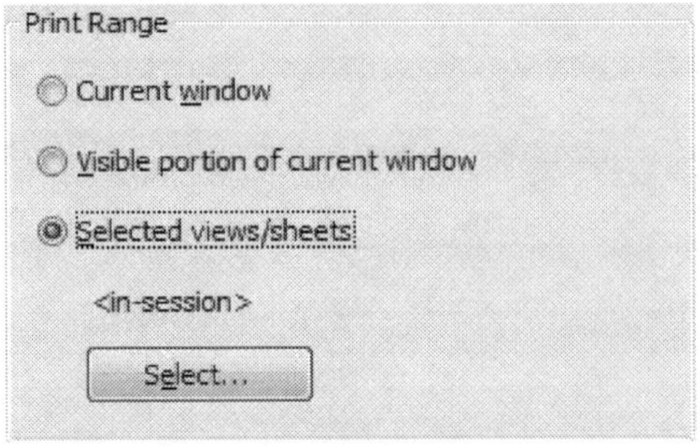

Figure 4–43

- **Current window**: Prints the entire current sheet or view you have open.
- **Visible portion of current window**: Prints only what is displayed in the current sheet or view.
- **Selected views/sheets**: Prints multiple views or sheets. Click **Select...** to open the View/Sheet Set dialog box to choose what to include in the print set. You can save these sets by name so that you can more easily print the same group again.

Options

If your printer supports multiple copies, you can specify the number in the *Options* area, as shown in Figure 4–44. You can also reverse the print order or collate your prints. These options are also available in the printer properties.

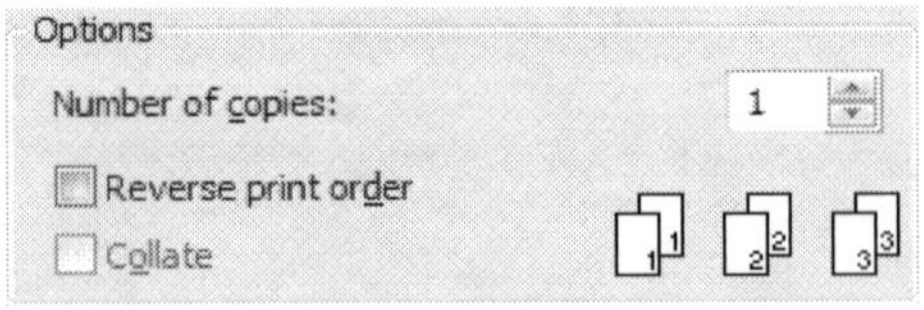

Figure 4–44

Settings

Click **Setup**... to open the Print Setup dialog box, as shown in Figure 4–45. Here, you can specify the *Orientation* and *Zoom* settings, among others. You can also save these settings by name.

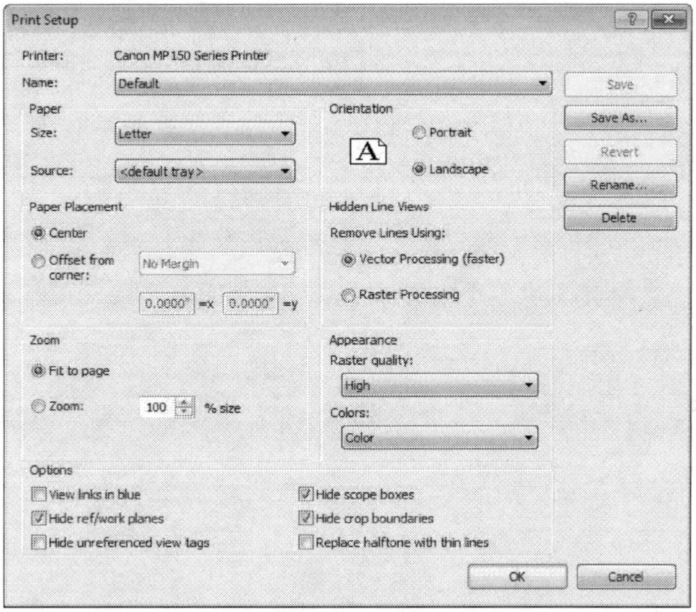

Figure 4–45

- In the *Options* area specify the types of elements you want to print or not print. Unless specified, all of the elements in a view or sheet print.

4.4 Exporting Files

If your company uses multiple CAD programs or works with consultants who use other CAD programs, prepare your Autodesk Revit files so that the other programs can use them as well. The Autodesk Revit software provides ways to export Autodesk Revit vector data to CAD formats, DWF, Building Site, Images and Animations, Reports, FBX, gbXML, IFC (Industry Foundation Classes), and ODBC databases, as shown in Figure 4–46.

Scroll down the Export list to see additional options.

Figure 4–46

- Find out if the users for which you are exporting need a 2D or 3D view. You can export any view, but only 3D views export the entire building model; other views create 2D files.

Enhanced in 2017

- Text character size, location, and other text related properties is rendered faithfully when exported to other CAD file formats.

Export Types

- **CAD Formats:** Exports projects to AutoCAD DWG or DXF, MicroStation DGN, or ASIC SAT files for 3D modeling.
- **DWF/DWFx:** Exports views and sheets to DWF or DWFx files to be used in Autodesk® Design Review for review and redlining.
- **Building Site:** Exports ADSK exchange files that can be used with Civil Engineering programs.
- **FBX:** Exports 3D files for Autodesk® MotionBuilder®, as well as Autodesk® Maya®, Autodesk® 3ds Max®, and Viz plug-ins. You must be in a 3D view for this to display.
- **Family Types:** Exports family type information to a text (.TXT) file that can be imported into a spreadsheet program to verify that all of the parameters for each type are correct. You must be in a family file for this to display.
- **gbXML:** Exports model information that can be used in other programs for energy or load analysis.
- **IFC:** Exports the Autodesk Revit model to Industry Foundation Class objects. These can be used by CAD programs that do not use RVT file formats. It uses established standards for typical objects in the building industry. For example, an Autodesk Revit wall element translates to an IfcWall object. Additional mapping for specialty items can be set up.
- **ODBC Database:** Exports Autodesk Revit information to an Open Database Connectivity database file. It creates tables of the model element types and instances, levels, rooms, key schedules, and assembly codes.
- **Images and Animations:** Exports walkthroughs, solar studies, and images.
- **Reports:** Exports information from Schedules and Room/Area. Schedules are exported as delimited text files that can be imported into a spreadsheet. You must be in a schedule view to export. Room/Area reports are saved as HTML files.

Enhanced in 2017

- **Options:** Sets up the options for Export Setups for DWG/DXF, DGN, and IFC options.

Exporting CAD Format Files

Exporting Autodesk Revit Projects to various CAD file formats is a common need in collaboration with consultants and engineers. Using this process, you can export individual views or sheets, or sets of views or sheets to DWG, DXF, DGN, and SAT files. You can also create and save sets of views/sheets.

How To: Export a CAD Format File

1. If you are exporting only one view, open the view you want to export. If you are exporting the model, open a 3D view.
2. In the Application Menu, expand  (Export), click  (CAD Formats), and select the type of format you want to export as shown in Figure 4–47.

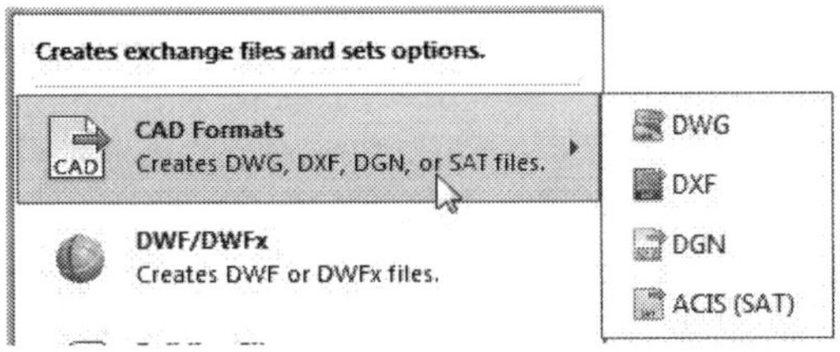

Figure 4–47

- The examples in this section show the process for DWG files. It is the same for other types of files.

3. The Export CAD Formats dialog box displays, as shown in Figure 4–48.

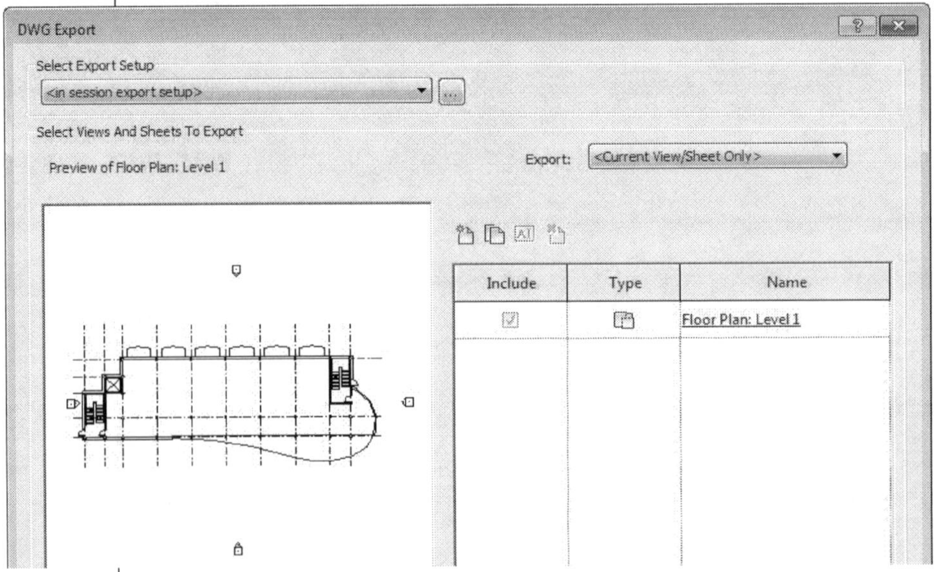

Figure 4–48

4. If you have an existing export setup, you can select it from the drop-down list as shown in Figure 4–49, or click  (Modify Export Setup) to create a new one.

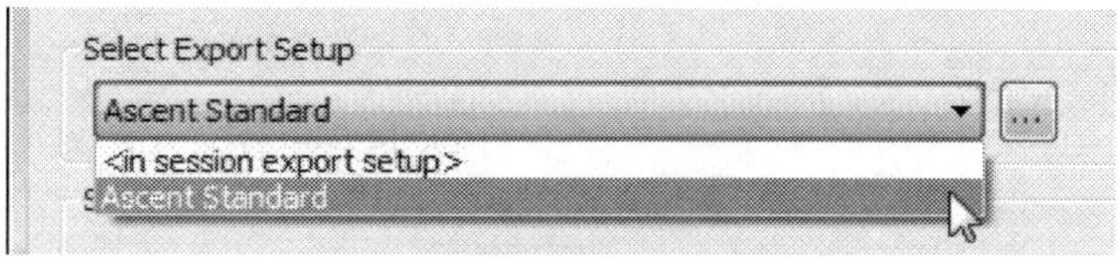

Figure 4–49

5. Select the view(s) you want to export from the Export drop-down list as shown in Figure 4–50.

Figure 4–50

   - To export only the active view, select **<Current View/ Sheet Only>**.
   - To export any views or sheets that are open in the session of the Autodesk Revit software, select **<In session view/sheet set>**.
   - To export a predefined set of views or sheets, select the name from the list if it is available. You can create new sets of views and sheets to export.

6. When everything is set up correctly, click **Next...**.
7. In the Export CAD Formats - Save to Target Folder dialog box, select the folder location and name. If you are exporting to DWG or DXF, select the version in the Files of type drop-down list.
8. Click **OK.**

- The Project Base Point of the Autodesk Revit project becomes the 0,0 coordinate point in other CAD formats.

How To: Create an Export Setup

1. In the DWG, DXF, or DGN Export dialog box, next to the Select Export Setup list, click (Modify Export Setup) or in the Application Menu, expand (Export), scroll down to (Options), expand it, and select (Export Setups DWG/DXF) or (Export Setups DGN).
2. The Modify DWG/DXF or Modify DGN Export Setup dialog box contains all of the elements and types you can export. You can select an existing Layer standard provided with the program (as shown in Figure 4–51), or create a new one.

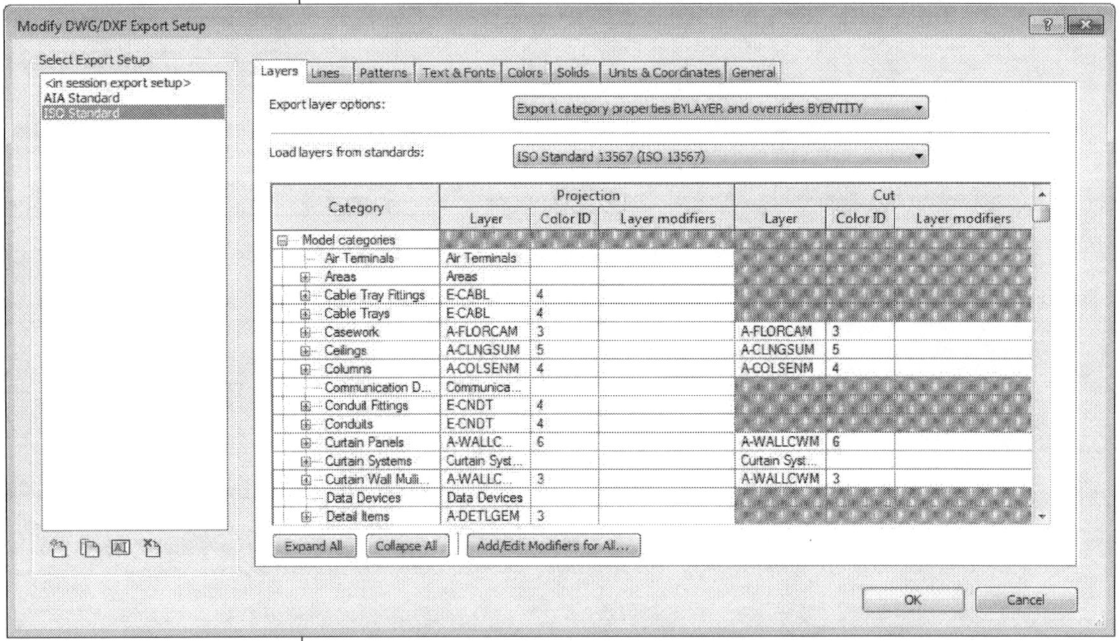

Figure 4–51

3. Select each of the tabs and apply the appropriate information.
   - In the *Layers* tab, map the Categories in the Autodesk Revit software to the Layers (or Levels).
   - In the *Lines*, *Patterns*, and *Text & Fonts* tabs map the styles required.
   - In the *Colors* tab, select to export either Index colors (255 colors) or True color (RGB values).
   - In the *Solids* tab (3D views only), select to export to either Polymesh or ACIS solids.

- In the *Units & Coordinates* tab, specify what unit type one DWG unit is and the basis for the coordinate system.
- In the *General* tab, you can set up how the rooms and room boundaries are exported, what to do with any non-plottable layers, how scope boxes, reference planes, coincident lines, and unreferenced view tags are handled, how views on sheets and links are treated, and which version of the DWG file format to use.

- Export setups can be created in a template file or shared between open projects using Transfer Project Standards.

How To: Create a New Set of Views/Sheets to Export

1. Start the appropriate Export CAD Formats command.
2. In the Export CAD Formats dialog box, click (New Set).
3. In the New Set dialog box, type a name and click **OK**.
4. The tab displays with the new set active and additional information, as shown in Figure 4–52.

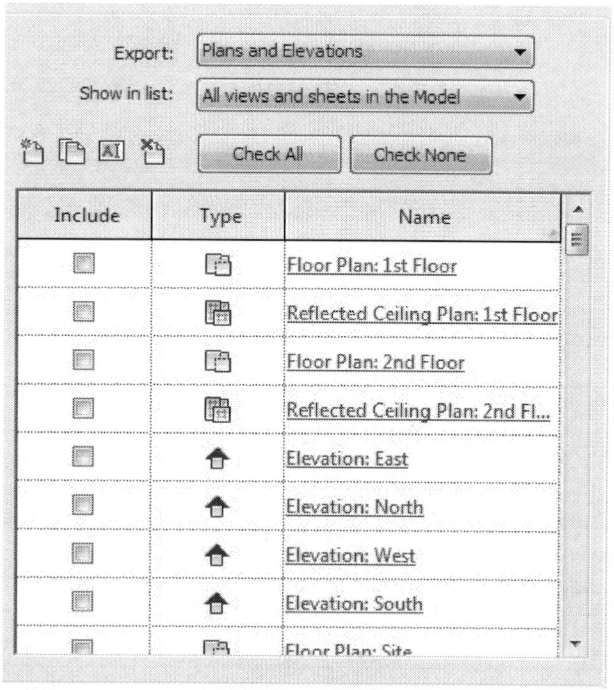

Figure 4–52

5. Use *Show in List* to limit the number of items that display in the table.
6. Select the views and/or sheets that you want to export from the project.
    - Use **Check all** or **Check none** to aid in selection.
7. When you finish with the set, continue the export process.

Exporting to DWF

Exporting DWF/DWFx (Design Web Format) files gives you a safe and easy way to share Autodesk Revit project information without sending the actual file. For example, a client does not have to have the Autodesk Revit software on their machine to view the file and they cannot make any changes directly to it. DWF/DWFx files are also much smaller than project files and are therefore easier to email or post on a website. DWF/DWFx files can include element data that can be viewed in Autodesk Design Review.

The process of exporting a DWF file is similar to CAD Format exports. You can export individual views or sheets, as shown in Figure 4–53, or you can create sets of multiple views/sheets.

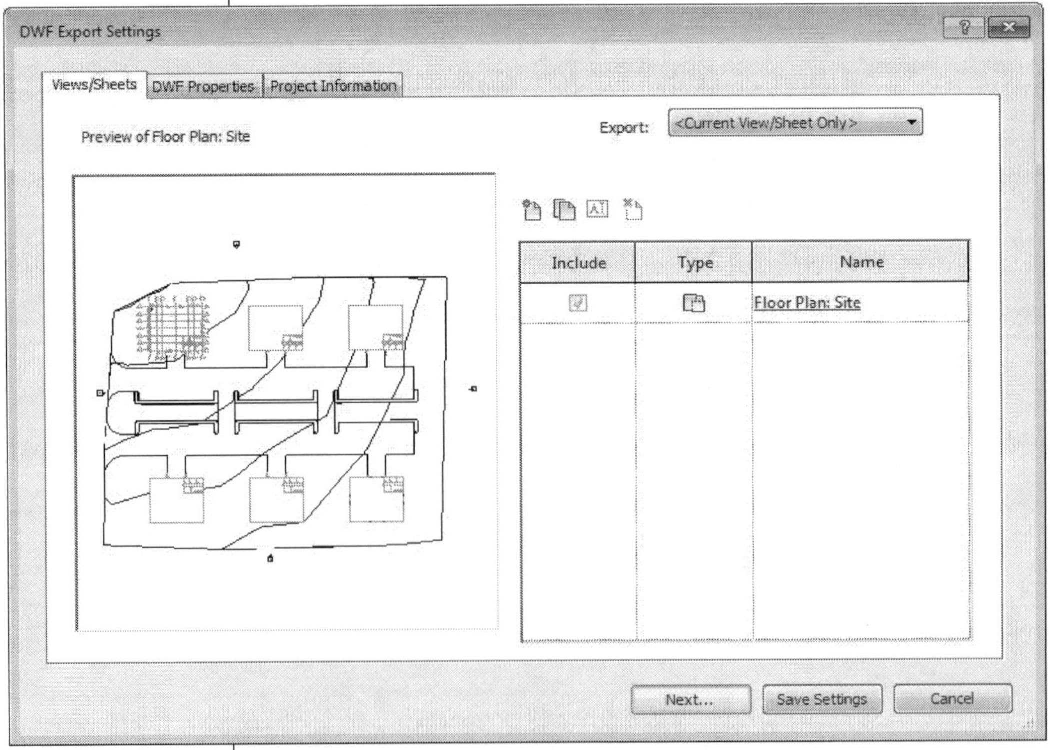

Figure 4–53

- In the *DWF Properties* tab, set up the export object data, the graphics settings, and print setup.
- The *Project Information* tab, shown in Figure 4–54, can be updated and included in a DWF export.

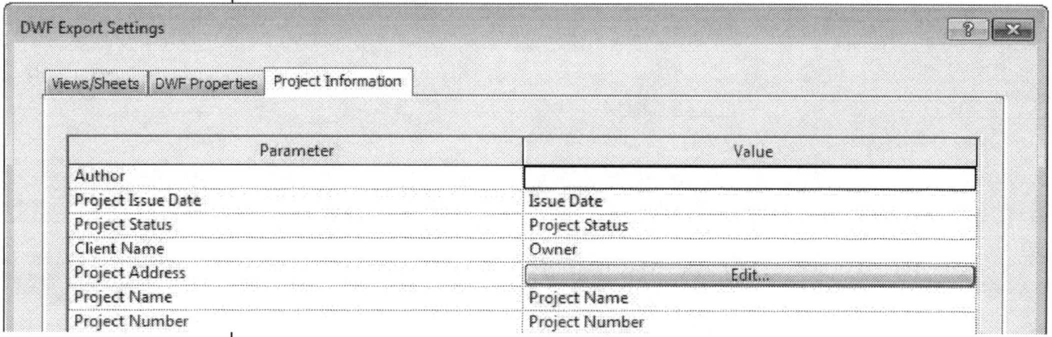

Figure 4–54

- Files can be exported to the DWF or DWFx format.
- You can mark up (redline) DWF/DWFx files using a program such as Autodesk Design Review. The markups can then be linked back into the Autodesk Revit project, where the original user can make changes.
- Textures, line patterns, line weights, and text are included in 3D DWF exports.

Practice 4d Export Files

Practice Objective

- Export views to AutoCAD drawing files and DWF viewing files.

Estimated time for completion: 5 minutes

In this practice you will export several views to AutoCAD drawing files and to DWF files, as shown in Autodesk Design Review in Figure 4–55.

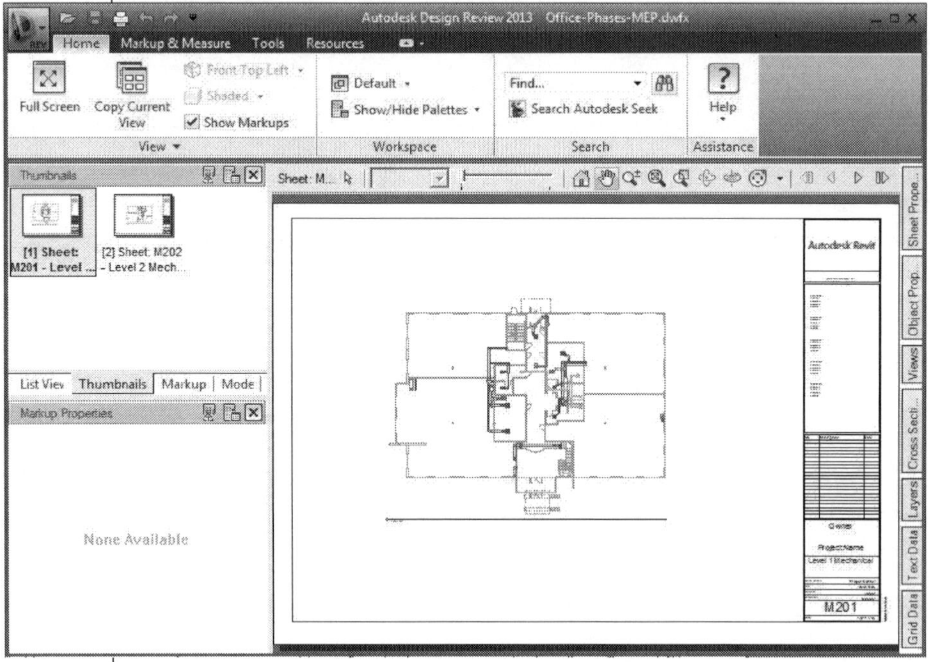

Figure 4–55

Task 1 - Set up and Export a Set of 2D Views to a DWG File.

1. Open the project **Office-Export.rvt**.

2. In the Application Menu, expand (Export), expand (CAD Formats), and click (DWG).

3. In the DWG Export dialog box, in the *Select Export Setup* area, click  (Modify Export Setup).

4. In the Modify DWG/DXF Export Setup dialog box, *Layers* tab, *Load layers from standards* list, select the standard you are most likely to use.

5. In the *Text & Fonts* tab for *Text behavior when exported*, select **Preserve visual fidelity**.

6. Scroll down in the list of fonts and map *Arial* to **Arial Narrow**, as shown in Figure 4–56.

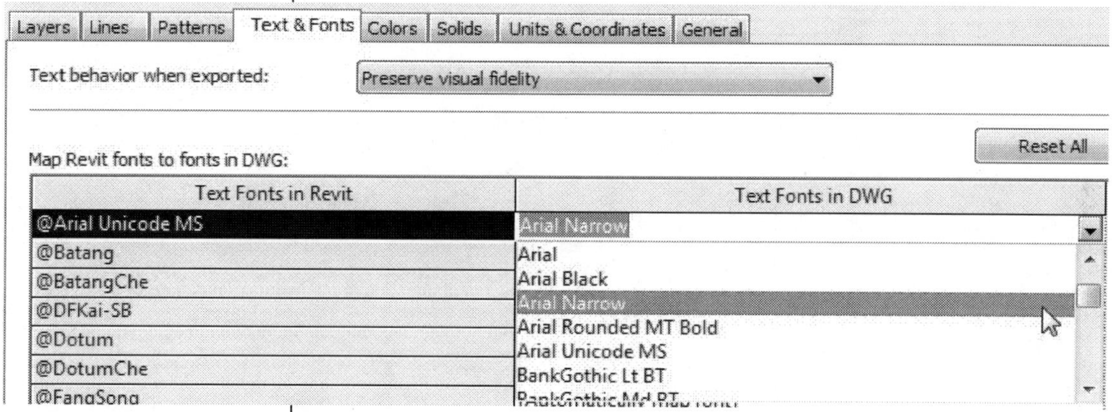

Figure 4–56

7. In the *General* tab, select **Export rooms, spaces and areas as polylines**. Click **OK**.

8. In the DWG Export dialog box, click  (New Set).

9. In the New Set dialog box, type the name **Plans** and click **OK**.

10. Select at least two floor/structural plan views, as shown in Figure 4–57.

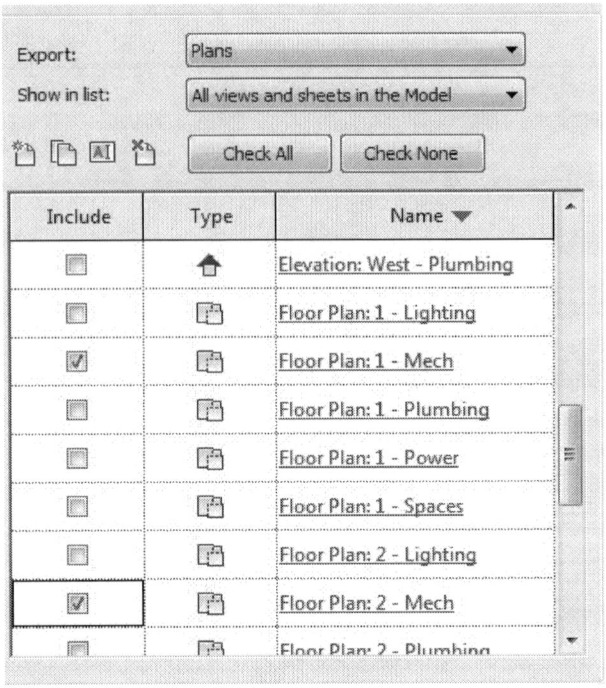

Figure 4–57

11. Click **Next...**.

12. In the Export CAD Formats - Save to Target Folder dialog box, set the *Save In:* folder to the practice files folder. Set the *Files of Type:* to **AutoCAD 2013 DWG** files.

13. Set the *Naming* to **Automatic-Long (Specify prefix)** and type **Plans** in the *File name/Prefix* field.

14. Click **OK**. The software generates DWG files for the each selected view using the setup you defined.

Task 2 - Export a 3D View to AutoCAD.

1. Switch to a 3D view if you are not already in one.

2. In the Application Menu, expand (Export), expand (CAD Formats), and click (DWG Files).

3. In the DWG Export dialog box, set *Export* to **<Current View/Sheet only>**, as shown in Figure 4–58.

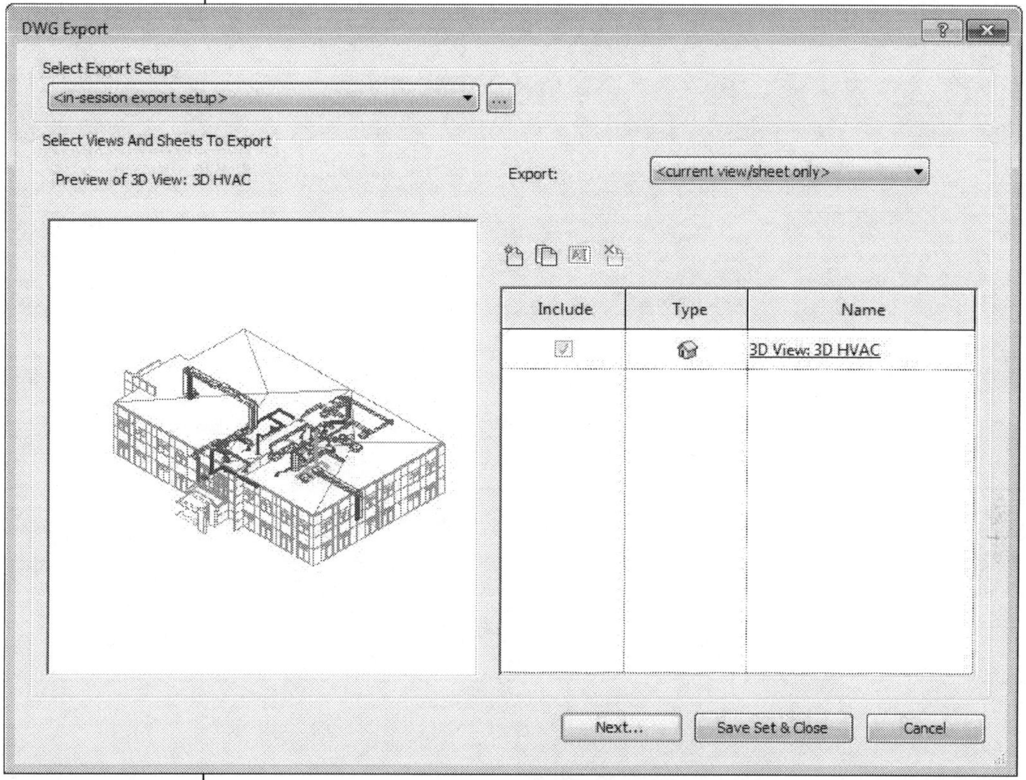

Figure 4–58

4. Click **Next...**. In the Export CAD Formats - Save to Target Folder dialog box, type a filename as required, and click **OK**.

5. If you have access to AutoCAD, you can open the files to see the exported geometry or view them in Windows Explorer, as shown in Figure 4–59 in the Extra Large Icons view.

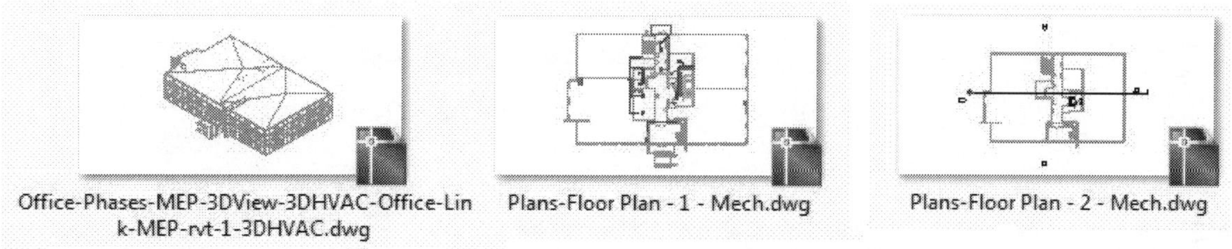

Figure 4–59

Task 3 - Export to DWF.

1. In the Application Menu, expand (Export) and click (DWF/DWFx).
2. In the DWF Export Settings dialog box, click (New Set).
3. In the New Set dialog box, type the name **Sheets** and click **OK**.
4. Change the *Show in list:* to **Sheets in the Model** and select the sheets, as shown in Figure 4–60.

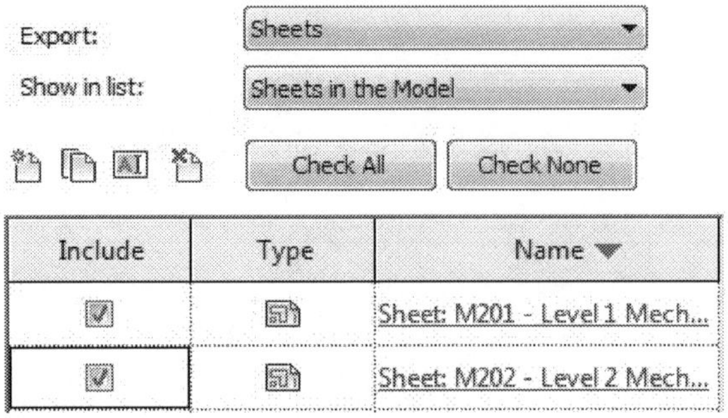

Figure 4–60

5. Switch to the *DWF Properties* tab and verify that **Element Properties** is selected.
6. Click **Next...**.
7. In the Export DWF - Save to Target Folder dialog box, note that **Combine selected views and sheets into a single dwf file** is selected by default.
8. Click **OK**.
9. If you have Autodesk Design Review, view the file.
10. If you have time, create a 3D DWF of the model and view the file.

Chapter Review Questions

1. How do you specify the size of a sheet?
   a. In the Sheet Properties, specify the **Sheet Size**.
   b. In the Options Bar, specify the **Sheet Size**.
   c. In the New Sheet dialog box, select a title block to control the Sheet Size.
   d. In the Sheet view, right-click and select **Sheet Size**.
2. How is the title block information filled in as shown in Figure 4–61? (Select all that apply.)

Figure 4–61

   a. Select the title block and select the label that you want to change.
   b. Select the title block and modify it in Properties.
   c. Right-click on the Sheet in the Project Browser and select **Information**.
   d. Some of the information is filled in automatically.
3. On how many sheets can a view be placed?
   a. 1
   b. 2-5
   c. 6+
   d. As many as you want.

4. Which of the following is the best method to use if the size of a view is too large for a sheet, as shown in Figure 4–62?

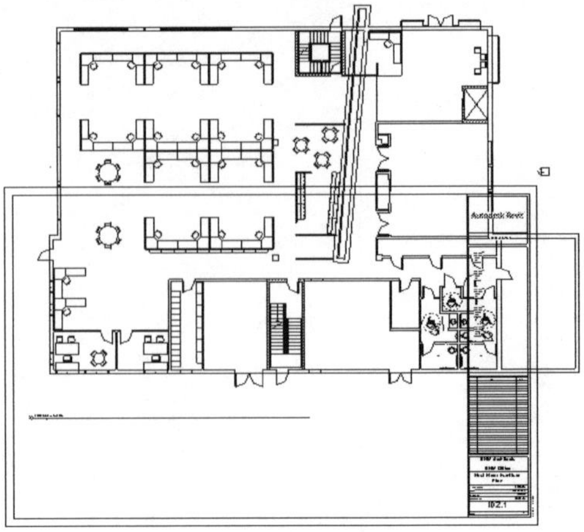

Figure 4–62

   a. Delete the view, change the scale and place the view back on the sheet.
   b. Activate the view and change the View Scale.

5. How do you set up a view on a sheet that only displays part of a floor plan, as shown in Figure 4–63?

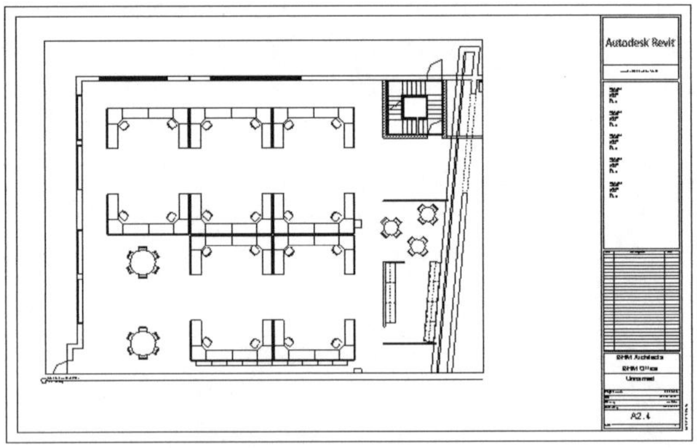

Figure 4–63

   a. Drag and drop the view to the sheet and use the crop region to modify it.
   b. Activate the view and rescale it.
   c. Create a callout view displaying the part that you want to use and place the callout view on the sheet.
   d. Open the view in the Project Browser and change the View Scale.

6. Which of the following settings can be specified when you export a project to DWG/DXF or DGN? (Select all that apply.)
   a. Line Weight to Color
   b. Text
   c. Units
   d. Patterns

Command Summary

Button	Command	Location
Sheets and Printing		
	Activate View	• **Ribbon:** (*select the view*) *Modify | Viewports* tab>Viewport panel • **Double-click:** *(in viewport)* • **Right-click:** (*on view*) Activate View
	Deactivate View	• **Ribbon:** *View* tab>Sheet Composition panel>expand Viewports • **Double-click:** *(on sheet)* • **Right-click:** (*on view*) Deactivate View
	Place View	• **Ribbon:** *View* tab>Sheet Composition panel
	Print	• **Application Menu**
	Sheet	• **Ribbon:** *View* tab>Sheet Composition panel
Exporting		
	ACIS (SAT)	• **Application Menu: Expand Export> CAD Formats**
	Building Site	• **Application Menu: Expand Export**
	CAD Formats	• **Application Menu: Expand Export>**
	DGN	• **Application Menu: Expand Export> CAD Formats**
	DWF/DWFx	• **Application Menu: Expand Export**
	DWG	• **Application Menu: Expand Export> CAD Formats**
	DXF	• **Application Menu: Expand Export> CAD Formats**
	Export	• **Application Menu**
	Export Setups DGN	• **Application Menu: Expand Export> Options**
	Export Setups DWG/DWF	• **Application Menu: Expand Export> Options**
	Family Types	• **Application Menu: Expand Export**

	FBX	• **Application Menu: Expand Export**
	gbXML	• **Application Menu: Expand Export**
	IFC	• **Application Menu: Expand Export**
	IFC Options	• **Application Menu: Expand Export> Options**
	Images and Animations	• **Application Menu: Expand Export**
	Mass Model gbXML	• **Application Menu: Expand Export**
	ODBC Database	• **Application Menu: Expand Export**
	Options	• **Application Menu: Expand Export**
	Reports	• **Application Menu: Expand Export**

Starting Multi-discipline Projects

Files from other CAD programs can be imported (and in some cases linked) into an Autodesk® Revit® project. These elements can be traced over or used as is to create a hybrid project. Imported CAD files can be manipulated and even exploded into individual elements, which can then take on Revit properties. Autodesk® Revit® models can be linked into other projects. Linking models can be used to create multiple copies of one building that are placed in a site plan, or to link an architectural model into a structural or MEP project.

Learning Objectives in this Chapter

- Import or link files that were created in other CAD programs into an Autodesk Revit project.
- Link Autodesk Revit models into a host project.
- Modify link display settings in views.

5.1 Importing and Linking Vector Files

You can print a hybrid drawing - part Autodesk Revit project and part imported/linked drawing.

Many firms have legacy drawings from vector-based CAD programs and could be working with consultants that use them. For example, you may want to link a DWG plan into your project, as shown in the Link CAD Formats dialog box in Figure 5–1, that you would then trace over using Autodesk Revit tools. Other non-CAD specific file formats including ADSK, IFC. Point clouds can also be opened or linked into Autodesk Revit projects.

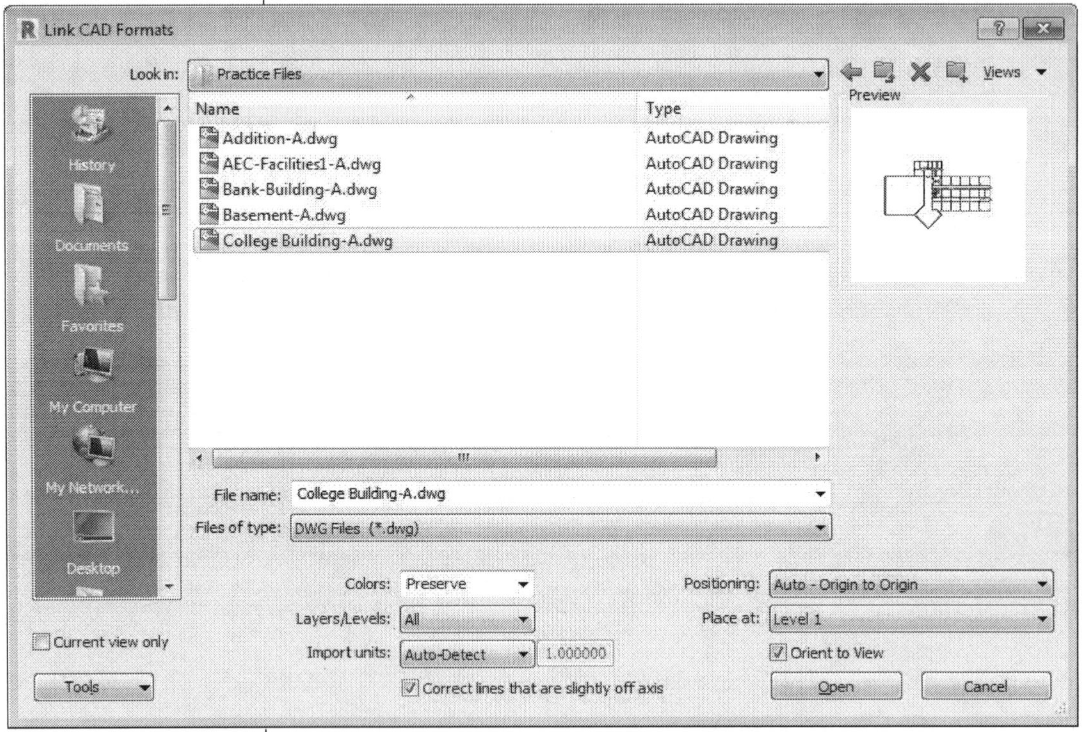

Figure 5–1

CAD Files can be either linked or imported into a project.

- **Link:** A connection is maintained with the original file and the link updates if the original file is updated.
- **Import:** No connection is maintained with the original file. It becomes a separate element in the Autodesk Revit model.

- CAD file formats that can be imported or linked include: AutoCAD® (DWG and DXF), MicroStation (DGN), 3D ACIS modeling kernel (SAT), and SketchUp (SKP).

How To: Import or Link a CAD File

1. In the *Insert* tab>Import panel, click  (Import CAD), or in the *Insert* tab>Link panel, click  (Link CAD).
2. Fill out the Import CAD (or Link CAD) dialog box. The top part of the dialog box holds the standard select file options. The bottom outlines the various options for importing or linking, as shown in Figure 5–2.

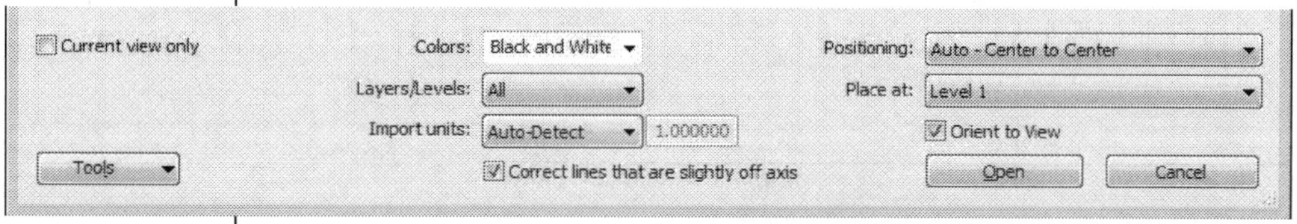

Figure 5–2

3. Click **Open**.
4. Depending on the selected Positioning method, the file is automatically placed or you can place it with the cursor.

Import/Link Options

Current view only	If selected, the file is imported/linked into the current view and not into other views. You might want to enable this option if you are just working on a floor plan and do not want the objects to display in 3D and other views.
Colors	The Autodesk Revit software works mainly with black lines of different weights on a white background to describe elements, but both AutoCAD and MicroStation use a variety of colors. To make the move into the Autodesk Revit software easier, you can select to turn all colors to Black and White, Preserve colors, or Invert colors
Layers	You can select which layers from the original drawing are imported/linked. The options are All, Visible (those that are not off or frozen), and Select. Select opens a list of layers or levels from which you can select when you import the drawing file.
Import units	Autodesk Revit software can auto-detect the units in the imported/linked file. You can also specify the units that you want to use from a list of typical Imperial and Metric units or set a Custom scale factor.
Correct lines that are slightly off axis	Corrects lines that are less than 0.1 degree of axis so that any elements based on those line are created correctly. It is on by default. Toggle it off if you are working with site plans.

Positioning	Select from the methods to place the imported/linked file in the Autodesk Revit host project. 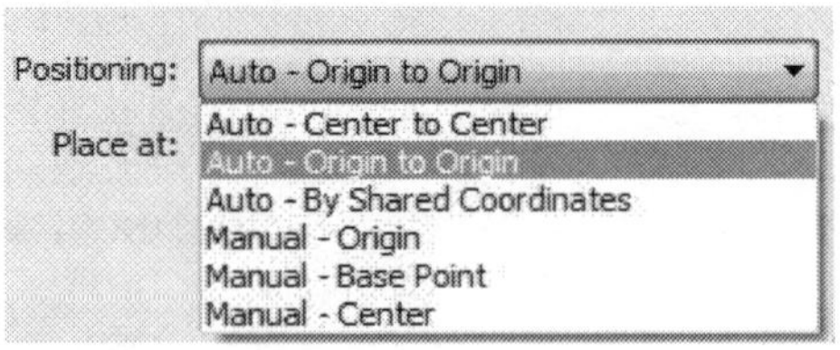
Place at:	Select a level in the drop-down list to specify the vertical positioning for the file. This is grayed out if you have selected Current view only.
Orient to View	Select this to place the file at the same orientation as the current view.

- The default positioning is **Auto - Origin to Origin**. The software remembers the most recently used positioning type as long as you are in the same session of Autodesk Revit. (The CAD Links dialog box remembers the last positioning used separately from the RVT Links dialog box.)
- If you are linking a file, an additional Positioning option, **Auto-By Shared Coordinates**, is available. It is typically used with linked Autodesk Revit files. If you use it with a CAD file, an alert box opens, as shown in Figure 5–3, containing information about the coordinate systems and what the Autodesk Revit software does.

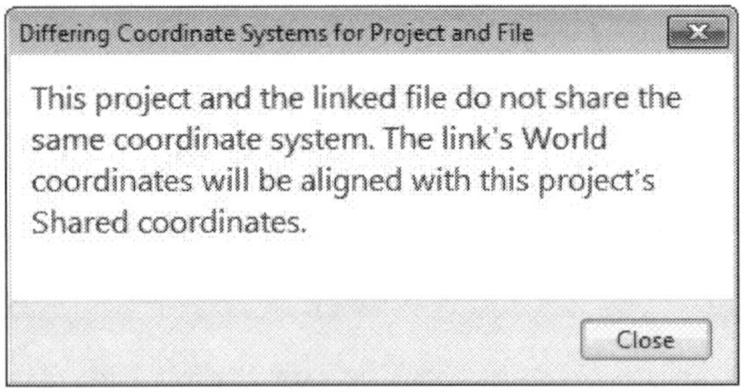

Figure 5–3

- When you link a drawing that includes reference files (XREFS), only the top level drawing is linked in and excludes any of the reference files. You need to bind the reference files to the main drawing before linking them into the project or you can link in each one separately.
- When you import a drawing that includes references (XREFS), the references come in as well.

Importing Line Weights

One significant setting for imported drawings is the line weight. Both AutoCAD and MicroStation can use line weights as well as colors. Typically, AutoCAD line weights are associated with a color. Therefore, the Autodesk Revit software imports them by color.

How To: Import Line Weights

Clicking in the title bar of a panel typically opens a settings dialog box related to the commands in the panel.

1. Before you import a CAD file, in the *Insert* tab>Import panel, click (Import Line Weights), as shown in Figure 5–4.

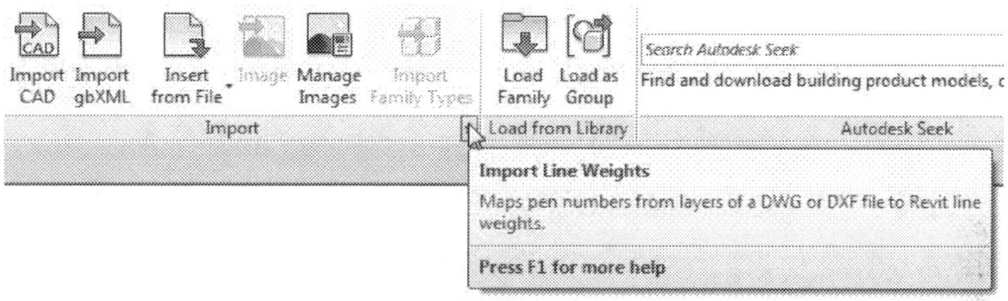

Figure 5–4

2. In the Import Line Weights dialog box shown in Figure 5–5, load a text file that holds the relationships or type them in the dialog box. You can then save them for later use.

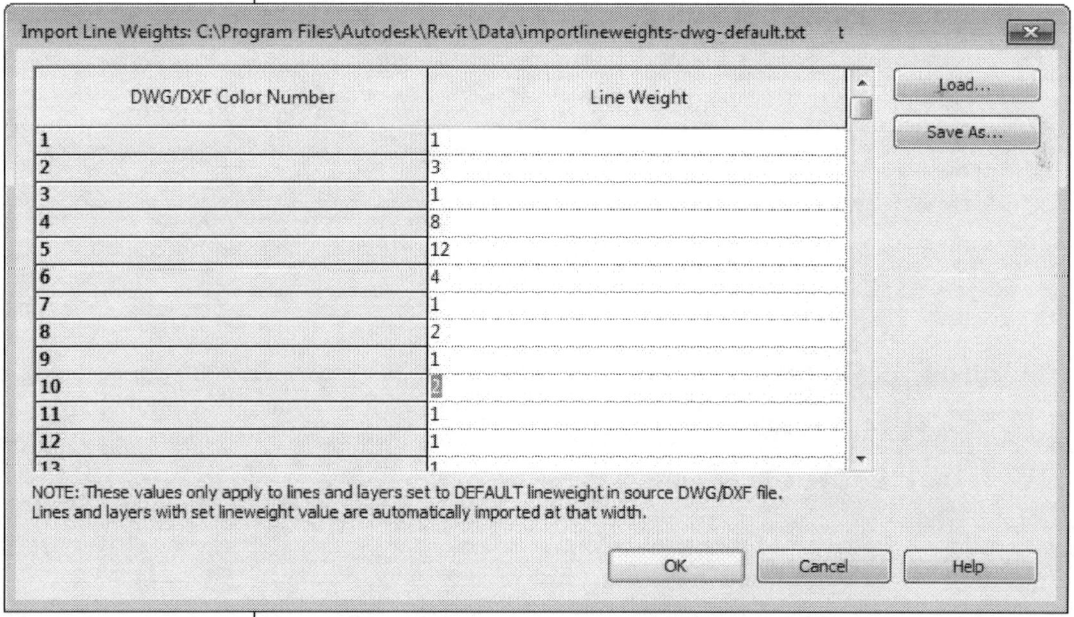

Figure 5–5

3. Click **OK** and then import the CAD file.

- To load information from an existing text file, click **Load...** and select the file that you want to use. Several files are included in the *Data* folder, as shown in Figure 5–6.

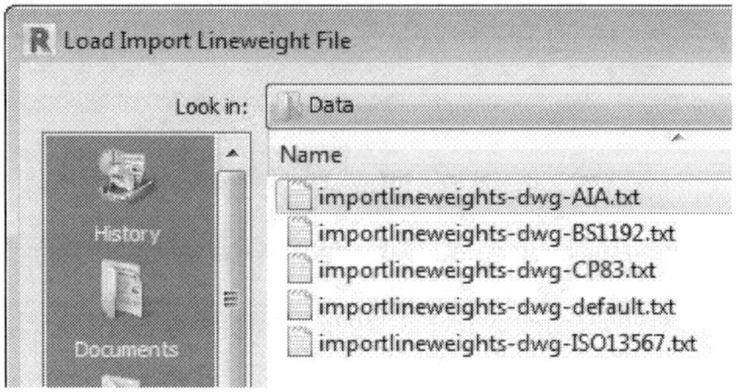

Figure 5–6

- To create a custom text file for specific projects, set up a sequence and click **Save As...**.
- Save your custom import line weight text files to a folder that is accessible to everyone that might need to use it. Do not save any custom files to the Autodesk Revit folders because they might be deleted if the program is upgraded or reinstalled.

Hint: Linking AutoCAD Civil 3D DWG Files

AutoCAD Civil 3D creates DWG files but the process of using them accurately in Autodesk Revit requires some extra steps. The Project Base Point in Revit is basically the same as the 0,0,0 origin point in an AutoCAD DWG. However, Civil 3D files typically use real world site locations established by surveyors. You can request a reference point (Northing, Easting, Elevation) from the civil engineer and add that information to the Survey Point in the Revit project before linking the site into the model.

Working with Other File Formats

There are additional file formats that can be opened or linked into Autodesk Revit projects, including IFC (Industry Foundation Class) elements, ADSK (Autodesk Exchange) files and point clouds.

IFC (Industry Foundation Classes)

The IFC specification is an international data neutral format. Models created in any building design program can be saved or exported to this file format. You can open IFC files directly (Application Menu>Open> (IFC)) or link them into the current project (in the *Insert* tab>Link panel, click (Link IFC)).

- If you are opening an IFC file, first setup the default template and manage the mapping of IFC classes to Revit Categories (Application Menu>Open> (IFC Options).
- Autodesk Revit models can be exported to IFC.

Autodesk Exchange Files

Building Component files, such as the blower created in Inventor shown in Figure 5–7, can be imported as a family into an Autodesk Revit project. They display the real size of the equipment and can also include connectors to related MEP elements. They must first be saved in the original program as an Autodesk® Exchange (ADSK) file.

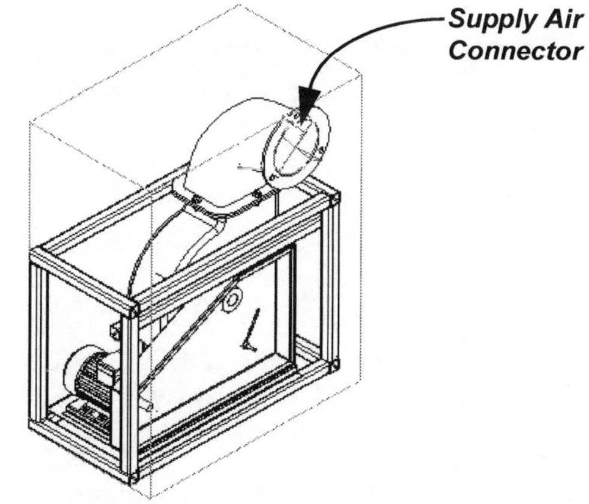

Figure 5–7

- To use an ADSK file, first load it into the project (*Insert* tab> Load from Library panel, click (Load Family)) and then use the **Component** command to place it.

- ADSK files can be saved as an RFA family file. In the Application Menu, expand (Open), expand (Building Component) and select the ADSK file to open. Then, in the Application Menu, expand (Save As) and click (Family).

Point Clouds

Point clouds are created using 3D laser scanners and are frequently used to establish accurate existing information. Once you link a point cloud (in the *Insert* tab>Link panel click (Point Cloud)) into a project, as shown in Figure 5–8, you can snap to alignment planes and individual points.

Figure 5–8

There are three file formats that you can link:

- **RCS** - Individual indexed scanned models.
- **RCP** - Groups of indexed scanned models.
- **Raw** - Non-indexed scans from multiple types of scanners.

Enhanced in **2017**

- If you are using one of the raw formats, Revit will automatically index it. You will then need to return to the original command to load the new RCS or RCP.

Practice 5a

Work with Vector Files - Architectural

Practice Objective

- Import an AutoCAD file into an Autodesk Revit project and use it as a basis to add elements for a hybrid drawing.

In this practice you will create a hybrid CAD/Autodesk Revit project for an addition to an existing building. You will import an AutoCAD file into a project and add some Autodesk Revit elements, as shown in Figure 5–9.

Estimated time for completion: 5 minutes

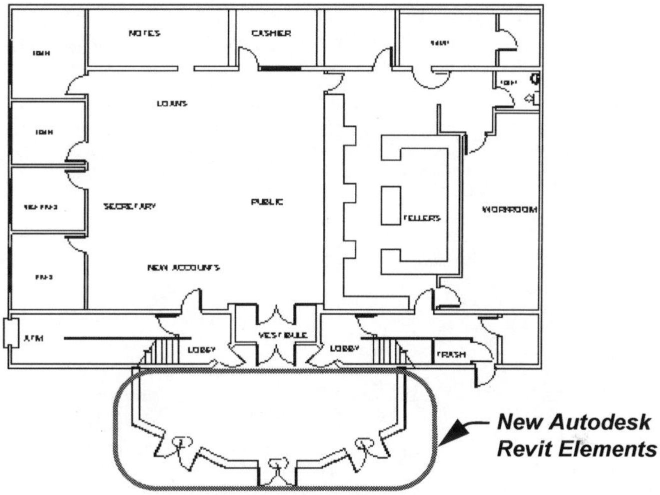

Figure 5–9

Task 1 - Import a CAD file.

1. Start a new project based on the Architectural template.
2. Verify that you are in the **Floor Plans: Level 1** view.

The CAD file is not going to change. So you can Import rather than link this file.

3. In the *Insert* tab>Import panel, click (Import CAD).

4. In the Import CAD dialog box, in the practice files folder, select the AutoCAD drawing file **Bank-Existing.dwg** and set the following options:

    - Select **Current View Only**.
    - *Colors*: **Black and White**
    - *Layers:* **All**
    - *Import Units:* **Auto-Detect**
    - Select **Correct lines that are slightly off axis**.
    - *Positioning*: **Auto-Center to Center**

5. Click **Open**.

6. Switch to an elevation view. No elements are in that view—the imported information is 2D only.

7. Switch back to the **Floor Plans: Level 1** view.

8. Use the outline to draw walls (with a Height to Level 2). Add doors and windows in front of the existing entrance of the building as a new entrance, similar to that shown in Figure 5–10.

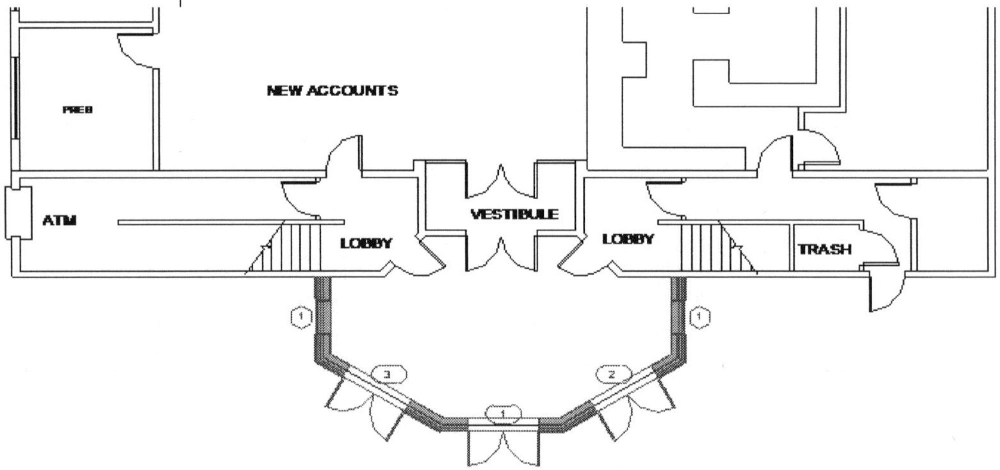

Figure 5–10

9. Switch to the **Elevations (Building Elevations): South** view. You should see the Autodesk Revit objects in the view.

10. Save the project as **Bank Addition Architectural.rvt**.

Practice 5b

Work with Vector Files - Structural

Practice Objective

- Import an AutoCAD file into an Autodesk Revit project and use it as a basis to add elements for a hybrid drawing.

Estimated time for completion: 5minutes

In this practice you will create a hybrid CAD/Autodesk Revit project for an addition to an existing building. You will import an AutoCAD file into a project and add some Autodesk Revit elements, as shown in Figure 5–11.

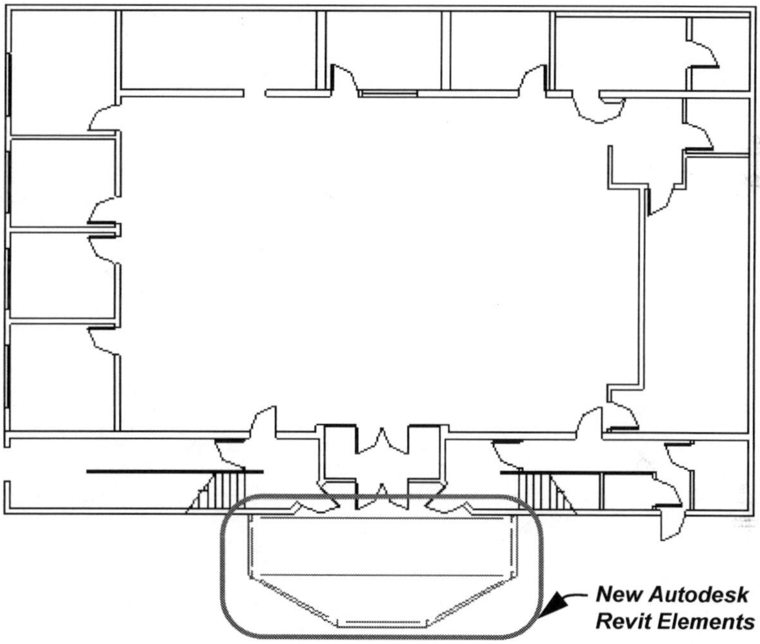

Figure 5–11

Task 1 - Import a CAD file.

1. Start a new project based on the Structural template.
2. Verify that you are in the **Structural Plans: Level 2** view.
3. In the *Insert* tab>Import panel, click  (Import CAD).

4. In the Import CAD dialog box, in the practice files folder, select the AutoCAD drawing file **Bank-Existing.dwg** and set the following options:
   - Select **Current View Only**.
   - *Colors*: **Black and White**
   - *Layers:* **All**
   - *Import Units:* **Auto-Detect**
   - Select **Correct lines that are slightly off axis**.
   - *Positioning*: **Auto-Center to Center**
5. Click **Open**.
6. Switch to an elevation view. No elements are in that view—the imported information is 2D only.
7. Switch back to the **Structural Plans: Level 2** view.
8. Select the imported CAD file and change it to half-tone.
9. Add columns (with a *Depth* set to **Level 1**) and beams to the top of them using the outline in front of the existing entrance of the building for a new entrance, similar to that shown in Figure 5–12.

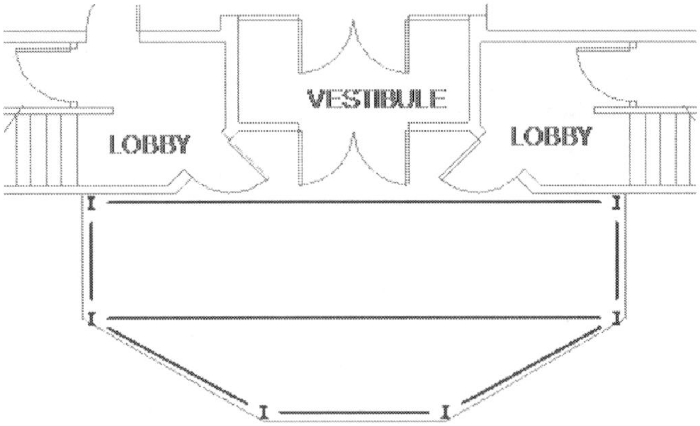

Figure 5–12

10. Switch to the **Elevations (Building Elevations): South** view. You should see the Autodesk Revit objects in the view.
11. Save the project as **Bank Addition Structural.rvt**.

Practice 5c

Work with Vector Files - MEP

Practice Objective

- Import an AutoCAD file into an Autodesk Revit project and use it as a basis to add elements for a hybrid drawing.

In this practice you will create a hybrid CAD/Autodesk Revit project for an addition to an existing building. You will import an AutoCAD file and link an Autodesk Revit model into a project and add some Autodesk Revit elements, as shown in Figure 5–13.

Estimated time for completion: 5 minutes

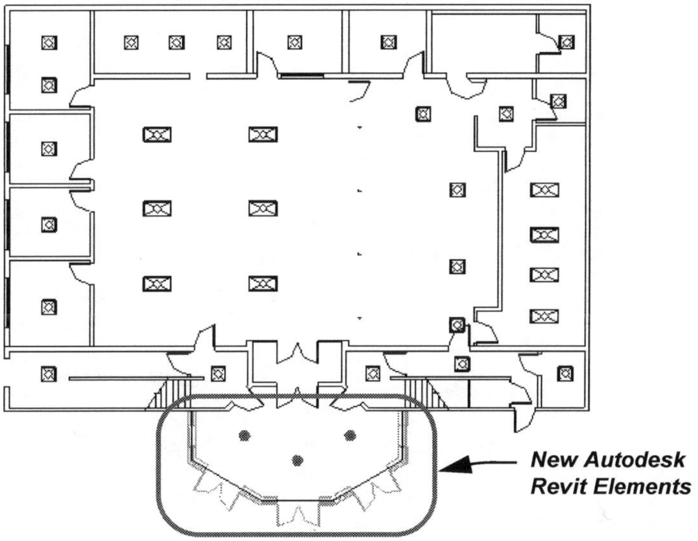

Figure 5–13

Task 1 - Import a CAD file.

1. Start a new project based on the Electrical or Systems template. (To access these templates, in the New Project dialog box, click **Browse...** and select the required template from the Autodesk Revit templates library.)
2. Open the Electrical>Lighting> **Floor Plans: 1- Lighting** view.
3. In the *Insert* tab>Import panel, click (Import CAD).

4. In the Import CAD dialog box, in the practice files folder, select the AutoCAD drawing file **Bank-MEP.dwg** and set the following options:
   - Select **Current View Only**.
   - *Colors*: **Black and White**
   - *Layers:* **All**
   - *Import Units:* **Auto-Detect**
   - Select **Correct lines that are slightly off axis**.
   - *Positioning*: **Auto-Center to Center**
5. Click **Open**.
6. Switch to an elevation view. No elements are in that view—the imported information is 2D only.
7. Switch back to the **Floor Plans: 1 - Lighting** view.
8. Link in the Autodesk Revit model, **Bank-Addition-A**.rvt from your practice files folder using Origin - to - Origin positioning.
9. Open the Electrical>Lighting>Ceiling Plans>**1 - Ceiling Elec** view. The linked Autodesk Revit elements display in this view but the imported CAD elements do not.
10. Add several new lights in the new entry area similar to that shown in Figure 5–14. (This example uses pendant lights placed on the ceiling face.)

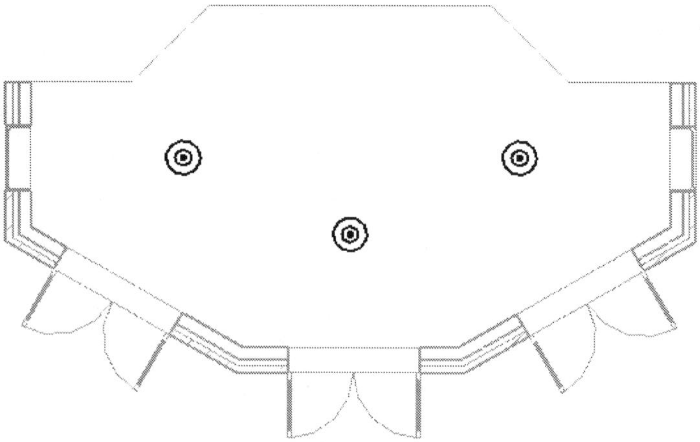

Figure 5–14

11. Switch to the **Elevations (Building Elevations): North- Elec** view. You should see the Autodesk Revit objects in the view.
12. Save the project as **Bank Addition-MEP.rvt**.

5.2 Linking Models

You can link an Autodesk® Revit® project into any other project. A linked model automatically updates if the original file is changed. This method can be used in many ways. For example, use this method when you have a number of identical buildings on one site plan, as shown in Figure 5–15.

The more links that are in a project, the longer it can take to open.

Figure 5–15

For architectural projects you can use links for multiple floors of one building that are identical to each other, or for repeated elements in a floor, such as identical room plans in a hospital, hotel, or apartment building. You can create one link and then copy the link to the host project.

Structural and MEP projects typically use the architectural model as the base for their projects. But there are times when an architect should link consultants files into the architectural file as well.

Standard practice on collaborative projects is that the architect and all consultants are on the same release.

- Architectural, structural, and MEP models created in the Autodesk® Revit® software can be linked to each other as long as they are from the same release cycle.
- When you use linked models, clashes between disciplines can be detected, and information can be passed between disciplines.
- Elements can be copied and monitored for even better coordination.

- Linked models can be constrained to elements in the host project and to each other. You can select references in linked models as a work plane and can schedule elements from the linked model in the host project.

Hint: Project Base Point

The origin of a project coordinate system is specified by the project base point, as shown in Figure 5–16. This should be set early in the project and before you start linking files together. It can be (but is not always) connected with the Survey Point, which is set to exact survey information.

Figure 5–16

- Project base points and survey points are visible in the Site view of the default architectural template. You can toggle them on in any view. In the Visibility/Graphic Overrides dialog box, in the *Model Category* tab, expand the **Site** category.
- Spot Coordinates and Spot Elevations are relative to the project base point.

How To: Add a Linked Model to a Host Project

1. In the *Insert* tab>Link panel, click (Link Revit).
2. In the Import/Link RVT dialog box, select the file that you want to link. Before opening the file, set the *Positioning*, as shown in Figure 5–17.

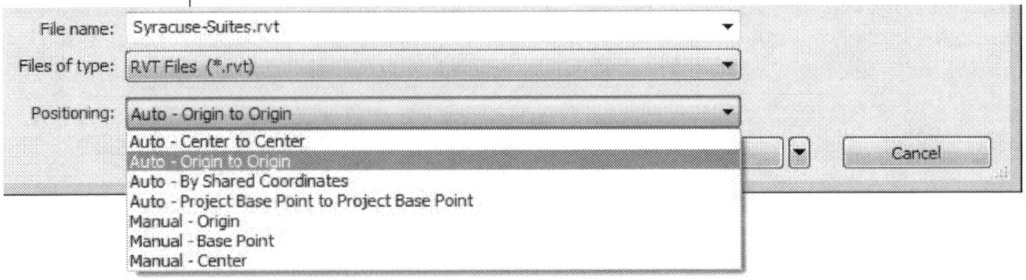

Figure 5–17

3. Click **Open**.
4. Depending on how you decide to position the file, it is automatically placed in the file or you can manually place it with the cursor.

- The default positioning is **Auto - Origin to Origin**. The center of a linked model is the center of the geometry. Therefore, if you modify the extents of the original model, its exact location changes in the host project if you link **Center to Center**.

New in 2017

- **Auto - Project BasePoint to Project Base Point** aligns the base points of the projects rather than the default origins.

- The software remembers the most recently used positioning type as long as you are in the same session of Autodesk Revit. (The CAD Links dialog box remembers the last positioning used as well, but separately from RVT Links)

- As the links are loading, do not click on the screen or click any buttons. The more links that are present in a project, the longer it takes to load.

New in 2017

- Linked models can be moved once you have placed them in the project. If you want to return them to the original location, right-click on the link and select either **Reposition to Project Base Point** or **Reposition to Internal Origin**, as shown in Figure 5–18

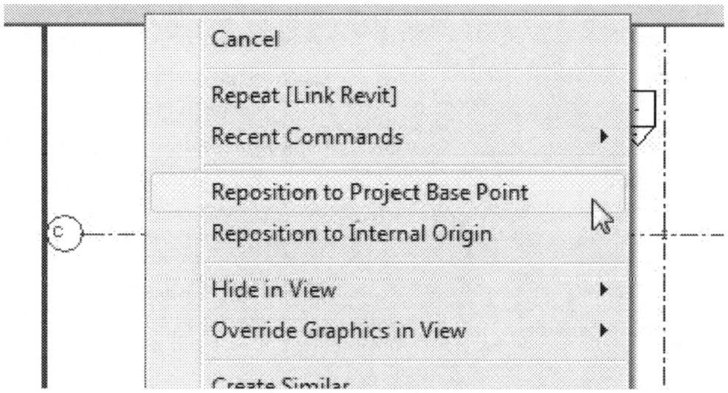

Figure 5–18

Hint: Preventing Linked Model from being moved

Once a linked model is in the correct location, you can lock it in place to ensure that it does not get moved by mistake, or prevent the linked model from being selected.

- To toggle off the ability to select links, in the Status Bar, click (Select Links).
- To pin the linked model in place, select it and in the *Modify* tab>Modify panel, click (Pin).
- To prevent pinned elements from being selected, in the Status Bar, click (Select Pinned Elements).

Multiple Copies of Links

Copied instances of a linked model are typically used when creating a master project with the same building placed in multiple locations, such as a university campus with several identical student residences.

- Linked models can be copied, rotated, arrayed, and mirrored.
- You only link a model once, but you can place as many copies as are required into the host project. The copies are numbered automatically, and the name can be changed in Properties when the instance is selected. There is only one linked model, and the copies are additional instances of that link.
- When you have placed a link in a project, you can use the Project Browser, as shown in Figure 5–19, to drag and drop additional copies of the link into the project.

Figure 5–19

Annotation and Linked Models

Many annotations can be added to the host model that reference elements in the linked model. For example, in Figure 5–20, the walls columns and grids are part of the linked model but the dimensions and tags are placed in the host project.

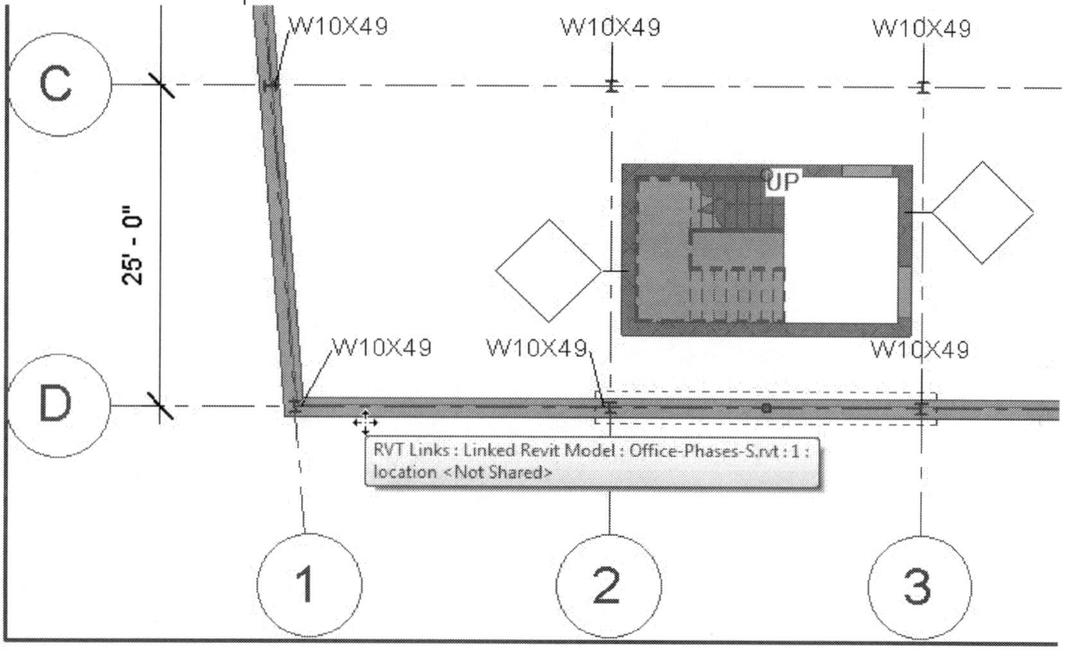

Figure 5–20

- Elements in the linked model can also be scheduled in the host project.

Managing Links

A linked model reloads each time the host project is opened. You can also reload the model by right-clicking on the Revit Link in the Project Browser, and then selecting **Reload** or **Reload From**, as shown in Figure 5–21.

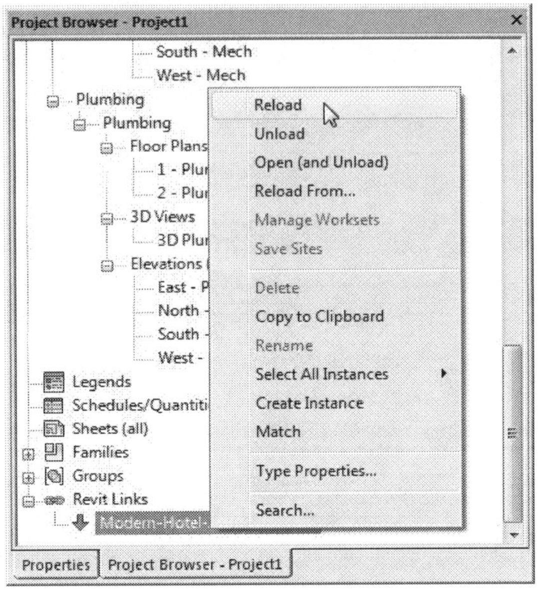

Figure 5–21

The Manage Links dialog box (shown in Figure 5–22) enables you to reload, unload, add, and remove links. Additionally, it provides access to other options. To open the Manage Links dialog box, in the *Insert* tab>Link, panel click (Manage Links). The Manage Links dialog box also displays when you select a link in the *Modify | RVT Links* tab.

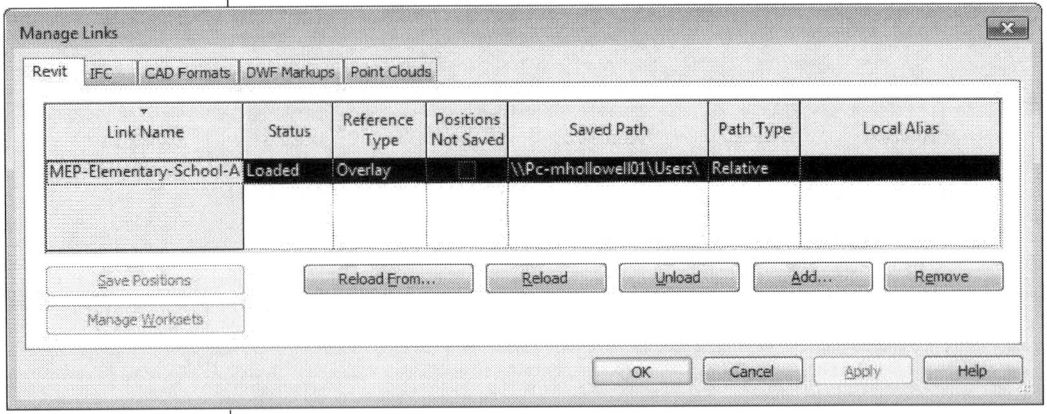

Figure 5–22

The options available in the Manage Links dialog box include the following:

- **Reload From:** Opens the Add Link dialog box, which enables you to select the file you want to reload. Use this if the linked file location or name has changed.
- **Reload:** Reloads the file without additional prompts.
- **Unload:** Unloads the file so that it the link is kept, but the file is not displayed or calculated in the project. Use **Reload** to restore it.
- **Add:** Opens the Import/Link RVT dialog box, which enables you to link additional models into the host project.
- **Remove:** Deletes the link from the file.

Links can be nested into one another. How a link responds when the host project is linked into another project depends on the option in the *Reference Type* column:

- **Overlay:** The nested linked model is not referenced in the new host project.
- **Attach:** The nested linked model displays in the new host project.

The option in the *Path Type* column controls how the location of the link is remembered:

- **Relative**
    - Searches the root folder of the current project.
    - If the file is moved, the software still searches for it.
- **Absolute**
    - Searches the entire file path where the file was originally saved.
    - If the original file is moved, the software is not able to find it.
- Other options control how the linked file interfaces with Worksets and Saved Positioning.
- In the Manage Links dialog box, when you have multiple links, you can sort rows by clicking the column header.

Linked Model Properties

Linked models have both instance properties and type properties. Instance Properties, as shown in Figure 5–23, include the *Name* for the individual copy of the link. This is automatically updated as you insert more than one. You can also change the name to help you identify it later. It also shows if it is part of a *Design Option* and if it is set to a *Shared Site*.

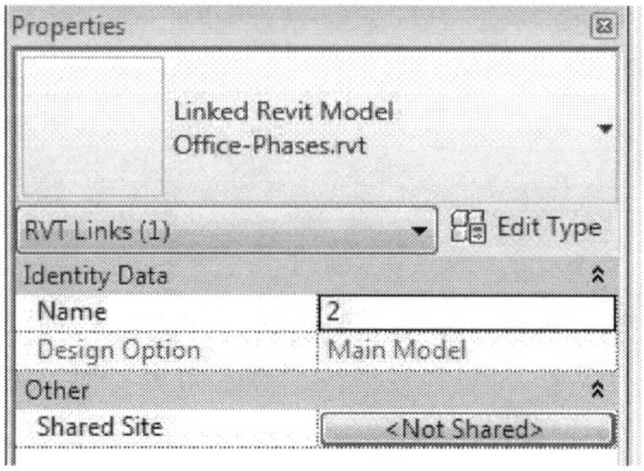

Figure 5–23

Type Properties, as shown in Figure 5–24, include *Room Bounding* which is required if you want to be able to place rooms or spaces from the information in the linked model. It also includes *Reference Type* (Overlay or Attachment) and *Phase Mapping*.

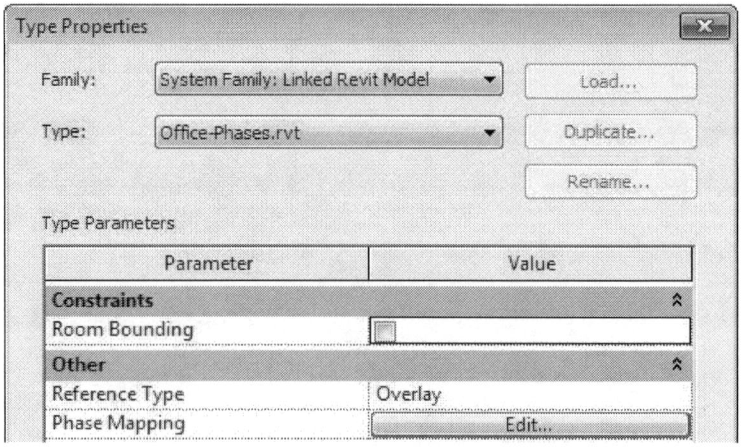

Figure 5–24

The phases in linked models can be mapped to the host project phasing so that the phasing schemes from different projects can be displayed consistently. Edit the Type Properties of the linked model and next to *Phase Mapping*, click **Edit...**. In the Phases dialog box, as shown in Figure 5–25, select the Phase from the linked model to match the corresponding phase in the host project.

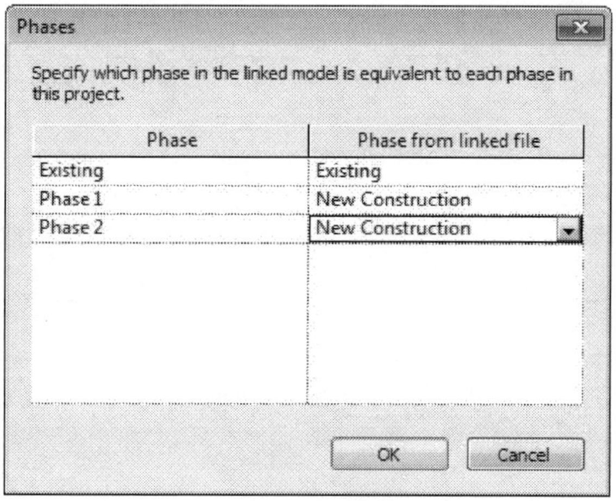

Figure 5–25

Practice 5d Link Models

Estimated time for completion: 10 minutes

Practice Objectives

- Link several models into a host project.
- Make copies of linked models in a project.

In this practice you will link architectural, structural, and MEP models into a host building site project. You will make copies of the linked models and place them on the site, as shown in Figure 5–26.

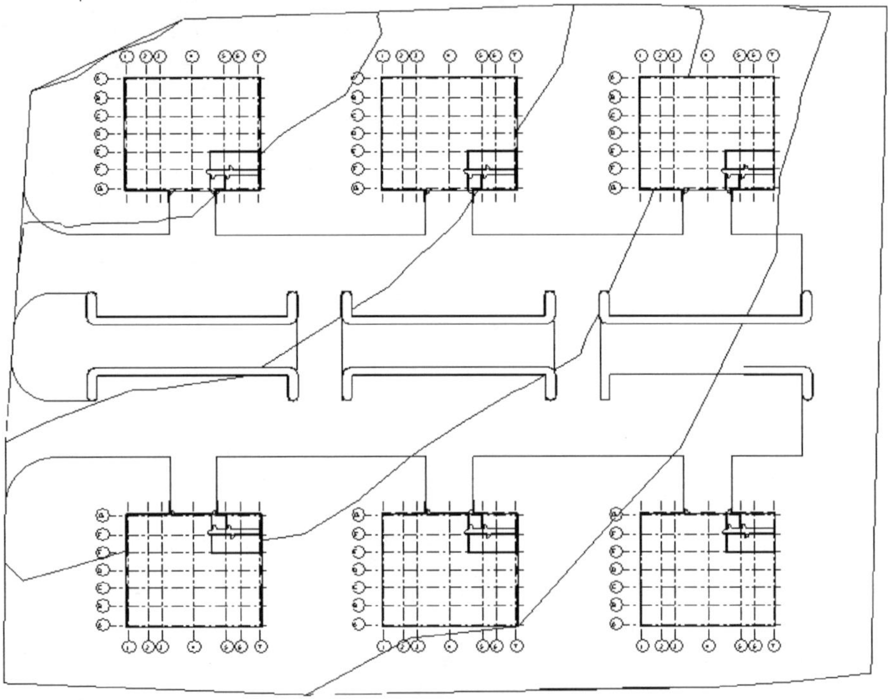

Figure 5–26

Task 1 - Link several models into a host project.

1. In the practice files folder, open **Industrial-Park.rvt**. The site has six rectangular pads for warehouse buildings.

2. In the *Insert* tab>Link panel, click (Link Revit).

The links do not come in directly on a pad. They need to be moved to the correct location.

3. In the Import/Link RVT dialog box, select the file **Industrial-Building-A.rvt**. Verify that the *Positioning* is set to **Auto - Origin to Origin.**
4. Click **Open**.
5. Select the new link. In Properties, verify that the *Name* of this instance is **1**. This makes tracking the rest of the instances easier.
6. Click (Link Revit) again and link in **Industrial-Building-MEP.rvt** at the same position.
7. An alert box opens, warning you that the model has another model linked to it and that it is not visible in this project. This is because it was linked in that file as an overlay rather than an attachment. Close the dialog box.
8. Repeat the process one more time and link in **Industrial-Building-S.rvt** at the same position.
9. Select all of the linked models that are on top of each other and move them to one of the pads at the top of the site. You might need to zoom in to place it precisely.
10. Copy the linked models to the other pads on the same side of the parking lot.
11. Mirror the links from the north side of the parking to the south side and move them into place, as shown in Figure 5–26.
12. Save the project.

Chapter Review Questions

1. Which of the following types of vector files can you import into the Autodesk Revit software? (Select all that apply.)
   a. DGN
   b. DWG
   c. DOC
   d. DXF
2. Which of the following settings can be specified before you import AutoCAD files (as shown in Figure 5–27) or Microstation files into a project?

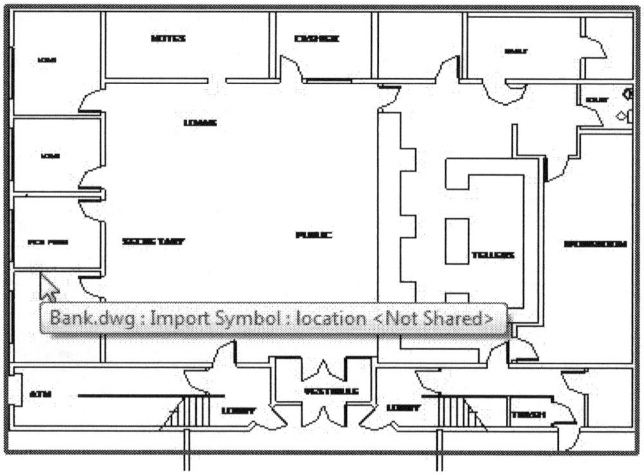

Figure 5–27

   a. Color to Line Weight
   b. Text and Dimension Styles
   c. Units
   d. Patterns

3. When linking an Autodesk Revit model into another project, which of the positioning methods keeps the model in the same place if the extents of the linked model changes in size?
    a. Auto - Center to Center
    b. Auto - Origin to Origin
    c. Manual - Basepoint
    d. Manual - Center

Command Summary

Button	Command	Location
	**Import CAD**	• **Ribbon**: *Insert* tab>Import panel
	**Link CAD**	• **Ribbon:** *Insert* tab>Link panel
	**Link Revit**	• **Ribbon:** *Insert* tab>Link Panel>Link Revit
	**Manage Links**	• **Ribbon**: *Insert* tab>Link panel> Manage Links or *Modify RVT Links* tab>Link panel>Manage Links (if selected)

Project Team Collaboration

Project team collaboration happens on many levels in a firm and between disciplines. When you have a very large project with more than one person working on that project at one time, you need to create and use worksets. Worksets enable you to work in one part of a project while someone else is working in another part of the same project. Not everyone needs to know how to set up worksets, but everyone can benefit from learning how to work with them.

Learning Objectives in this Chapter

- Understand worksharing workflow and definitions.
- Create and open a local file based on the central file.
- Synchronize a local file with the central file.
- Set the active workset and work in the local file.
- Request and approve permission to edit elements.
- Close the workshared project correctly.
- Control workset visibility by view.
- Investigate tips for using worksets,

6.1 Introduction to Worksets

When a project becomes too big for one person, it needs to be subdivided so that a team of people can work on it. Since Autodesk® Revit® projects include the entire building model in one file, the file needs to be separated into logical components (as shown in Figure 6–1), without losing the connection to the whole. This process is called "worksharing" and its main component is worksets.

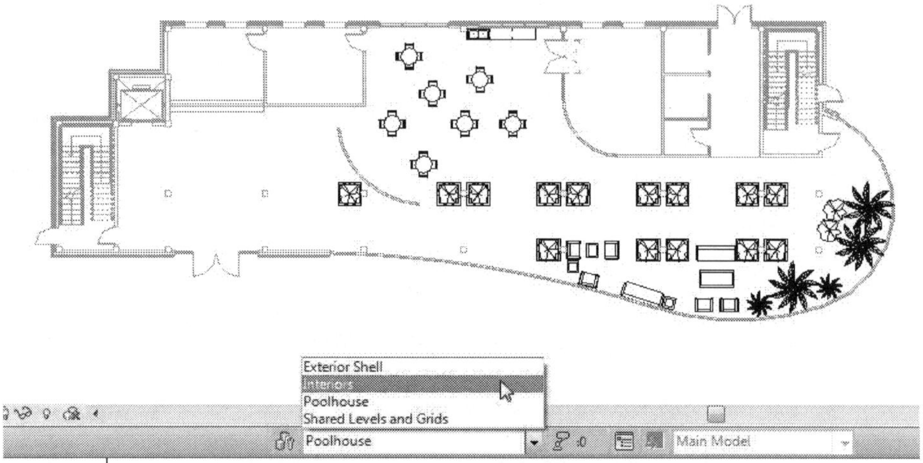

Figure 6–1

When worksets are established in a project, there is one **central file** and as many **local files** as required for each person on the team to have a file, as shown in Figure 6–2. All local files are saved back to the central file, and updates to the central file are sent out to the local files. This way, all changes remain in one file and all parts of the project, model views, and sheets are automatically updated.

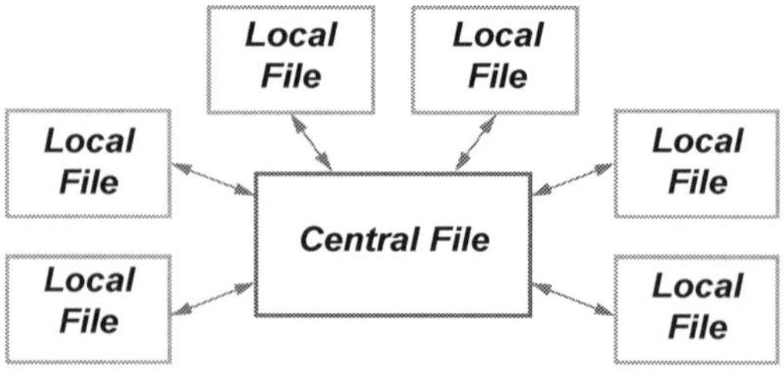

Figure 6–2

- The central file is created by the BIM Manager, Project Manager, or Project Lead, and stored on a server, enabling multiple user access.

Workset Definitions

Workset: A collection of related elements in a project. Each user-created workset matches a part of the project that an individual team member would work on (such as the exterior shell, site, or interior partitions). There are also worksets created automatically for Families, Project Standards (such as materials and line styles), and Views. Worksets can be checked out so that others cannot modify them without permission.

Central File: The main file that holds all of the worksets. This is the file to which everyone saves their changes. Typically, the file is not edited directly.

Local File: A copy of the central file that is saved to your local computer. This is the file that you modify. You then save the file locally and synchronize it with the central file.

Element borrowing: Refers to the process of modifying items in the project that are not part of the workset you have checked out. This either happens automatically (if no one else has checked out a workset), or specifically, when you request to have control of the elements (if someone else has a workset checked out).

General Process of Using Worksets

Close any worksets to which you do not need access. This saves system memory and frees up elements for other project team members to edit.

1. Create a local file from the central file that is set up by the project manager.
2. Open the local file and select the worksets on which you need to work.
3. Set a workset active. This is the workset on which any new elements are placed.
4. Add and modify elements, as required.
   - You may need to request access to elements in worksets that are currently checked out by other project team members.
5. Save the local file frequently as you would save any other project.
6. Synchronize the local file with the central file several times a day or as required by company policy or project status.
   - This reloads any changes from the central file to your local file and vice versa.
7. Save the local file every time you save to the central file.

6.2 Opening and Saving Workset-Related Projects

Some people recommend that you create a new local file every morning to ensure that you have the most up-to-date information.

The first step in using a workset-related project is to create a local file. This is the file you use to add and modify any of the elements in a project. Once you have a local file created, you can open it with only specific worksets opened. Local files are saved directly to your computer. You can also synchronize the local file with the central file.

How To: Create a Local File

1. Open the central file. This is typically on a server and might have "Central" in its name. Do not work in this file.
2. In the Open dialog box, when a central file is selected, use the **Create New Local** option, as shown in Figure 6–3.
3. Verify that it is selected and click **Open**.

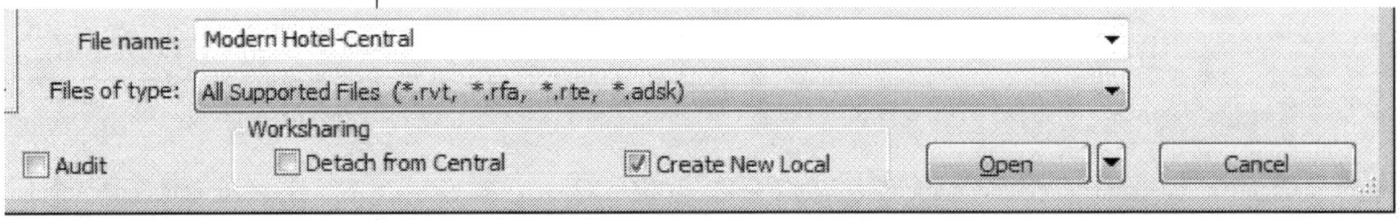

Figure 6–3

4. A copy of the project is created. It has the same name as the central file with Autodesk Revit *User Name* added to the end.
5. In the Quick Access Toolbar, click (Save) if you want to use the default filename (*Central File Name-Local*.rvt). Alternatively, in the Application Menu, select **File>Save As>Project** and name the file according to your office standard. It can include "Local" in the name to indicate that it is saved on your local computer or that you are the only one working with that copy of the file.
6. Click **Save**.

Hint: Setting the Username and Default File Location

The Autodesk Revit software checks the current *Username* to assign the local file name and determine which worksets are available for you to open after you create a local file. By default, it uses the login name you provided when you entered the operating system. You can change the *Username* in the Options dialog box (**Application Menu>Options**) in the *General* pane, as shown in Figure 6–4.

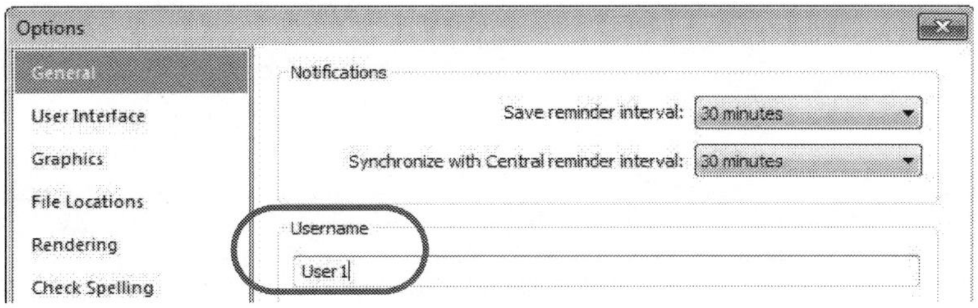

Figure 6–4

- This pane is also where you can set reminders to save and synchronize the local file with the central file.

In the *File Locations* pane, set the *Default path for user files*, as shown in Figure 6–5.

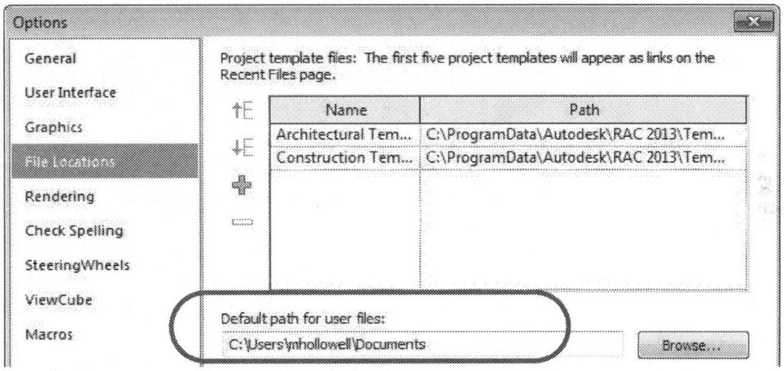

Figure 6–5

- This pane is also where you set location for project template files, family template files, and point cloud files.

How To: Open a Local File with Specific Worksets Editable

Once you have created a local file, you can open it with specific worksets editable.

1. Start the (Open) command.
2. In the Open dialog box, select the local file set up on your computer.
3. Click beside **Open** and select which worksets you want to open, as shown in Figure 6–6.

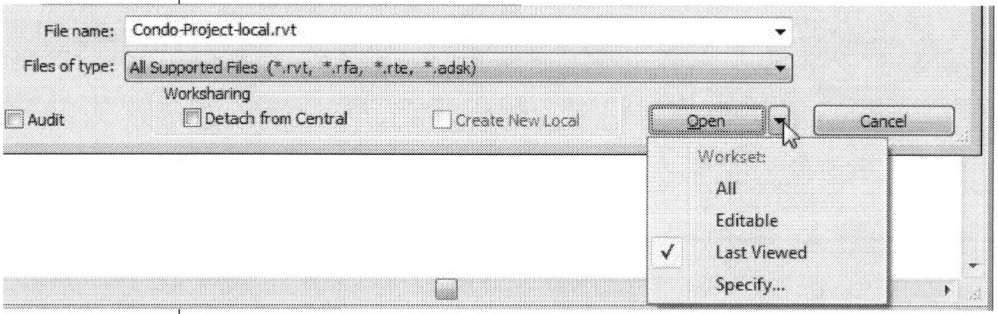

Figure 6–6

4. Click **Open**.

Open Worksets Options

All	Opens all worksets.
Editable	Opens all worksets that are editable (not checked out by someone else).
Last Viewed	Opens the worksets that were viewed last time you saved the local file. This is the default after the local file has been saved once.
Specify	Opens the Opening Worksets dialog box (once you click **Open**) where you select the worksets you want opened or closed.

Enhanced in **2017**

- A rarely used option, **Detach from Central**, opens the file and detaches it from the central file. The new file name automatically has "detached" appended to the end of the name. You can either detach and preserve worksets, which you can then save as a different central file, or detach and discard worksets and all the related elements which removes all worksharing options from the file.

How To: Specify Opened or Closed Worksets

If you select **Specify...** when you open a workset-related file, it opens the Opening Worksets dialog box.

1. In the Opening Worksets dialog box (shown in Figure 6–7), select the name of the workset you want to open or close.

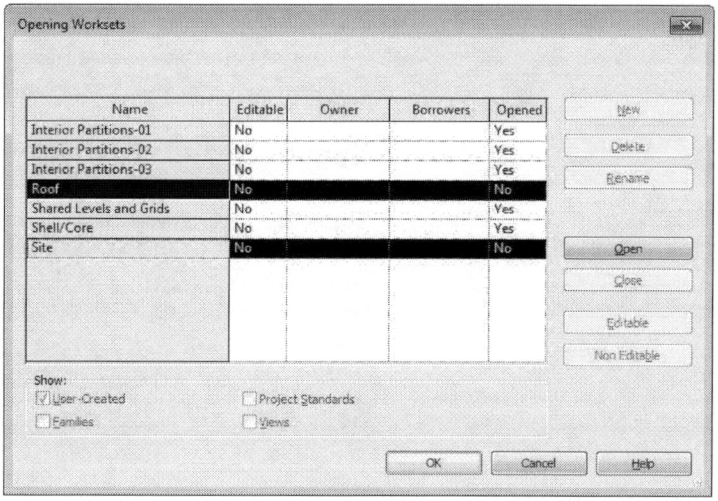

Figure 6–7

2. Click **Close** if a workset is opened and you want to close it. Click **Open** if a workset is closed and you want to open it.
3. Click **OK** to finish.

- You can select more than one workset by holding <Ctrl> or <Shift>. To select all of the worksets, press <Ctrl>+A.

Notes on Local Files

- When you open a local file, select only those worksets you need to open. Limiting the number of worksets speeds up the process of opening and saving the file.
- Only the user who created a local file should work on it, although others can open it. If you do open someone else's file, an alert box displays recommending that you change the user name or stop working on the file.
- If you try to save a file listed in someone else's name, you are alerted that it cannot be saved.

Saving Workset Related Files

To save workset-related files, you save them to your local machine as you would any other file. You also synchronize the file with the central file periodically and at the end of the day.

- Save the local file frequently (every 15-30 minutes). In the Quick Access Toolbar, click (Save) to save the local file as you would any other project.
- Synchronize to the central file periodically (every hour or two) or after you have made major changes to the project.

Synchronizing to the Central File

There are two methods for synchronizing to the central file.

Synchronize Now: Updates the central file and then the local file with any changes to the central file since the last synchronization without prompting you for any settings. It automatically relinquishes elements borrowed from any workset but retains worksets used by the current user.

The last used command is active if you click the top level icon.

- In the Quick Access Toolbar or *Collaborate* tab>Synchronize panel, expand (Synchronize and Modify Settings or Synchronize with Central), and click (Synchronize Now).

Synchronize and Modify Settings: Opens the Synchronize with Central dialog box, as shown in Figure 6–8, where you can set the location of the central file, add comments, save the file locally before and after synchronization, and set the options for relinquishing worksets and elements.

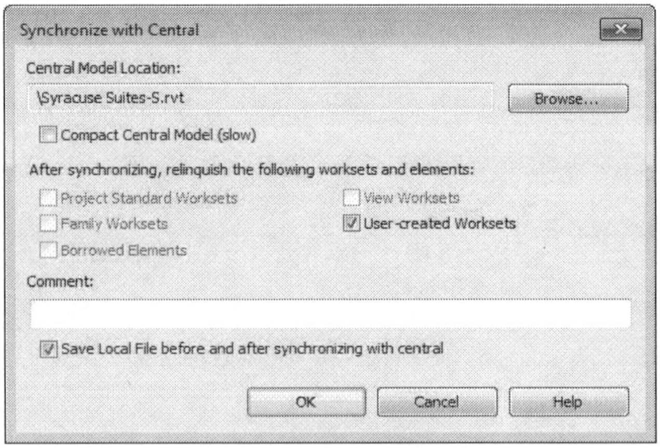

Figure 6–8

- In the Quick Access Toolbar or *Collaborate* tab>Synchronize panel, expand (Synchronize and Modify Settings or Synchronize with Central), and click (Synchronize and Modify Settings).
- Always save the local file after you have synchronized the file with central. Changes from the central file might have been copied into your file.
- When you close a local file without saving to the central file you are prompted to do so as shown in Figure 6–9.

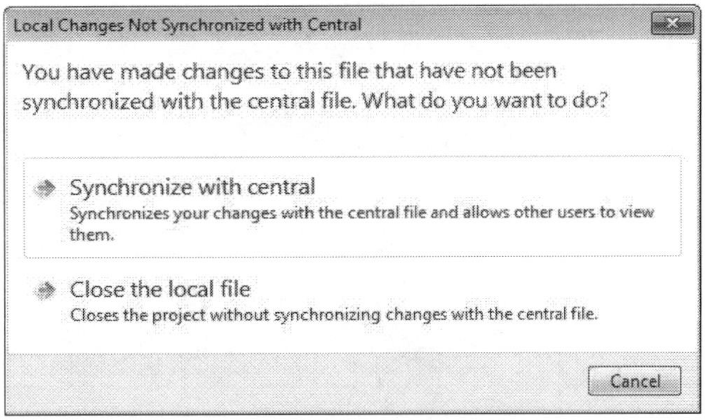

Figure 6–9

Hint: Save As Options

If you want to save the central file as a new central file, use **Save As**. In the Save As dialog box, click **Options...**. In the File Save Options dialog box, select **Make this a Central File after save**, as shown in Figure 6–10. This option is toggled off by default because you typically create local files from the central file.

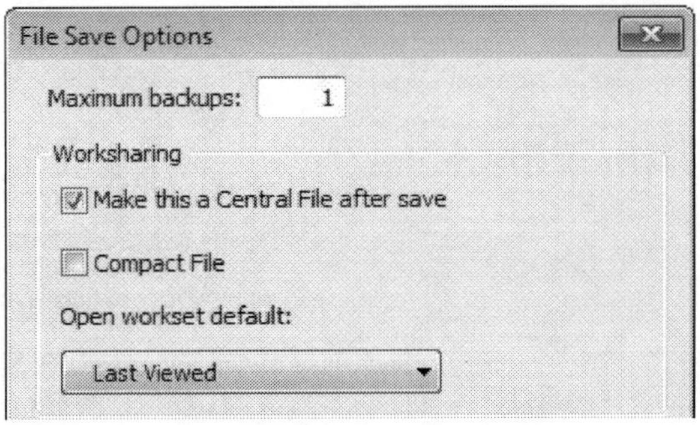

Figure 6–10

Practice 6a Open Workset-Related Projects - Architectural

Practice Objectives

- Set up two copies of the Autodesk Revit software with different user names.
- Update an existing central file for use in the practice.
- Create a local file of the central file from each copy of the software.

Estimated time for completion: 10 minutes

In this practice you create two local files using two different copies of the Autodesk Revit software. You open the local files and select specific worksets to open in each project, as shown in Figure 6–11.

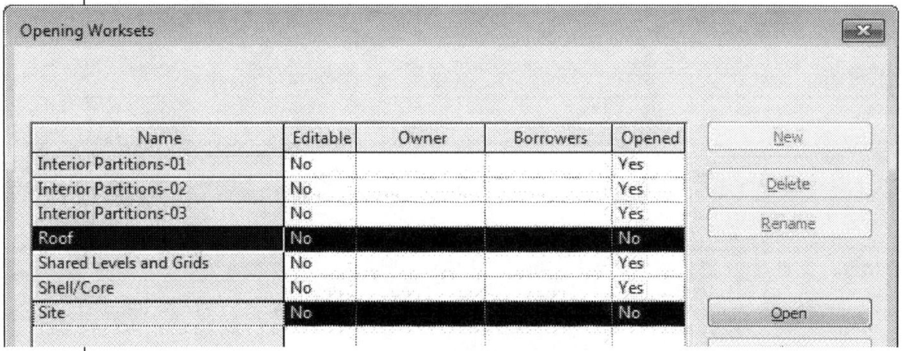

Figure 6–11

This practice uses a project that has been subdivided into worksets. To simulate a worksharing environment, you will open two sessions of the Autodesk Revit software and change the *Username* to **User1** and **User2**.

- **User1** focuses on the interiors of the condo units.
- **User2** focuses on the Exterior and Core.

Task 1 - Setup Two Copies of Autodesk Revit Using Different User Names.

1. Start the first copy of the Autodesk Revit software. You do not need to be in a project.
2. In the Application Menu, click **Options**.
3. In the Options dialog box, in the *General* tab, sign out of Autodesk® A360 if required, and change the *Username* to **User1**, as shown in Figure 6–12.

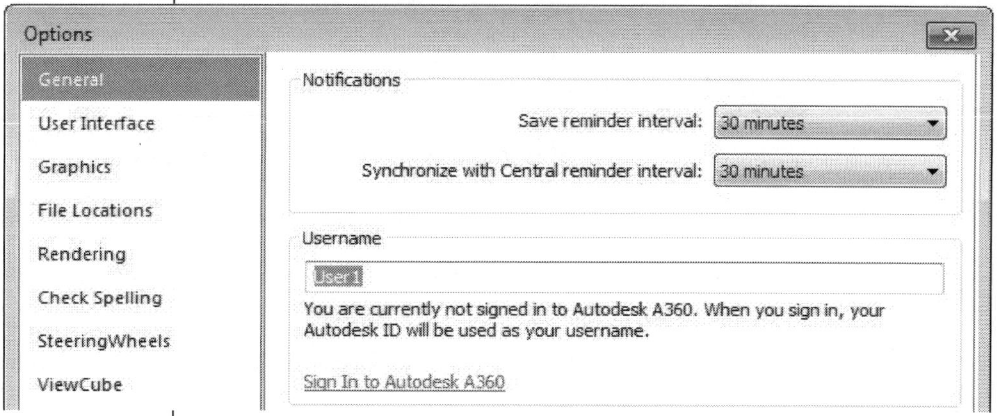

Figure 6–12

- Write down the existing name before you change it, so that you can return it to the original name at the end of these practices.

4. In the *File Locations* tab, change the *Default path for user files* to the practice files folder.
5. Click **OK** to close the dialog box.
6. Open a second copy of Autodesk Revit and repeat the steps above changing the *User Name* to **User 2**.

Task 2 - Update the Central File.

A central file needs to be repathed if it has been relocated. This typically does not happen in an office environment, but does in the training environment, depending on where the central file is saved.

1. Working in the **User1** copy of Autodesk Revit, in the Quick Access Toolbar, click (Open). In the practice files folder, open **Condo-Project-A.rvt**.
2. Alert boxes about a Copied Central Model display. Read and then close the alert boxes.
3. In the Application Menu, expand (Save As) and click (Project).
4. In the Save As dialog box, click **Options.**...
5. In the File Save Options dialog box, select **Make this a Central File after save** and then click **OK**.
6. Verify that the name is still set to **Condo-Project-A.rvt**, and then click **Save**.

7. When the Workset File Already Exists dialog box displays, click **Yes** to replace the existing file.
8. Close the project.

Task 3 - Create the Local File for User1.

1. Continue working in the **User1** copy of Autodesk Revit. In the Quick Access Toolbar, click (Open). In the practice files folder, open **Condo-Project-A.rvt**.
   - Do not select central files from the startup screen, as that opens the central file itself. Instead, use the **Open** command to create a new local file.
2. Verify that **Create New Local** is selected and click **Open**. A file with the name **Condo-Project-A_User1.rvt** is opened.
3. In the *Collaborate* tab>Manage Collaboration panel, click (Worksets) or in the Status Bar, click (Worksets).
4. In the Worksets dialog box, make **Interior Partitions-01** the Active Workset. Set *Editable* to **Yes** and select **Visible in all views** for this workset. Select the worksets **Roof** and **Site**. Click **Close** so that the worksets are not open in this session, as shown in Figure 6–13.

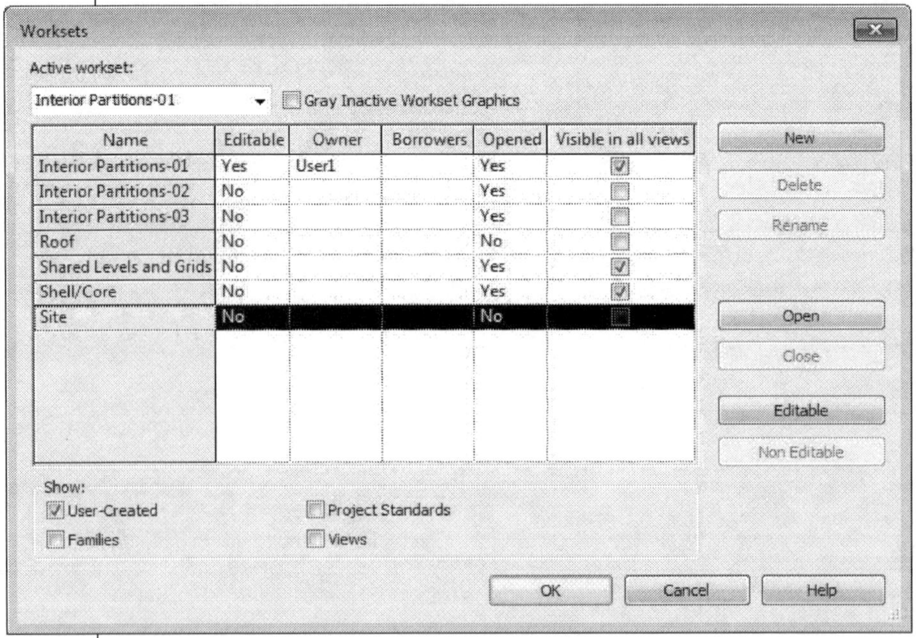

Figure 6–13

5. Click **OK** to finish.

6. In the Quick Access Toolbar, click (Save) to save the local file.

Task 4 - Create the Local File for User2.

1. Work in the **User2** copy of Autodesk Revit.

2. In the Quick Access Toolbar, click (Open) and select the file **Condo-Project-A.rvt**. Verify that **Create New Local** is selected, click the arrow next to **Open**, and select **Specify...** in the drop-down list, as shown in Figure 6–14.

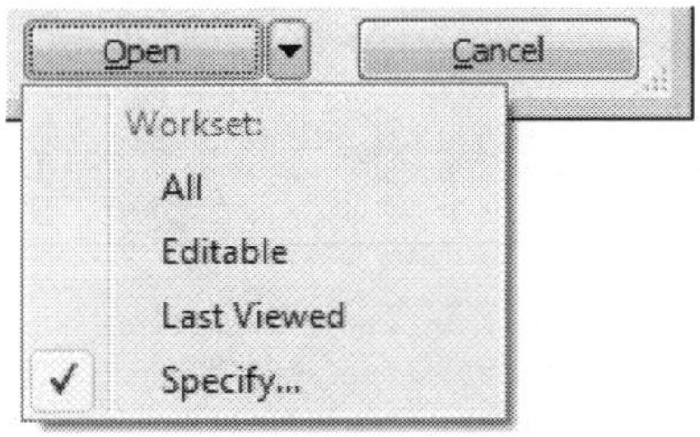

Figure 6–14

3. Click **Open** to open the project.

4. In the Opening Worksets dialog box, select the three **Interior Partition** worksets and click **Close** so that these worksets are not opened in this session, as shown in Figure 6–15.

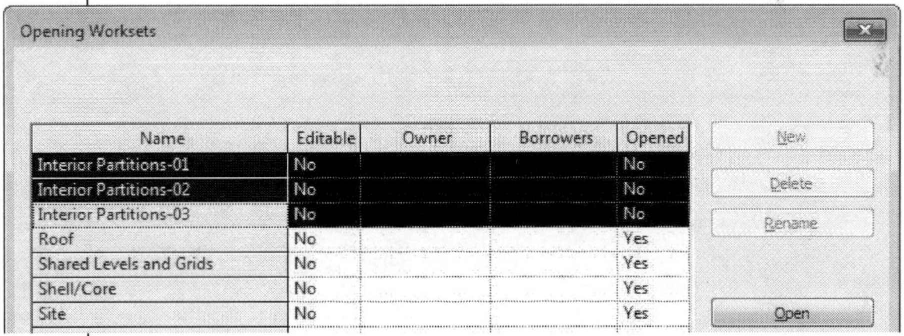

Figure 6–15

5. Click **OK** to finish. The file is opened and automatically named **Condo-Project-A_User2.rvt**.

6. Save the local file.

7. Leave both copies of the Autodesk Revit software open for the next practices.

Practice 6b Open Workset-Related Projects - Structural

Practice Objectives

- Set up two copies of the Autodesk Revit software with different user names.
- Update an existing central file for use in the practice.
- Create a local file of the central file from each copy of the software.

Estimated time for completion: 10 minutes

In this practice you create two local files using two different copies of the Autodesk Revit software. You open the local files and select specific worksets to open in each project, as shown in Figure 6–16.

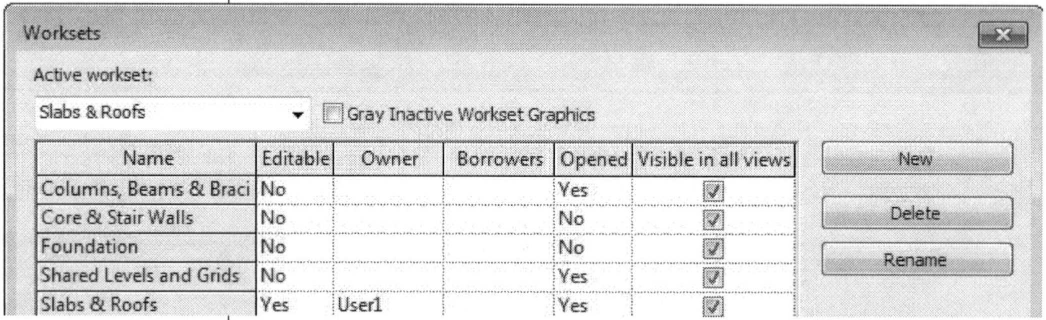

Figure 6–16

This practice uses a project that has been subdivided into worksets. To simulate a worksharing environment, you will open two sessions of the Autodesk Revit software and change the **Username** to **User1** and **User2**.

- **User1** focuses on the floor slabs.
- **User2** focuses on the core and stair walls.

Task 1 - Setup Two Copies of Autodesk Revit Using Different User Names.

1. Start the first copy of the Autodesk Revit software. You do not need to be in a project.
2. In the Application Menu, click **Options**.

3. In the Options dialog box, in the *General* tab, sign out of Autodesk A360 if required, and change the *Username* to **User1**, as shown in Figure 6–17.

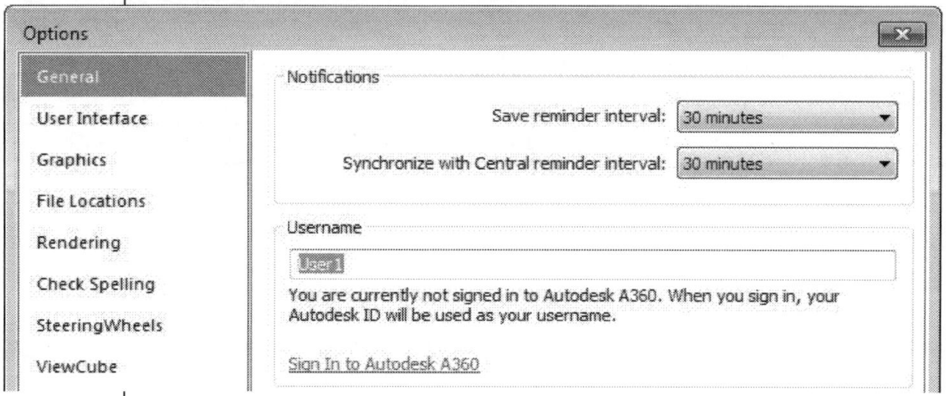

Figure 6–17

- Write down the existing name before you change it, so that you can return to the original name at the end of these practices.

4. In the *File Locations* tab, change the *Default path for user files* to the practice files folder.
5. Click **OK** to close the dialog box.
6. Open a second copy of Autodesk Revit and repeat the steps above changing the *User Name* to **User 2**.

Task 2 - Update the Central File.

1. Working in the **User1** copy of Autodesk Revit, in the Quick Access Toolbar, click (Open). In the practice files folder, open **Syracuse-Suites-S.rvt**.

A central file needs to be repathed if it has been relocated. This typically does not happen in an office environment, but does in the training environment, depending on where the central file is saved.

2. Alert boxes about a Copied Central Model display. Read and then close the alert boxes.
3. In the Application Menu, expand (Save As) and click (Project).
4. In the Save As dialog box, click **Options...**.
5. In the File save Options dialog box, select **Make this a Central File after save**, and then click **OK**.

6. Verify that the name is still set to **Syracuse-Suites-S.rvt** and then click **Save**.

7. When the Worksets File Already Exists dialog box displays, click **Yes** to replace the existing file.

8. Close the project.

Task 3 - Create the Local File for User1.

1. Continue working in the **User1** copy of Autodesk Revit. In the Quick Access Toolbar, click (Open). In the practice files folder, open **Syracuse-Suites-S.rvt**.
   - Do not select central files from the startup screen as it opens the central file directly. Instead, use the **Open** command and create a new local file.

2. Verify that **Create New Local** is selected and click **Open**. A file with the name **Syracuse-Suites-S_User1.rvt** is opened.

3. In the *Collaborate* tab>Manage Collaboration panel, click (Worksets) or in the Status Bar, click (Worksets).

4. In the Worksets dialog box, make **Slabs & Roofs** the Active Workset. Set *Editable* to **Yes** and select **Visible in all views** for this workset. Select the **Core & Stair Walls** and **Foundation** worksets. Click Close so the worksets are not open in this session, as shown in Figure 6–18.

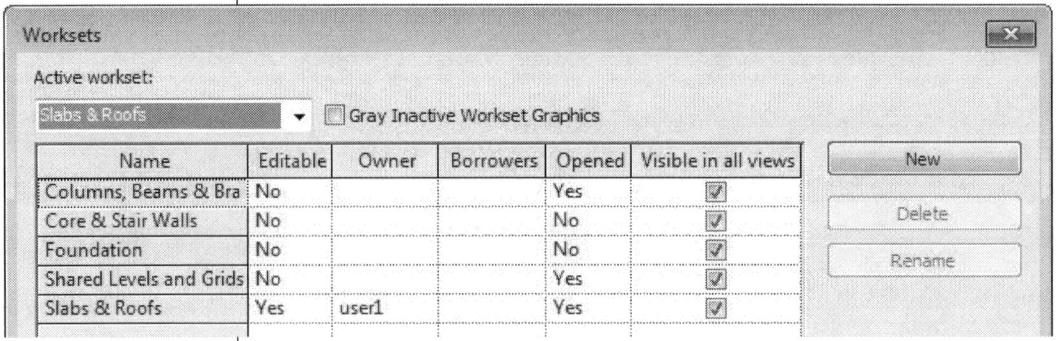

Figure 6–18

5. Click **OK** to finish.

6. In the Quick Access Toolbar, click (Save) to save the local file.

Task 4 - Create the Local File for User2.

1. Work in the **User2** copy of Autodesk Revit.

2. In the Quick Access Toolbar, click  (Open) and select the file **Syracuse-Suites-S.rvt**. Verify that **Create New Local** is selected, click the arrow next to **Open**, and select **Specify...** in the drop-down list, as shown in Figure 6–19.

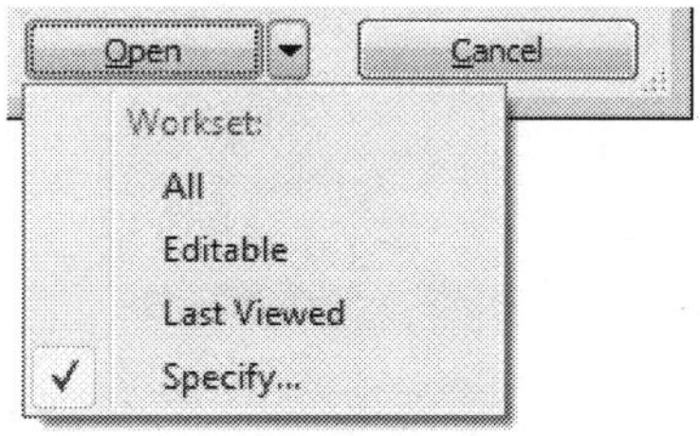

Figure 6–19

3. Click **Open** to open the project.

4. In the Opening Worksets dialog box, select the **Columns, Beams & Bracing**, and **Slabs & Roofs** worksets and click **Close** so these worksets are not opened in this session, as shown in Figure 6–20.

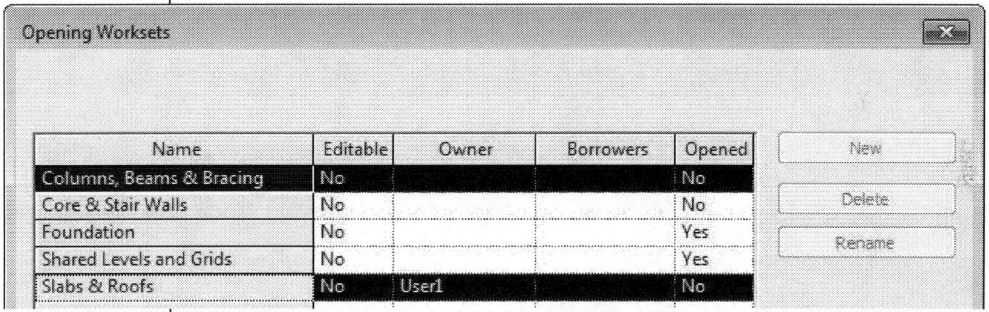

Figure 6–20

5. Click **OK** to finish. The file is opened and automatically named **Syracuse-Suites-S_User2.rvt**.

6. Save the local file.

7. Leave both copies of the Autodesk Revit software open for the next practices.

Practice 6c Open Workset-Related Projects - MEP

Practice Objectives

- Set up two copies of the Autodesk Revit software with different user names.
- Update an existing central file for use in the practice.
- Create a local file of the central file from each copy of the software.

Estimated time for completion: 10 minutes

In this practice you create two local files using two different copies of the Autodesk Revit software. You open the local files and select specific worksets to open in each project, as shown in Figure 6–21.

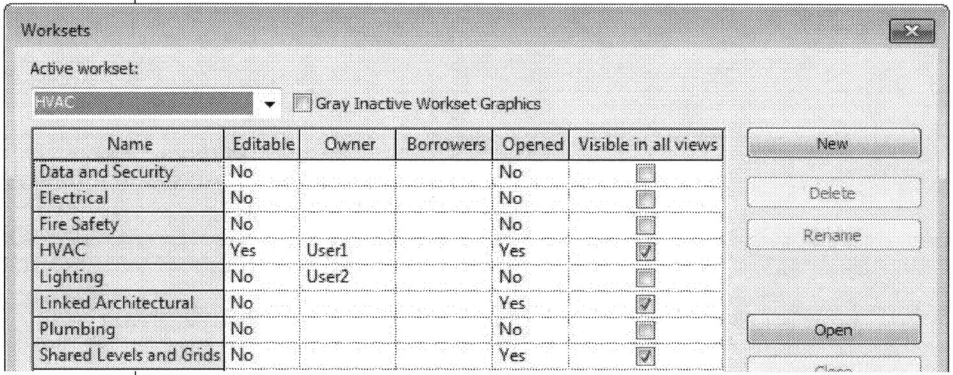

Figure 6–21

This practice uses a project that has been subdivided into worksets. To simulate a worksharing environment, you will open two sessions of the Autodesk Revit software and change the **Username** to **User1** and **User2**.

- **User1** focuses on the HVAC portion of the project.
- **User2** focuses on the Lighting portion of the project.

Task 1 - Setup Two Copies of Autodesk Revit Using Different User Names.

1. Start the first copy of the Autodesk Revit software. You do not need to be in a project.
2. In the Application Menu, click **Options**.

3. In the Options dialog box, in the *General* tab, sign out of Autodesk A360 if required, and change the *Username* to **User1**, as shown in Figure 6–22.

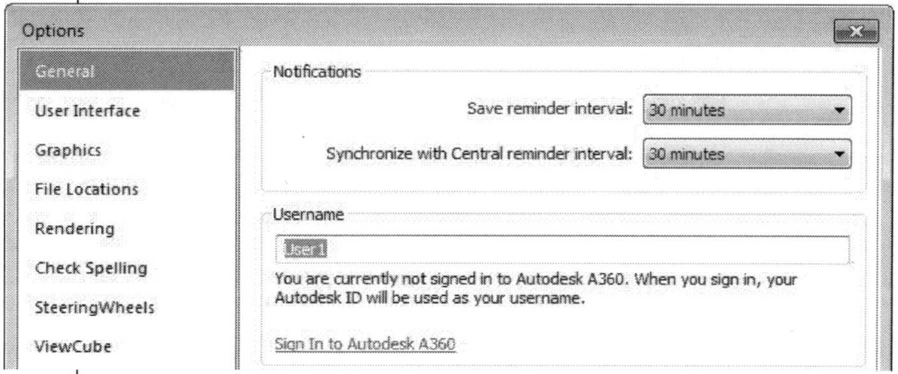

Figure 6–22

- Write down the existing name before changing it, so that you can return to the original name at the end of these practices.

4. In the *File Locations* tab, change the *Default path for user files* to the practice files folder.

5. Click **OK** to close the dialog box.

6. Open a second copy of Autodesk Revit and repeat the steps above, changing the *User Name* to **User 2**.

Task 2 - Update the Central File

1. Working in the **User1** copy of Autodesk Revit, in the Quick Access Toolbar, click (Open). In the practice files folder, open **Elementary-School-MEP.rvt**.

A central file needs to be repathed if it has been relocated. This typically does not happen in an office environment, but does in the training environment, depending on where the central file is saved.

2. Alert boxes about a Copied Central Model display. Read and then close the alert boxes.

3. In the Application Menu, expand (Save As) and click (Project).

4. In the Save As dialog box, click **Options...**.

5. In the File save Options dialog box, select **Make this a Central File after save** and then click **OK**.

6. Verify that the name is still set to **Elementary-School-MEP.rvt** and then click **Save**.

7. When the Workset File Already Exists dialog box displays, click **Yes** to replace the existing file.

8. Close the project.

Task 3 - Create the Local File for User1.

1. Continue working in the **User1** copy of Autodesk Revit. In the Quick Access Toolbar, click (Open). In the practice files folder, open **Elementary-School-MEP.rvt**.

   - Do not select central files from the startup screen as it opens the central file directly. Instead, use the **Open** command and create a new local file.

2. Verify that **Create New Local** is selected and click **Open**. A file with the name **Elementary-School-MEP_User1.rvt** is opened.

3. In the *Collaborate* tab>Manage Collaboration panel, click (Worksets) or in the Status Bar, click (Worksets).

4. In the Worksets dialog box, make **HVAC** the Active Workset. Set *Editable* to **Yes** and select **Visible in all views** for this workset.

5. Select all the other worksets except **Linked Architectural** and **Shared Levels and Grids**. Click **Close** so that the worksets are not open in this session, as shown in Figure 6–23.

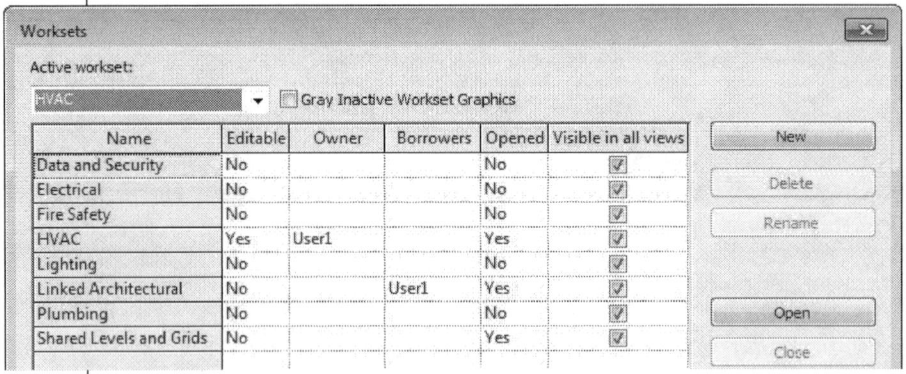

Figure 6–23

6. Click **OK** to finish.

7. In the Quick Access Toolbar, click (Save) to save the local file.

Task 4 - Create the Local File for User2.

1. Work in the **User2** copy of Autodesk Revit.

2. In the Quick Access Toolbar, click  (Open) and select the file **Elementary-School-MEP.rvt**. Verify that **Create New Local** is selected, click the arrow next to **Open**, and select **Specify...** in the drop-down list, as shown in Figure 6–24.

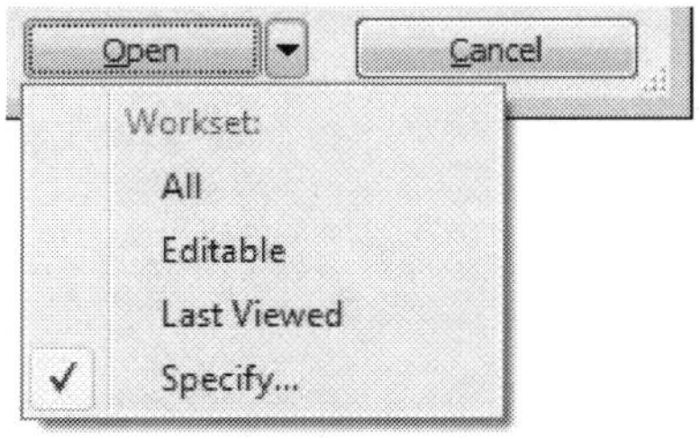

Figure 6–24

3. Click **Open** to open the project.

4. In the Opening Worksets dialog box, select **Data and Security**, **Fire Safety**, **HVAC**, and **Plumbing** worksets and click **Close** so that these worksets are not opened in this session, as shown in Figure 6–25.

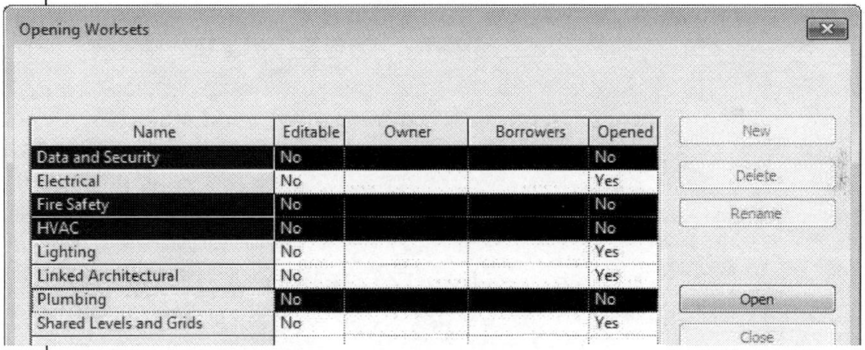

Figure 6–25

5. Click **OK** to finish. The file is opened and automatically named **Elementary-School-MEP_User2.rvt**.

6. Save the local file.

7. Leave both copies of the Autodesk Revit software open for the next practices.

6.3 Working in Workset-Related Projects

Most of the work you do in a workset is no different to working in any other project. You draw and modify elements. You create views, sheets, and schedules. You even create families and modify family types, if you have permissions to do so.

Several workset-specific methods and tools can increase your effectiveness as you work. You can edit elements in worksets that you have not checked out, check out worksets, request and receive editing permissions, and save the worksets locally and to the central file.

- Once you are in a workset-related project, select the *Collaborate* tab, as shown in Figure 6–26. The workset-related tools are in the Worksets and Synchronize panels.

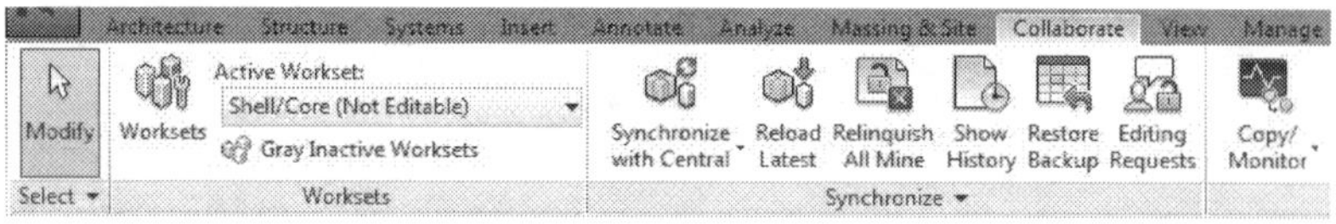

Figure 6–26

Setting the Active Workset

When new elements are added to the project, they are placed on the active workset. It is therefore important to set the active workset correctly before adding new elements. Not doing so can result in visibility and permissions-related issues.

How To: Set the Active Workset

1. Open your local file.
2. In the Status Bar, expand the *Active Workset* list and select a workset, as shown in Figure 6–27.

You can also set the active workset in the Collaborate tab>Manage Collaboration panel.

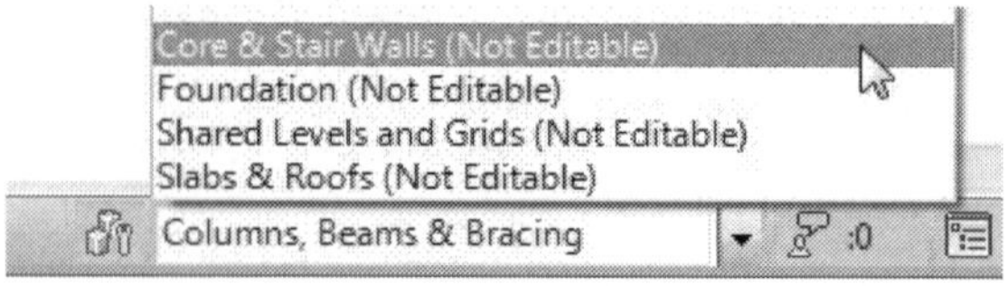

Figure 6–27

- It does not matter if the workset says (**Not Editable**); you can still add elements to it. **Not Editable** means that you have not checked out the workset but are working on the basis of borrowing elements.
- You can gray out inactive worksets in a view to easily distinguish between active and inactive worksets, as shown in Figure 6–28. In the *Collaborate* tab>Manage Collaboration panel, toggle (Gray Inactive Workset Graphics) on. You can also select **Gray Inactive Workset Graphics** in the Worksets dialog box.

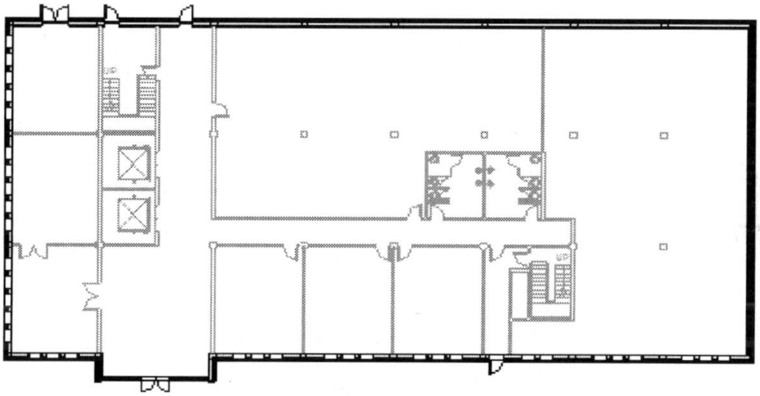

Figure 6–28

Editing Elements in Worksets

There are two different ways to edit elements in worksets:

1. Borrow elements: If you *borrow* the elements as you make changes, no one has to wait for permission to make modifications even if someone else is working on the same workset. This can speed up the work if you have a fairly small group of people working on the project, especially when there is some overlap between the purposes of the users or when the project has only been divided into a few worksets.
2. Check out a workset: When you *check out* a specific workset and make it editable, no one else can modify elements in that workset without expressed permission.

Check with your project coordinator to see which method your office uses.

Borrowing Elements

When you select an element and see the **Make element editable** icon, as shown in Figure 6–29, it means you have not checked out that particular workset or that you are not currently borrowing the element.

It is not necessary to click the icon; simply proceed to edit the element as required.

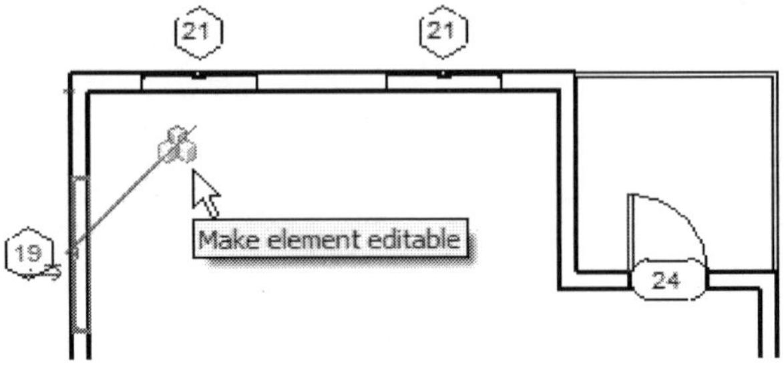

Figure 6–29

- If you modify the element and it enables you to do so, then no one else has that workset checked out and you were given automatic permission to modify this element.
- If someone else has borrowed the element or checked out the workset to which it belongs, you are prompted to request permission to edit the element.

How To: Check Out Worksets

You can also open the Worksets dialog box from the Status Bar.

1. In the *Collaborate* tab>Manage Collaboration panel, click (Worksets).
2. In the Worksets dialog box, select **Yes** in the *Editable* column next to the workset name that you want to checkout and edit, as shown in Figure 6–30. More than one workset can be checked out and made editable at a time, but ensure that you only check out those that you really need.

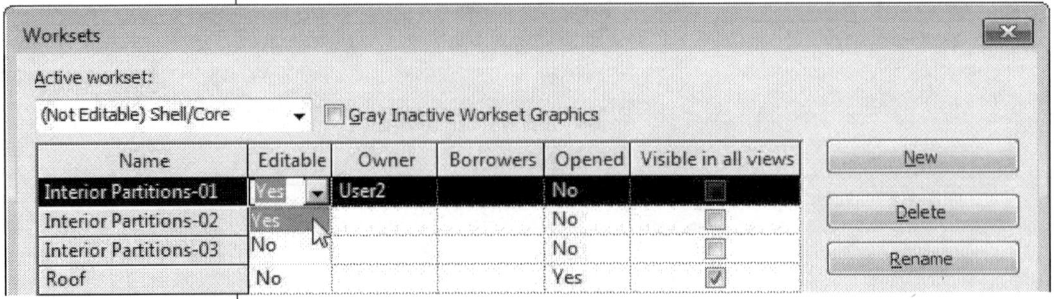

Figure 6–30

3. Select **Active workset** in the menu. You can also set the active workset from the list in the Manage Collaboration panel and Status Bar.
4. Click **OK**.

- When editing elements, you can control which ones can be picked by selecting **Editable Only** in the Options Bar, as shown in Figure 6–31. If **Editable Only** is selected, you can only select items that are available in the editable worksets or those which you borrowed. If it is cleared, you can select anything.

Figure 6–31

Permissions to Edit

If you try to edit an element that is being used by someone else, an alert box opens stating that you cannot edit the element without their permission, as shown in Figure 6–32. First, you must request an edit. Second, the owner of the workset either grants or denies the request. If the request is granted, you can update your local file and have control of the element until you relinquish it.

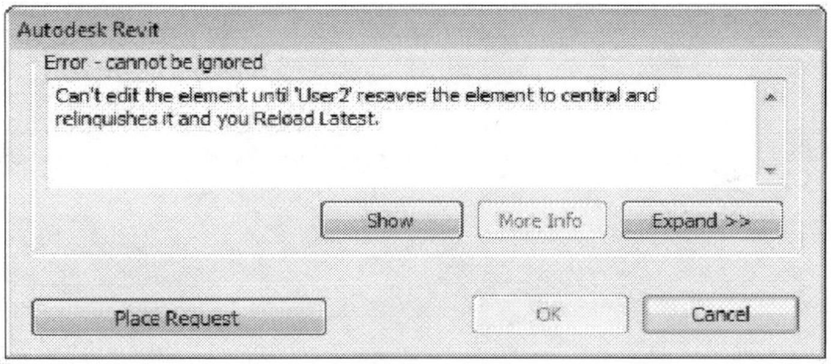

Figure 6–32

How To: Request an Edit

1. When the alert box opens stating that you need to have permission to modify an element, click **Place Request** to ask to borrow the element.
2. An alert box opens, stating the request has been made, as shown in Figure 6–33. If you expect a quick reply, leave the message in place. If you want to continue working, click **Close** and cancel out of the alert box. The request is still active.

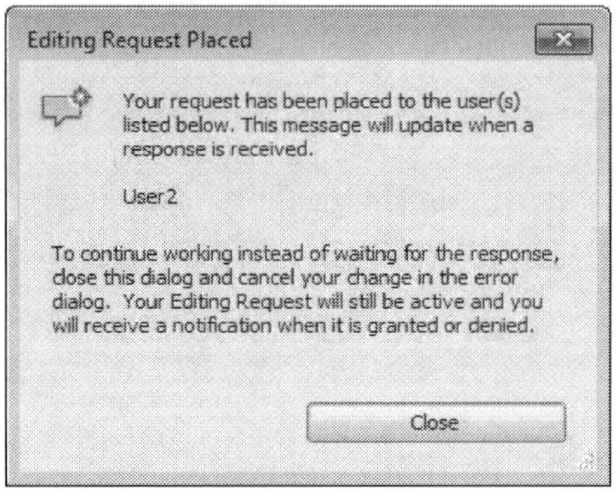

Figure 6–33

How To: Grant or Deny an Editing Request

1. When a user sends an editing request for an element you are currently borrowing or which belongs to a workset which you have checked out (editable), an alert displays as shown in Figure 6–34.

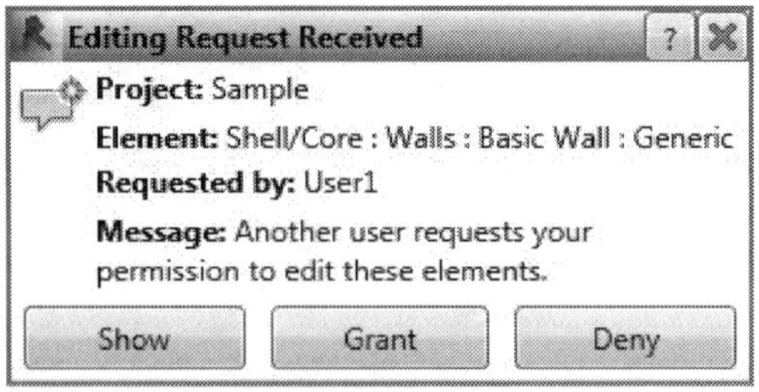

Figure 6–34

2. In the Editing Request Received dialog box, click **Show** to zoom into the element requested, **Grant** to allow the other user to modify the element, or **Deny** to stop the other user from modifying the element.

3. If you do not respond right away to the editing request, you can always access it again. In the *Collaborate* tab>Synchronize panel, click  (Editing Requests) or in the Status Bar, click  (Editing Request). The information on the Status Bar includes the number of requests outstanding, as shown in Figure 6–35.

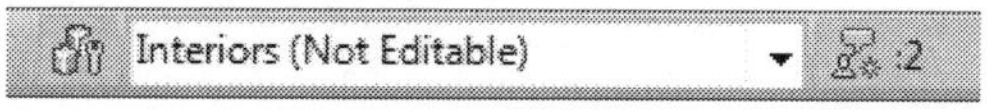

Figure 6–35

4. In the Editing Requests dialog box, as shown in Figure 6–36, select the pending request. Click on the date.

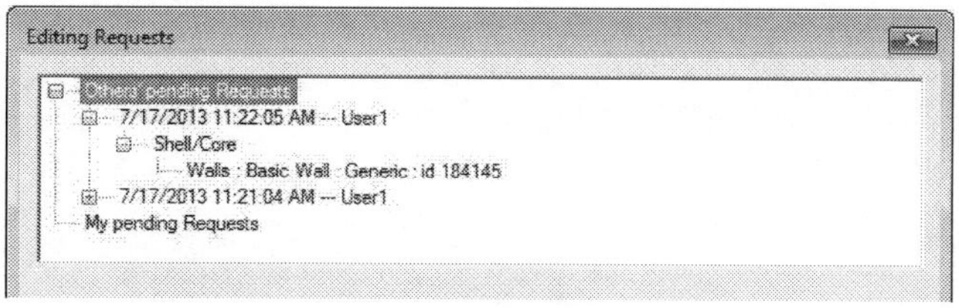

Figure 6–36

- When you select the editing request date, the elements included in the request are highlighted in the project. Click **Show** to zoom in on the elements if required.

5. Click **Grant** to enable the other user to make the changes or **Deny/Retract** to deny the request. (The original user can also retract the request with this button.) You can also grant the request by saving the entire workset back to the central file and relinquishing the items.

Applying an Editing Request

When an editing request is granted, a confirmation alert box opens in the program of the user who requested it, as shown in Figure 6–37. Close the alert box.

Once a request is granted, you can make modifications to the element again without having to request to edit the feature, although the icon still displays.

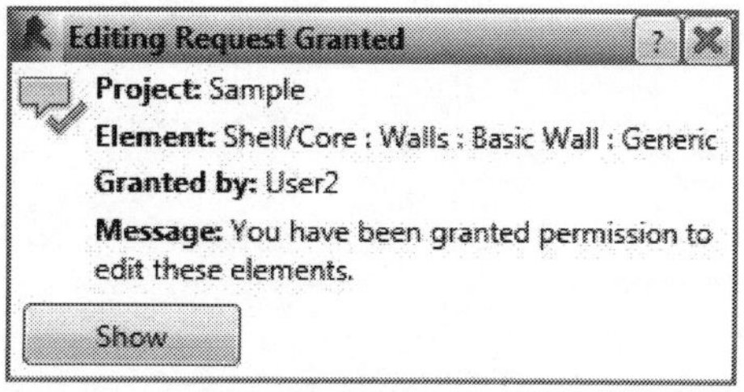

Figure 6–37

- If the requesting user canceled out of the Error dialog box, when they are notified that they have permission, click (Reload Latest) or type **RL** to make the ownership modification.
- If the Error dialog box is still open, the Editing Request Placed dialog box displays that the request has been granted, as shown in Figure 6–38. Click **Close** and the element is modified.

An additional note "Reload Latest is required to edit the elements" might display in the dialog box depending on what the other user did with the borrowed elements.

Figure 6–38

Editing Request Frequency

To control the frequency of updates to editing requests (and worksharing display modes), in the Options dialog box, in the *General* tab, move the slider bar between *Less Frequent* and *More Frequent*, as shown in Figure 6–39.

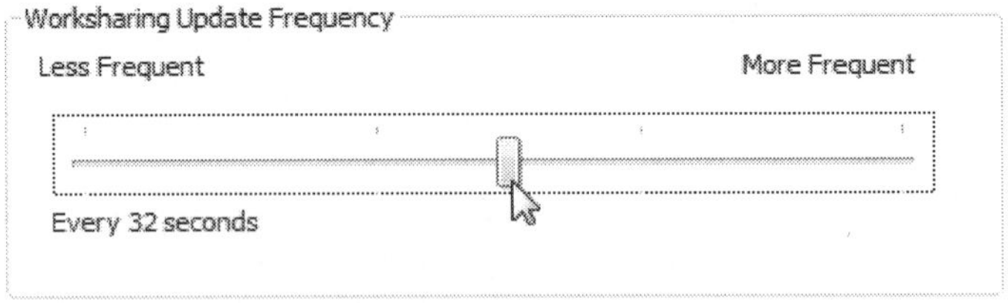

Figure 6–39

- If the bar is moved to the far side of *Less Frequent*, it changes to manual and updates only when you borrow elements or synchronize with the central file. This can improve the performance of the program but also causes the other user to wait until you receive the request.

Relinquishing Worksets

After you have been working with borrowed elements or have checked out worksets, you should return them to the central file when you are finished. In the Quick Access Toolbar or *Collaborate* tab>Synchronize panel, click (Synchronize and Modify Settings). The Synchronize with Central dialog box displays, as shown in Figure 6–40. In this dialog box, select the worksets and/or elements you want to relinquish. Only those of which you have ownership are available.

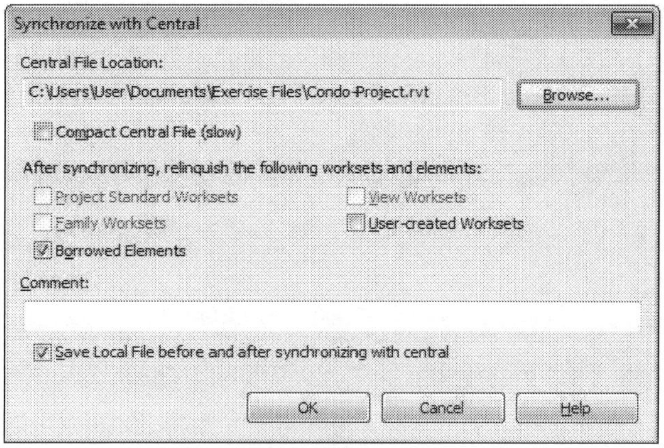

Figure 6–40

Synchronize with Central Options

- The **Borrowed Elements** option is selected by default. This relinquishes any elements you borrowed from another workset.
- Select **Save the Local File before and after synchronizing with central** to save extra steps.
- If the central file location changes, select the new central file using **Browse...**.
- Periodically, use the **Compact Central File (slow)** option when you save to the central file. This reduces the file size, but also increases the time required to save.

Adding comments at key points and for significant changes in the project is useful in case the project backup needs to be restored in the future.

- You can add comments to the central file for others to see. To view the comments, in the *Collaborate* tab>Synchronize panel, click (Show History), and select the central file whose history you want to view. The History dialog box displays with the *Date/Time Stamp*, *Modified by*, and *Comments* columns populated with information, as shown in Figure 6–41.

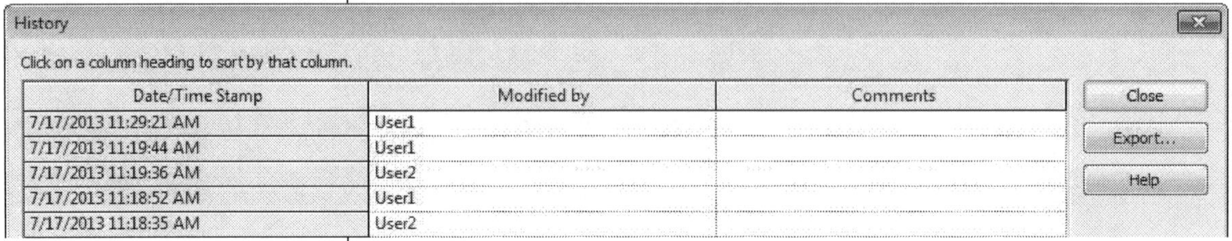

Figure 6–41

Ending the Day Using Worksets

IMPORTANT: When you have finished working on the project for the day, you need to save to the central file and relinquish all user-created editable worksets. Then, you must save your local file before exiting the Autodesk Revit software. This way, the two files are in sync and you are able to save to the central file next time you work on the local file.

- If you close a project, but have not relinquished all worksets when you saved to the central file, the alert shown in Figure 6–42 displays.

If you are working on a project with other people, you need to relinquish all your worksets when closing a project so they can edit them. This is correct worksharing etiquette.

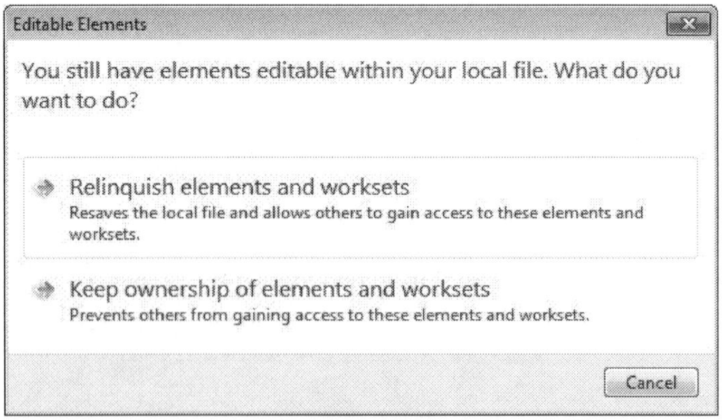

Figure 6–42

- To relinquish worksets without saving to the central file, in the *Collaborate* tab>Synchronize panel, click (Relinquish All Mine)

Do not delete any files in these directories.

- The backup directory for central and local files, as shown in Figure 6–43, holds information about the editability of worksets, borrowed elements, and workset/element ownership. If required, you can restore the backup directory. In the *Collaboration* tab>Synchronize panel, click (Restore Backup).

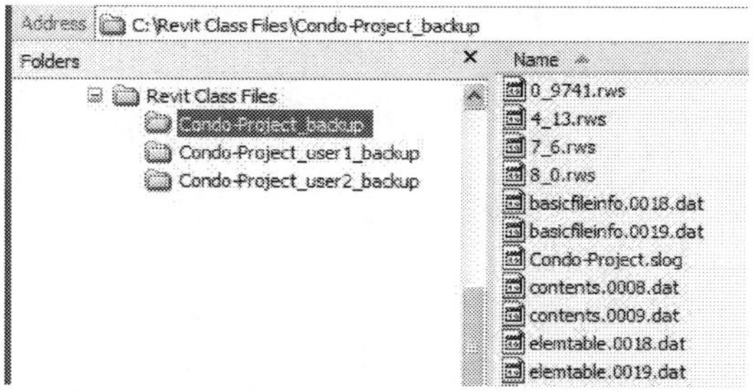

Figure 6–43

6.4 Visibility and Display Options with Worksharing

While using worksets, there are certain display tools to help you as you work. Worksets can be toggled off and on in the Visibility/Graphics dialog box. You can use the Worksharing Display settings to graphically show by color information, such as the Owners of different elements and the elements that need to be updated.

Controlling Workset Visibility

Not all worksets need to be visible in every view. For example, the exterior shell of a building should display in most views, but interior walls or the site features only need to be displayed in related views. The default workset visibility is controlled when the workset is first created, but can be managed in the Visibility/Graphics dialog box, as shown in Figure 6–44.

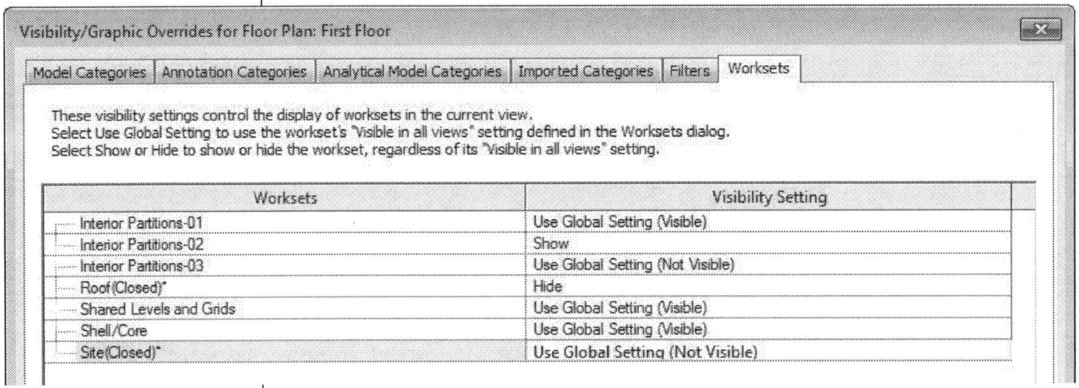

Figure 6–44

How To: Change the Visibility of Worksets

1. Type **VV** or **VG** to open the Visibility/Graphics dialog box.
2. Select the *Worksets* tab. Modify the *Visibility Setting* for each workset, as required. Changing the setting to **Show** or **Hide** only impacts the current view.
3. Click **OK** to close the dialog box.

- Worksets marked with an asterisk (*) have not been opened in this session of the Autodesk Revit software and are therefore not visible in any view.

- Closing worksets toggles off element visibility in all views. It also saves more computer memory than just toggling off the display of worksets.

- The *Worksets* tab in the Visibility/Graphics dialog box is only available if worksets have been enabled.
- These overrides can also be setup in a view template.

Worksharing Display Options

A handy way to view the status of elements in worksharing is to set the Worksharing Display. For example, when you set the Worksharing Display to Worksets, as shown in Figure 6–45, the elements in each workset are highlighted in a different color.

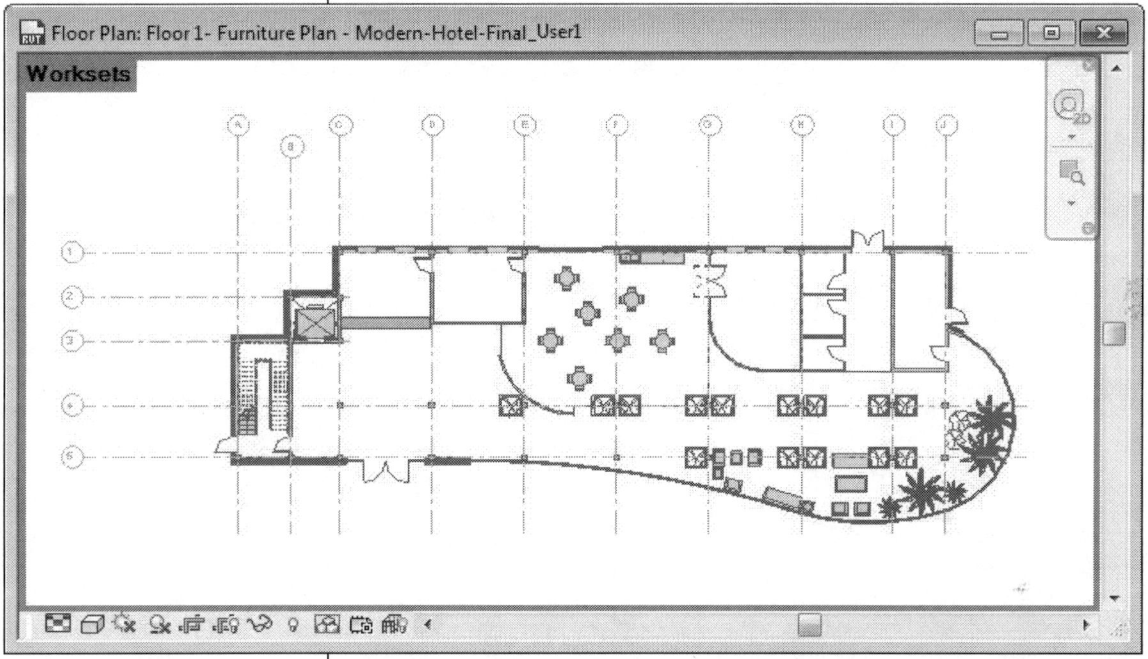

Figure 6–45

There are several type of Worksharing displays: Checkout Status, Owners, Model Updates, and Worksets. You can access those in the Status Bar, as shown in Figure 6–46.

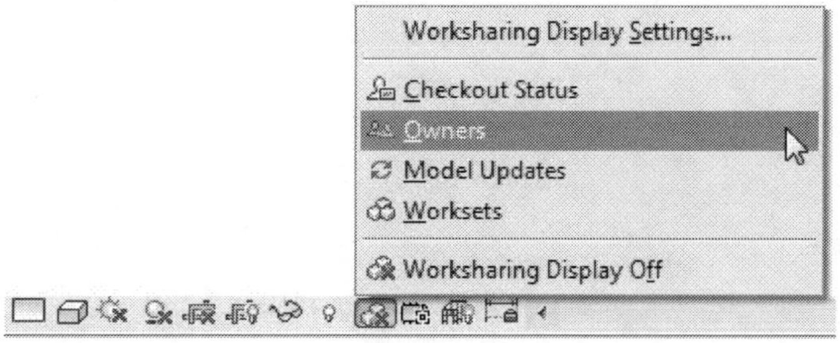

Figure 6–46

Toggling on Gray Inactive Worksets while using Worksharing Display might change the display status of elements in two tones of the same color.

- As you hover the cursor over elements in a view, with Worksharing Display selected, information about the element displays, depending on the type you selected, as shown in Figure 6–47.

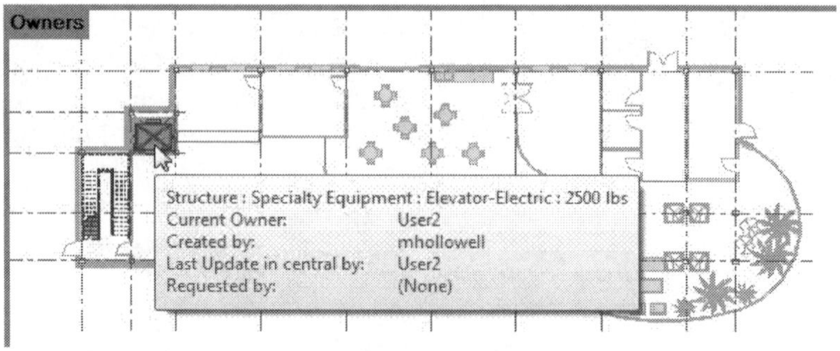

Figure 6–47

- You can modify the colors in the Worksharing Display Settings, as well as select which items you want to display, as shown in Figure 6–48.

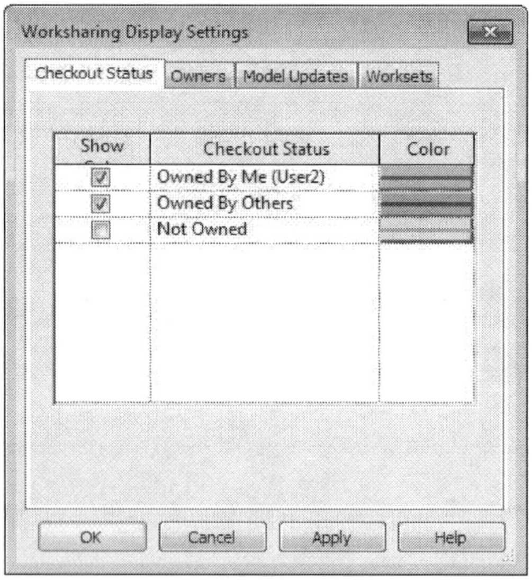

Figure 6–48

Practice 6d

Work in Workset-Related Projects - Architectural

Practice Objectives

- Add and Modify Elements in Worksets.
- Request and grant permissions to edit.
- Save, synchronize, and reload files to display the changes made by each user.

Estimated time for completion: 20 minutes

In this practice you will work with two different sessions of the Autodesk Revit software. In the first session, you will make worksets visible and add, modify elements in worksets without having to get permission. You will then switch to a different user and make a workset editable. The first user requests an edit to the workset owned by the second user. Permission will be granted and the first user will make the change. You save the local file, save to central file, and reload the latest file. An example of Worksets dialog box used in this practice is shown in Figure 6–49.

Name	Editable	Owner	Borrowers	Opened	Visible in all views
Interior Partitions-01	Yes	User1		Yes	☑
Interior Partitions-02	No			Yes	☐
Interior Partitions-03	No			Yes	☐
Roof	No			No	☐
Shared Levels and Grids	No			Yes	☑
Shell/Core	No	User2	user1	Yes	☑
Site	No			No	☐

Figure 6–49

- You must complete **Practice 6a: Open Workset-Related Projects - Architectural** before beginning this practice.

Task 1 - Add and Modify Elements in Worksets.

1. Working as **User1** in the file **Condo-Project-A_User1.rvt**, verify that you are in the **Floor Plans: First Floor** view.

2. Zoom in on Unit 1C, and add several walls using an interior wall type with the *Height* set to **Second Floor**. Include one that butts up against an existing window, as shown in Figure 6–50. A warning displays, noting that the Insert conflicts with the joined wall.

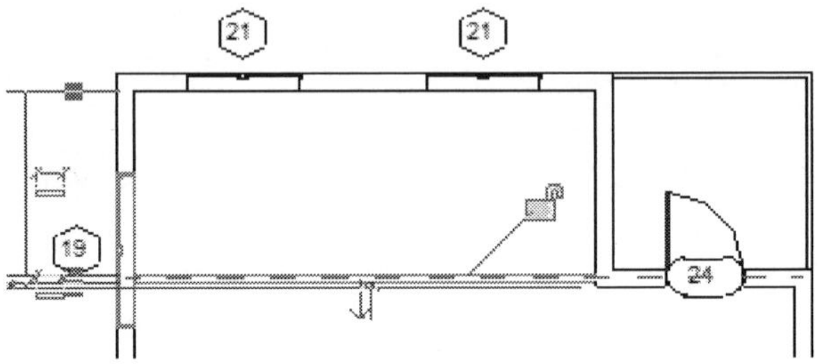

Figure 6–50

3. Close the warning.

4. Click (Modify) and select the window. It has an icon connected to it (as shown in Figure 6–51), indicating that it belongs to another workset. Click the **Make element editable** icon.

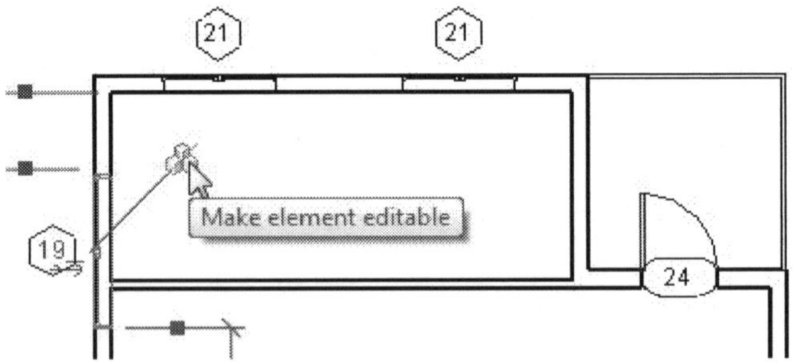

Figure 6–51

5. Move the window so it does not conflict with the wall.

6. Open the Worksets dialog box. **User1** is noted as the *Owner* of the **Interior Partitions-01** workset and a *Borrower* of **Shell/Core** workset, as shown in Figure 6–52.

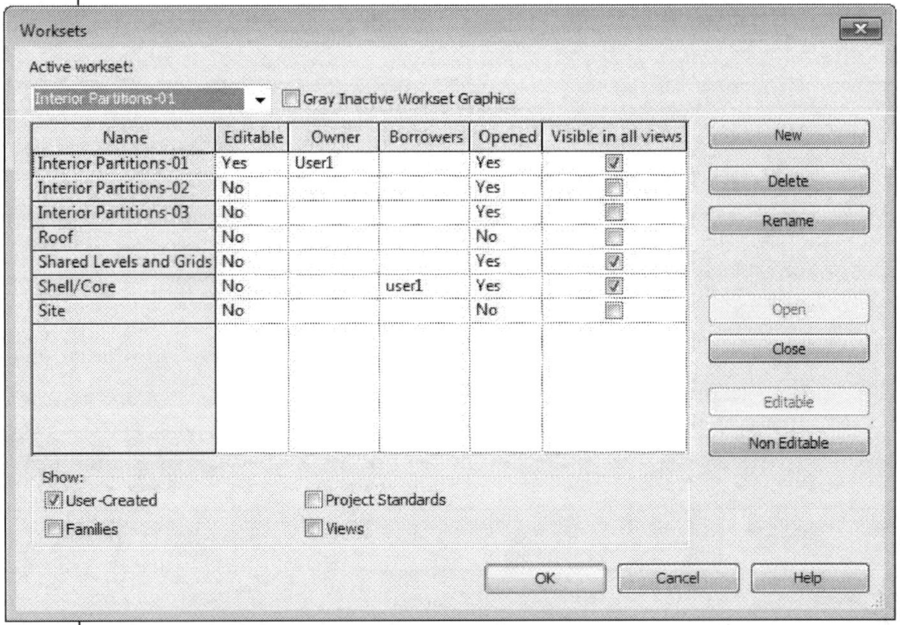

Figure 6–52

7. Click **OK** to close the dialog box.

8. In the Quick Access Toolbar, click  (Synchronize and Modify Settings) to open the Synchronize with Central dialog box, as shown in Figure 6–53. The **Borrowed Elements** option should be selected. Add a comment about moving the window and select **Save Local File before and after synchronizing with central**.

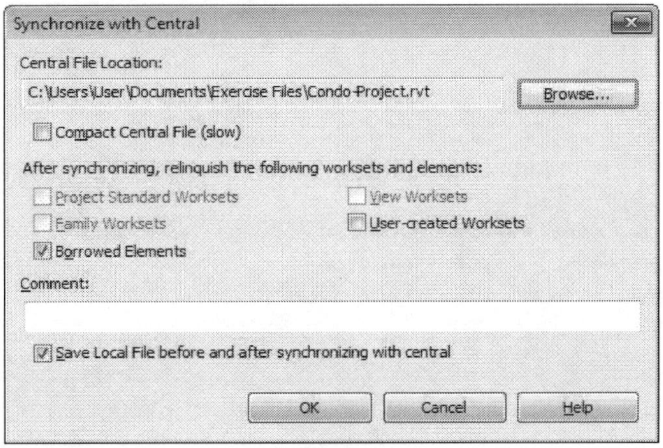

Figure 6–53

9. Click **OK**.

Task 2 - Check out a Workset.

1. Open the session of the Autodesk Revit software used by **User2** and open the **Floor Plans: First Floor** view if it is not already open. None of the changes show in the local file.
2. In the *Collaborate* tab>Synchronize panel, click (Reload Latest or type **RL**. The window location changes but you do not see the new walls because that workset is not open.
3. Click (Worksets) to open the dialog box.
4. Select **Shell/Core** in the *Active workset* drop-down list and make it editable (select **Yes** in the *Editable* column). The *Owner* should display **User 2**, as shown in Figure 6–54.

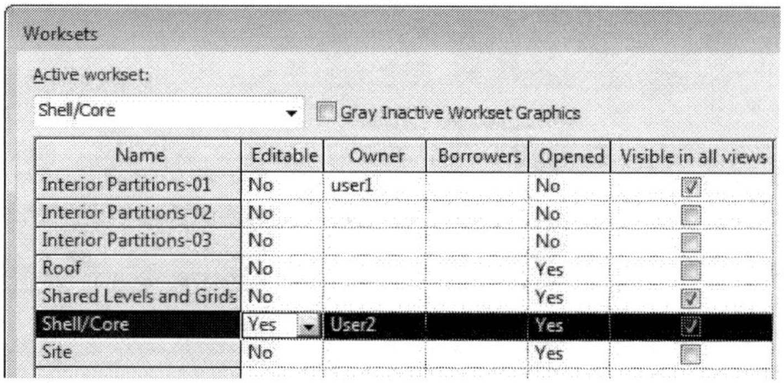

Figure 6–54

5. Click **OK** to close the dialog box.
6. Move door number 5 in Unit 1A down in the wall so that it is no longer opposite to door number 6.
7. In the Quick Access Toolbar, click (Save) to save the local file.
8. Switch to the **User1** session and type **RL** (Reload Latest). There are no new changes to load, as shown in Figure 6–55, because User 2 has not saved back to the central file. Close the dialog box.

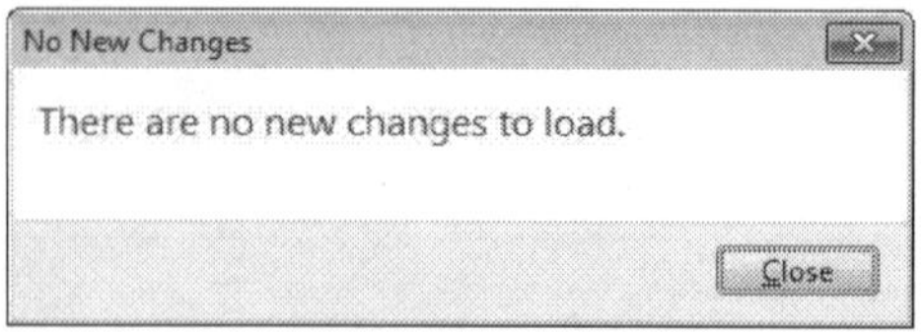

Figure 6–55

9. Switch to the **User2** session and click (Synchronize Now). This saves the changes to the central file without relinquishing the Shell/Core workset.

Task 3 - Request Permission to Edit.

1. Switch to the **User1** session and type **RL** (Reload Latest) again. This time, the door moves in response to the change made in the central file.

2. Try to move the door back where it was. This time, an error message displays that cannot be ignored, as shown in Figure 6–56. **User2** has made the Shell/Core workset editable. Therefore, anyone else cannot edit elements in it without permission.

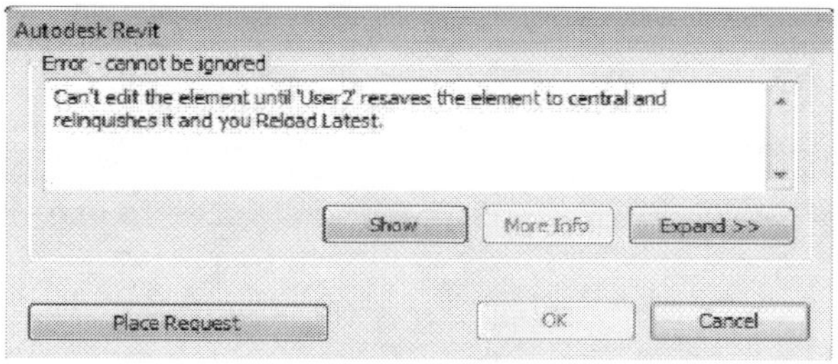

Figure 6–56

3. Click **Place Request**. The Editing Request Placed dialog box opens. Close the dialog boxes.

4. Switch to the **User2** session. An alert box displays, as shown in Figure 6–57.

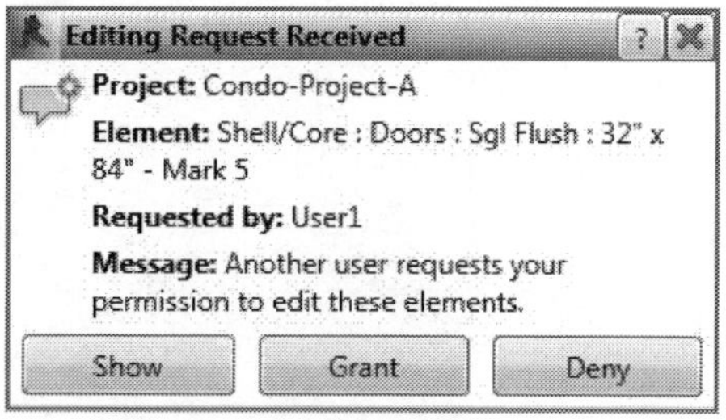

Figure 6–57

5. Hover the cursor over the **Show** button to highlight the door. Move the dialog box out of the way if required, to see the door.

6. The other user can have permission to modify the placement of this door. Click **Grant**. By doing this, you enable the other user full control over this one element in the workset.

7. Switch to the **User1** session. The Editing Request is granted, as shown in Figure 6–58.

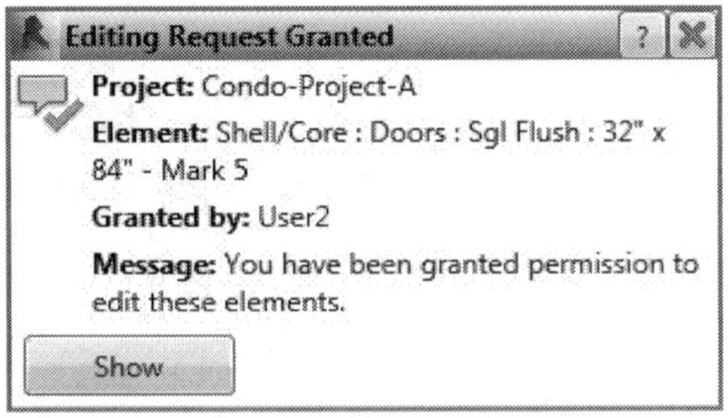

Figure 6–58

8. Close the Editing Request Granted dialog box. Your request was granted and the door moves.
9. Move the door again to exactly where you want it. This time, you are not prompted to ask to move the door because you are still borrowing it.
10. Try to move another door. You do not have permission to move this door. Click **Cancel** rather than place the request. The door returns to its original location.
11. In the View Control Bar, expand the Worksharing display and click  (Owners). Different colors highlight the elements and their respective owners. Hover the cursor over one of the walls to display information about the owner, as shown in Figure 6–59.

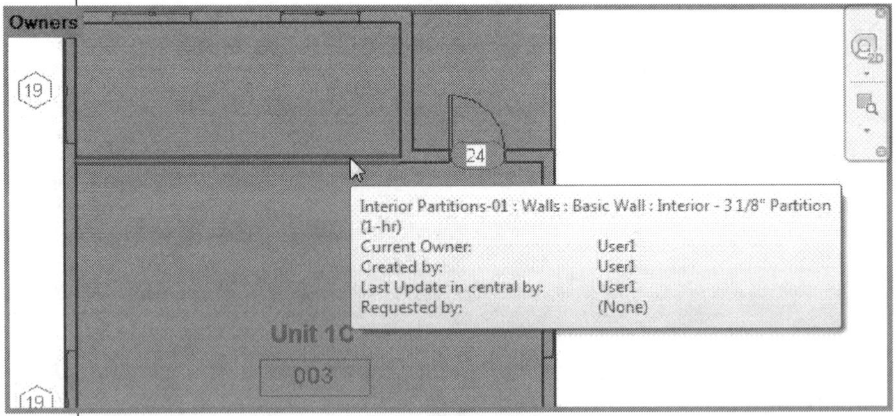

Figure 6–59

- The color on your display might be different.

12. Zoom out so you can see the full floor plan.

13. Click (Synchronize and Modify Settings) and relinquish **User created Worksets** and **Borrowed Elements.**

14. The new interior walls once displayed as owned by **User1** are now not in color and the door that was borrowed returns to the original owner User 2.

15. Toggle the Worksharing Display off.

16. Save the local file.

17. Switch to the **User2** session.

18. Click (Synchronize Now). The door moves to the location where **User1** moved it. When you save to the central file, it also reloads the latest changes.

19. Close the project. When the Editable Elements dialog box opens, as shown in Figure 6–60, click **Relinquish elements and worksets**.

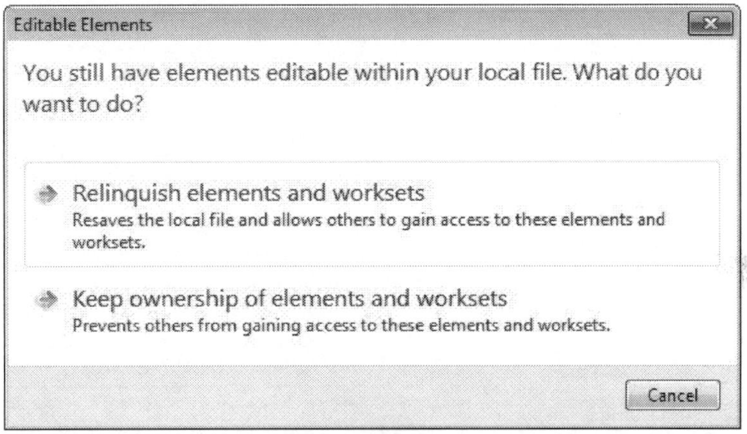

Figure 6–60

20. Close the **User2** session of the Autodesk Revit software.

21. In the **User1** session of the Autodesk Revit software, return the *Username* to the original name at the start of this set of practices.

22. Close the project and synchronize with central if required.

Practice 6e Work in Workset-Related Projects - Structural

Estimated time for completion: 20 minutes

Practice Objectives

- Add and Modify Elements in Worksets.
- Request and grant permissions to edit.
- Save, synchronize, and reload files to display the changes made by each user.

In this practice you will work with two different sessions of the Autodesk Revit software. In the first session, you will make worksets visible and add, modify elements in worksets without having to get permission. You will then switch to a different user and make a workset editable. The first user requests an edit to the workset owned by the second user. Permission will be granted and the first user will make the change. You save the local file, save to central file, and reload the latest file. An example of Worksets dialog box used in this practice is shown in Figure 6–61.

Name	Editable	Owner	Borrowers	Opened	Visible in all v
Columns, Beams & Bracing	No			Yes	☑
Core & Stair Walls	No	User2	User1	Yes	☑
Foundation	No			No	☐
Shared Levels and Grids	No			Yes	☑
Slabs & Roofs	Yes	User1		Yes	☑

Figure 6–61

- You must complete **Practice 6b: Open Workset-Related Projects - Structural** before beginning this practice.

Task 1 - Add and Modify Elements in Worksets.

1. Working as **User1** in the file **Syracuse-Suites-S_User1.rvt**, open the **Structural Plans: 1ST FLOOR** view.

2. Zoom in on the beam system between grids 6 and 7 and C and D. Stay far enough out so that you can see the edge of the building as shown in Figure 6–62. Do not select the beam system.

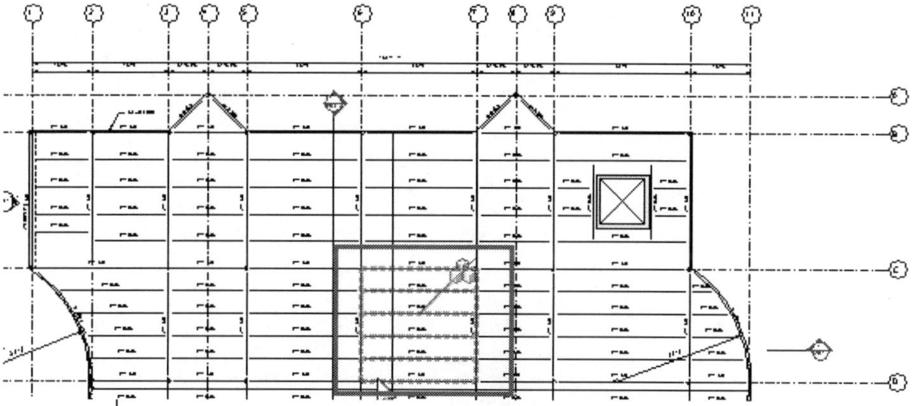

Figure 6–62

3. Select the second beam from the top and type **UP** to unpin it from the beam system. Move it **2'-0"** up so that the distance between the beams is **7'-0"** as shown in Figure 6–63.

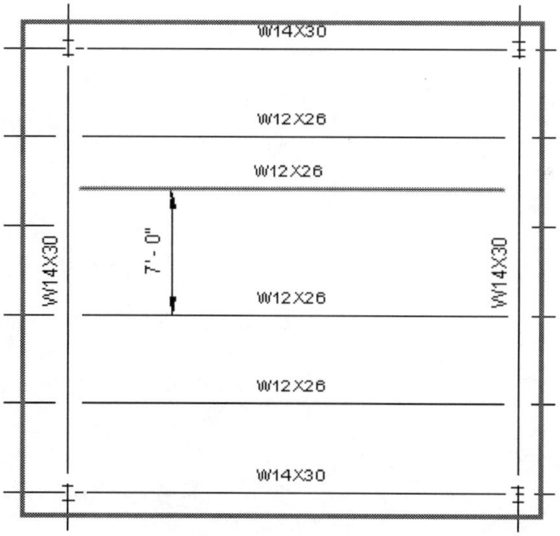

Figure 6–63

4. Hover the cursor over the edge of the building and press <Tab> until the floor is highlighted. Select the floor.

5. In the *Modify | Floors* tab>Mode panel, click (Edit Boundary).

6. In the Draw panel, click (Boundary Line) and draw a rectangle approximately **4'-0"x6'-0"** to add a new opening in the floor. Move the opening inside the framing system between two beams, as shown in Figure 6–64. An exact location is not required for this practice.

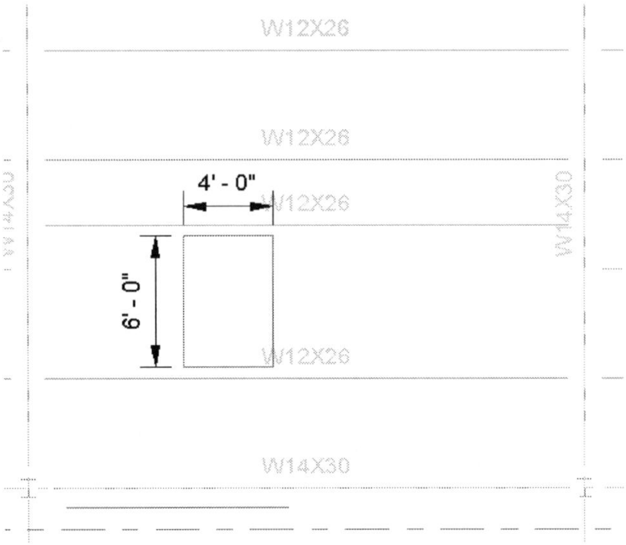

Figure 6–64

7. Click (Finish Edit Mode).

8. In the *Collaborate* tab>Manage Collaboration panel, in the Active Workset drop-down list, select the **Columns, Beams & Bracing** workset to make it the active workset. It should be listed as (Not Editable).

9. In the *Structure* tab>Structure panel, click (Beam).

10. In the *Modify | Place Beam* tab>Tag panel, click (Tag on Placement) to toggle it, on as required.

11. In the Type Selector, verify that the selected beam is **W-Wide Flange: W12x26**. In the Options Bar, set the *Structural Usage* to **Joist**, and verify that the **Chain** option is cleared, as shown in Figure 6–65.

Figure 6–65

12. Add two beams to frame the new opening on the unsupported sides, as shown in Figure 6–66.

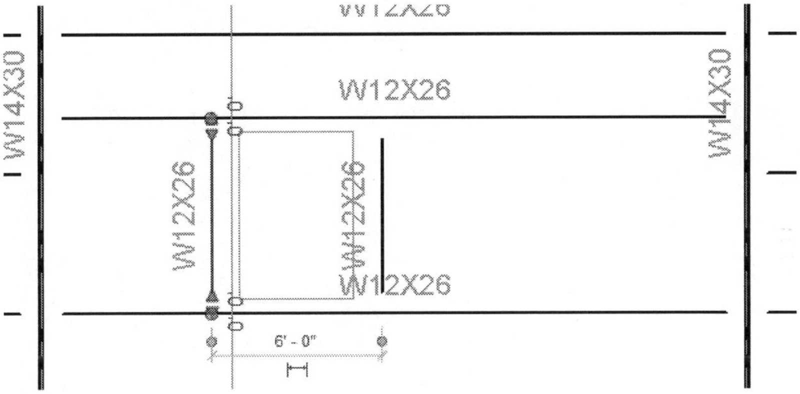

Figure 6–66

13. In the *Collaborate* tab>Manage Collaboration panel or in the Status Bar, click (Worksets).

14. In the Worksets dialog box, **User1** is noted as the Owner of the Slabs & Roofs workset and as a Borrower of Columns, Beams & Bracing, as shown in Figure 6–67.

Name	Editable	Owner	Borrowers	Opened	Visible in all v
Columns, Beams & Bracing	No		User1	Yes	☑
Core & Stair Walls	No			No	☑
Foundation	No			No	☑
Shared Levels and Grids	No			Yes	☑
Slabs & Roofs	Yes	User1		Yes	☑

Figure 6–67

15. Close the dialog box.

16. In the Quick Access Toolbar, click (Synchronize and Modify Settings).

17. In the Synchronize with Central dialog box, the **Borrowed Elements** option should be selected. Add a comment about adding an opening to the First Floor Slab, and select the **Save the Local File before and after synchronizing with central** option, as shown in Figure 6–68.

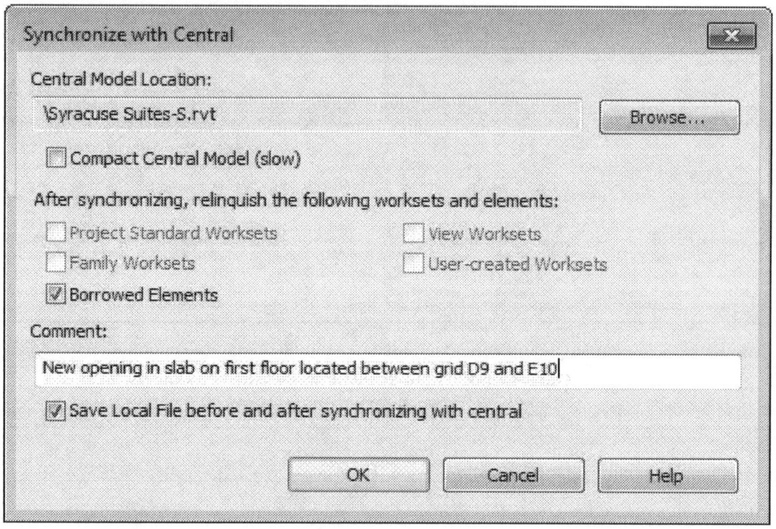

Figure 6–68

18. Click **OK** to finish synchronizing.

Task 2 - Check Out a Workset.

1. Open the session of the Autodesk Revit software that is designated to **User2**.

2. Open the **Structural Plans: 1ST FLOOR** view if it is not already open. None of the changes display in the local file yet.

3. In the Status Bar, click (Worksets).

4. In the Worksets dialog box, open the **Columns, Beams & Bracing** and **Slabs & Roofs** worksets by setting the *Opened* column to **Yes**, as shown in Figure 6–69. Click **OK**.

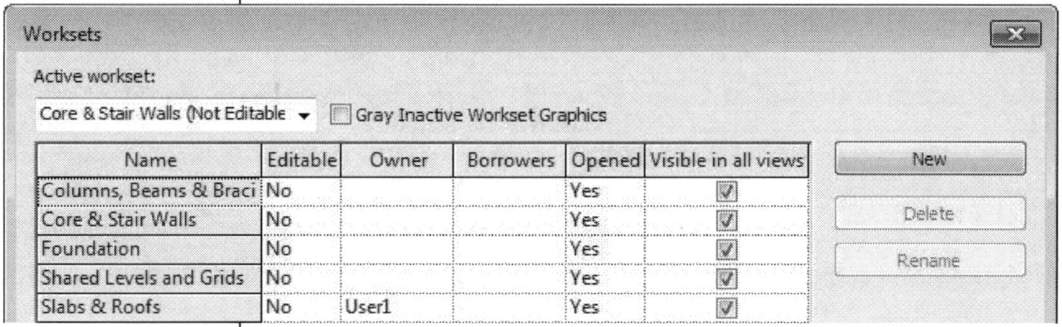

Figure 6–69

5. In the **Structural Plans: 1ST FLOOR** view, the changes are still not displayed.

6. In the *Collaborate* tab>Synchronize panel, click (Reload Latest) or type **RL**. The new opening and joist display.

7. Open the Worksets dialog box.

8. In the Worksets dialog box, select **Core & Stair Walls** in the list of worksets and make it **Editable**. The Owner should change to **User2**, as shown in Figure 6–70.

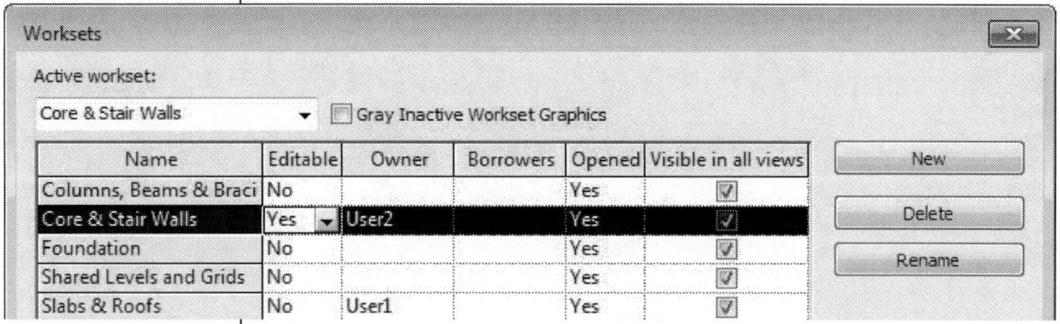

Figure 6–70

9. Click **OK**.

10. Zoom in on the elevator in the upper right of the building.

11. Move the core's north wall approximately **1'-0"** up.

12. In the Quick Access Toolbar, click (Save) to save the local file.

13. Switch to the **User1** session and type **RL** (**Reload Latest**). There are no new changes to load because User2 has not saved back to the central file.

14. Switch to the **User2** session and click (Synchronize Now). This saves the changes to the central file without relinquishing the Core & Stair Walls workset.

Task 3 - Request Permission to Edit.

1. Switch to the **User1** session.

2. Open the Worksets dialog box.

3. Select **Core & Stair Walls** in the list of worksets and click **Open**. Click **OK** to exit the dialog box.

4. Type **RL** (**Reload Latest**) again. This time, the core wall moves in response to the change made by **User2**.

5. Try to move the core wall back to its previous position. An error message opens that cannot be ignored. **User2** has made the Core & Stair Walls workset editable. Therefore, no one else can edit elements in it without permission, as shown in Figure 6–71.

Figure 6–71

6. Click **Place Request**. The Editing Request Placed dialog box opens. Leave it open.

7. Switch to the **User2** session.

8. The Editing Request Received dialog box opens as shown in Figure 6–72.

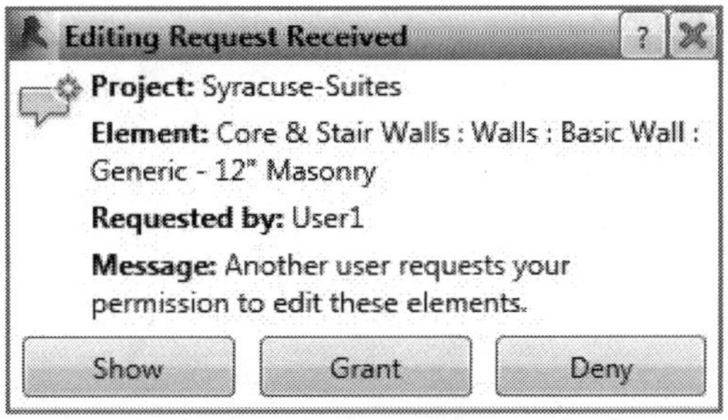

Figure 6–72

9. Hover the cursor over the **Show** button to highlight the door. (Move the box out of the way as required to display the modified wall.)

10. The other user can have permission to modify the placement of this core wall. Click **Grant**. By doing so, you enable the other user to have full control over this element in the workset.

11. Switch to the **User1** session.

12. The Editing Request Granted dialog box opens.

13. After a moment or two, the Editing Request Placed dialog box updates to prompt you that your request has been granted. Because your request was granted, the core wall moves.

14. Close the dialog boxes.

15. Move the core wall again. This time, you are not prompted to ask permission to move the core wall because you are still borrowing it.

16. Try to move another core wall. You do not have permission to move this wall. Cancel rather than place the request. The core wall returns to its original location.

Task 4 - View Information About the Worksets.

1. Continue working as **User1**.
2. In the Status Bar, expand the Worksharing display, and select **Owners** as shown in Figure 6–73.

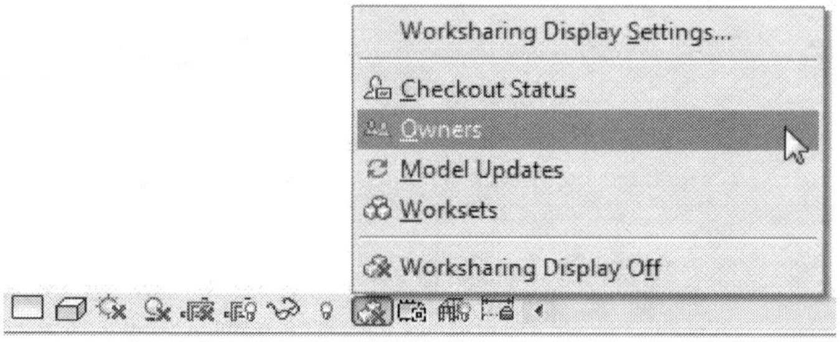

Figure 6–73

3. The view displays in color showing the two owners. Different colors highlight the elements and their respective owners. as shown in Figure 6–74. Hover the cursor over one of the walls to display information about the owner.

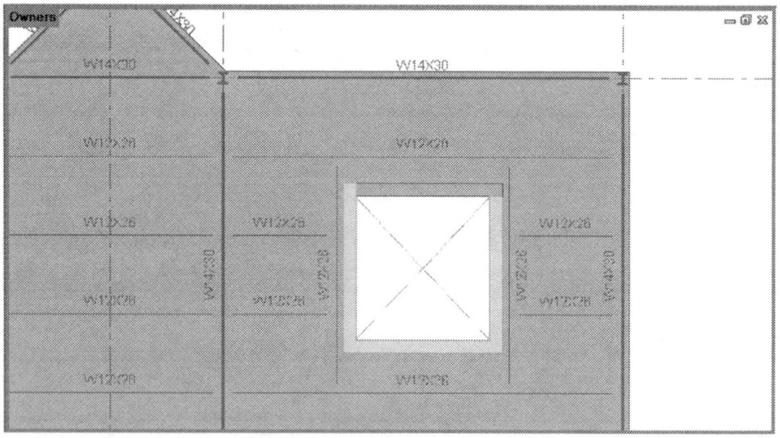

Figure 6–74

4. Open the Worksets dialog box. The owner of Core & Stair Walls is listed as **User2**, but **User1** is also listed as a borrower. Click **Cancel**.
5. Toggle the **Worksharing Display** off and zoom out to see the full building.

6. In the *Collaborate* tab>Manage Collaboration panel, click (Gray Inactive Worksets) to gray-out the elements that you cannot modify without requesting permission. This also grays out the core walls, although you have a right to edit the wall that you borrowed.
7. Click (Synchronize and Modify Settings) and verify that all of the worksets will be relinquished before clicking **OK**.
8. Close the project.
9. Switch to the **User2** session.
10. Click (Synchronize Now). The core wall moves to the location selected by **User1**. When you sync with the central file, it also reloads the latest changes.
11. Close the project. When the Editable Elements dialog box opens, select **Relinquish elements and worksets**.
12. If you will not be continuing into the next section, close the **User2** session of the Autodesk Revit software. In addition, in the **User1** session of the Autodesk Revit software, return the Username to the original name used at the beginning of this practice.

Practice 6f Work in Workset-Related Projects - MEP

Practice Objectives

- Add and Modify Elements in Worksets.
- Request and grant permissions to edit.
- Save, synchronize, and reload files to display the changes made by each user.

Estimated time for completion: 20 minutes

In this practice you will work with two different sessions of the Autodesk Revit software. In the first session, you will make worksets visible and add, modify elements in worksets without having to get permission. You will then switch to a different user and make a workset editable. The first user requests an edit to the workset owned by the second user. Permission will be granted and the first user will make the change. You save the local file, save to central file, and reload the latest file. An example of Worksets dialog box used in this practice is shown in Figure 6–75.

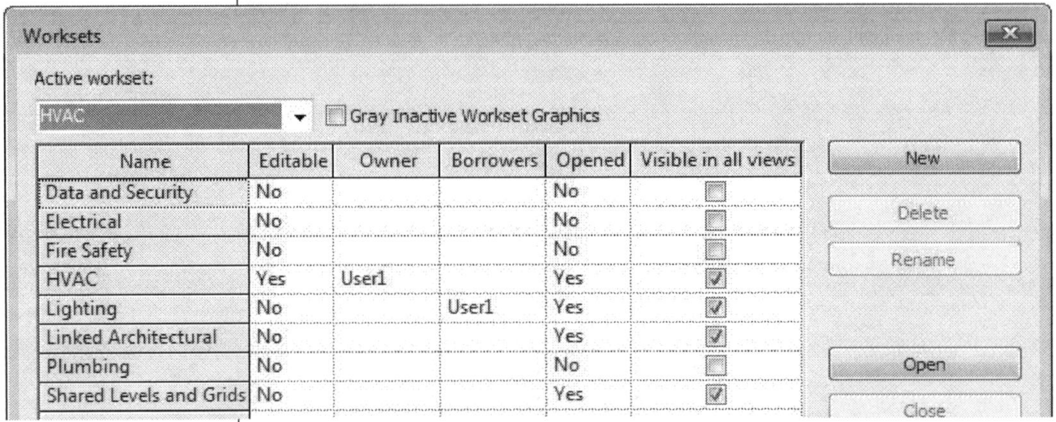

Figure 6–75

- You must complete **Practice 6c: Open Workset-Related Projects - MEP** before beginning this practice.

Task 1 - Add and Modify Elements in Worksets.

1. Working as **User1** in the file **Elementary-School-MEP_User1.rvt**, open the **Coordination>MEP>Ceiling Plans:01 RCP** view.

2. Zoom in on the lower left classroom. You should see elements related to HVAC.

3. Move a couple of air terminals similar to that shown in Figure 6–76. Reattach the flex duct, if required.

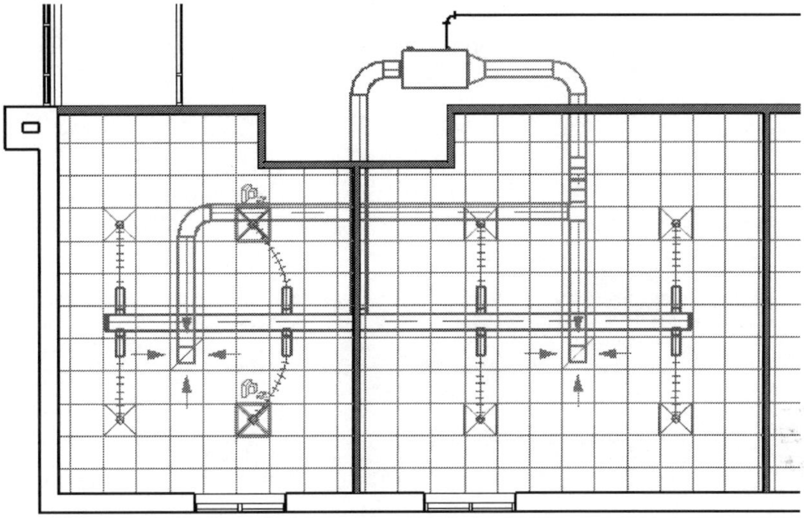

Figure 6–76

4. Open the Worksets dialog box and select the Lighting workset. Open it and make it visible in all views. Click **OK**. Now the air terminals are on top of lights.

5. Select one of the lighting fixtures. It has an icon connected to it, as shown in Figure 6–77, indicating that it belongs to another workset. Click the icon to make the element editable.

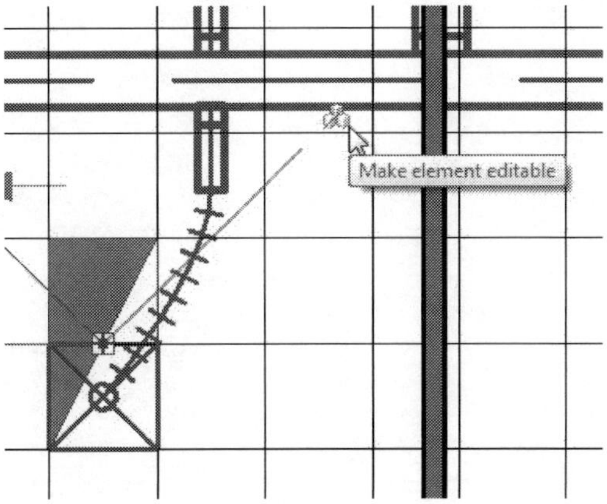

Figure 6–77

6. Move the lighting fixture so it does not conflict with the air terminal.

7. Open the Worksets dialog box. **User1** is noted as the *Owner* of the **HVAC** workset and a *Borrower* of **Lighting** and **Linked Architectural** worksets, as shown in Figure 6–78.

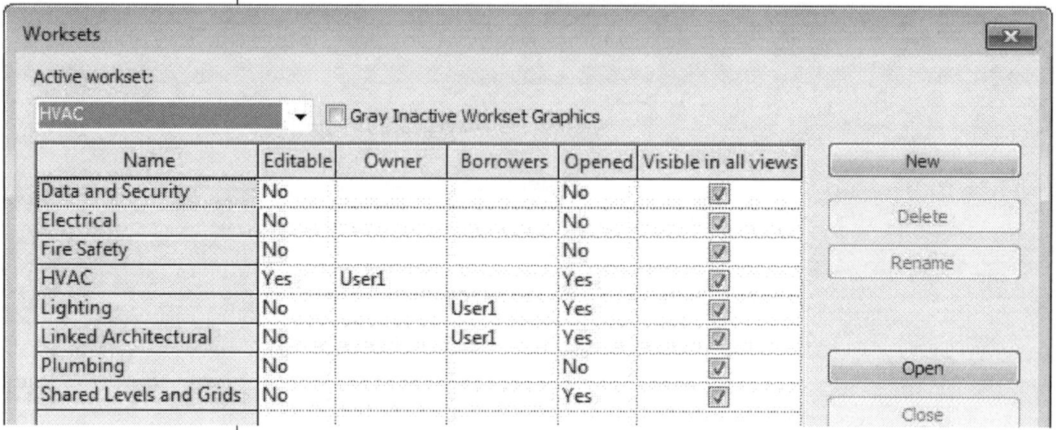

Figure 6–78

8. Click **OK** to close the dialog box.

9. In the *Collaborate* tab>Synchronize panel, or the Quick Access Toolbar, click (Synchronize and Modify Settings) to open the Synchronize with Central dialog box, as shown in Figure 6–79. The **Borrowed Elements** option should be selected. Add a comment about moving the light and select **Save Local File before and after synchronizing with central**.

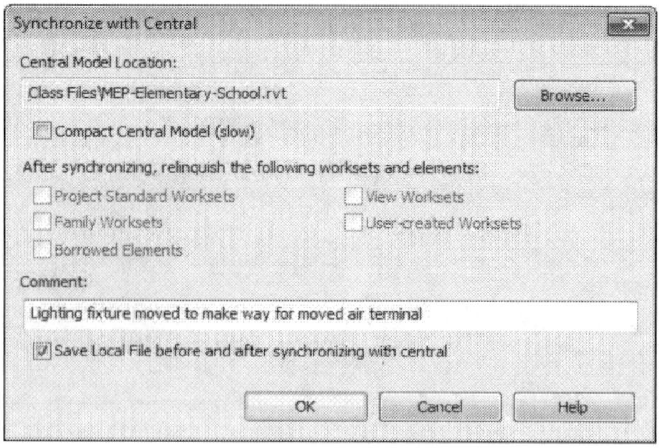

Figure 6–79

10. Click **OK**.

Task 2 - Check out a Workset.

1. Work in **User2** and open the **Coordination>MEP>Ceiling Plans: 01 RCP**. Neither the HVAC elements nor the changes show in the local file.

2. In the *Collaborate* tab>Synchronize panel, click (Reload Latest or type **RL**. The light fixture location changes but you do not see the air terminals because that workset is not open.

3. Click (Worksets) to open the dialog box and open the HVAC workset. Verify that it is Visible in all views.

4. Select **Lighting** in the *Active workset* drop-down list and make it editable (select **Yes** in the *Editable* column). The *Owner* should display **User 2**, as shown in Figure 6–80.

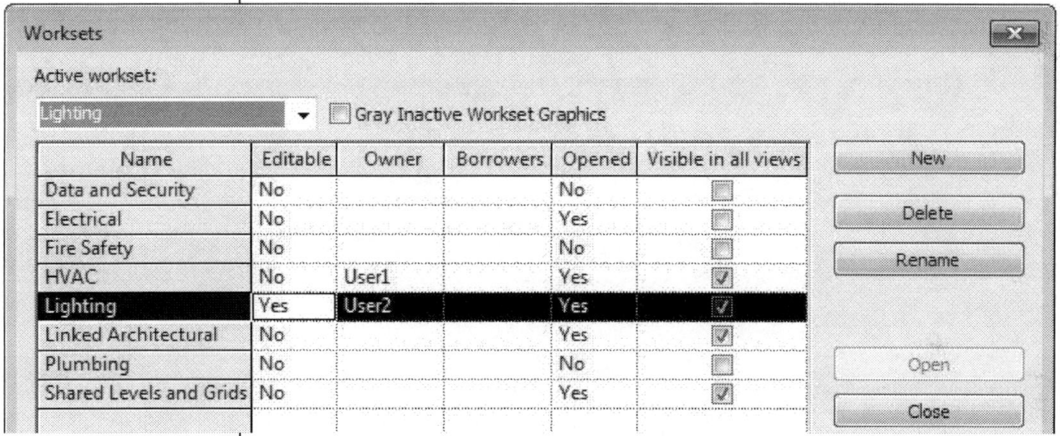

Name	Editable	Owner	Borrowers	Opened	Visible in all views
Data and Security	No			No	☐
Electrical	No			Yes	☐
Fire Safety	No			No	☐
HVAC	No	User1		Yes	☑
Lighting	Yes	User2		Yes	☑
Linked Architectural	No			Yes	☑
Plumbing	No			No	☐
Shared Levels and Grids	No			Yes	☑

Figure 6–80

5. Click **OK** to close the dialog box.

6. Add another lighting fixture in the room.

7. In the Quick Access Toolbar, click (Save) to save the local file.

8. Switch to the **User1** session and type **RL** (Reload Latest). There are no new changes to load, as shown in Figure 6–81, because User 2 has not saved back to the central file. Close the dialog box.

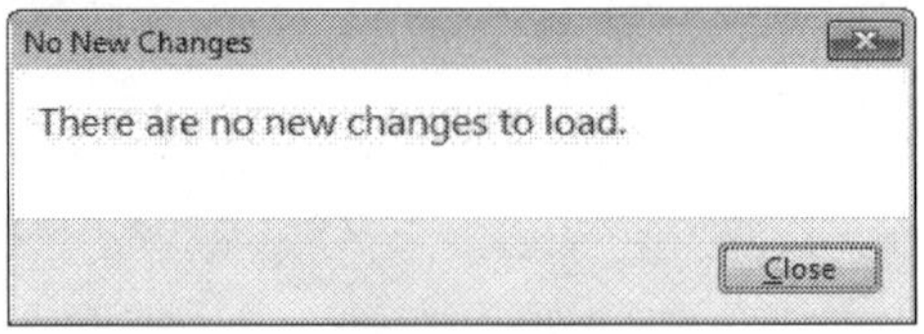

Figure 6–81

9. Switch to the **User2** session and click  (Synchronize Now). This saves the changes to the central file without relinquishing the Lighting workset.

Task 3 - Request Permission to Edit.

1. Switch to the **User1** session and type **RL** (Reload Latest) again. This time, the new lighting fixture displays because it was saved to the central file.
2. Try to move one of the lighting fixtures. This time, an error message displays that cannot be ignored, as shown in Figure 6–82. **User2** has made the Lighting workset editable. Therefore, no one else can edit elements in it without permission.

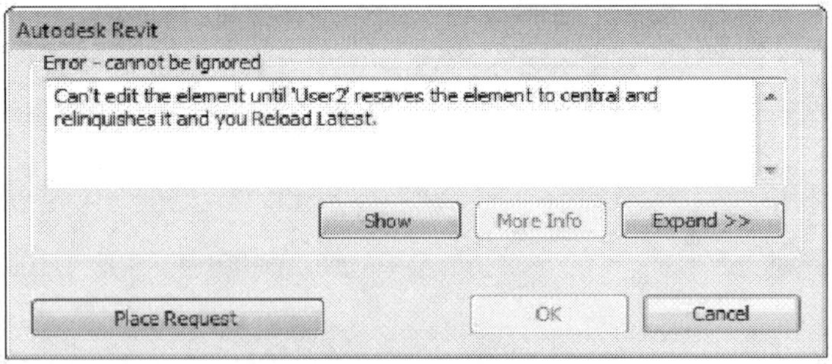

Figure 6–82

3. Click **Place Request**. The Editing Request Placed dialog box opens.

4. Switch to the **User2** session. An alert box displays, as shown in Figure 6–83.

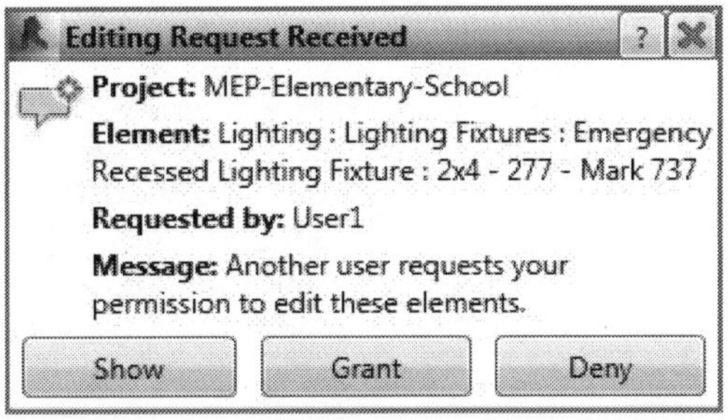

Figure 6–83

5. Hover the cursor over the **Show** button to highlight the door. Move the dialog box out of the way if required to see the modified lighting fixture.

6. The other user can have permission to modify the placement of this lighting fixture. Click **Grant**. By doing this, you enable the other user full control over this one element in the workset.

7. Switch to the **User1** session. The Editing Request is granted, as shown in Figure 6–84.

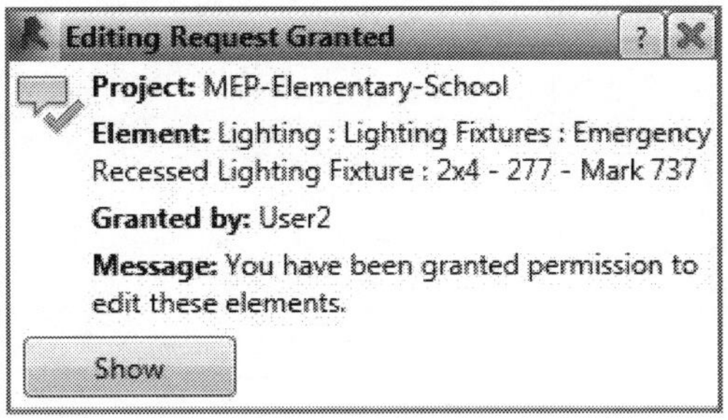

Figure 6–84

8. Close the Editing Request Granted dialog box. Your request was granted and the lighting fixture moves.

9. Move the lighting fixture again to exactly where you want it. This time, you are not prompted to ask to move the element because you are still borrowing it.

10. Try to move another lighting fixture. You do not have permission to move this or any others. Click **Cancel** rather than place the request. The lighting fixture returns to its original location.

11. In the View Control Bar, expand the Worksharing display and click (Owners). Different colors highlight the elements and their respective owners. Hover the cursor over one of the elements to display the information about the owner, as shown in Figure 6–85.

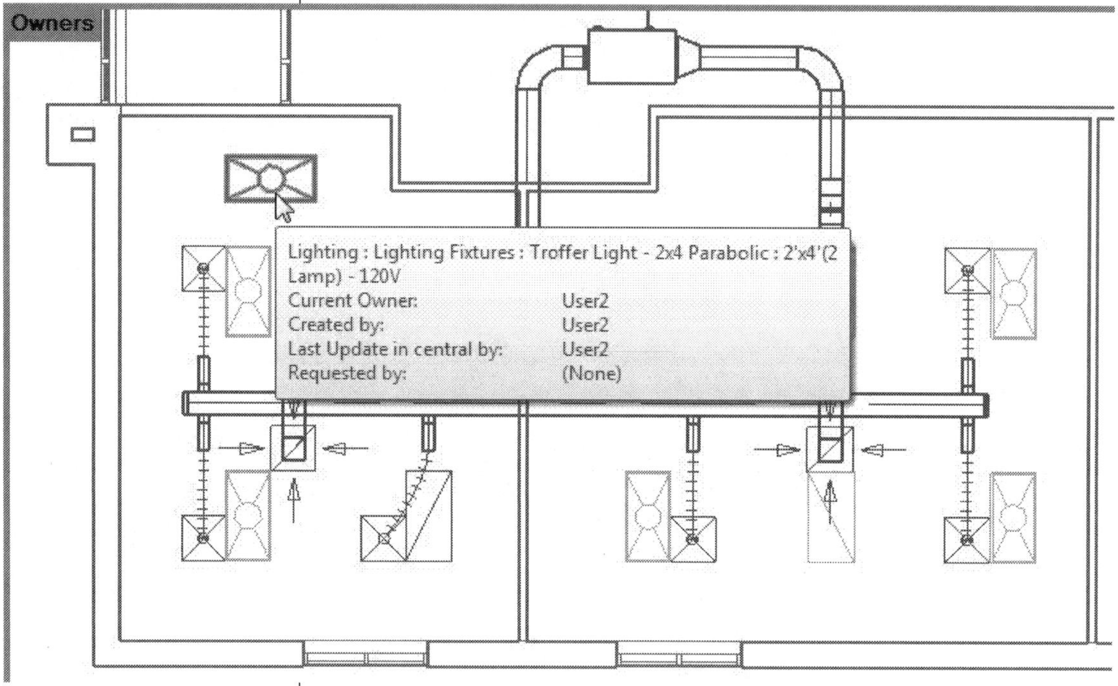

Figure 6–85

- The color on your display might be different.

12. Click (Synchronize and Modify Settings) and relinquish **User created Worksets** and **Borrowed Elements.**

13. Toggle the Worksharing Display off and zoom out to see the full building.

14. Save the local file.

15. Switch to the **User2** session.

16. Click (Synchronize Now). The lighting fixture moves to the location where **User1** moved it. When you save to the central file, it also reloads the latest changes.

17. Close the project. When the Editable Elements dialog box opens, as shown in Figure 6–86, click **Relinquish elements and worksets**.

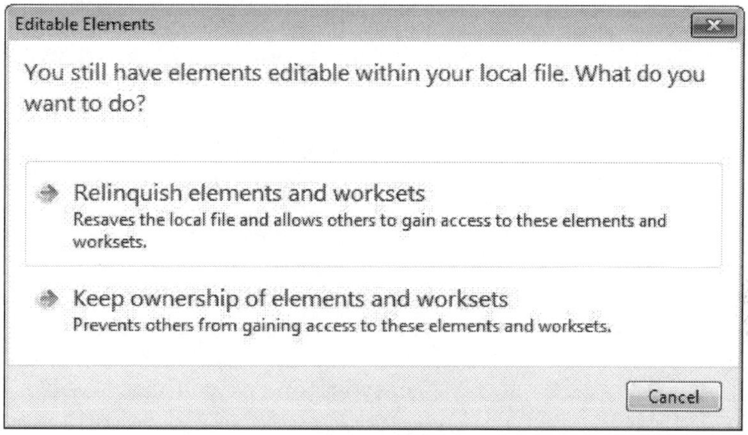

Figure 6–86

18. Close the **User2** session of the Autodesk Revit software.

19. In the **User1** session of the Autodesk Revit software, return the *Username* to the original name at the start of this set of practices.

20. Close the project.

6.5 Best Practices for Worksets

Working with Company Policies

There are different practices regarding the frequency of synchronizing with central. Some companies ask users to synchronize before lunch and at the end of the day. Other companies require users to synchronize every 30 - 60 minutes. As the file size gets larger, synchronizing more often prevents the loss of data and also makes the synchronization finish quicker than if there are several hours worth of work to synchronize. However, there can be many reasons to change this frequency or to do additional synchronizations at specific points in time. They are:

- Major or critical changes to the project, such as moving an elevator core, reorienting the building on the site, etc.
- Users working in close proximity inside the model, to reduce permission issues.

When users need to leave their work for an hour or more (for lunch or a meeting, or at the end of the day), it is best to synchronize and relinquish all. Then, upon returning, they should create a new local file (with a new name if you want the previous file saved as a backup). This ensures their file is up to date and eliminates the update time.

Tips for Using Worksets

Working with the Local File

- Be selective about which worksets you open. Avoid opening worksets that are not required for the work you are doing in the project. Limiting the number of worksets speeds up the process of opening and saving the file.
- Close unused views on a regular basis as you are working on a project.
- Use a Starting View that is a drafting view, 2D plan, or elevation view. The Autodesk Revit software only loads into memory what it displays, so this saves memory the next time the file is opened. This can also be used before plotting to increase the amount of available RAM.
- If you have been away from an active project for some time, it is better to create a new local file rather than depend on the **Reload Latest** command to update your current local file for you.

- If you are not sure what workset to put certain elements in, you can use *Workset1* or a specific temporary workset to put them in until the decision can be finalized.
- Restart the software before performing memory-intensive operations, such as printing an entire document set.

Saving to the Central File

- Stagger your saves to the central file.
- Type **RL** (Reload Latest) to update your copy of the project without changing the central file. This saves time by eliminating the need to reload as part of the **Synchronize and Modify Settings** command.
- Periodically synchronize with the central file using the **Compact File** option. This takes longer to save, but frees up more memory.
- If you get an error, such as *Unable to Save* or *File not found*, you might have run out of memory. Close the major worksets so that the Autodesk Revit software releases some of the virtual memory that can be used to then save the file.

Requesting Edits

- Enable elements, not worksets, whenever possible. The Autodesk Revit software automatically borrows the unowned elements without user intervention. This saves time by not having to request an edit in the first place.
- Communicate with the team members working on a project to avoid working on the same elements at the same time.

Tips for Creating Worksets

Worksets and the Team

- Assign one person to create worksets.
- Create your project team structure to correspond with the new way of working with the building model. For example, architects and engineers do much of the work directly without needing an intern or drafter to create working drawings until the later parts of a project.
- Divide worksets according to components of a building rather than drawing types (such as plans, elevations, and sections), as these are created automatically.

- Key considerations when determining how to divide a project into worksets, include the ability to load only those worksets that are required at the time and the ability to control visibility by worksets.
- As the project progresses, more worksets can be added.
- Using worksets does not negate the need for good team communication. You still need to have scheduling and planning meetings.
- Be sure that everyone knows exactly which part of the model for which they are responsible.
- File sharing should be a tool that is used in the workflow of the project; it should not be something that is disruptive.

Creating Worksets

- A multi-floor building does not need to have a workset for each floor until you are working on the floor-specific layouts.
- If you have a project with a large floor plate that needs to be divided by match lines to fit on sheets, you should divide the various parts of the building into separate worksets.
- If you have imported files into a project, each import should be in a separate workset that is not visible by default. They should also be closed when not in use.
- Every linked file should also be in a separate workset not visible by default. They should also be closed when not in use.
- Worksets cannot be included in templates.

Default Workset Visibility

- As you create worksets, you should set the visibility. For example, the exterior and core of a building should be visible in all views, but furniture layouts or tenant partitions only need to be visible in specific views.
- Set up a standard for typical workset visibility designations. There are always exceptions, but working with the standard first is simpler.

Chapter Review Questions

1. When you want to update the work that you have done and receive any changes others have made, but you do not want to change anything else, which command do you use?

   a.  (Synchronize and Modify Settings)

   b.  (Synchronize Now)

   c.  (Relinquish All Mine)

   d.  (Reload Latest)

2. Where should a local file be located?

   a. On the project manager's computer.

   b. On the company server.

   c. On each team member's computer.

3. What do you need to do so that any new elements you add are placed in a particular workset, as shown in Figure 6–87?

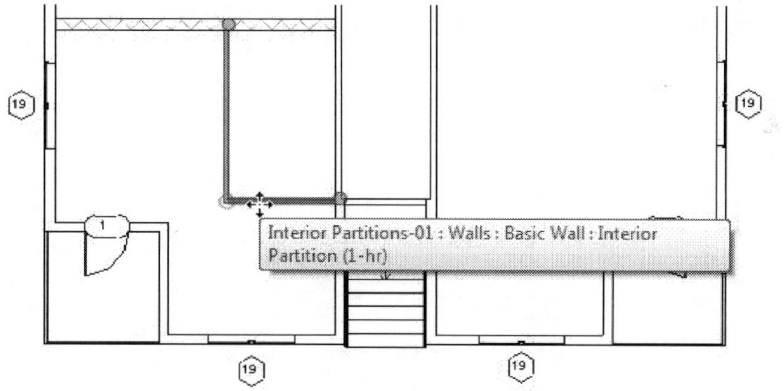

Figure 6–87

   a. Gray out inactive worksets so you know not to work in them.

   b. Make the workset editable.

   c. Set the workset active.

   d. Create a new workset.

4. When selecting an element to edit, the icon shown in Figure 6–88 displays. What do you need to do?

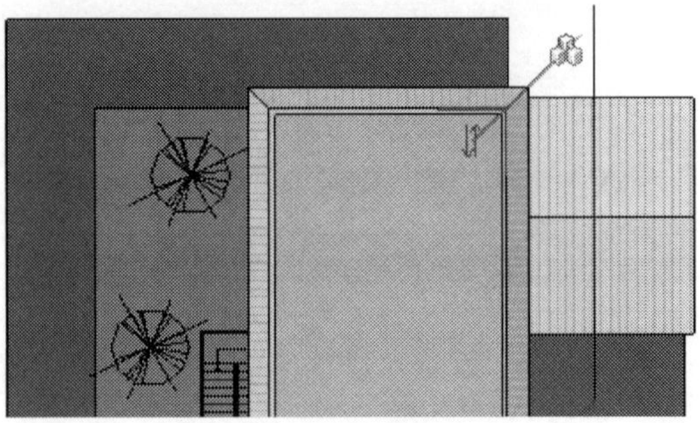

Figure 6–88

   a. Nothing, you can edit the element without checking it out.
   b. Click the icon and an error dialog box displays indicating that you cannot edit the element.
   c. Click the icon and an error dialog box displays indicating that you cannot edit the element but you can request permission to edit it.
   d. Click the icon and a dialog box displays granting you permission to edit the element.

5. You have the most recent updates from the central file but some elements in a workset are not displaying, as shown in Figure 6–89. Which of the following should you check? (Select all that apply.)

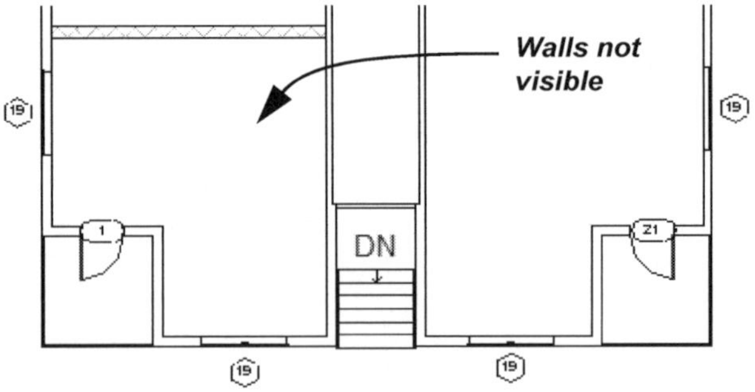

Figure 6–89

   a. In the Visibility/Graphics Overrides dialog box, change the Visibility Setting of the workset to **Visible**.
   b. In the Worksets dialog box, request permission to edit.
   c. Set the workset as active.
   d. On the Status Bar, change the Worksharing Display.
   e. In the Worksets dialog box, verify if the workset is open.

Command Summary

Button	Command	Location
	**Collaborate**	• **Ribbon**: *Collaborate* tab>Manage Collaboration panel
 	**Editing Requests**	• **Ribbon**: *Collaborate* tab> Synchronize panel • **Status Bar**
	**Gray Inactive Worksets**	• **Ribbon**: *Collaborate* tab>Manage Collaboration panel
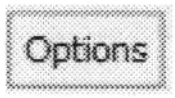	**Options**	• **Application Menu**
	**Owners (Display)**	• **Status Bar:** expand Worksharing Display Off
	**Relinquish All Mine**	• **Ribbon**: *Collaborate* tab> Synchronize panel
	**Reload Latest**	• **Ribbon**: *Collaborate* tab> Synchronize panel • **Shortcut**: RL
	**Restore Backup**	• **Ribbon**: *Collaborate* tab> Synchronize panel
	**Show History**	• **Ribbon**: *Collaborate* tab> Synchronize panel
	**Synchronize and Modify Settings**	• **Quick Access Toolbar** • **Ribbon**: *Collaborate* tab> Synchronize panel>expand Synchronize with Central
	**Synchronize Now**	• **Quick Access Toolbar** • **Ribbon**: *Collaborate* tab> Synchronize panel>expand Synchronize with Central
 	**Worksets**	• **Ribbon**: *Collaborate* tab>Manage Collaboration panel>Worksets • **Status Bar**
	**Worksets (Display)**	• **Status Bar:** expand Worksharing Display Off
	**Worksharing Display Off**	• **Status Bar**

Creating Details

Creating details is a critical part of the design process, as it is the step where you specify the exact information that is required to build a construction project. The elements that you can add to a model include detail components, detail lines, text, keynotes, tags, symbols, and filled regions for patterning. Details can be created from views in the model, but you can also draw 2D details in separate views.

Learning Objectives in this Chapter

- Create drafting views where you can draw 2D details.
- Add detail components that indicate the typical elements in a detail.
- Annotate details using detail lines, text, tags, symbols, and patterns that define materials.

A.1 Setting Up Detail Views

Most of the work you do in the Autodesk® Revit® software is exclusively with *smart* elements that interconnect and work together in the model. However, the software does not automatically display how elements should be built to fit together. For this, you need to create detail drawings, as shown in Figure A–1.

Details are created either in 2D drafting views, or in callouts from plan, elevation, or section views.

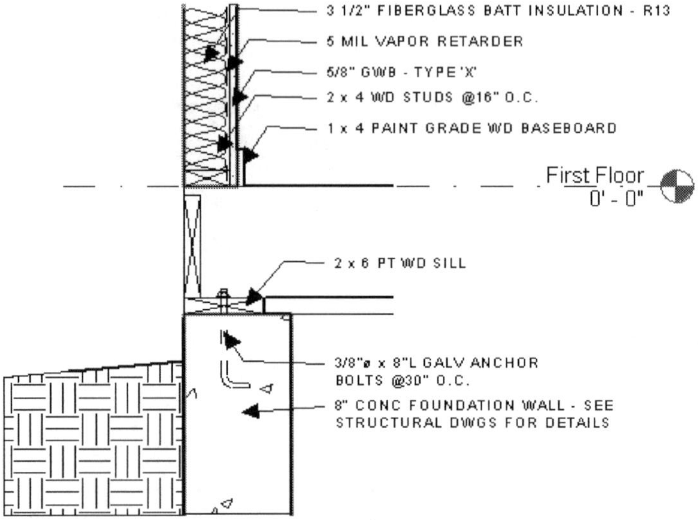

Figure A–1

How To: Create a Drafting View

1. In the *View* tab>Create panel, click (Drafting View).
2. In the New Drafting View dialog box, enter a *Name* and set a *Scale*, as shown in Figure A–2.

Drafting views are listed in their own section in the Project Browser.

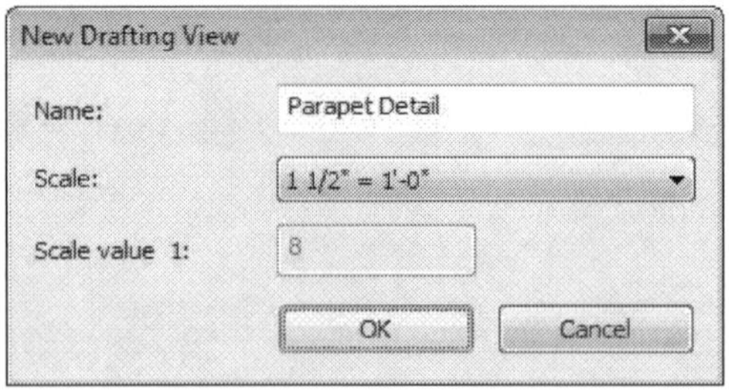

Figure A–2

3. Click **OK**. A blank view is created with space in which you can sketch the detail.

Callouts also have a Detail View Type that can be used in the same way.

How To: Create a Detail View from Model Elements

1. Start the **Section** or **Callout** command.
2. In the Type Selector, select the **Detail View: Detail** type.
   - The marker indicates that it is a detail, as shown for a section in Figure A–3.

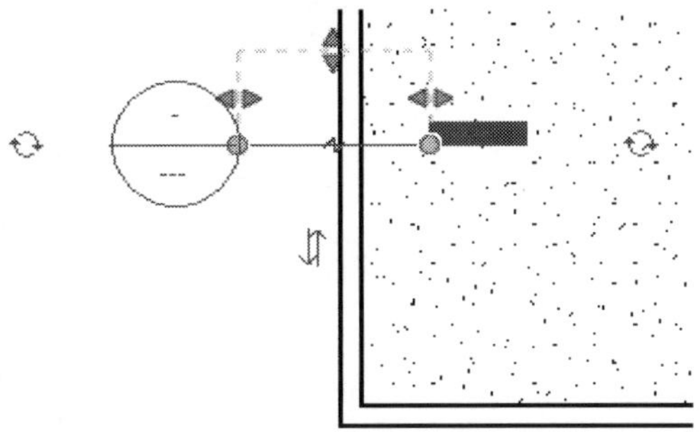

Figure A–3

3. Place the section or a callout of the area you want to use for the detail.
4. Open the new detail. Use the tools to sketch on top of or add to the building elements.

- In this type of detail view when the building elements change, the detail changes as well, as shown in Figure A–4.

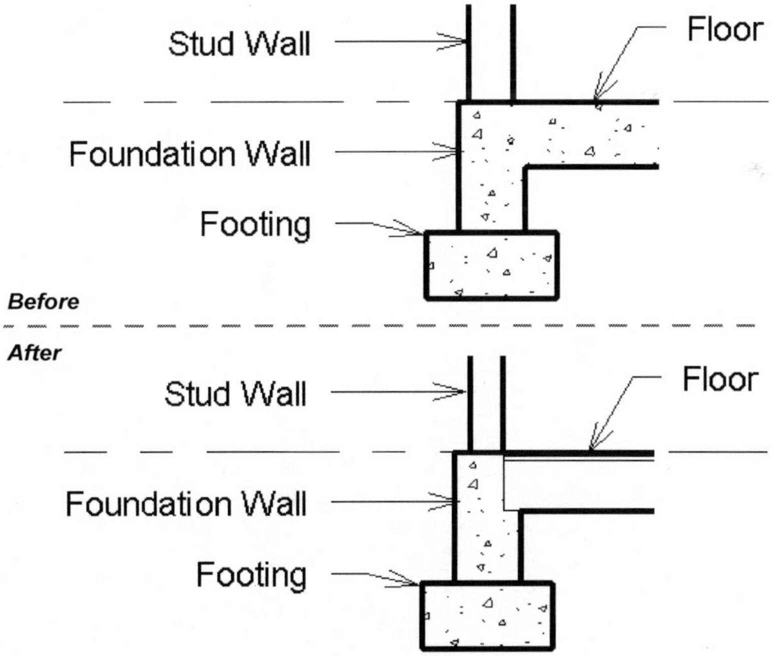

Figure A–4

- You can create detail elements on top of the model and then toggle the model off so that it does not show in the detail view. In Properties, in the *Graphics* area, change *Display Model* to **Do not display**. You can also set the model to **Halftone**, as shown in Figure A–5.

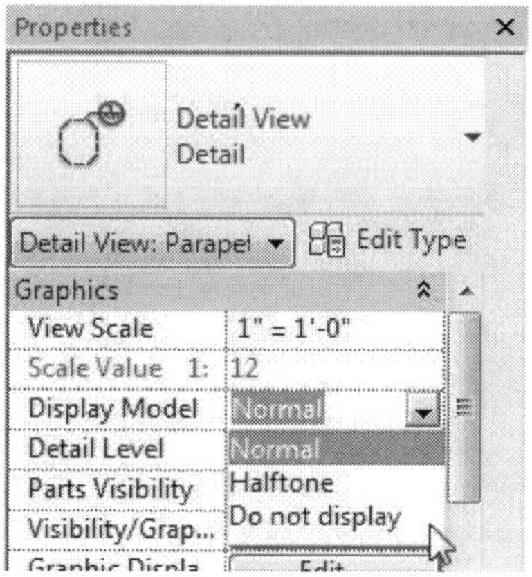

Figure A–5

Referencing a Drafting View

Once you have created a drafting view, you can reference it in another view (such as a callout, elevation, or section view), as shown in Figure A–6. For example, in a section view, you might want to reference an existing roof detail. You can reference drafting views, sections, elevations, and callouts.

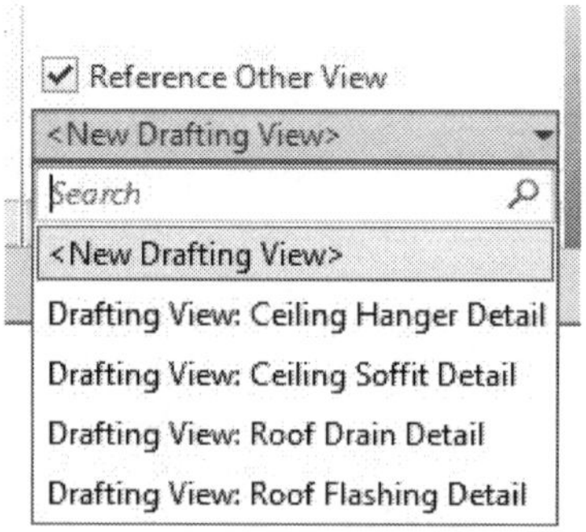

Figure A–6

- You can use the search feature to limit the information displayed.

How To: Reference a Drafting View

1. Open the view in which you want to place the reference.
2. Start the **Section, Callout,** or **Elevation** command.
3. In the *Modify* | *<contextual>* tab>Reference panel, select **Reference Other View**.
4. In the drop-down list, select **<New Drafting View>** or an existing drafting view.
5. Place the view marker.
6. When you place the associated drafting view on a sheet, the marker in this view updates with the appropriate information.

- If you select **<New Drafting View>** from the drop-down list, a new view is created in the *Drafting Views (Detail)* area in the Project Browser. You can rename it as required. The new view does not include any model elements.

- When you create a detail based on a section, elevation, or callout, you do not need to link it to a drafting view.

- You can change a referenced view to a different referenced view. Select the view marker and in the ribbon, select the new view from the list.

Saving Drafting Views

To create a library of standard details, save the non-model specific drafting views to your server. They can then be imported into a project and modified to suit. They are saved as .RVT files.

Drafting views can be saved in two ways:

- Save an individual drafting view to a new file.
- Save all of the drafting views as a group in one new file.

How To: Save One Drafting View to a File

1. In the Project Browser, right-click on the drafting view you want to save and select **Save to New File...**, as shown in Figure A–7.

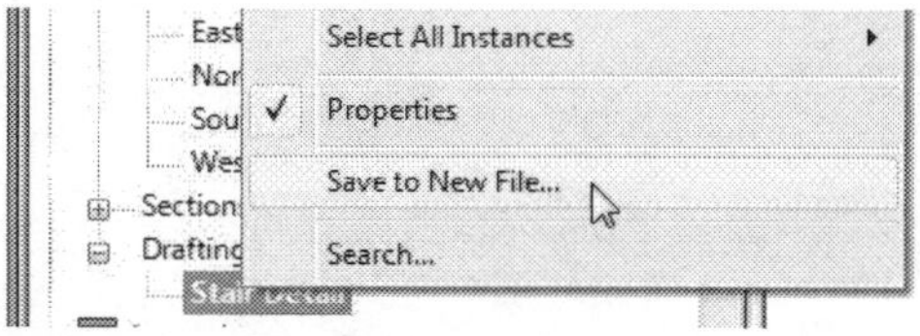

Figure A–7

2. In the Save As dialog box, specify a name and location for the file and click **Save**.

You can save sheets, drafting views, model views (floor plans), schedules, and reports.

How To: Save a Group of Drafting Views to a File

1. In the Application Menu, expand (Save As), expand (Library), and click (View).
2. In the Save Views dialog box, in the *Views:* pane, expand the list and select **Show drafting views only**.
3. Select the drafting views that you want to save as shown in Figure A–8.

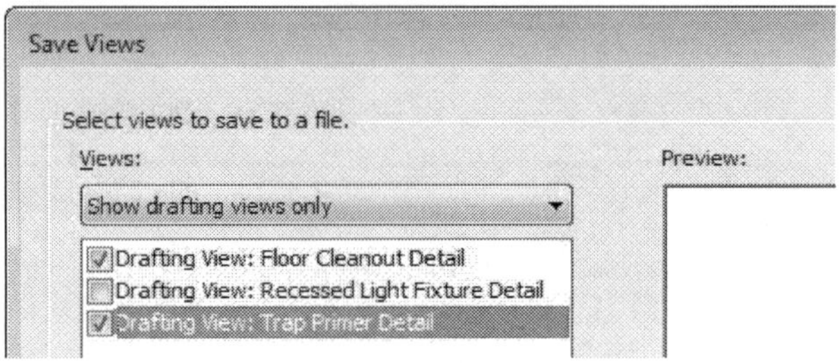

Figure A–8

4. Click **OK**.
5. In the Save As dialog box, specify a name and location for the file and click **Save**.

How To: Use a Saved Drafting View in another Project

1. Open the project to which you want to add the drafting view.
2. In the *Insert* tab>Import panel, expand (Insert from File) and click (Insert Views from File).
3. In the Open dialog box, select the project in which you saved the detail and click **Open**.
4. In the Insert Views dialog box, limit the types of views to **Show drafting views only**, as shown in Figure A–9.

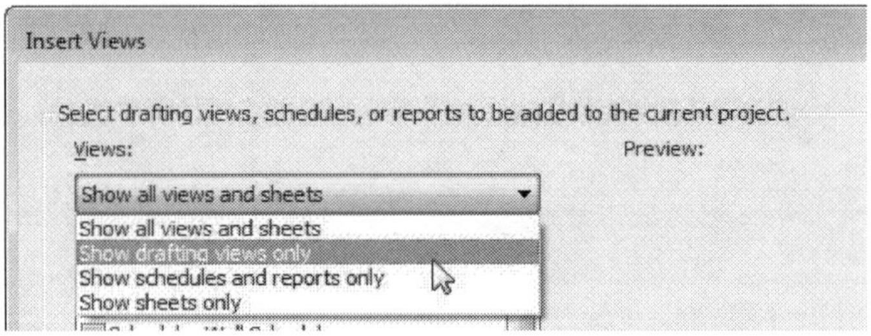

Figure A–9

5. Select the view(s) that you want to insert and click **OK**.

Hint: Importing Details from Other CAD Software

You might already have a set of standard details that have been used in various projects. You can reuse them in the Autodesk Revit software, even if they were created in other software, such as the AutoCAD® software. Import the detail into a new project, clean it up, and save it as a view before bringing it into your project.

1. Create a drafting view and make it active.
2. In the *Insert* tab>Import panel, click (Import CAD).
3. In the Import CAD dialog box, select the file to import. Most of the default values are what you need. You might want to change the *Layer/Level colors* to **Black and White**.

Click **Open**.

- If you want to modify the detail, select the imported data. In the *Modify | [filename]* tab>Import Instance panel, expand (Explode) and click (Partial Explode) or (Full Explode). Click (Delete Layers) before you explode the detail. A full explode greatly increases the file size.
- Modify the detail using tools in the Modify panel. Change all the text and line styles to Autodesk Revit specific elements.

A.2 Adding Detail Lines and Components

Autodesk Revit elements (such as the heat pump detail shown in Figure A–10) typically require additional information to ensure that they are constructed correctly. To create details, you add detail components, detail lines, and various annotation elements. These elements are drawn in a 2D drafting view and are not directly connected to the full model.

Figure A–10

How To: Draw Detail Lines

1. In the *Annotation* tab>Detail panel, click  (Detail Line).
2. In the *Modify | Place Detail Lines* tab>Line Style panel, select the type of line you want to use, as shown in Figure A–11.

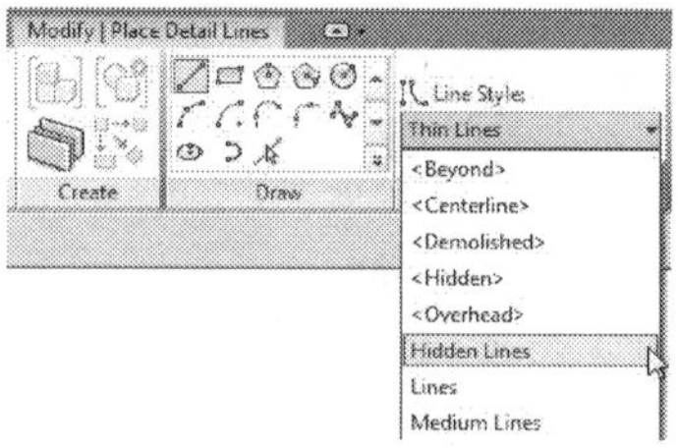

Figure A–11

3. Use the tools in the Draw panel to create the detail lines.

- Detail lines and symbols are view-specific, which means that they only display in the view in which they were created.

Detail Components

You can also load detail components from Autodesk Seek.

Detail components are families made of 2D and annotation elements. Over 500 detail components organized by CSI format are found in the *Detail Items* folder of the library, as shown in Figure A–12.

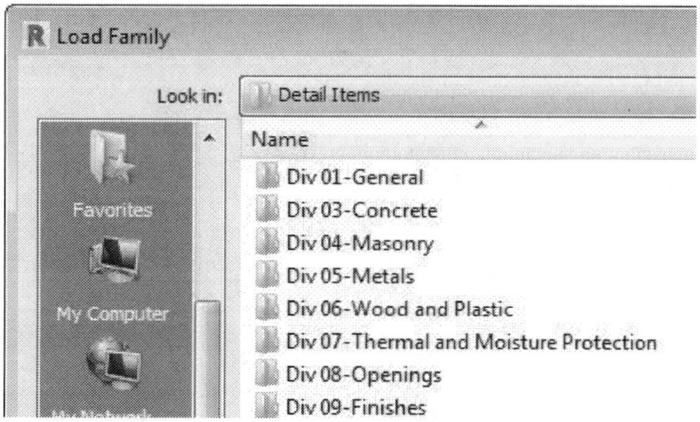

Figure A–12

How To: Add a Detail Component

1. In the *Annotate* tab>Detail panel, expand (Component) and click (Detail Component).
2. In the Type Selector, select the detail component type. You can load additional types from the Library.
3. Many detail components can be rotated as you insert them by pressing <Spacebar>. Alternatively, select the **Rotate after placement** option in the Options Bar, as shown in Figure A–13.

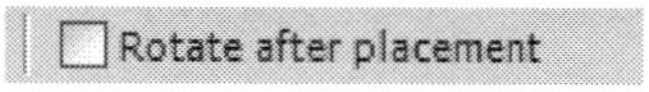

Figure A–13

4. Place the component in the drawing. Rotate it if required.

Adding Break Lines

The Break Line is a detail component found in the *Detail Items\ Div 01-General* folder. It consists of a rectangular area (shown highlighted in Figure A–14) which is used to block out elements behind it. You can modify the size of the area that is covered and change the size of the cut line using the controls.

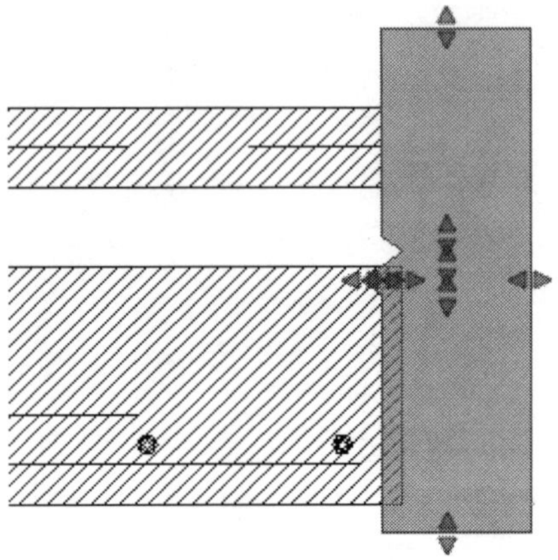

Figure A–14

Hint: Working with the Draw Order of Details

When you select detail elements in a view, you can change the draw order of the elements in the *Modify | Detail Items* tab> Arrange panel. You can bring elements in front of other elements or place them behind elements, as shown in Figure A–15.

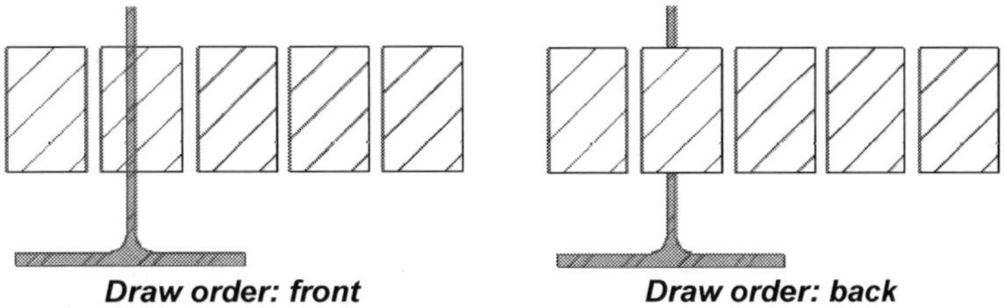

Figure A–15

- **(Bring to Front):** Places element in front of all other elements.
- **(Send to Back):** Places element behind all other elements.
- **(Bring Forward):** Moves element one step to the front.
- **(Send Backward):** Moves element one step to the back.

You can select multiple detail elements and change the draw order of all of them in one step. They keep the relative order of the original selection.

Repeating Details

Instead of having to insert a component multiple times (such as with a brick or concrete block), you can use (Repeating Detail Component) and draw a string of components, as shown in Figure A–16.

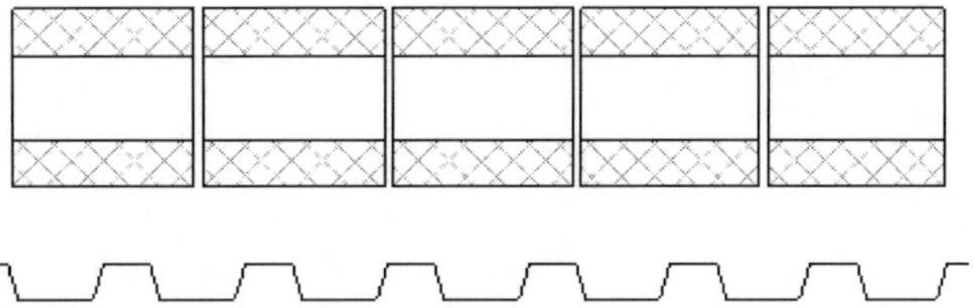

Figure A–16

How To: Insert a Repeating Detail Component

1. In the *Annotate* tab>Detail panel, expand (Component) and click (Repeating Detail Component).
2. In the Type Selector, select the detail you want to use.
3. In the Draw panel, click (Line) or (Pick Lines).
4. In the Options Bar, type a value for the *Offset*, if required.
5. The components repeat as required to fit the length of the sketched or selected line, as shown in Figure A–17. You can lock the components to the line.

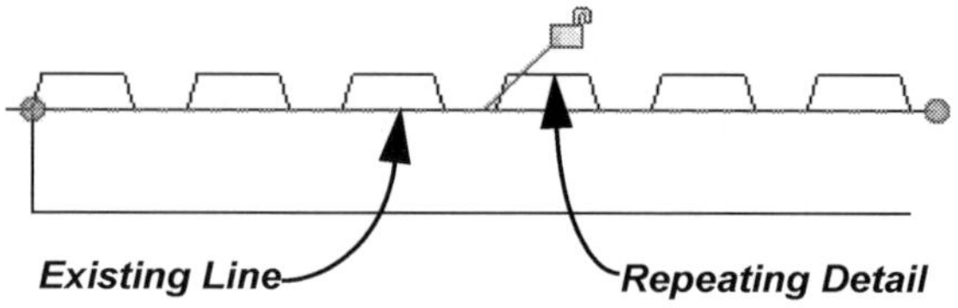

Figure A–17

> **Hint: (Insulation)**
>
> Adding batt insulation is similar to adding a repeating detail component, but instead of a series of bricks or other elements, it creates the linear batting pattern, shown in Figure A–18.
>
> 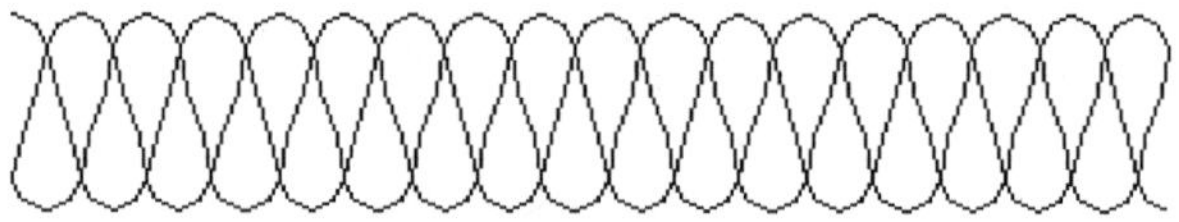
>
> **Figure A–18**
>
> Before you place the insulation in the drawing, specify the *Width* and other options in the Options Bar, as shown in Figure A–19.
>
> 
>
>
> **Figure A–19**

A.3 Annotating Details

After you have added components and drawn detail lines, you need to add annotations to the drawing. You can use standard annotation tools to place text notes, dimensions, and symbols, as shown in Figure A–20. You can also fill regions with a pattern to indicate materials.

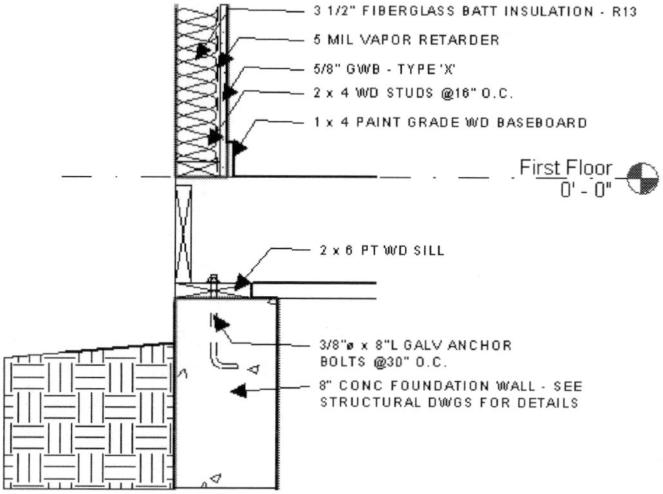

Figure A–20

Working with Dimensions

You can create permanent dimensions using aligned, linear, angular, radial, diameter, and arc length dimensions. These can be individual or a string of dimensions, as shown in Figure A–21. With aligned dimensions, you can also dimension entire walls with openings, grid lines, and/or intersecting walls.

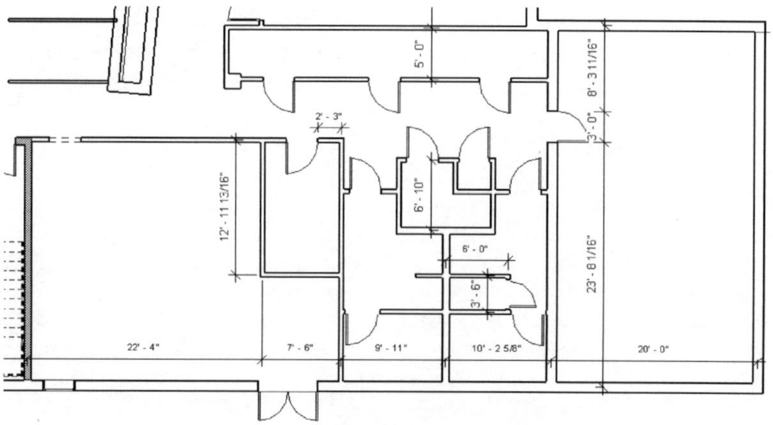

Figure A–21

- Dimensions referencing model elements must be drawn on a model in an active view. You can dimension on sheets, but only to items drawn directly on the sheets.
- Dimensions are available in the *Annotate* tab>Dimension panel and the *Modify* tab>Measure panel, as shown in Figure A–22.

 *(Aligned) is also located in the Quick Access Toolbar.*

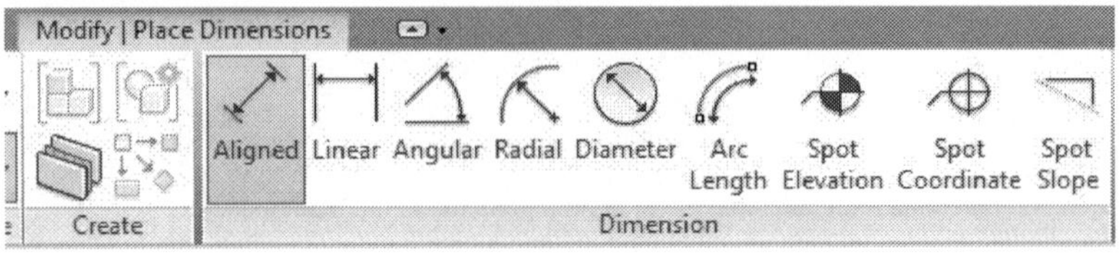

Figure A–22

How To: Add Aligned Dimensions

1. Start the  (Aligned) command or type **DI.**
2. In the Type Selector, select a dimension style.
3. In the Options Bar, select the location line of the wall to dimension from, as shown in Figure A–23.
   - This option can be changed as you add dimensions.

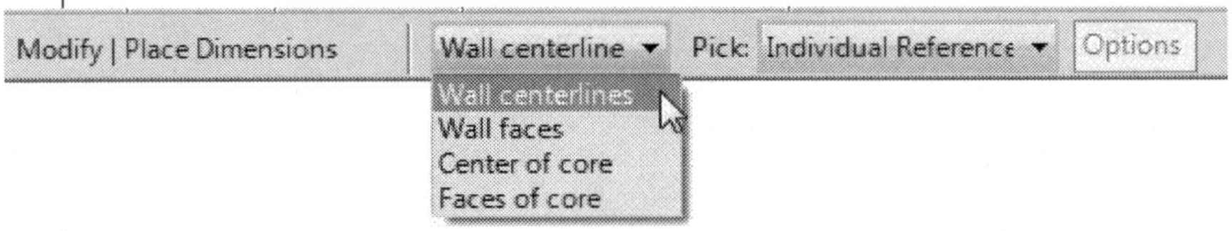

Figure A–23

4. In the Options Bar, select your preference from the *Pick* drop-down list:
   - **Individual References**: Select the elements in order (as shown in Figure A–24) and then click in empty space to position the dimension string.

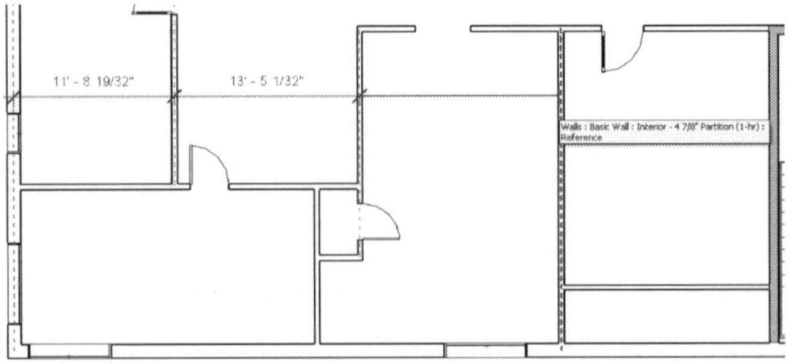

Figure A–24

- **Entire Walls**: Select the wall you want to dimension and then click the cursor to position the dimension string, as shown in Figure A–25.

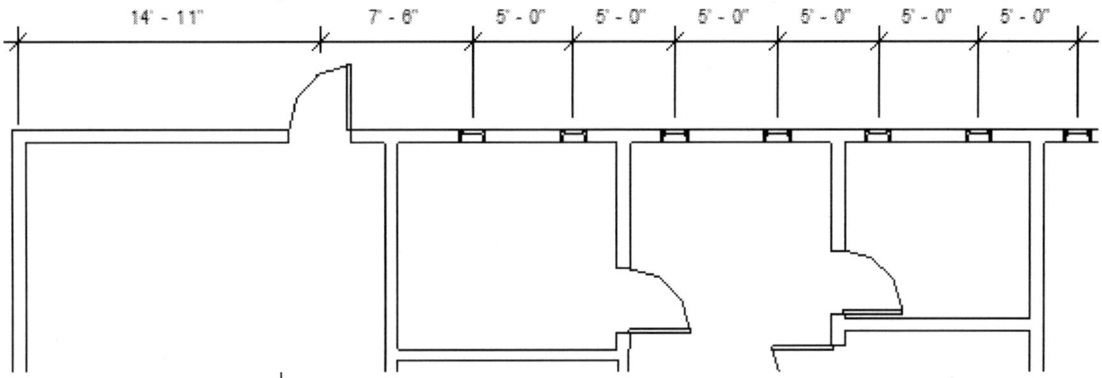

Figure A–25

- When dimensioning entire walls you can specify how you want *Openings*, *Intersecting Walls*, and *Intersecting Grids* to be treated by the dimension string. In the Options Bar, click **Options**. In the Auto Dimension Options dialog box (shown in Figure A–26), select the references you want to have automatically dimensioned.

*If the **Entire Wall** option is selected without additional options, it places an overall wall dimension.*

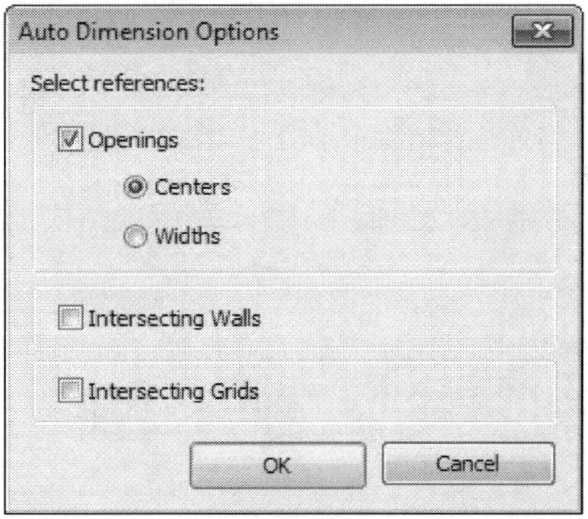

Figure A–26

Working With Text

The **Text** command enables you to add notes to views or sheets, such as the detail shown in Figure A–27. The same command is used to create text with or without leaders.

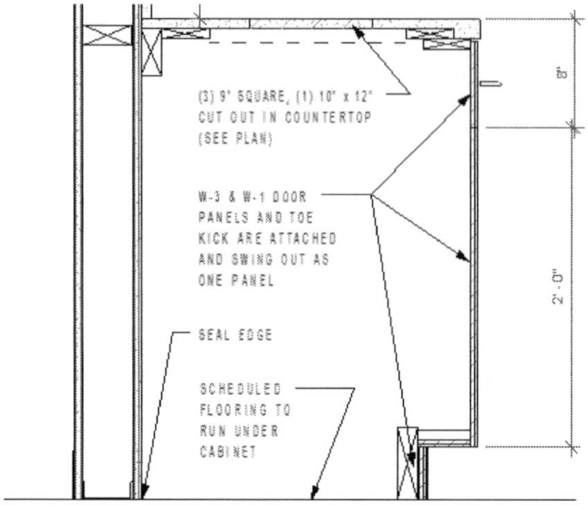

Figure A–27

The text height is automatically set by the text type in conjunction with the scale of the view (as shown in Figure A–28, using the same size text type at two different scales). Text types display at the specified height, both in the views and on the sheet.

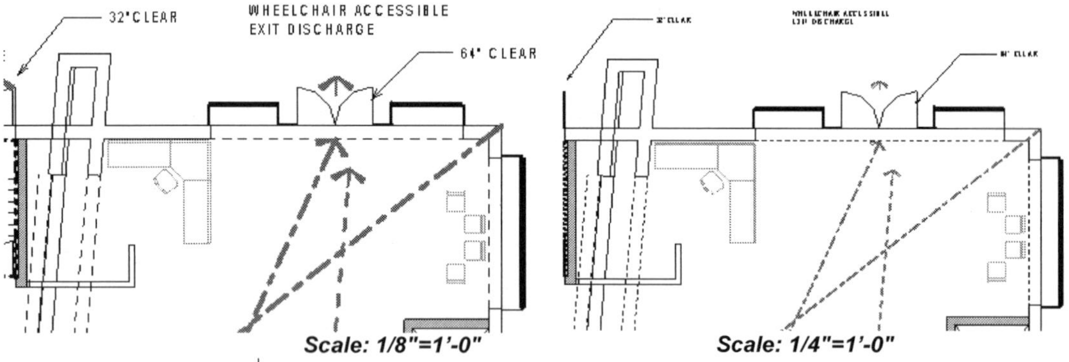

Figure A–28

How To: Add Text

The text type sets the font and height of the text.

1. In the Quick Access Toolbar or *Annotate* tab>Text panel, click A (Text).
2. In the Type Selector, set the text type.
3. In the *Modify | Place Text* tab>Leader panel, select the method you want to use: A (No Leader), A (One Segment), A (Two Segments), or A (Curved).
4. In the Paragraph panel, set the overall justification for the text and leader, as shown in Figure A–29.

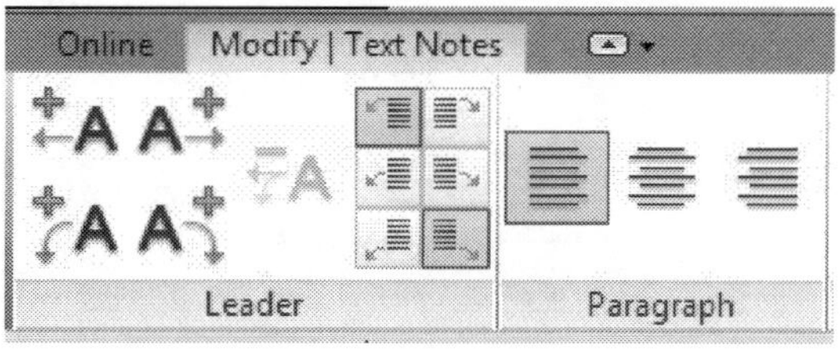

Figure A–29

Use alignment lines to help you align the text with other text elements.

5. Select the location for the leader and text.
   - If **No leader** is selected, select the start point for the text and begin typing.
   - If using a leader, the first point places the arrow and you then select points for the leader. The text starts at the last leader point.
   - To set a word wrapping distance, click and drag to set the start and end points of the text.

Enhanced in 2017

6. Type the required text. In the *Edit Text* tab, specify additional options for the font and paragraph, as shown in Figure A–30.

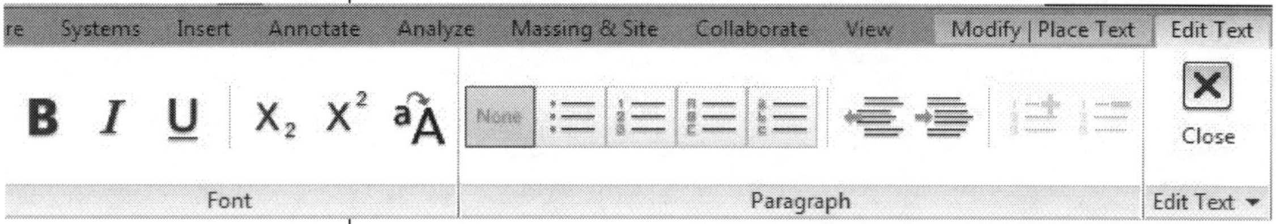

Figure A–30

7. In the Edit Text tab>Edit Text panel, click (Close) or click outside the text box to complete the text element.
   - Pressing <Enter> after a line of text starts a new line of text in the same text window.

Using Symbols

Symbols are 2D elements that only display in one view, while components can be in 3D and display in many views.

Many of the annotations used in architectural drawings are frequently repeated. Several of them have been saved as symbols in the Autodesk Revit software, such as the North Arrow, Center Line, and Graphic Scale annotations as shown in Figure A–31.

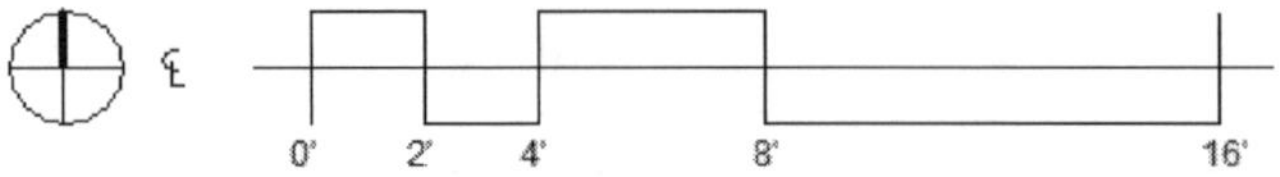

Figure A–31

- You can also create or load custom annotation symbols.

How To: Place a Symbol

1. In the *Annotate* tab>Symbol panel, click (Symbol).
2. In the Type Selector, select the symbol you want to use.
3. In the *Modify | Place Symbol* tab>Mode panel, click (Load Family) if you want to load other symbols.
4. In the Options Bar, as shown in Figure A–32, set the *Number of Leaders* and select the **Rotate after placement** option if you want to rotate the symbol as you insert it.

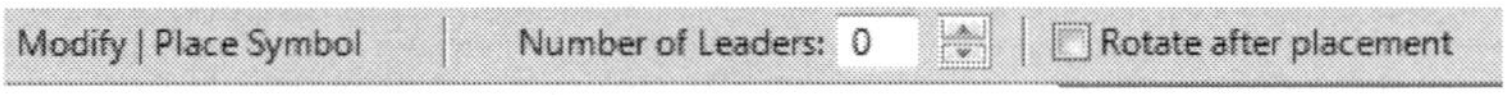

Figure A–32

5. Place the symbol in the view. Rotate it if you selected the **Rotate after placement** option. If you specified leaders, use the controls to move them into place.

Adding Detail Tags

Besides adding text to a detail, you can tag detail components using (Tag By Category). The tag name is set in the Type Parameters for that component, as shown in Figure A–33. This means that if you have more than one copy of the component in your drawing, you do not have to rename it each time you place its tag.

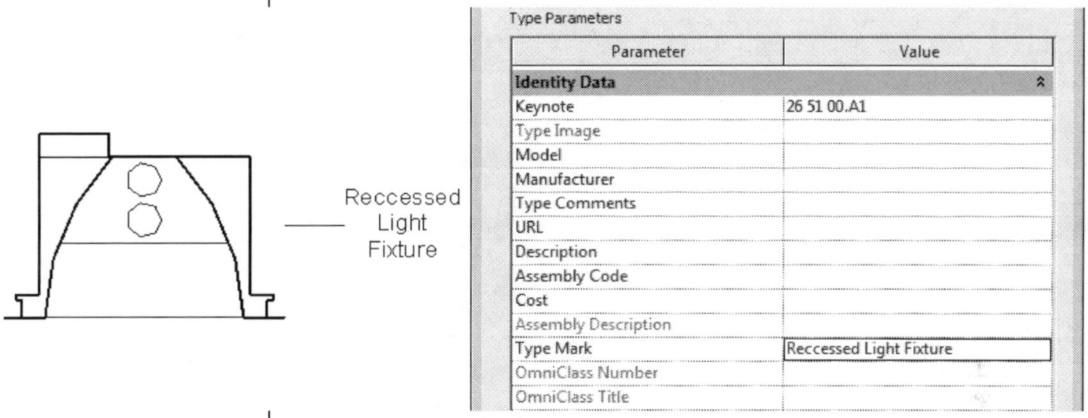

Figure A–33

- The **Detail Item Tag.rfa** tag is located in the *Annotations* folder in the library.

Creating Filled Regions

Many elements include material information that displays in plan and section views, while other elements need such details to be added. To add patterns manually for details, you create filled regions, as shown in Figure A–34.

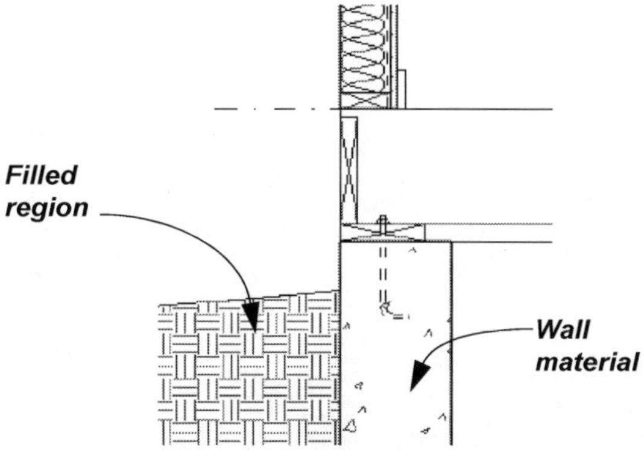

Figure A–34

The patterns used in details are *drafting patterns*. They are scaled to the view scale and update if you modify it. You can also add full-size model patterns to the surface of some elements.

How To: Add a Filled Region

1. In the *Annotate* tab>Detail panel, expand (Region) and click (Filled Region).
2. Create a closed boundary using the Draw tools.
3. In the Line Style panel, select the line style for the outside edge of the boundary. If you do not want the boundary to display, select the <Invisible lines> style.
4. In the Type Selector, select the fill type, as shown in Figure A–35.

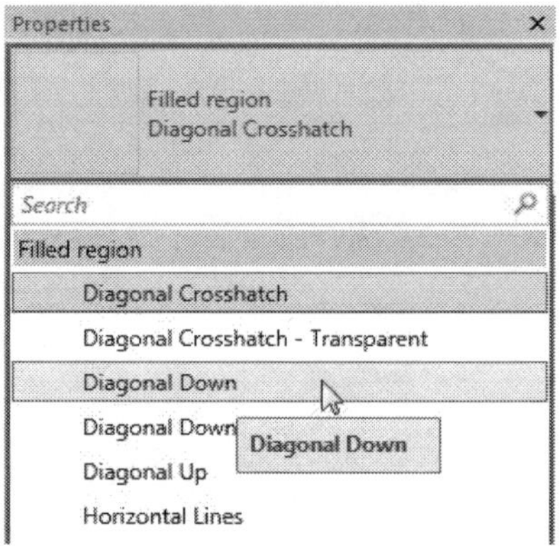

Figure A–35

5. Click (Finish Edit Mode).

- You can modify a region by changing the fill type in the Type Selector or by editing the sketch.
- Double-click on the edge of the filled region to edit the sketch.

  If you have the Selection option set to (Select elements by face) you can select the pattern.

Practice A1

Create Details - Architectural

Estimated time for completion: 15 minutes

Practice Objectives

- Create a detail based on a section.
- Add filled regions, detail components, and annotations.

In this practice you will create a detail based on a callout of a wall section. You will add repeating detail components, break lines, and detail lines, create filled regions, and add annotation to complete the detail, as shown in Figure A–36.

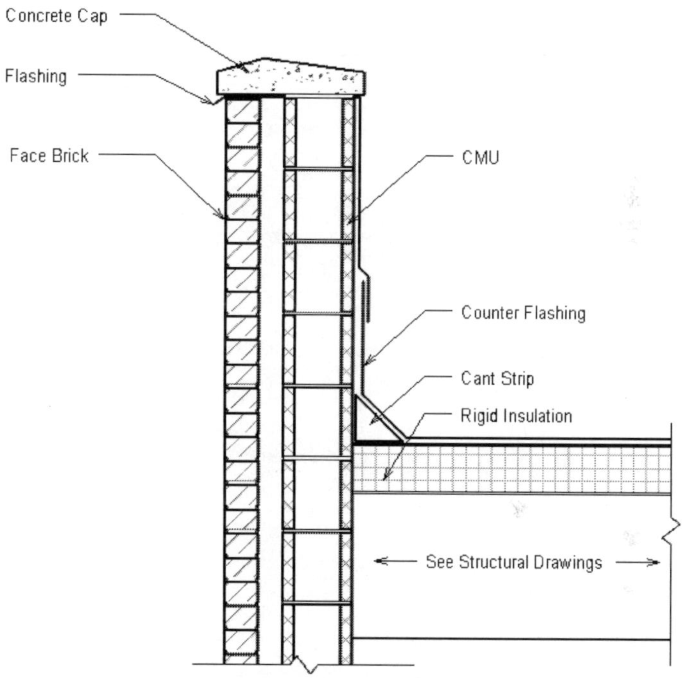

Figure A–36

Task 1 - Create a callout of a wall section.

1. Open the project **Modern-Hotel-Detailing.rvt**.
2. Open the **Floor Plans: Floor 1** view.

3. Double click on the wall section head shown in Figure A–37. This guarantees that you open the right section.

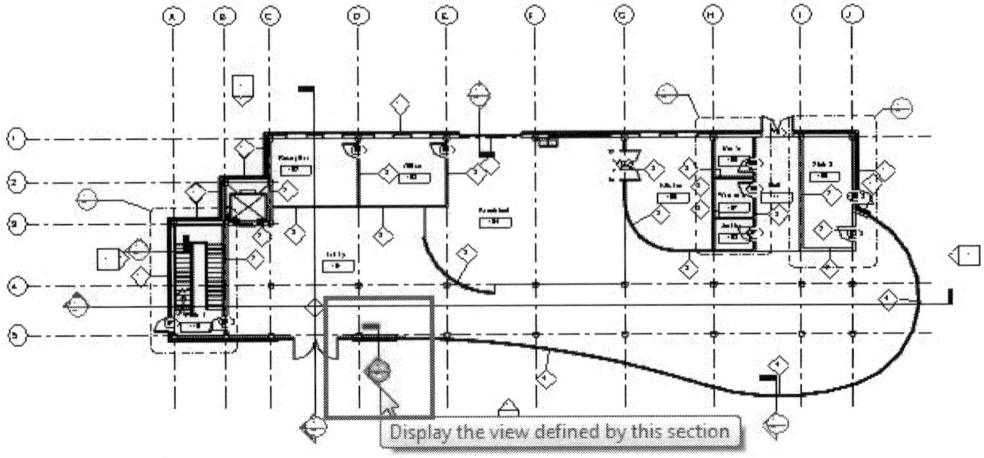

Figure A–37

4. Zoom in to the top of the wall showing the parapet and the roof.

5. In the *View* tab>Create panel, click (Callout).

6. In the Type Selector, select **Detail View: Detail**.

7. Create a callout as shown in Figure A–38. Open the callout.

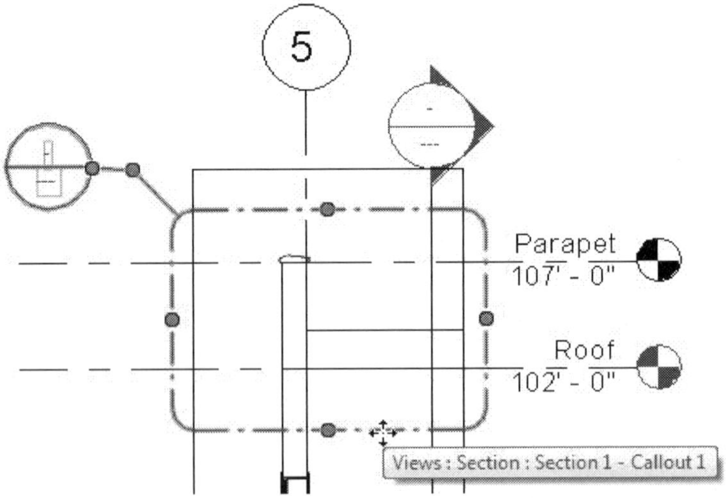

Figure A–38

8. In the View Control Bar, set the following parameters:
   - *Scale*: **1"=1'-0"**
   - *Detail Level*: (Fine)
9. Hide the levels, grids, and section markers (if displayed).
10. Toggle off the Crop Region.
11. In the Project Browser, in the *Detail Views (Detail)* node, rename the view to **Parapet Detail**.
12. Save the project.

Task 2 - Add repeating detail components and break lines.

1. In the *Annotate* tab>Detail panel, expand (Component) and then click (Repeating Detail Component).
2. In the Type Selector, verify that the type is set to **Repeating Detail: Brick**.
3. Draw the brick line from the top of the parapet cap down, as shown in Figure A–39.

Drawing from the top down insures that "mortar" is between the cap and the brick. This is how the detail elements were created.

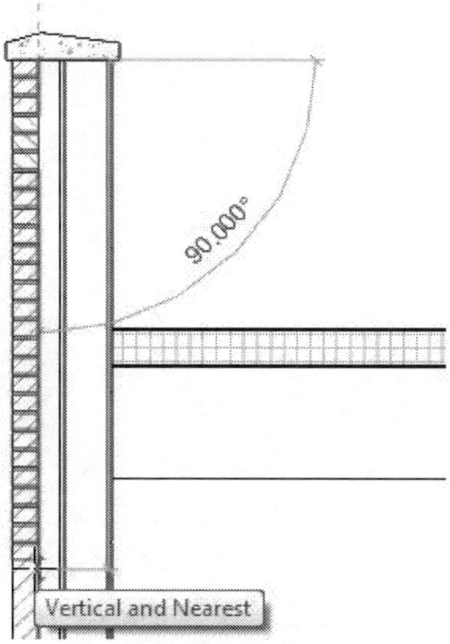

Figure A–39

4. In the Type Selector, select **Repeating Detail: CMU**. Draw over the other side of the wall.

The Autodesk Revit software lists the last tool you used at the top of the drop-down list.

5. In the *Annotate* tab>Detail panel, expand (Repeating Detail Component) and click (Detail Component).
6. In the *Modify | Place Detail Component* tab>Mode panel, click (Load Family).
7. In the Load Family dialog box, navigate to the *Detail Items> Div 01-General* folder, select **Break Line.rfa**, and then click **Open**.
8. Add break lines to the bottom and right side of the detail. Press <Spacebar> to rotate the Break Line as required and use the controls to modify the size and depth, as shown in Figure A–40

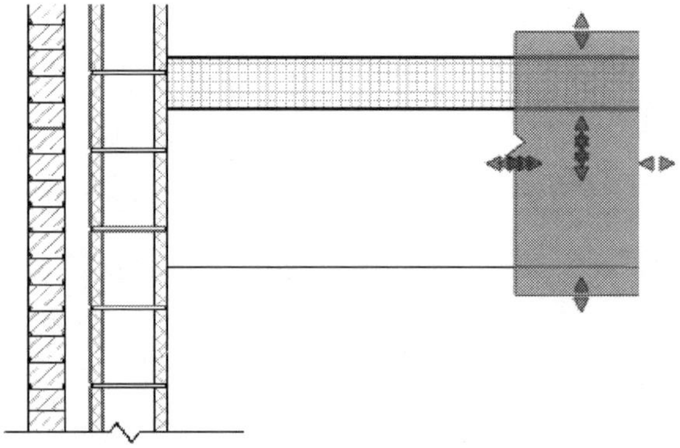

Figure A–40

9. Save the project.Draw flashing using detail lines.

Task 3 - Draw flashing using detail lines.

1. In the *Annotate* tab>Detail panel, click (Detail Line).
2. In the *Modify | Place Detail Lines* tab>Line Style panel, verify that **Wide Lines** is still selected.
3. Draw flashing similar to that shown in Figure A–41.

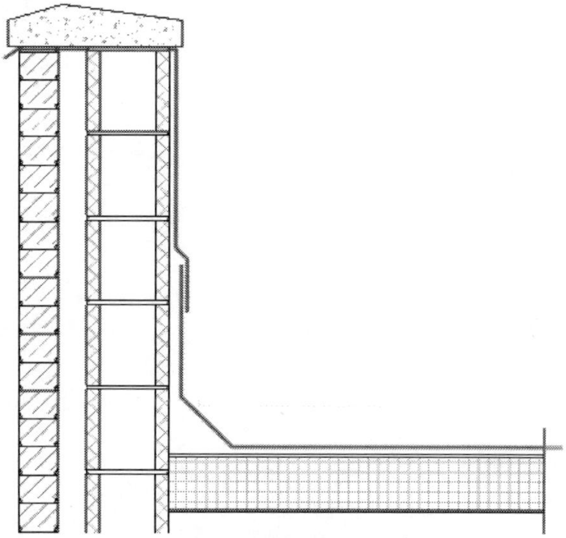

Figure A–41

4. Using Detail Lines, add a cant strip under the flashing.
5. Save the project

Task 4 - Annotate the detail.

1. In the Quick Access Toolbar or on the *Annotate* tab>Text panel, click (Text).
2. In the *Modify | Place Text* tab>Format panel, select (Two-Segments).

3. Add the text and leaders shown in Figure A–42. Use Alignments to place the leader points and text.

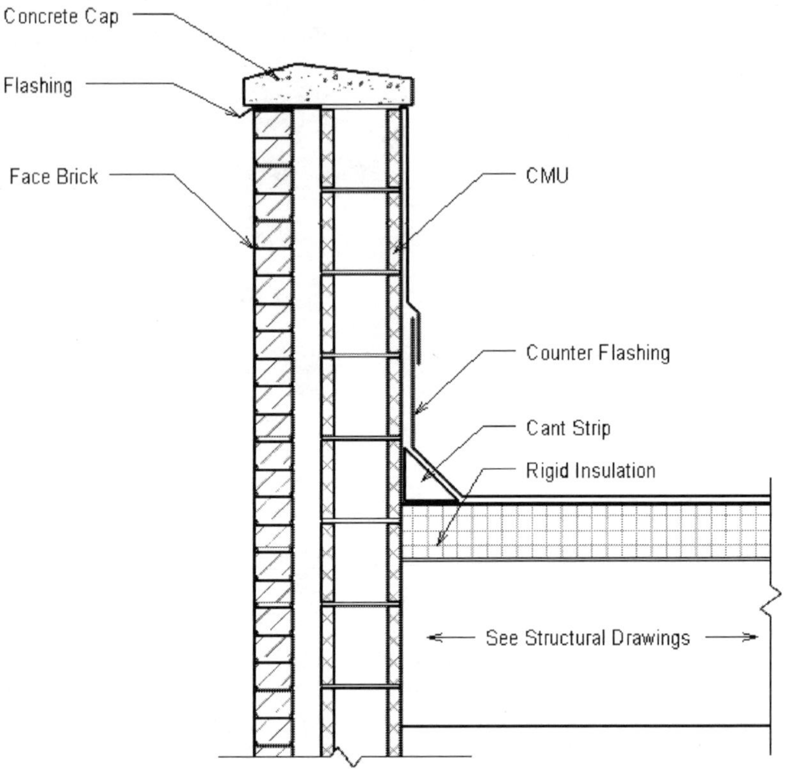

Figure A–42

4. Save the project.

- At this point you have a hybrid between detail items and model items. You can continue to add detail items to replace the roofing. You can also add structural elements if you have time.

Practice A2

Create Details - MEP

Practice Objectives

- Create a drafting view.
- Add detail lines, components, filled regions, and text.

Estimated time for completion: 10 minutes

In this practice you will create a drafting view. In the new view you will add detail lines of different weights, insulation, and filled regions. You will also add detail components, including Break Lines and text notes. Next, you will place the detail view on a sheet (as shown in Figure A–43) and place a reference section. Finally, you will create a second detail using detail components.

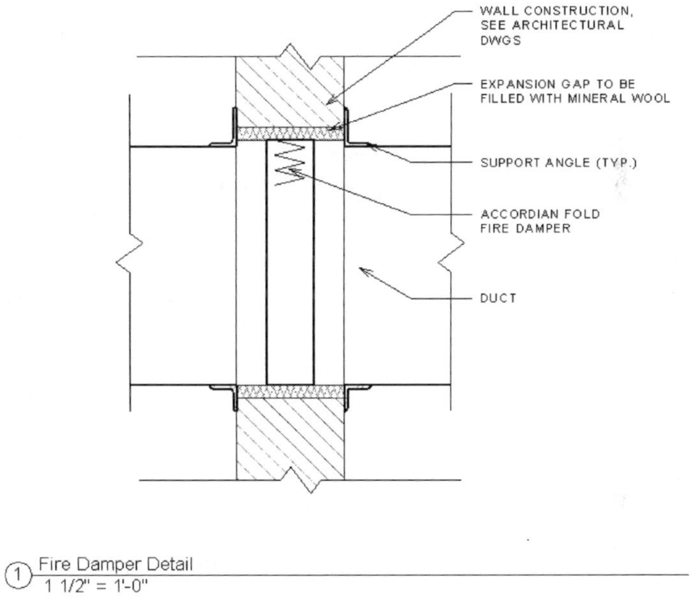

Figure A–43

Task 1 - Create a drafting view.

1. Open the project **MEP-Elementary-School-Detailing.rvt**.
2. In the *View* tab>Create panel, click (Drafting View).
3. In the New Drafting View dialog box, set the name and scale as follows:
   - *Name*: **Fire Damper Detail**
   - *Scale*: **1 1/2"=1'-0"**

4. In the Project Browser, expand the **Coordination** node until you can see the new detail view. Select the view, as shown in Figure A–44.

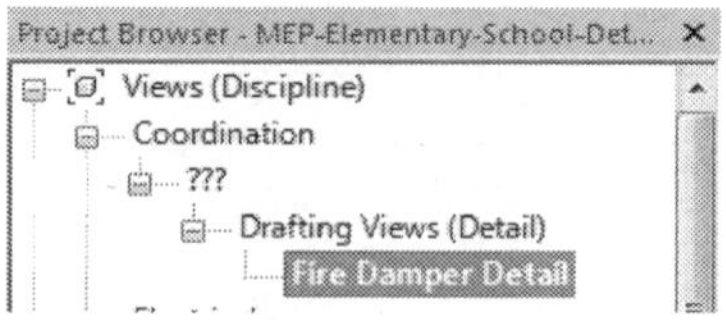

Figure A–44

5. In Properties, change *Discipline* to **Mechanical** and *Sub-Discipline* to **HVAC**. The new view moves to that node in the Project Browser.

Task 2 - Draw detail lines.

1. In the *Annotate* tab>Detail panel, click (Detail Line).
2. In the *Modify | Place Detail Lines tab*, ensure that the *Line Style* is set to **Thin Lines**. Draw the two vertical lines shown in Figure A–45.
3. Change the *Line Style* to **Wide Lines** and draw the two horizontal lines shown in Figure A–45. These become the primary duct and wall lines.

The dimensions are for information only.

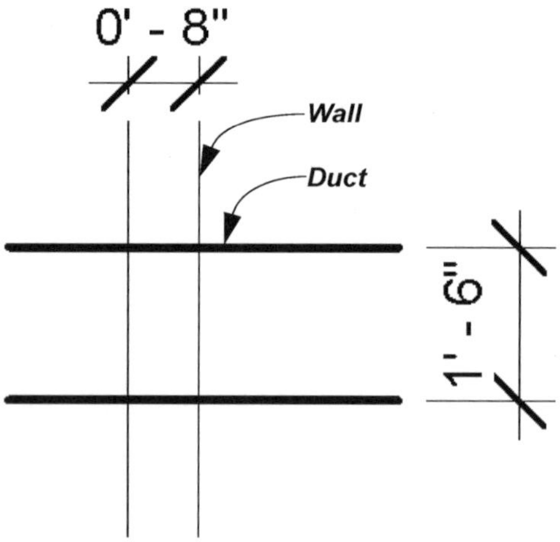

Figure A–45

- If the difference in the line weights does not display clearly, zoom in and, in the Quick Access Toolbar, toggle off (Thin Lines).

4. Continue adding and modifying detail lines to create the elements shown in Figure A–46. Use modify commands (such as **Split** and **Offset**) and the draw tools.

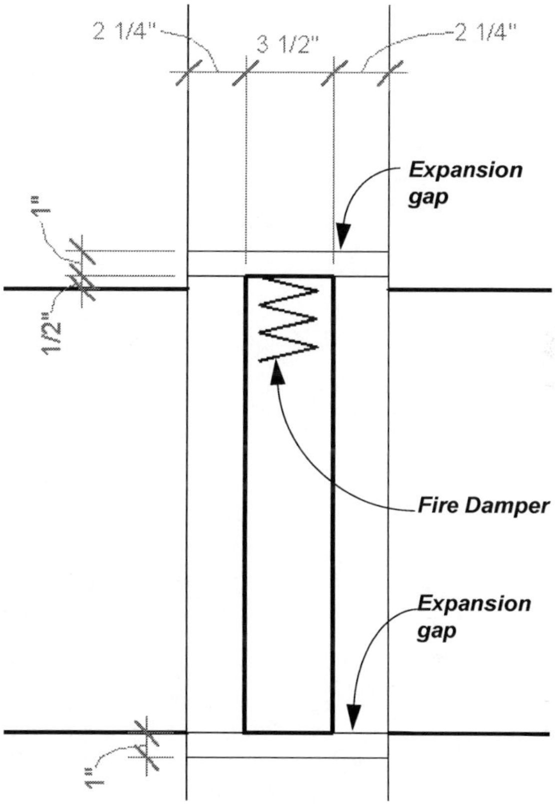

Figure A–46

5. Save the project.

Task 3 - Add detail components.

1. In the *Annotate* tab>Detail panel, click (Component).
2. In the Type Selector, select **AISC Angle Shapes - Section L3X2X1/4**.

3. Place the angle on the top left. as shown in Figure A–47.
    - Press <Spacebar> to rotate the angle before placing it.
4. Change the type **to AISC Angle Shapes - Section L2X2X1/4** and place the angle on the bottom of the duct, as shown in Figure A–47.

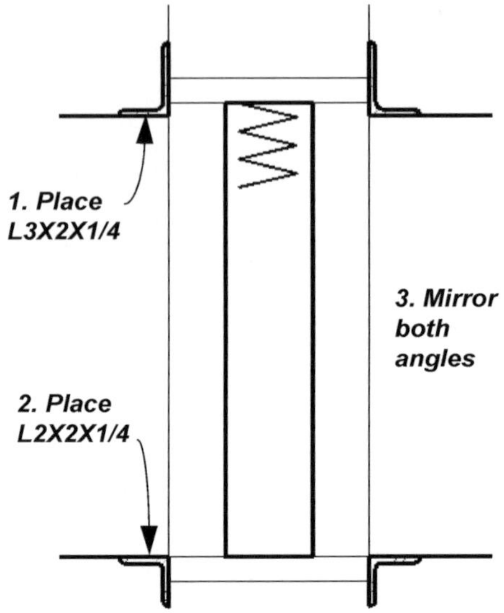

Figure A–47

5. Select the two angle components and mirror them to the other side, as shown in Figure A–47.
6. Add four Break Line components. Rotate and use the controls to modify the size until all of your excess lines are covered, as shown in Figure A–48.

The exact location and size of your break lines might vary.

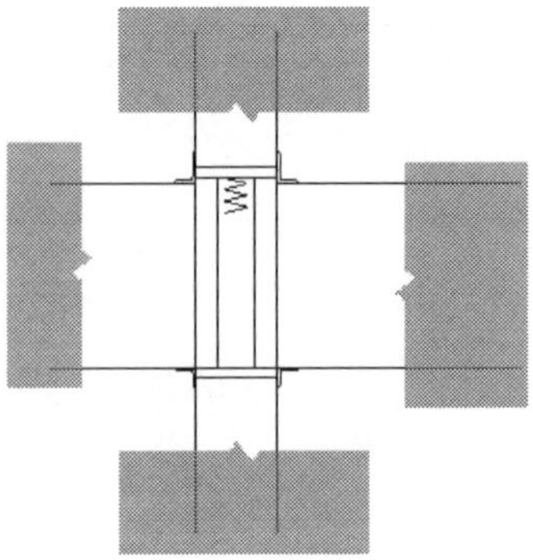

Figure A–48

7. Save the project.

Task 4 - Add insulation and filled regions.

1. In the *Annotate* tab> Detail panel, click (Insulation).
2. In the Options Bar, set the *Width* to **1"**.
3. Draw the insulation lines in the two expansion gaps, as shown in Figure A–49.
4. In the *Annotate* tab> Detail panel, click (Filled Region)
5. In the Type Selector, select F**illed region: Diagonal Down**.
6. Draw rectangles around the wall areas as shown in Figure A–49.
7. Click (Finish). The filled regions display.

The filled region pattern does not display until you finish the process.

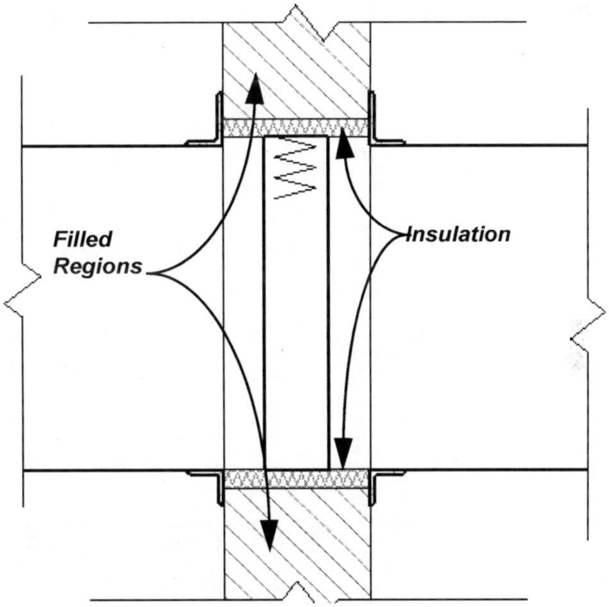

Figure A–49

8. Save the project.

Task 5 - Add text notes.

1. In the *Annotate* tab> Text panel click **A** (Text).
2. In the *Modify | Place Text* tab> Format panel, select (Two Segments) as the leader style.
3. In the Type Selector, select **Text: 3/32" Arial**.
4. Add text notes, as shown in Figure A–50.

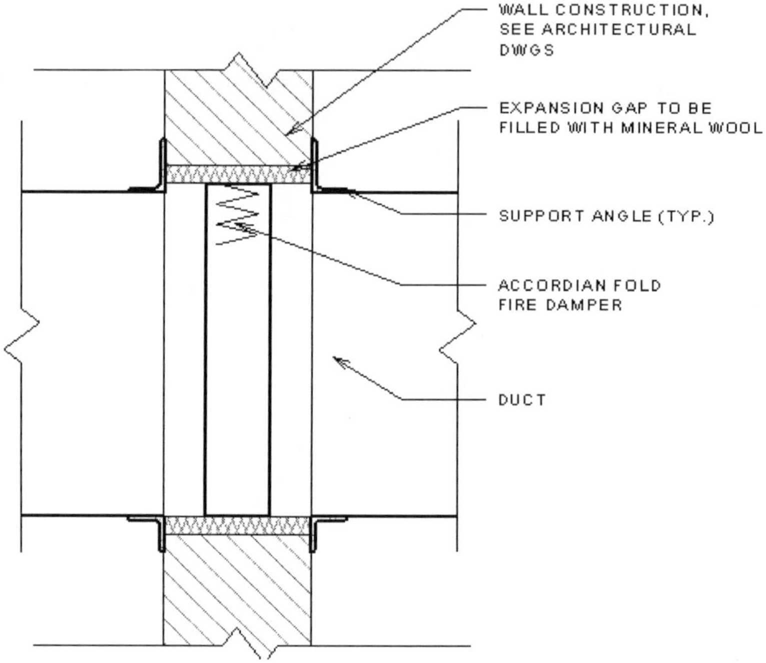

Figure A–50

5. Save the project.

Task 6 - Place the detail on a sheet and reference it in the project.

1. In the Project Browser, open the sheet **M601 - HVAC Details**.
2. In the Project Browser, drag the **Fire Damper Detail** view to the sheet.
3. Open the Mechanical>HVAC>**1 - Mech** view.

4. Zoom in on one of the duct systems.

5. In the *View* tab> Create panel, click  (Callout).

6. In the *Modify | Callout* tab>Reference panel, select **Reference Other View**.

7. Expand the drop-down list and select the new **Fire Damper Detail**, as shown in Figure A–51.

8. Place the callout at the intersection of a duct and the wall, as shown in Figure A–51. The information is filled out based on the location of the detail view on the sheet.

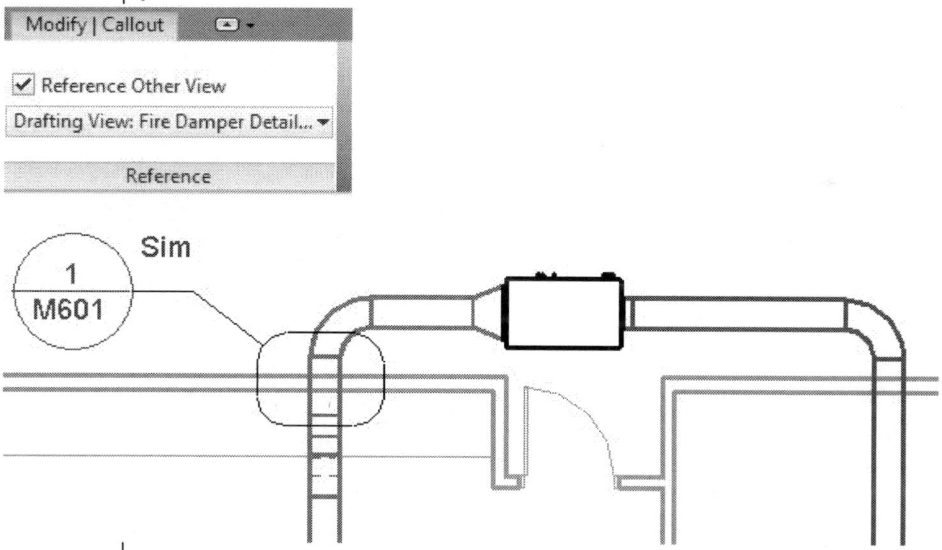

Figure A–51

9. Save the project.

Practice A3 Create Details - Structural

Estimated time for completion: 20 minutes

Practice Objectives

- Create a detail based on a section.
- Add filled regions, detail components, and annotations.

In this practice you will create an enlarged detail based on a section, modify lineweights, create filled regions, and add detail components, and annotation as shown in Figure A–52.

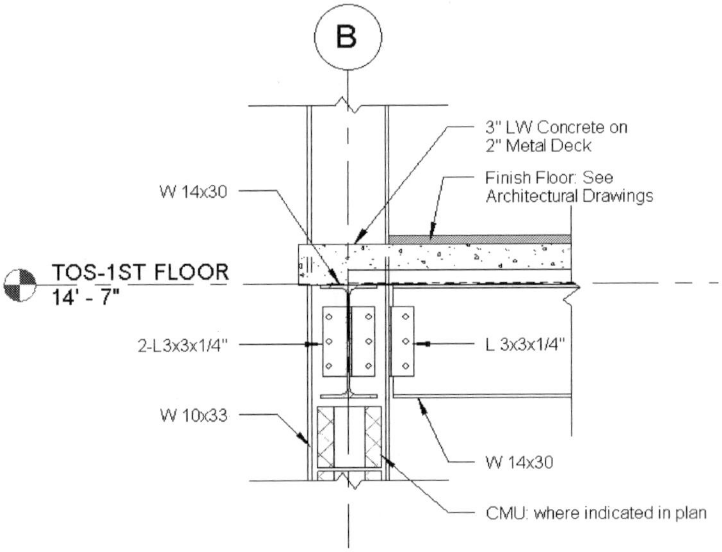

Figure A–52

Task 1 - Create an enlarged detail.

1. Open the project **Syracuse-Suites-Detailing.rvt**
2. Open the **Sections (Building Section): North-South Section** view.
3. Zoom in on the intersection of the **TOS-1ST FLOOR** level and **Grid B** (on the left). Adjust the crop region as required.
4. In the *View* tab>Create panel, click (Callout).

5. Create a callout as shown in Figure A–53 and double click on the callout head to open it.

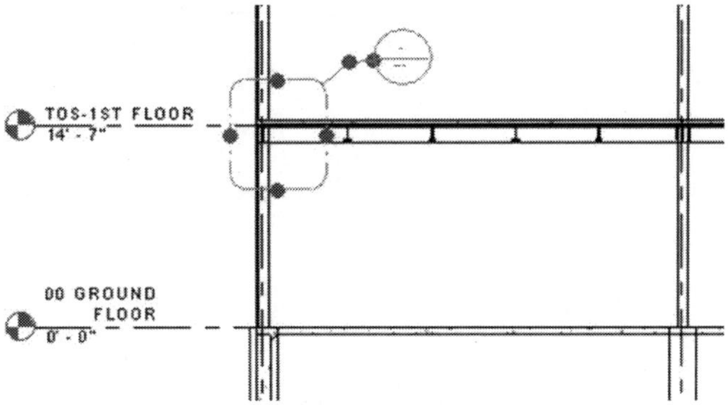

Figure A–53

Set the Detail Level to (Fine), if required.

6. In the View Control Bar, set the *Scale* to **3/4"=1'-0"**.
7. Select the **TOS-1ST FLOOR** level datum and use the **Hide Bubble** control to hide the bubble on the right.
8. Zoom in close to the intersection to display the line thicknesses. The slab and beam section cut lines are too heavy.
9. Select the slab. Right-click and select **Override Graphics in View> By Element...**
10. In the View-Specific Element Graphics dialog box, change the *Cut Lines Weight* to **2** as shown in Figure A–54.

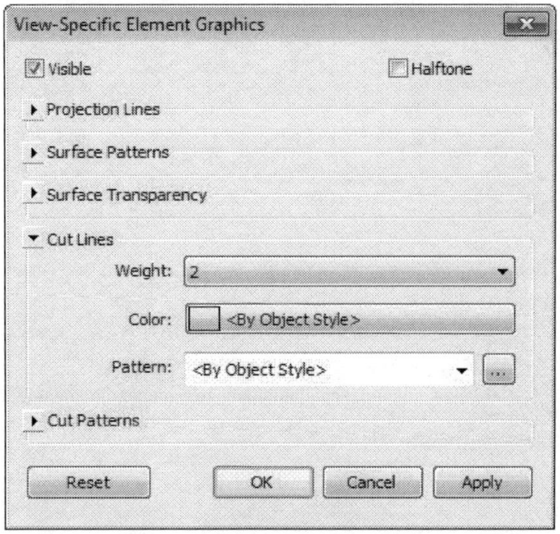

Figure A–54

11. Click **OK**.
12. Select the beam that is cut in section and change the *Cut Lines Weight* to **3**.
13. Save the project.

Task 2 - Create filled regions to display an architectural floor.

1. In the *Annotate* tab>Detail panel, click  (Filled Region).
2. In the Type Selector, select **Filled Region: Solid Black.**
3. Click  (Edit Type).
4. In the Type Properties dialog box, click **Duplicate...** and create a new type named **Solid Gray**.
5. In the Type Parameters, change the *Color* to a light gray.
6. Click **OK** twice to return to the sketch.
7. In the *Modify | Create Filled Region Boundary* tab>Draw panel, use the drawing tools to create a **1"** thick boundary above the floor slab, as shown in Figure A–55.

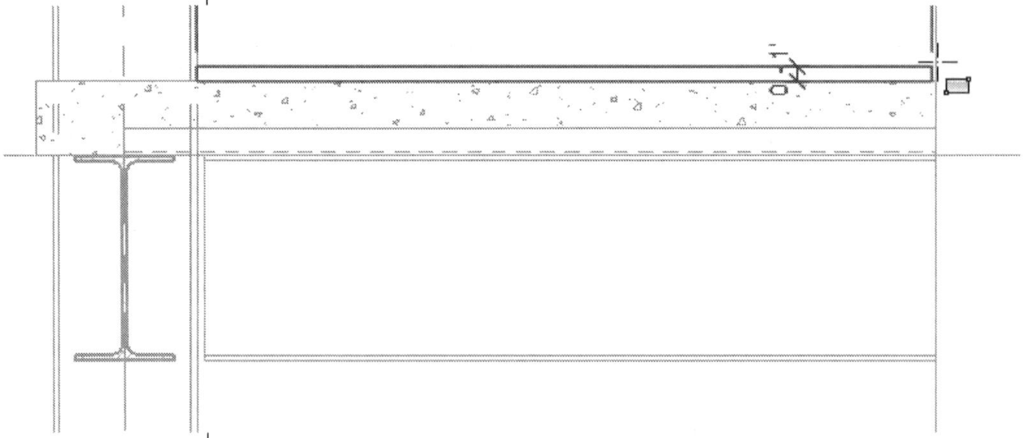

Figure A–55

8. Click (Finish Edit Mode) in the Mode panel. The region representing an architectural floor, displays as shown in Figure A–56.

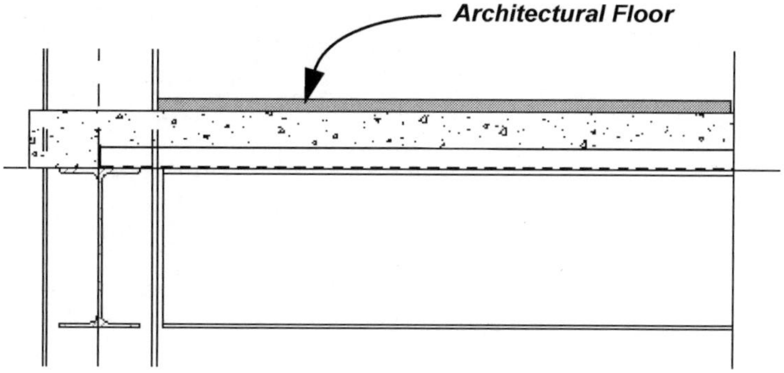

Figure A–56

Task 3 - Add detail components.

1. In the *Annotate* tab>Detail panel, click (Detail Component).
2. In the *Modify | Place Detail Component* tab>Mode panel, click (Load Family).
3. Browse to the *Detail Items>Div-05-Metals>050500-Common Work Results for Metals>050523-Metal Fastenings* folder. Open the files **L-Angle-Bolted Connection-Elevation.rfa** and **L-Angle-Bolted Connection-Section.rfa**. Press <Ctrl> to select both files.
4. In the Type Selector, select **L-Angle-Bolted Connection-Elevation: L3x3x1/4"**.
5. Click (Edit Type).
6. In the Type Properties dialog box, change the *Number Of Bolts* to **3**. Click **OK**.

7. Place the component at the intersection of the midpoint on the beam in elevation and the column it frames into as shown in Figure A–57.

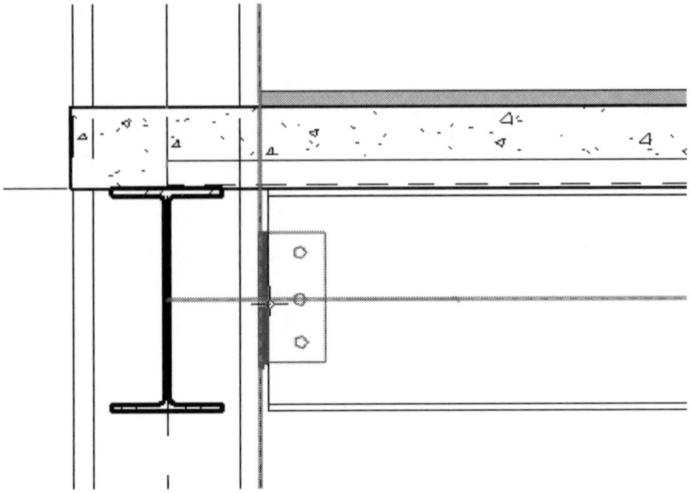

Figure A–57

8. Repeat the procedure. This time place the **L-Angle-Bolted Connection-Section** on the sectioned beam. After it is placed, select it and stretch the grips ◄ ► to be tight around the member as shown in Figure A–58.

To make it easier to see, toggle on (Thin Lines) in the Quick Access Toolbar.

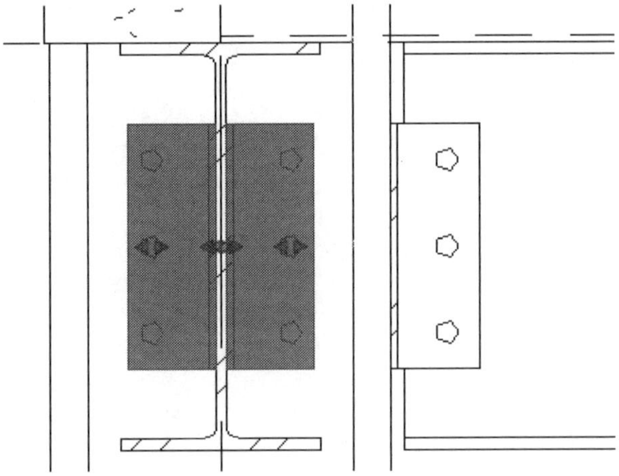

Figure A–58

9. Save the project.

Task 4 - Add repeating detail components.

1. In the *Annotate* tab>Detail panel, expand Component, and click (Repeating Detail Component).
2. In the Type Selector, select **Repeating Detail: CMU**.
3. In the Options Bar, set the *Offset* to **0' 3 13/16"** (or **=7 5/8" / 2**). (Hint: You can type formulas wherever a number can be added.)
4. Select the bottom midpoint of the **W14x30** section and draw a line down to display at least 2 CMU blocks, as shown in Figure A–59.

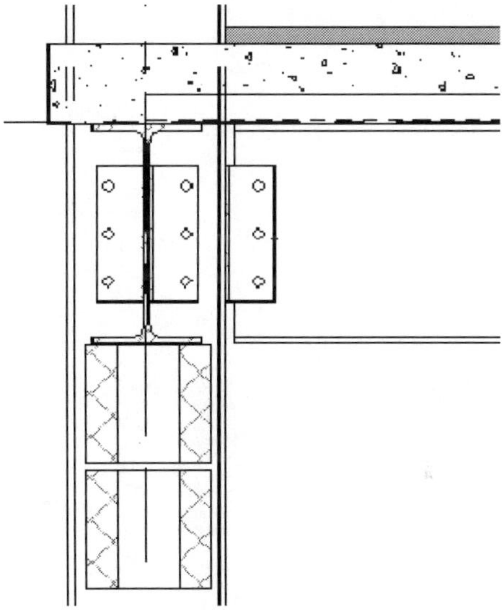

Figure A–59

5. Select the new CMU wall, and in the *Modify | Detail Items>Arrange* tab, click (Send to Back).
6. Click (Move) to move the entire CMU wall down **1"** to create space for a bearing plate for the beam.
7. Save the project.

Task 5 - Annotate the detail.

1. In the *Annotate* tab>Detail panel, click (Detail Component). Click (Load Family) to add a break line.
2. Browse to the *Detail Items>Div 01-General* folder and open the file **Break Line.rfa**.
3. Add break lines to the top, bottom, and right side of the detail as shown in Figure A–60. Press <Spacebar> to rotate the Break Line as required.

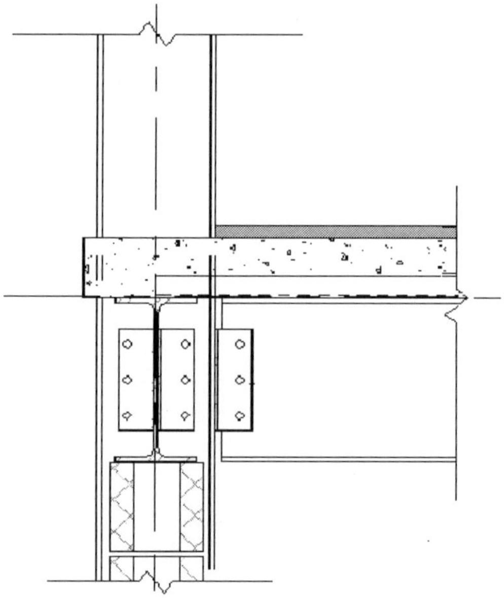

Figure A–60

Modify the crop region so that excess elements do not display on the outside of the break lines.

4. Leave plenty of room for annotation by making the annotation crop region larger.
5. In the *Annotate* tab>Text panel, click **A** (Text).

6. Add notes to complete the detail as shown in Figure A–61.

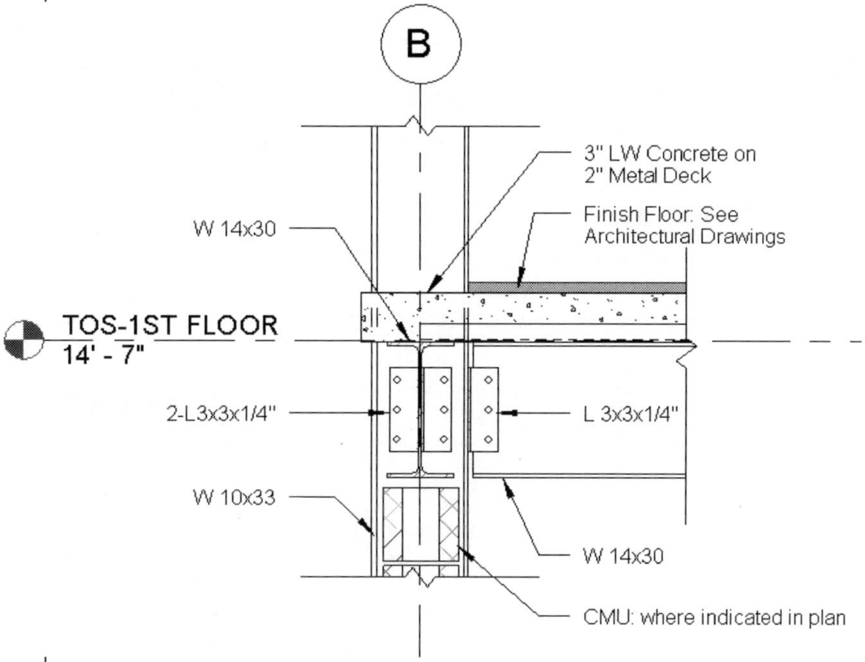

Figure A–61

7. In the View Control Bar, click (Hide Crop Region).
8. Save the project.

Chapter Review Questions

1. Which of the following are ways in which you can create a detail? (Select all that apply.)
   a. Make a callout of a section and draw over it.
   b. Draw all of the elements from scratch.
   c. Import a CAD detail and modify or draw over it.
   d. Insert an existing drafting view from another file.
2. In which type of view (access shown in Figure A–62) can you NOT add detail lines?

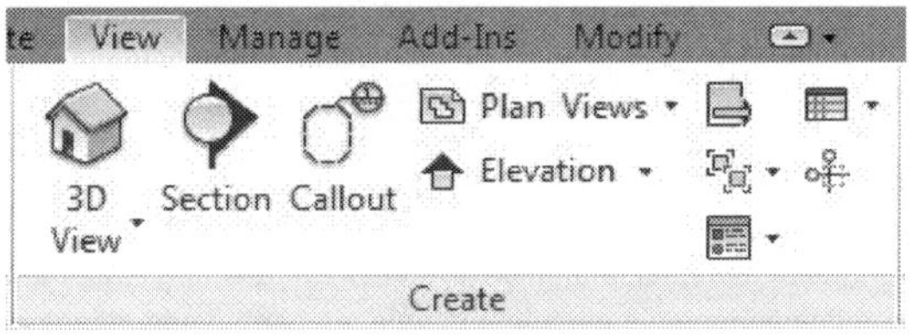

Figure A–62

   a. Plans
   b. Elevations
   c. 3D views
   d. Legends
3. How are detail components different from building components?
   a. There is no difference.
   b. Detail components are made of 2D lines and annotation only.
   c. Detail components are made of building elements, but only display in detail views.
   d. Detail components are made of 2D and 3D elements.
4. When you draw detail lines they are...
   a. Always the same width.
   b. Vary in width according to the view.
   c. Display in all views associated with the detail.
   d. Display only in the view in which they were created.

5. When a wall is moved (as shown in Figure A–63), how do you update the dimension?

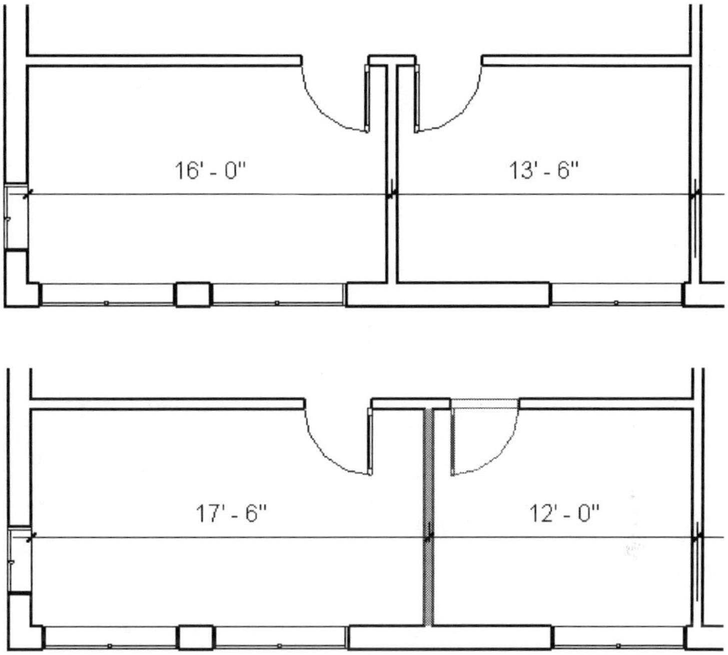

Figure A–63

a. Edit the dimension and move it over.

b. Select the dimension and then click **Update** in the Options Bar.

c. The dimension automatically updates.

d. Delete the existing dimension and add a new one.

6. When you edit text, how many leaders can be added using the leader tools shown in Figure A–64?

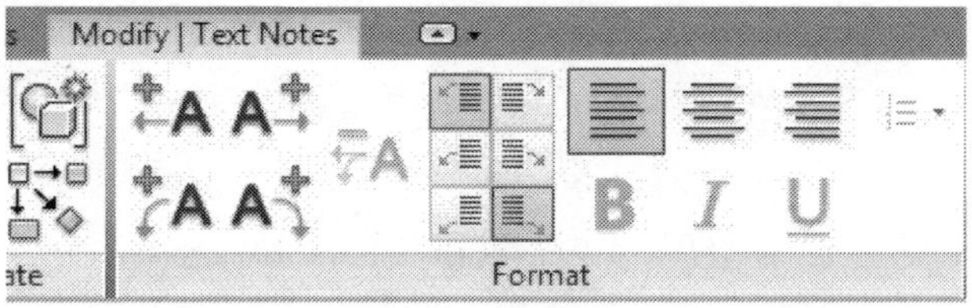

Figure A–64

a. One

b. One on each end of the text.

c. As many as you want at each end of the text.

7. Which command do you use to add a pattern (such as concrete or earth as shown in Figure A–65) to part of a detail?

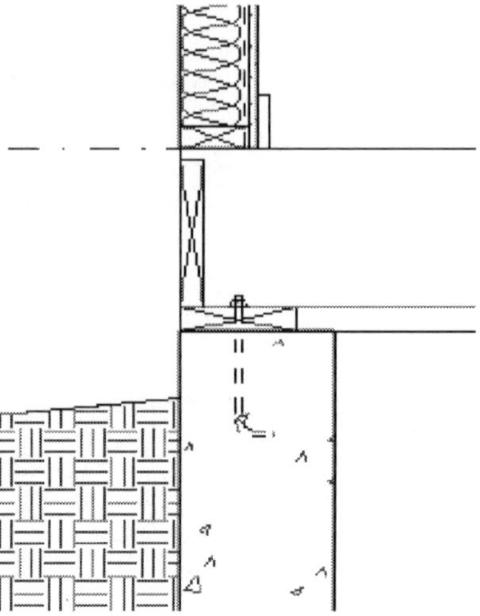

Figure A–65

a. **Region**

b. **Filled Region**

c. **Masking Region**

d. **Pattern Region**

Command Summary

Button	Command	Location
Detail Tools		
	**Aligned Dimension**	• **Ribbon:** *Annotate* tab>Dimension panel>Aligned • **Ribbon:** *Modify* tab>Measure panel> Aligned Dimension • **Quick Access Toolbar:** Aligned Dimension • **Shortcut:** DI
	**Detail Component**	• **Ribbon:** *Annotate* tab>Detail panel> expand Component
	**Detail Line**	• **Ribbon:** *Annotate* tab>Detail panel
	**Insulation**	• **Ribbon:** *Annotate* tab>Detail panel
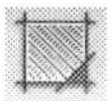	**Region**	• **Ribbon:** *Annotate* tab>Detail panel
	**Repeating Detail Component**	• **Ribbon:** *Annotate* tab>Detail panel> expand Component
	**Text**	• **Ribbon:** *Annotate* tab>Text panel • **Quick Access Toolbar** • **Shortcut:** TX
View Tools		
	**Bring Forward**	• **Ribbon:** *Modify* | *Detail Items* tab> Arrange panel
	**Bring to Front**	• **Ribbon:** *Modify* | *Detail Items* tab> Arrange panel
	**Drafting View**	• **Ribbon:** *View* tab>Create panel
	**Insert from File: Insert Views from File**	• **Ribbon:** *Insert* tab>Import panel> expand Insert from File
	**Send Backward**	• **Ribbon:** *Modify* | *Detail Items* tab> Arrange panel
	**Send to Back**	• **Ribbon:** *Modify* | *Detail Items* tab> Arrange panel

CAD Import Tools

	Delete Layers	• **Ribbon:** *Modify* | *<imported filename>* tab>Import Instance panel
	Full Explode	• **Ribbon:** *Modify* | *<imported filename>* tab>Import Instance panel>expand Explode
	Import CAD	• **Ribbon:** *Insert* tab>Import panel
	Partial Explode	• **Ribbon:** *Modify* | *<imported filename>* tab>Import Instance panel> expand Explode

Index

Made in the USA
Monee, IL
08 November 2026

67858076R10219